Writing Back

Writing Back

Sylvia Plath and Cold War Politics

Robin Peel

Madison • Teaneck
Fairleigh Dickinson University Press
London: Associated University Presses

Associated University Presses
440 Forsgate Drive
Cranbury, NJ 08512

Associated University Presses
16 Barter Street
London WC1A 2AH, England

Associated University Presses
P.O. Box 338, Port Credit
Missisauga, Ontario
Canada L5G 4L8

The paper used in this publication meets the requirements of the American National Standard for Permanence of Paper for Printed Library Materials Z39.48-1984.

Library of Congress Cataloging-in-Publication Data

Peel, Robin.
  Writing back : Sylvia Plath and Cold War politics / Robin Peel.
      p.   cm.
  ISBN 0-8386-3868-6
  1. Plath, Sylvia—Political and social views.   2. Politics and literature—Great Britain—History—20th century.   3. Political poetry, American—History and criticism.   4. Americans—England—History—20th century.   5. Politics in literature.   6. Cold War in literature.   I. Title.

PS 3566.L27 Z826 2002
811′.54—dc21   2002023112

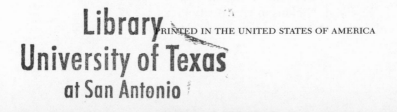

I mop up the universe

.　.　.　.　.　.　.

The business of sullen continents is my news
              —Discarded lines from "Fever" (January 1962), MRBR

And then there were other faces. The faces of nations,
Governments, Parliaments, societies,
The faceless faces of important men.

It is these men I mind:
They are so jealous of anything that is not flat! They are jealous gods
That would have the whole world flat because they are.
                    —"Three Women" (1962), *CP:* 179

Contents

7

Acknowledgments

Barbara Blumenthal for helping me identify 'The Lady or the Tiger?' and for supplying answers to numerous other questions.
Susan Sanborn Barker for information about "Venus in the Seventh."

Karen Kukil for her unfailing support, help, and advice throughout the semester at Smith College and afterwards.

Paul Lawley for his careful reading of the manuscript and his many helpful suggestions.

Richard Larschan for his invaluable comments on a draft of the manuscript, and the Wellesley doors he helped open.

Mary Reeves for her knowledge of Plath, Graves, and Laura Riding.

Clarissa Roche, Elizabeth Sigmund, "Father Michael" and Elizabeth Jenkins for their recollections and access to unpublished manuscripts.

Al Alvarez for provoking fresh reading and thinking.

Sheila Jones of C.N.D. and Pat Arrowsmith for their comments and suggestions.

The Helm Fellowship and Lilly Library for the research award which made possible a visit to the Plath Archive at the University of Indiana at Bloomington.

Jo Gill for reading the manuscript and providing Anne Sexton references.

Mary Peel for being the bedrock that supports the whole structure.

The Anti-Military Collage which appears as the cover illustration is used with the permission of Smith College and the Plath estate.

Excerpts from *The Collected Poems* by Sylvia Plath, edited by Ted Hughes. Copyright © 1960, 1965, 1971, 1981 by the Estate of Sylvia Plath. Editorial material © by Ted Hughes. Used by permission of Faber and Faber Ltd and HarperCollins Publishers, Inc.

Johnny Panic and the Bible of Dreams and Other Prose Writings by Sylvia Plath. Used by permission of Faber and Faber Ltd and HarperCollins Publishers.

The Journals of Sylvia Plath by Ted Hughes (ed.) copyright 1982 by Ted Hughes as executor of the estate of Sylvia Plath. Used by permission of Doubleday, a division of Random House, Inc.

Sylvia Plath: Letters Home. Selected and edited with commentary by Aurelia Schober Plath. Used by permission of Faber and Faber Ltd.

The Bell Jar by Sylvia Plath. Used by permission of Faber and Faber and Random House Inc, Publishers.

"Hughes Depicts Cambridge Scene" by Bonnie Joseph, *The Sophian,* 7 November 1957. Used with permission of Smith College Archives.

Unpublished poetry and pose by Sylvia Plath used by courtesy of Faber and Faber Ltd. The Lilly Library, Indiana University, Bloomington, Indiana, and Mortimer Rare Book Room, Smith College, Northampton, Massachusetts.

Some of the material in chapter 4 was originally published in the summer 2000 *Journal of Modern Literature.*

Lines from the poetry and prose of Laura (Riding) Jackson reprinted by permission of Carcanet Press, Manchester, Persea Books, New York, and the author's Board of Literary Management. The Board requires, as one of its conditions, that the following statement is printed:

> In conformity with the late author's wish, her Board of Literary Management asks us to record that, in 1941, Laura (Riding) Jackson renounced, on grounds of linguistic principle, the writing of poetry: she had come to hold that "poetry obstructs general attainment to something better in our linguistic way-of-life than we have."

Finally, it has not been possible to trace the original letters from Sylvia Plath to Lynne Lawner, copies of which are kept in the Mortimer Rare Book Room, but the author wishes to acknowledge the copyright holders in anticipation of their making themselves known to the publishers.

The two stanzas from "My Friend, My Friend" by Anne Sexton reprinted by permission of Sterling Lord Literistic, Inc. Copyright by Anne Sexton.

List of Abbreviations

CP   Sylvia Plath, *Collected Poems*, ed. Ted Hughes (London: Faber and Faber 1981)

JP   Sylvia Plath *Johnny Panic and the Bible of Dreams and other Prose Writings*, ed. Ted Hughes (London : Faber and Faber 1975)

JPl   Sylvia Plath *The Journals of Sylvia Plath* ed. Karen V. Kukil (London Faber and Faber 2000)

J   Sylvia Plath, *The Journals of Sylvia Plath*, ed. Frances McCullough and Ted Hughes (New York : Ballantine—Random House, 1982)

LH   Sylvia Plath, *Letters Home : Correspondence 1950–1963*, ed, Aurelia Plath (London : Faber, 1975)

MRBR   Sylvia Plath manuscript held at Smith College, Mortimer Rare Book Room

BJ   Sylvia Plath, *The Bell Jar* (1963) (London: Faber and Faber 1988)

LL   Manuscript held at Lilly Library, Indiana University

Writing Back

1

Sylvia Plath: Writing, History, and Politics

> We shall by morning
> Inherit the earth.
> Our foot's in the door.
> "Mushrooms" (1959)

> I just wish England had the sense to be neutral, for it is quite obvious
> that she would be 'obliterated' in an nuclear war, and for this reason
> I am very much behind the nuclear disarmers here.
> —Sylvia Plath, Letters Home 7 December 1961

> I want to study, learn history, politics, language.
> —Sylvia Plath, Letters Home 23 October 1962

THIS BOOK OFFERS A DETAILED EXPLORATION OF THREE ISSUES WHICH,
despite the steady growth of studies of Sylvia Plath and her writings, remain neglected. The first issue, virtually ignored by the main body of
Plath criticism, is the extent to which Plath's later writing was influenced
by the reporting of the Cold War politics and events of the early 1960s.
The second issue involves an assessment of the effect on Plath's writing
of her transatlantic shuttling, and the relationship of her work to specific
places. The third issue is, perhaps, the most contentious, and concerns
the extent to which some of the writing constitutes an act of deliberate
and conscious performance. Discussion of this third issue will interpret
the idea of "performance" in two quite distinct ways. One of these identifies particular writings as conscious experiments in voice. The other,
suggested by the expression "writing back," reads Plath's poetry and fiction as performed responses to the would-be controlling forces of state
and institutions, forces that operate on a national or global scale.

Linking all three issues is the idea of disguise, for the relationship between Plath's poetry and the public events of her time is a concealed relationship. In attempting to uncover it, certain objections have to be acknowledged and overcome. Allen Tate, speaking on behalf of those who
make poetry, argued that what matters is the completed poem, not where
it came from or why.[1] Other poets, such as Robert Graves, believed that

15

the Machiavellian and internecine world of the daily exercise of power is a distraction to the making of poems. Those national agencies of power and enemies of creativity, the organizations, institutions, and bureaucracies of public life, are avoided by any poets wishing to preserve their artistic integrity.

This view of art as a detached aesthetic is attractive, but suspect. It is particularly suspect with regard to the middle section of the twentieth century, when international events, impacting on individuals in a way only made possible by global technology, threatened to wipe out the familiar world altogether. In October 1962, Cold War anxiety translated itself into widespread fears of an imminent apocalypse, fuelling a heightened sense of the significance and urgency of the present. Hardly anyone was sheltered from these influences; even the remotest cottage or cabin could have access to global communication.

Until relatively recently Sylvia Plath has not been regarded as a very political writer, except on the very specific subject of sexual politics. Her poetry avoided references to contemporary events and where she draws on the imagery of such recent history as Hiroshima and the concentration camps this is usually understood to be Plath's way of using the politics of history to represent in striking metaphor the more generic dehumanization of the individual. It is in this sense—if at all—that her own claim, made in an interview just before she died, that she was "rather a political person"[2] is usually interpreted.

Nor is her work usually discussed in terms of its intimate relationship with place. The shuttling between America and England, added to the number of addresses Plath had in those two countries during her short life, suggests a rootless, shifting lifestyle. Her reminiscence of Winthrop, "Ocean 1212W," highlights an affectionate and intimate memory of place that contrasts with the disturbing—and sometimes menacing—representation of features of landscape and environment elsewhere in her writing, where, again, metaphor seems to have left specificity behind.

Instead, to account for the power and density of Plath's writing, there were for a long time two dominant lines of explanation, each an echo of the other. As Jacqueline Rose has pointed out,[3] there is a certain irony in the fact that ostensibly Hughes and some feminist critics share a belief that in her final year Plath tapped into a core self. For Hughes, this is the "true" self, one that is not artificial, not superficial, not immature. It is the voice that appears when the poet has achieved a mystical connection with god, or truth. Rose argues that this effectively relocates Plath within the patriarchy.

For the kind of reading that we encounter in some feminist criticism, there is a different, but parallel discovery of an "authentic" voice involving a similar process of discarding, except that here the layers that Plath sheds in her *Ariel* period are the layers that have been imposed by the patriarchy. Thus, the essential voice that is released, like Ariel from his pine tree, is either androgynous, like Shakespeare's Ariel, or the voice of unmediated woman. Plath is Venus, Sapphic, Lilith, the Earth Mother, the female principle, the winged lioness. What strikes a reader such as Janice Markey[4] is what she sees as the celebration of women in relationship, sometimes erotic relationship, in poems such as "Leaving Early," "Ariel," "Fever 103°" and "Lesbos." Markey also acknowledges the importance of religion, the cinema, satire, and consumerism in Plath's work, but argues that her achievement lay in writing about women with a clarity and directness that had not been achieved before.

This latter reading is supported by Plath's enthusiasm for the voice she discovered in Anne Sexton's *All My Pretty Ones,* a copy of which she received in August 1962. In a letter of congratulation sent to Sexton, and dated 21 August,[5] Plath praises the poems for being "womanly in the greatest sense" and "blessedly *unliterary.*" The poems she singles out for special praise—'For God While Sleeping", 'Letter written during a January Northeaster," "The Black Art," and "Lament," for example—with their Jewish imagery, exploration of absence of a former lover, questions about what it means to be a woman writer, and the remorseless indifference of nature to human suffering, provide glimpses of subjects that Plath was to incorporate into her own distinctive verse in the months that followed. Plath seems to be consciously writing directly as a woman, in a language that is no longer controlled by an agenda set by others.

Such readings should not be discarded, but it is time to regard them as incomplete. The extent of this incompleteness becomes clear when we see how the poems and fiction are informed by Plath's experience of the contrasting ideologies and politics of England and America and her response to Cold War reporting. It is clear that Plath's response to Cold War and other international events at the historical moment in which her children were born, was as much a catalyst for her writing as was the end of her marriage. Though the *Ariel* poems are informed by the latter experience, they, and *The Bell Jar,* would not have been written as they were without Plath's reading of the interaction of childbirth and the language of conflict and the Cold War, as experienced in England between 1960 and 1963.

A materialist reading of Plath of the kind to be advanced here will always seek to locate her writing not only in relation to specific places and insitutitions, but among the many other preparatory discourses that she encountered during her childhood and life as an adult woman. These include the discourses of middle class white America, and the European critiques of those discourses. It will be seen that there is continuity in her life and work—Plath's desire for fame and success, the practice of writ-

ing—and, there is realignment. The early community security and certainties provided by family, Girl Scouts, and Winthrop beach is replaced
by the uncertainties and stresses of individualism and competition. The
experience of Europe and the brief return to the United States then
caused Plath to modify her reading of art and society. Put simply, the
move from England to America, back to America and then back to England stimulated an intellectual dialog and a dialectic with the politics of
each country. This she internalized alongside the previously established
vocabulary and discourse of myth and mysticism, and the one ground re-
morselessly against the "other." Plath's experience of motherhood and international tension combined to accelerate a re-evaluation of the importance of history, politics and institutions. In particular, the commentaries
on the Cold War and nuclear warfare, which she read, heard and responded to, contributed to the specific language of the *Ariel* sequence in
ways about which we cannot be categorical, but which should be admitted. Plath read widely and during her time in England the discourse of
the Cold War pervaded serious journalism, television and radio, protest
folk songs, and satire.

In one sense, Plath's work *has* frequently been considered as the product of a specific time and a specific place. And, here lies a problem. The
problem is that as new readers encounter her work there is enormous
pressure on them to interpret "specific time" and place in terms of Plath's
known life story, as if she were a character from some epic drama such
as *Gone With the Wind.* So much general reporting has discussed Plath's
work as the interiorizing of experience dictated by the politics of personal
relationships, that other possibilities have been overshadowed. This tendency has been fuelled by the succession of biographies, newspaper articles, documentaries, and films which explore her life. The Plath industry tends to distort Plath's own writing, for the endless discussion of her
relationships make it difficult to locate the published work in other
frames, in other contexts.

Yet, it is important to do this—to look at the writing in its relationship
to the public, often political discourses from which it emerged and in its
relationship to other texts. Here, "texts" do not refer principally to other
literary works that Plath read, very important though these are. They
mean newspapers, magazines, radio programs, and films, which all provided windows through which she regularly viewed her world.

More specifically, it is important to study Plath as a writer in her period, and both in and out of place. She left America to live on an island
at the edge of Europe at the height of the Cold War, not having seen or
experienced the war in Europe at first hand, but gradually discovering its
aftermath. The process would have been disorientating for any young
American. Plath's dream of England contrasted with an American mili-

tary view of England as a Cold War fort, just behind the frontier of the Iron Curtain (the garrisons placed in England during World War II now strengthened with nuclear weapons), which itself contrasted with England's post-war dreams of a new Elizabethan age. As a country, England offered Plath frustration and joy. The disappointing drabness of the English capital and coast was offset by her delight in the cottages and moors in Yorkshire and Devon.

An examination of these cultural reference points and their relationship to the writing will contribute to a greater recognition of the *density* of Plath's poetry and prose, which can increasingly be seen as reconstructed barometers of their time rather than diverse expressions of autobiography. Such an examination, which draws on new discoveries in the Plath manuscripts, will also encourage an appreciation of the *breadth* of her work.

WAYS OF READING SYLVIA PLATH: FROM MYTH TO POLITICS

Within the field of Plath criticism, there has been no extended study of Plath and politics, but there has been a shift towards an appreciation of the cultural specificity of her work. Over the four decades since Plath's death there has been a gradual move away from those readings which privilege the mythological, first in the direction of readings which emphasise the role of the subconscious, and more recently to those which emphasise the importance of gender and the significance of history and culture.

The body of work that Plath's writing has generated is so huge, that any brief summary must of necessity be indicative and partial. The purpose of attempting an overview, however, is to acknowledge the range of discourses into which Plath can be seen to have tapped. Like the criticism itself, her work shows continuities. The majority of these discourses are traceable in all the work, from the earliest to the very latest—and, the question that presents itself is the extent to which there is a shift in Plath's writing from the individual to the collective that corresponds to the shift in the criticism from the mythic to the socially engaged.

For many critics, an understanding of mythology has been the key to Plath's writing. Judith Kroll's early study[6] was one of the first to trace the poetry's moon imagery and other motifs back to the symbolism and mythology associated with Robert Graves's *The White Goddess*. At Smith College and Cambridge, Plath's extensive reading as an English major had brought her into contact with the rich world of myth, metaphor and metonymy, and her meetings with Richard Sassoon and Ted Hughes intensified this interest. Their shared immersion in European traditions of esotericism, mysticism, and the occult has been well documented, most recently by Mary Kurtzman[7] (who emphasizes the importance of Plath's cabalistic beliefs and her interest in the Tarot), and by Timothy Materer in *Modernist Alchemy.*[8]

In some ways, this interest in folklore and archetypes links directly with another discourse which has also been extensively discussed. One of the characteristics of esotericism that attracts followers of the magical and the concealed is the very idea that there may be such a thing as hidden knowledge accessible to only a few. The rich tradition of the occult, taken in its widest sense to include Astrology, Rosicrucianism, Sufiism, the Kabbala, Masonic ritual, the Knights Templar, Neo-platonism, the cult of Isis, Theosophy, and so on, has provided a rich source of material for those twentieth-century writers (such as Yeats), who identify with the nineteenth-century Romantic model of the poet as seer and transcendent magician whose wand is language. Influenced by the model of the medieval alchemist, such an individual was undertaking a Faustian search for knowledge which required the practitioner to withdraw from the world and dedicate himself/herself totally to the pursuit of the ineffable. This willingness to retreat and become solitary was more congenial to Hughes than it was to Plath, but initially, her own feelings about the seriousness of their shared project meant that she was willing to accept a reduced circle of friends in Cambridge, in Northampton (while she was teaching at Smith College), in London (in Chalcot Square), and, finally, during her first year at Court Green in Devon.

This voluntary isolation meant that Plath was encouraged by circumstances, as well as inclination to tap into the second discourse with which her work is associated, the discourse and practice of self-analysis. Encouraged by Freudian and Jungian theory, her psychotherapist, Ruth Beuscher, and her contact with Robert Lowell to believe that her established practice of writing in journals about the intensity of her personal experience, including her breakdown and attempted suicide in 1953— could be transmuted into crafted, hard-edged poems, Plath set about chronicling her own inner odyssey, in verse and prose. Much of the writing about Plath's poetry draws on the tools of psychoanalysis: David Holbrook's *Sylvia Plath*[9] with its shrill charges of nihilism and psychotic poetry, works backwards from the suicide and finds plentiful evidence of an obsession with death and negation, schizophrenia and a divided self. Later studies, such as Jacqueline Rose's *The Haunting of Sylvia Plath,*[10] have tried to offer less simplistic readings, uncoupling the writing/writer connection that any knowledge of Plath's life makes so inviting and attractive. This second reading practice, one which privileges psychoanalytic theory, thus complements the first, in that both emphasize sup-

pressed, hidden knowledge which expert analysis can reveal. The alchemist seeks to divine the world, the psychoanalyst the individual, the
psychoanalytical theorist the text.

It also intersects with a third critical approach. Feminist readings of
Plath emphasize her journey as a woman initially constructed by, and
then challenging and escaping, the patriarchy through a language and
discourse that is specifically female. Although Plath did not have access
to the specific discourse of the second wave of twentieth-century feminism—*The Feminine Mystique* was published in January 1963 in America, and in England after her death, and she does not appear to have
owned a copy of Simone de Beauvoir's 1949 study, *The Second Sex*. Some
feminist readings have tended to recognise in Plath those qualities which
have been associated with *l'écriture féminine*. These readings draw on
the arguments of Irigaray, Kristeva, and Cixous,[11] that women can write
themselves into being through a resistance to the patriarchal, linear language, which in accordance with male sexuality privileges conclusion and
resolution. With either the specifically female allusion to menstrual
blood, breasts, maternity, moon and lioness, or the androgynous spirit figures of Ariel and Lady Lazarus, Plath is seen to construct a gendered language, or rather a language which problematises gender. Sandra M.
Gilbert and Susan Gubar[12] take a slightly different angle, emphasizing
the way that Plath reworks the imagery and iconography of male writers,
such as Yeats and Lawrence. At the same time they show how she challenges the patriarchy and conceives of gender relations as conflict, de-
ploying the language of warfare in poems which become a site for the
clash between the sexes. In other recent feminist readings, where gender itself is seen as a social construct or *performance* (as argued by Judith
Butler),[13] Plath's later work can be seen in part as an acting-out, or un-
ravelling, of that performance. Jacqueline Rose develops a similar argument, and Susan Van Dyne also considers the performative element in
gender in her study of Plath's poetry.[14] Many of these debates about gender, subjectivity and language are brought together in Christina Britzolakis's *Sylvia Plath and the Theatre of Mourning*,[15] in which Plath's poetry is read as psychic theater.

Earlier critics, such as Hugh Kenner[16] and David Shapiro[17] had rejected the notion that there is a consciously performative element,
whether gendered or not, accusing Plath of "bogus spirituality" (Kenner)
or melodrama (Shapiro). Other critics included in the same study, edited
by Gary Lane in 1979,[18] read the performative element as comic per-
sonae. J. D. O'Hara[19] argues that the voice that we hear in the more furious and raging poems is a deliberately bizarre and eccentric one which
at times incorporates the gallows humor that characterizes some of Beckett's characters. Samuel Beckett is just one of the special influences that

have been traced in Plath's work. Other sources of inspiration include the more obvious, such as Robert Lowell, Dylan Thomas, Roethke, Yeats, Dostoyevsky and W. H. Auden, whose influence was often acknowledged by Plath. They also include Virginia Woolf, D. H. Lawrence, and J. D. Salinger, all of whom Plath admired and imitated. Less obvious influences include de Quincey, Stevie Smith and, in her final year, the satirical work of Spike Milligan and the *Beyond the Fringe*[20] team.

In the search for thematic readings the technical qualities of the poems—and, the prose—can be overlooked, and, it is salutory to read the middle section of Gilbert and Gubar's discussion of Plath.[21] Here, there is a reminder of the technical experiments with form that characterize the genesis of so many of the poems—both early, and late. Gilbert and Gubar show how it is possible to rearrange the broken final lines of "Ariel" into a "ghost text" of a regular quatrain. Such observations act as a corrective to the image of the poet with her thesaurus, an emphasis which tends to belittle her achievement. Plath's keen and practiced interest in form has been noted, particularly with respect to her early work. It is discussed by Daniel Weissbort [22] in his essay describing the background to her translation of four sonnets by the French sixteenth-century poet, Pierre de Ronsard. The Ronsard translations are remarkable for their skill in retaining the sonnet form. Plath was a deeply formal writer. She constantly experimented within the demands of traditional form, and found this liberating rather than a restraint. The emphasis is on the "form" of "perform," which comes from the Old French *fournir* "to finish," or complete.

There is yet another major discourse with which the poetry joins. Plath's most powerful writing was produced in England in an environment that at times seemed extraordinarily alien to her. But, not only did England appear alien, as we know from her own remarks and Hughes's recently published "Birthday Letters" poems, America itself became defamiliarized. Plath came to see her own country differently as she absorbed some of the pacifist dissent of English liberal political activism. This was a time when the active Campaign for Nuclear Disarmament movement in Britain targeted the American Polaris nuclear submarines at Holy Loch in Scotland and the presence of atomic bomb research center at Aldermaston in England. The significance of this twin alienation, and the use Plath made of it, is often overshadowed in studies of her life and writing which tend to concentrate on the rupture with Hughes, privileging notions of the confessional, of gender and the autobiographical over notions of the geo-political. Gilbert and Gubar, for example state a widely shared belief that "Although Plath claimed in a late radio interview to be deeply concerned with world politics, she did not have an explicitly political imagination."[23]

Even in the more recent studies, there is a tendency to downgrade the significance of politics. In the more simplistic readings, this has been used as an excuse to use the writing as if it were simply a route back into the life, in a rather unproductive attempt to discover a single "true" reading of this life, as in Sylvia Lehrer's study.[24] Even in studies which promise to take the reader in interesting new directions (such as the discussion of racial politics in Renée Curry's chapter "The Enactment of Whiteness in Plath's Poetry" there is a tendency to return to familiar positions:

> Plath's . . . investment in depicting a whiteness that lacks unless marked by features of racial Otherness, along with the sheer accumulation of color, whiteness and blackness in her poetry, evinces Plath as a poet both produced by the racial politics of the 1950s United States and superficially aware of a need to focus particular attention on racial politics. Although Plath might claim her own whiteness and its lack for particular purposes, the only real subject matter she scrutinizes in her poetry is that of the self spiraling in on the self.[25]

History, rather than contemporary global politics, has been the main focus for discussion which deals with cultural issues. In *The Holocaust and the Literary Imagination,* Lawrence Langer[26] quotes Adorno's "No Poetry after Auschwitz" and discusses Steiner's critical position, which questions Plath's need to confront the horrors of the atrocities of the Holocaust, and her appropriation of this discourse. This looks backward to Plath's relationship with her past, and is clearly an important cultural factor informing the writing. Later recognition of the political dimension in Plath's life and writing—by critics such as Mazzaro,[27] Uroff,[28] Sinfield,[29] Rose[30] and Strangeways[31]—does take discussion forward to consider the relevance of Cold War events in the late 1950s for an understanding of Plath's writing. Tracy Brain[32] has recently drawn attention to the relationship between Plath's work and concerns about the environment expressed in such books as Rachel Carson's *Silent Spring.* This approach will be taken an important stage further by concentrating on the relationship between Plath's later work and her reading of specific newspapers and magazines of the 1960s, and by considering Plath's relationship with radio.

That Plath became increasingly politicized in England, especially after 1960, is a claim never before examined in a full length study. It is not a claim that is ever made with much conviction, partly because other, more personal events in her life have seemed to offer a more obvious way into to the writing. Yet, there is a strong argument for paying attention to the public and the political, for once, to see how it alters the reading of Plath. In *The Political Unconscious,* Fredric Jameson argues for the "priority of the political interpretation of literary texts."[33] Unlike classic psychoanalytic theory which examines how mental processes such as fantasy operate at the individual level, articulations of political-unconscious theory, building on Jameson, "pave the way for understanding how fantasies operate at the individual and cultural level and are shaped by material forces".[34]

Plath's later writing was produced in specific places in England during a period of heightened world tension, and her interaction with the specificities of place and time including the textual environment, the physical and cultural environments and the global political environment, should not be overshadowed by the narrative of her marriage and premature death. Plath initially regarded many of these elements as background to her work, but they insisted on seeping into the writing, a seepage she came increasingly to accept and value. In the radio interview in which she called herself a "rather political person," Plath also acknowledged the importance of the gods of place for her as a writer, and her eagerness to pack as much as possible into the writing. This concern with the detail of the now would have earned disapproval from some of her artistic friends, but she distances herself from their male aesthetic: "I'm a woman, I like my little *Lares* and *Penates*. I like trivia, and I find that in a novel I can get more of life. . . .[35]

The message in the whole of this interview is clear. Politics and the "trivia" of place are not to be excluded from her art, and nor should they be excluded from a discussion of it. This may seem a rather banal thing to say, and since the argument is not that Plath's writing was political in its intent, but rather that it is informed by an anxiety about international politics, this may also appear to be giving undue prominence to things that can be taken for granted. Any sensitive, intelligent human being, any man or woman with young children, is likely to feel anxious about the damage being done to the environment and is likely to be affected by a rise in international tension. Yet, what is striking about the discussion of Plath's writing, is the remarkable dehistoricisation of it from the period 1960 to 1963. This surprising critical omission needs to be addressed. It seemed insufficient to mention world events and places and then pass over them: they needed to be evaluated as important contemporary discourses and sites with which Plath's work intersects.

POLITICS AND THE PRINT ENVIRONMENT: COLD WAR FEAR AND THE SPECIFICITIES OF PLACE

For you have got to remember that around 1960, at the height of the Cold War, everybody thought we were going to be blown up. These people—Lowell and then Sylvia, were very much writing about that strain.

—Al Alvarez, BBC Radio 4, 19 March 2000

Evidence of the strain caused by and reflected in the newspapers and magazines of this Cold War period can be found by turning to almost any issue of the weekly publications that Plath read. One example from the last few months of her life will illustrate the character of this discourse of anxiety.

On turning to page eight of their Sunday newspaper on 27 January 1963, readers of *The Observer,* among whose number was Sylvia Plath, whose novel *The Bell Jar* was reviewed by Anthony Burgess elsewhere in this edition of the London-based paper,—would have noticed an unusual half page advertisement under the bold heading "Operation Safety Catch." The privately sponsored advertisement was a long personal plea to end the dangerous Cold War crisis. It consisted entirely of small print, and provided evidence of the huge feeling of anxiety about nuclear war that was running through a significant section of the population of England at the beginning of 1963. The recent period of sustained international tension, from the Russian and American tank confrontation across the Berlin divide in October 1961 to the Cuban Missile Crisis of October 1962, had produced a prolonged period of anxiety, and the daily possibility of a nuclear exchange seemed, and was, very real. The advertisement was paid for by an anonymous self-styled "member of the World of faceless fission fodder" and although (or perhaps precisely because) it proposed what many would see as a politically naive solution to the confrontation of the nuclear Cold War Superpowers,[36] it is an indicator of just how fearful many people in England were at this time. The long statement, a "memorandum to governments of nuclear nations" concludes by moving from a global perspective to a very personal one:

> 3 A.M.—Awake in the silent hours as a high flying jet whispers across the night sky patrolling, perhaps, with an unsigned death warrant for some distant town. Somewhere, too, is a missile aimed at my own locality. This is no dream of fitful sleep but harsh reality. . . . Suppose it were to happen now, at this instant, how would it be? A lingering flash, more brilliant than the midday sun, followed by silence. The children cry out in terror. The shock wave is but seconds away, battering to dust all within its path. The Kingdom of Chaos and his dark pavilion is now at hand.[36]

This advertisement is a surface, textual expression of an anxiety that by January 1963 was being fed by a succession of newspaper and magazine articles on the arms race. The rhetoric and imagery of this journalism sustained and reinforced the widespread underlying fear about nuclear war. In September 1962, the "Science and the Citizen" column in *Scientific American* began as follows:

> In the past 12 months the nuclear testing game of follow-the-leader has loosed more megatons of nuclear energy than all the explosions in the entire 17 year

period since Alamogordo. The latest round began last September 1, when the U.S.S.R. broke the three-year test moratorium with a series of multimegaton atmospheric explosions. The U.S. retaliated first with a series of small underground tests and then, beginning in April, with atmospheric tests. The U.S series was drawing to a close when in early August the U.S.S.R. started up again with a test in the atmosphere.[38]

Such rhetoric, whether circulating among the scientific community or aimed at a more general reader (and journalists in daily papers trawl the specialist journalists for material), inevitably heightens the reader's sense of anxiety, apocalypse and human powerlessness. When placed alongside the poetry and fiction Plath produced in England between 1960 and 1963, common features can be observed, suggesting that certain aspects of these discourses have been absorbed by Plath. These are incorporated in Plath's poetry and novel and contribute to the shifts in voice, density and urgency that are traceable in her writing from this period.

This shift is especially noticeable when contrasting this later writing with her earlier 1950s work. In 1956, during her first stay in England, Plath wrote a poem called "Dialogue between Ghost and Priest." The title hints at one strand in Plath's writing traceable well beyond her student period. The emphasis is on the spiritual rather than the temporal, myth and religion rather than social commentary, and the romance of history rather than the historicity of politics. The Cold War was no less real in 1956, but for Plath its events occupied that interesting but distant hinterland called "politics."

The word "politics" is used here and throughout this text in the narrower sense in which it was used before more recent cultural theory broadened its meaning: that is, as the organization and administration of local, state or international affairs by governmental organisations. Politics, in other words, is what is defined by Hague, Harrop, Breslin, and glossed by Axford "as the process by which groups make collective decisions."[39] This is not to accept the binary categories of individual/state, questioned by gender theory which sees sexual politics in *all* relationships and by cultural theory which sees agency as a principle informing thought and behavior so pervasively that the category "individual" is itself questionable. It is precisely the case that Plath came to question the limits of her own autonomy and to reassess the forces impinging on her as a writer in ways which represent her own politicization. But, in the 1950s, Plath defined and discussed herself primarily in relation to imaginative writing, art, and immediate personal relationships. Her relationship to the state was secondary. She was well aware of cultural pressures (particularly on women,) but saw these as functions of society rather than of government. Later, global events forced her to reassess this separation, and to recognize greater continuity and connectedness between the operation of the individual and the world she inhabited. Cold War events forced into every citizen's consciousness a crude realization of the dangerous consequences of parties differing in their view of government, as acted out in the confrontation between the United States and the Soviet Union.

It is true that international politics involved sets of ideas and issues of which Plath became increasingly aware at Cambridge in the mid-1950s, but their expression in the behavior of states and politicians did not constitute a perceived *threat* to her personally. A visit to a reception for Khrushcev and Bulganin held by the Russian Embassy in London is a subject for an essentially light-hearted sketch in *Varsity*, and in a letter to her mother (LH: 242) she balances a report of the politicians she saw at the reception with the news that her husband, Ted Hughes, is teaching her about horoscopes.

The titles of other poems from that year ("Conversations Among the Ruins," "Bucolics," "Two Sisters of Persephone," "Faun," and "Crystal Gazer" point to experiments in poetry emerging from a university literature degree at Cambridge and Plath's contact with a circle of people interested in art, myth and the supernatural. Although she writes about political events in the letters and prose, these other preoccupations were more central to her other writing, and they never entirely disappear from her work. The poems from the 1960s incorporate ideas and images from mythology, religion, and literature, and in the last months of her life she was conducting a written dialog with an American priest from Oxford. But, by then the second experience of England at a time of Cold War political tension had contributed to a gradual, but significant shift in her writing. This transformation, involving a kind of crystallization of images which combine urgency and dense concentrations of thought and feeling, is obvious to even the casual reader, but is usually explained in terms which disregard the relevance of contemporary global politics and the specificities of place. The relationship between this later writing, history and contemporary political discussion, takes discussion into new territory.

The critical practice of historicizing is a well established one. In 1981, Fredric Jameson exhorted readers to "Always historicise!"[40] Catherine Belsey began her 1983 essay "Literature, history, politics" by acknowledging that even then there was nothing new in bringing together the three disciplines in her title. She argues that Raymond Williams, E. P. Thomson and Christopher Hill had been doing it throughout their lives, and a tradition of European Marxist criticism has always done it. Even T. S. Eliot, F. R. Leavis and E. M. W. Tillyard did it when they sought to construct a sense of a lost Elizabethan community, organic, unified and rich in language.[41]

In her essay, Belsey's interest in these three disciplines is Foucauldian, and she praises the way that Foucault's work "politicizes the polyphony of the signified."[42] Such an approach has had the effect of decentring literary criticism, focusing attention instead on phenomena such as power and discourse. Politics and history are not used as contexts to support readings of literature, but as discourses in their own right to be read alongside literary texts. The purpose of this critical practice is to see if such parallel readings provide evidence of exchanges of language that permit fresh readings of texts.

The search for evidence of such interaction and crosscurrents of discourse is by no means a new departure in Plath studies. In the opening section of his 1982 study of twentieth-century poetry Stan Smith wrote:

> All poetry, at its deepest levels, is structured by the precise historical experience from which it emerged, those conjunctures in which its author was formed, came to consciousness and found a voice. . . . [T]o Sylvia Plath, for example, identity itself is the primary historical datum: the self is a secretion of history, and therefore not initially "my" self at all, but the voice of its antecedents, its progenitors, a "mouthpiece of the dead."[43]

Smith argues that the specificity of place is very important for an understanding of Plath's writing, and this is a theme developed in the first part of this book, which locates Plath culturally in a the contrasting perspectives of post-war America and England. Smith also argues that an understanding of the specificity of experience, shaped as it by the historical now, is something that also informs the poetry. In discussing Plath's poems about birth Smith remarks, "What they embody, as their primary premise, is the *historicity* of the personal life, its status as a historical secretion, the precipitate of an order which precedes and will re-absorb it."[44]

Plath's interest in history is always rooted in the specific, seeking in "The Colossus," for example, an understanding of the limits of historical recovery, and of the obsession with the impossible task of remaking, reassembling, and restoring the past. This awareness of historical events overshadowing Plath's own past has been explored more recently by Sandra Gilbert and Susan Gubar. In their discussion of Plath's writing,[45] they assert that the *Ariel* poems show that throughout her entire life, the "real" world for Plath remained the marked world of her childhood, the world of the second world war. As evidence of this, readers are pointed towards the references to Hiroshima and the concentration camps in the 1962 *Ariel* poems. Subtler readings, such as this, avoid the trap of viewing poetry as sociology,[46] and there is much in Plath's writing to encourage readings which emphasize the way that the 1940s and the war cast a long shadow which influenced her writing in complex ways. The past is important to Plath, but she was also very actively engaged with the culture of her present. What she saw and heard either first hand or via cinema or radio excited her and was frequently a stimulus for her creative work.

PAINTINGS AND FILMS: IDIOGRAPHIC ELEMENTS IN THE VISUAL ENVIRONMENT

Plath possessed a highly developed visual imagination. She liked to paint and produced a series of pen drawings, mainly of buildings in Yorkshire, Cambridge and Spain. She wrote poems inspired by paintings such as Giorgio de Chirico's *The Disquieting Muses* and Rousseau's *The Dream* and by films such as Bergman's *Brink of Life*. In her biography of Plath, Linda Wagner-Martin[47] acknowledges George Steiner's interesting re- mark that Plath's 1962 poems can be compared to Picasso's anti-war painting, *Guernica*. Her later work can be compared to sophisticated col- lage, with each element carefully chosen for its individual effect, yet all contained within a tight form.

The collage effect is characteristic of the work of de Chirico and other artists associated with surrealism. A 1944 wartime painting by Salvador Dalí, *Dream Caused by the Flight of a Bee around a Pomegranate One Second Before Awakening*, contains several of the disturbing, displaced and sometimes surreal images that appear in Plath's writing. In the paint- ing, tigers leap surreally from the sky while a naked dreaming woman in the foreground is about to be awoken by the pouncing tigers or the rifle arrowing its way towards her, erasing the dream of the bee encircling the pomegranate. Such global political images of war and the unconscious have parallels in Plath's prose and poetry, which contains several allusions to the dreaming "lady," the rapacious tigers, and the flight of the bee. It is not unlikely that Plath knew the painting. The narrator in "Superman and Paula Brown's New Snowsuit," the short story which explores the ex- perience of a young girl growing up during the Second World War in America, describes the strange dreams she experiences, "My flying dreams were as believable as a landscape by Dali. . . ." (JP: 160).

There are echoes of Dalí in her own "political" picture, her 1960 anti- war and anti-patriarchy collage. In this image, kept at Smith College, Dalí's rifle bayonet of war threatening to pierce the woman finds a par- allel in the the spike of a jet plane carrying nuclear weapons that threat- ens Plath's cut-out woman. Both visual images draw on a common theme in which there is an interaction between the discourses and imagery of war and psychoanalysis.

The nuclear mushroom cloud was a potent and recurrent image haunt- ing the Cold War period. The image haunted both film and print. A much read 1946 book, *Hiroshima,* by John Hersey,[48] originally published in a single edition of *The New Yorker,* describes the immediate aftereffects of World War II nuclear explosion on the civilian population of Hiroshima. This text also contains images that are echoed in Plath's writing in England in the 1960s: the 103° fever that accompanies radiation sickness, the peeling skin, the baldness of the irradiated victims, and the presence of German Catholics priests suffering alongside the Japanese victims of the nuclear bomb. There seems to be no way of knowing if Plath read Hersey's book, but it is clear that the discourse into which it fed haunted her, and that Gilbert and Gubar's conclusion is right. In writing about her present world, Plath is drawing on the iconography, imagery, and discourses of her childhood and writing back to her past.

Such a view is consistent with psychological, feminist, mythological and historical readings of Plath, and it is one that fits in neatly with the view presented in the various biographies.[49] But, this presents a rather partial picture. It is fruitful to consider other readings, and rather than restricting discussion to the interaction of this writing with the cultural influence of World War II (1940s) or the Korean War (1950s) it is profitable to pay more attention to the relationship between Plath's writing and the more immediate discourses of the Cold War in the 1960s.

The fact that, in both her prose and poetry, Plath generally avoids direct reference to the issues, concerns and debates of the early 1960s should not be taken as evidence that she remained unaffected by them. Cultural influences can be absorbed, and produce unexpected symptoms in unexpected places. When children originally watched 1950s science fiction films about alien invasions and creatures from outer space, it did not occur to the majority of them to connect these films with the Cold War events outside the cinema, of which many children were only dimly aware. Contemporary critics, however, were quicker to make connections, arguing that films such as *The War of the Worlds* (1953), *The Invasion of the Body Snatchers* (1955), *The Incredible Shrinking Man* (1957), and *The Fly* (1958) were tapping into American anxieties about the possibility of world domination by Communism or the aftermath of nuclear war. As Thompson and Bordwell comment, "Such films were interpreted in immediate historical terms, often as commentaries on Cold War politics or the nightmarish effect of nuclear radiation."[50]

If films are the product of more complex influences than this simple interpretative reading suggest, then this is even truer of the greater textual density of some poetry and novels. Adam Bresnick[51] has written of the "density of signification" in poetry (he refers specifically to Homer) which allows for more powerfully condensed discussion. It would be over-simplistic to suggest that the Cold War determined the form that such science fiction films took. But, acknowledging the complexity of texts does not invalidate their possible dialectical relationship with contemporary global political discourses. It simply acknowledges that they do other things as well.

This density of allusion means that the cross over from film to poetry is implicit in some of Plath's poems, but very near the surface in the arrangement of the verse poem for three voices "Three Women," suggested by a Bergman film. By way of contrast, documentary film of either atomic bomb survivors, or concentration camp prisoners is the subject of the 1957 poem "The Thin People:"

> They are always with us, the thin people
> Meager of dimension as the gray people
>
> On a movie-screen. They
> Are unreal, we say:
>
> It was only in a movie, it was only
> In a war making evil headlines when we
>
> Were small

(CP: 64)

Although apparently specific in its World War II Holocaust reference, the poem also explores the continuous haunting of the mind, through dream and recollection rekindled by fresh images of war. Yet, in this poem, as in the later work, there is a seeming desire to allow the specificity of the past and present to be embraced by what Plath saw as the larger resonance of myth. For the sound recording made at Harvard in 1958 the poem was called "The Moon was a Fat Woman Once," a reference to the myth of the paring of the moon. The poem jumps to this myth, as if wanting to escape the very image it has conjured up, but the image will not disappear.

PLATH, WRITING, AND POLITICS

For anyone setting out to trace the interaction between the majority of Plath's writing in England and the contemporary discourse of global politics, the initial evidence is unpromising. As with 1950s science fiction films, there is little or nothing in Plath's poetry that directly provides a direct commentary on the Cold War conflict or other contemporary events. In her public statements Plath said that she deliberately avoided writing about the newspaper headlines. Plath's small, personal library, held at Smith College, is predominantly literary, containing books ranging alphabetically from Auden to Yeats. Her letters and journals seem to concern themselves largely with matters of immediate personal interest, most obviously her family (letters) and her writing and relationship with those around her (journals). As far as we know, Plath never worked for a political group such as the Democratic Party (in America), nor the Liberal, Labour or Communist Party (in England), although she was broadly in sympathy with at least some of the aims of several of these groups. And, although we know that she endorsed the work of the Campaign for Nuclear Disarmament, this endorsement did not translate into political disobedience and activism. She did not vote until she was well into her twenties and this cannot be wholly explained by the exigencies of a student life which meant that she was away from home during important elections.

There are explanations for such political reticence, however. In the 1950s America in which Plath grew to adulthood increased prosperity, the rise of corporatism and the fear of communism stifled reasoned political thinking. In the practice of literature there had been a retreat from the high water mark of radical positions taken in the 1930s by writers and critics such as Lionel Trilling, Alfred Kazin, and Philip Rahv. Such critics now shared common ground with the increasingly dominant New Criticism philosophy espoused by conservative Southerners (such as Warren, Brooks, and Ransom), who were now teaching in Northern universities. In junior high school, Plath was given *Understanding Poetry* by Cleanth Brooks and Robert Penn Warren as her prize for being the outstanding student of her final year. At Smith, influential mentors such as Alfred Kazin and the visiting W. H. Auden were long past their overtly Marxist days. In the words of Alan Trachtenberg, in the United States "there was a growing post-war consensus . . . that the difficult and vital issues of American capitalist society lay in the realm of culture."[52] In Britain, there had been a similar turning away from the explicit political engagement of writers such as Orwell, Auden, and Shaw in the 1930s. England of the mid-1950s, that Plath experienced as a Fulbright scholar, had slipped back into a narrow conservatism that made the visionary program of the 1945 Labour Government seem a lifetime away. In both America and England there were some dissident voices, but the incipient rebellion of the Beat Movement did not initially strike much of a chord at Smith or Cambridge, and though Plath's discovery of Hughes seemed to link her with the black corduroy of rebellion, it took her away from political involvement. Hughes, like many English writers in the Romantic tradition before him, felt that the way to cope with the modern world was to withdraw from it. Although sometimes it was expedient to work for society, the city was a soulless place, and therefore, the poet must seek inspiration in isolation. The poets that Hughes later cited as influential on his own practice[53] (Lawrence, Dylan Thomas and Graves) were part of this tradition of withdrawal. Without this conscious separation of the artist from the world Hughes's work would perhaps not have had the specific intensity that marked it, but it is arguable that some of the new English poets of post 1945 Britain paid a price for turning their backs on their contemporary environment:

> Like their readers, most of the poets came from provincial, lower-middle class backgrounds; and they were therefore in a position to speak for and from an England not commonly met with in poetry. At first it looked as though they would seize this opportunity. Soon, however, their scholarship-boy ambition to achieve a certain classlessness led them to identify weaknesses as strengths, to overvalue Graves, and to turn their back on history, including the history of their own times.[54]

In her avoidance of overt political references in her poems, therefore, Plath was part of a trend. This was not confined to England. The pressures to avoid politics were brought to bear on other American writers of the period. One of the poets she identified as a "rival," Adrienne Rich, has written of the learning process that awakened her political awareness, and its impact on her poetry:

> The poems . . . were written by a woman growing up and living in the fatherland of the United States of North America. One task for the nineteen- or twenty-year-old poet who wrote the earliest poems here was to learn that she was neither unique nor universal, but a person in history, a woman and not a man, a white and also Jewish inheritor of a particular Western consiousness, from the making of which most women have been excluded.[55]

The early, formative voices to which Plath paid most heed (her English teachers, then Ted Hughes and Robert Lowell) all encouraged a very different kind of learning process, emphasizing poetry as something uniquely individual rather than collective, Romantic rather than historicized. All encouraged her to turn inwards for inspiration, and to experiment with images drawn from myth rather than Marx.

The biographies have tended to confirm this picture of a person absorbed in the more personal events of her own life, in her relationships, career and ambitions as a writer. More recently, however, there has been some acknowledgement that the evidence occasionally suggests that matters are more complex. It is odd that it *is* only recently that this interaction between her writing and contemporary political events has been more widely acknowledged, because even the most cursory examination of the way Plath lived and the way she responded to the world provides evidence of a remarkably active, visually aware, perceptive, and practical person engaged with the outer world at every level and at every moment.

She paints and sketches. She drives, she rides a horse, she cooks, she paints furniture, she tends her garden, amd she keeps bees. She responds to the visual stimulus of paintings, photographs and films, as well as to the nature around her. At the moment when she does her most remarkable writing, she has two very young children to look after. She is anxious that they have the very best chance in life: they are a rich source of joy, and she is determined to protect them from the ravages of a world which at times seems determined to destroy them.

This in itself does not amount to politicization in the narrower, more commonly used sense, but it does shift the contextualization of Plath's writing into that borderland between politics and art. The occupation of this territory has a significance for a reading of the 1960s texts that is not true of Plath's pre-England 1950s writing, where the political awareness is often perfunctory. Her experiences of the discourses and political discussion in England changed the way that Plath read, and this change is documented in the writing. The change is implicit in Stan Smith's assessment that

> Plath is, in fact, a profoundly political poet, who has seen the generic nature of these private catastrophes, their origin in a civilization founded on mass manipulation and collective trickery, which recruits its agents by those processes of repression and sublimation, denial and deferment which brings the ego to its belated birth in a family, a class, a gender.[56]

There is evidence that Plath was greatly disturbed by contemporary accounts and representations of inhumanity, whether these concerned events from the recent past or those being reported in the news. According to Al Alvarez,[57] during her time in England, Plath watched and was impressed by Resnais's film *Hiroshima Mon Amour* (1959), in which an affair between a Japanese man and a French woman actor who has come to perform in an anti-war film is played out against flashbacks to Hiroshima and World War II. The inter-relationship of history and present is emphasised in the opening sequence in which the lingering shot of falling ash coating the naked lovers is juxtaposed with stark newsreel film of Hiroshima victims with peeling skin. Flashbacks to the woman's experiences at the end of the War, when she driven to hide in the basement in her French village by hostile villagers who have shorn her hair for loving a German soldier, together with the subsequent despair and hospitalization, would have had a particular resonance for Plath.

That films and magazines could disturb Plath is shown by these journal entries written in 1958 following her return from England to teach at Smith College:

> August 27th (T)hen we got stupidly involved reading magazines in the library at Smith which always sickens me: vitriol between critics, writers, politicians:

an arsonist burnt to a black crisp death depicted in *Life* in the space before death, his skin hanging and curling away like peeled black paint; cremation fires burning in the dead eyes of Anne Franck: horror on horror, injustice on cruelty—all accessible, various—how can the soul keep from flying to fragments—disintegrating in one wild dispersal? Sept 5th War is talked of again—Chinese communists, fareast news breaks in grimly. Moonshot rivalry. Death sentence of negro stealing $1.95. How? Hatred, madness, bigotry. (JPl: 414, 419)

WRITING, REVISING, AND ROLE PLAYING: CASE STUDIES IN PROCESS

In her years as a student at Smith, from 1950–1955, the political is not absent from Plath's writing, but her reading was more likely to be applied to her continuing study of herself, to feed her constant goal of self-improvement and be related to her own immediate perceptions and experience. However, the focus on self-development and achievement itself reflects the dominant American ideology of the period. Plath imbibed this so deeply that "success or death" became the rhetorical options to which this ideology was reduced.

For Christmas 1949, Plath's mother gave Sylvia a copy of Nietzsche's *Thus Spake Zarathustra,* and when she was re-reading it for her Dosteyevski dissertation in 1954 (there are several cross-references to Dostoyevski's novels in the margins) she put one of her carefully drawn little stars next to the following paragraph which appears under the heading "Voluntary Death:" "And whoever wanteth to have fame, must take leave of honour betimes and practise the difficult art of—going at the right time."[58]

And, next to this she has written in neat, black ink "August 1953," the date of her suicide attempt during that bleak summer in Wellesley. Because her life offers such a powerful narrative itself, it is all too easy to be alert to the way that her writing seems to mirror that life, and in Yeats's terms, to relate everything to the dancer and not the dance. For that reason it helpful to contextualize and historicise the discussion of the 1960s writing in England by offering a reading of the 1950s journals as early experiments in performance and masquerade. Like much writing produced in juvenile years, this provides evidence of fierce protest, but is insuffiently rooted in experience and political awareness to become an effectively analytical discourse in its own right. The Smith College journals are zestful, passionate, and peppered with interesting insights and good writing, but Plath was only 18 when she started to write them, and they were not intended for publication. They nevertheless provide important evidence of writerly experiments in masquerade and performativity, specifically gendered strategies and discourses discussed by Joan Riviere in 1929[59] and Judith Butler in 1990.[60]

Role playing and performance have always been identified as characteristics of Plath's writing that should be weighed alongside the claims of those who would push the writing into the "confessional" camp. In "Dying is an Art," a review of *Ariel* originally published in 1965 and reprinted in *Language and Silence*, George Steiner[61] spoke of her "tricks of voice." Psychoanalytic and gender theory, drawing on notions of performativity and masquerade, provide a theoretical base for a reading of these earlier critical observations.

There are other—perhaps more obvious—reasons for acknowledging the importance of psychoanalytic theory in a reading of Plath, before moving the attention to the wider frame of social and global politics. In a very late piece, "Ocean 1212W" (JP: 117) (a reminiscence of the early years of her childhood at her grandmother's house in Winthrop, Massachusetts) Plath describes coming across a starfish with a missing arm, an image which resonates with reminders of her father's amputated leg (not to mention the plastic starfish that Esther gives the baby in *The Bell Jar*). The psychological effect of losing her father when Plath was only eight was tremendous, and it is inscribed in much of her writing, whether the subject is bees (his academic specialism), the haunting power of the past, disfigurement and amputation, recent German history, or male power. The sense of loss, which in Lacanian terms is the origin of desire, is manifest throughout her writing. Moreover, following the publicity surrounding the release of Hitchcock's *Psycho* in 1960 there was considerable popular discussion of issues such as schizophrenia and mother fixation. Even if Plath did not see the film (despite the French New Wave's admiration for Hitchcock he did not quite have the cachet of Resnais), it would have been hard to avoid the posters and the publicity.

The evolution of the writing, the reappearance and reworking of image and phrase, the appearance on the page and resources used in the production of the writing are the features of the texts which provide specific evidence of the process of composition and the relationship of the writing to the surrounding culture. Karen Kukil, the editor of the recent complete edition of all journal material kept at Smith (JP1), has pointed out how noticeable it is that the form of "journal" or typescript varies enormously, from the bound, lined book used during her student years at Smith, to the carbon-book with tear-out pages used for notes during her travels, to the typed sheets of foolscap used for her notes on the North Tawton people she was writing about during her last summer in Devon. When Plath writes about the English scene she most frequently writes on English paper. When she writes about America, in the fiction of *The Bell Jar*, she writes initially on American pink memo paper from Smith, even though she is living in England and has English stationery in her house. New evidence is uncovered in the sections of this book which pay close attention to the process of composition, using manuscript evidence relating to *The Bell Jar* manuscripts and the draft poems of early 1962, to "Little Fugue," to "Withens" and to the November 1962 poem "Thalidomide." In each case the aim is to trace the interaction between the writing and the surrounding cultural and political rhetorics.

The Influence of Geo-Politics: England, America, and the Reporting of Contemporary Events

Supporting these sections which focus on an analysis of specific manuscripts is a development of the the main political argument. This involves a discussion of the the exploratory and more perfunctory social and political allusions produced while Plath was being shaped by her American environment and milieu in the 1940s and 1950s. This contrasts with the writing produced by a different Plath, who reviews and reassesses that environment following the influence of her experiences in England, first as a student, and then later (and finally) as a writer, mother and politically concerned woman approaching and passing her thirtieth birthday. From 1960 onwards, Plath becomes more politically aware and politicized by international discourses. This new political awareness is reflected in the poetry and prose in ways which suggest that there is much more consistent and evolutionary development in the writing from 1960 to 1963 than is acknowledged by those who argue that the rupture with Hughes was *the* moment of transformation, was *the* watershed. Because the political is often interpeted in that rather problematic phrase "the personal is the political," the marital events of the summer of 1962 are readily, and understandably, seen as the crucial ones, with Plath liberating herself from the dominance (whether symbolic or real) of the masculine, of the father and husband. This reading ignores the events being played out on the international stage and the conjunction of the birth of her children and the threat of nuclear war. The importance of the interaction between these two events should not be overshadowed by Plath's later separation from Hughes.

From 1960 onwards, Plath begins to read the world as a representative of a small community rather than solely as an artist detached from society. By 1962, her children are written into her poetry, and global politics (in the form of extreme Cold War tension) brings issues of the present, and the threatened curtailment of the future into sharp focus—not simply her own future, but also her children's. She had a miscarriage in 1961. By moving to North Devon later that year she was entering one alien world, and by dwelling on the Cold War rush towards nuclear war as reported in the newspapers that world became not just alien, but completely lacking in protection. North Tawton was not—and, is not—a cozy, country village. There is a former World War II airfield nearby. The significance of place for Plath's writing is an important strand in the discussion that follows, as politics is mediated through sub-groups, institutions and local communities, and an awareness of history.

This approach, therefore, concentrates on the apparently ephemeral texts that surrounded Plath during this period, and on the significance of the places with which she had a close relationship, all in the context of the global conflict being acted out and argued over alongside the domestic one. To concentrate exclusively on the juxtaposition of the end of a personal relationship and the outpouring of poems narrows our reading of those poems and does them a disservice. As Michael Hulse said, in a review of *The Collected Poems,*

> Her distinctive authority derives from her stern, almost harsh insistence on submitting the responses of the emotions to the scrutiny of the intellect, on wedding the result of this scrutiny to images and ideas distilled by acts of indefatigable will and active curiosity from the life around her.[62]

Plath's life in England necessarily included world politics. This was a time of extraordinary world tension, and the way that national and international events were discussed and represented on radio, in magazines and newspapers and in anti-nuclear protest affected all consumers of those media. The journal entry quoted earlier, describing the effect of browsing among the magazines at Smith, provides early evidence of an interaction between Plath's writing and the detail of newspaper reporting. But, in England the immediacy and proximity of war would have felt much, much closer. Travels in Europe had opened Plath's eyes to the drabness and bleakness of post-war conditions. London still had its bomb sites; Berck-Plage had its hospital for war wounded. More important even than this reminder of the past conflict, was the real possiblity that the next war was imminent and would be nuclear. Even Ted Hughes, who is not noted for such writing, had been moved to write a poem ("A Woman Unconscious") that addressed directly the possiblity of nuclear war and global extinction.

Plath had a voracious appetite for serious journalism and films. News magazines (such as *Time* and *The New Statesman*) and newspapers (such as *The Observer*)[63] represented the threat of nuclear war, radiation and the flattening of cities in a relentless, chilling discourse. Newspaper reporting of the effects of radioactivity in the atmosphere show that the "flashback" techniques employed in Resnais's *Hiroshima Mon Amour* were not flashbacks from a calm present to a nightmare past that thankfully had gone, but a warning of what might be to come before very long. New magazines were full of reminders of the nuclear threat. A letter written to George Macbeth at the British Broadcasting Corporation (BBC) in April 1962[64] shows that Plath had read the 9 March issue of *Time* Magazine for she refers to a specific article. At the beginning of the magazine, there is a prominent feature on Christmas Island and other atomic bomb test sites; *Time* offered its readers a reminder of nuclear warfare in every issue.

References to Hiroshima and Nagasaki were frequently employed to illustrate events in the present, not the past. In *The Observer* of 3 February 1963, one of the last that Plath would have had the opportunity to read, there is a feature on Polaris nuclear submarines. Under the heading "Towards nuclear impasse," the article begins:

> On August 6th, 1945, the first atomic bomb was dropped on Hiroshima. It had a power of 15 kilotons (equals 15,000 tons of T.N.T.). The city was 60 per cent obliterated: casualties numbered 306,000—78,000 of them killed. Last week the House of Commons voted its acceptance of an agreement that Britain should equip herself with four or five submarines, each able to carry 16 Polaris missiles. One of these missiles, assuming a one-megaton warhead, is more than 60 times as powerful as the Hiroshima bomb.[65]

A reappraisal of Plath's "ephemeral" reading of news permits a term such as "Hiroshima" to be read as a signifier of Plath's 1960s present no less than her 1940s past.

The discourses of world politics in the early 1960s contained another strand, involving the invasion of the present by the past, and this *has* been considered in discussion of Plath's work. Adolf Eichmann, who was charged with crimes against humanity for his part in the administration of the mass murder of the Jewish population of Europe during the Nazi years, had been arrested in May 1960, and was brought to trial in Jerusalem in April 1961. The trial lasted the whole summer, and the court adjourned in August for four months. In December, it reconvened and convicted Eichmann on all fifteen accounts of the indictment. An appeal was lodged, rejected and on the 31 May 1962 Eichmann was executed.

These events were extensively reported in newspapers and can be mapped alongside Plath's time in England. Once again, they should not be seen as a reference to a past that has gone forever. At times the two discourses—Eichmann/Nazism and the threat of nuclear war—overlap and are seen to have clear parallels. One instance is this report of an exchange at a trial in which Pat Pottle, a Campaign for Nuclear Disarmament protestor, had been charged (along with five others) with conspiracy to incite others to commit a breach of the Official Secrets Act by entering a Royal Air Force station at Wethersfield. In the process of conducting his own defence, Pottle questioned the Air Commodore Graham Magill:

> Pottle: Air Commodore, is there any official order you cannot accept?
> Judge: Is there what? . . . He is an officer in the forces of Her Majesty.
> Pottle: So actually there is no order you would not accept?
> Magill: It is my duty to carry out any order that is given to me.
> Pottle: Would you press the button that you know is going to annihilate millions of people?
> Magill: If the circumstances so demanded it, I would.
> Pottle: Would you slit the throats of all the two-year-old children in this country, Air Commodore?
> Judge: I think you must stop all that.
> Pottle: I feel it was comparable with the effects of nuclear weapons. It was the same as saying he would press the button to explode the nuclear bomb. Have you read the summing-up of the judge at the Eichmann trial?[66]

Plath was haunted by dreams of cut-throats during this period, and whether the source is this image, the news reports from Algeria or some other news story, the image becomes written into her January and February 1962 poetry.

There is a related body of writing that Al Alvarez[67] has said was discussed by the circle of which he and Plath formed a part. As a way of confronting the arbitrariness of genocide and individual death, Plath had read Eugen Kogon's account of the German concentration camps and the psychology of those who ran them.[68] Kogon was a survivor, and had written *The Theory and Practice of Hell: The German Concentration Camps and the System Behind Them* in the years immediately following his liberation in 1945. The title of the book, which contains a catalog of unimaginable cruelty, sadism, and depravity, indicates not only the horror but his yearning to understand how such a thing could come about and be systematized.

Plath also read Hannah Arendt, whose studies of state power and the human condition in the contemporary world form the subject of *Between Past and Future* (1954), *The Human Condition* (1958), and *The Origins of Totalitarianism* (1961).[69] Plath died just before Arendt's most famous study *Eichmann in Jerusalem: A Report on the Banality of Evil* (1963)[70] was serialized in *The New Yorker,* but by then Alvarez—possibly with conversations with Plath partly in mind—had already identified a possible reason for this fascination with the holocaust:

> I once suggested (in a piece for *Atlantic Monthly,* December 1962) that one of the reason why the camps continued to keep such tight hold on our imaginations is that we see in them a small scale trial run for a nuclear war.[71]

Strangeways makes the point[72] that through her reading (of Eric Fromm, Arendt, and newspapers) Plath was alert to the rhetorical deceit practiced by those powers which sought to disguise the horror of war and genocide. Fromm used the Nazi regime to illustrate the behavior of which all societies and governments were capable, and he was active in the American nuclear-disarmament movement. The Nazi regime's bureacratic and euphemistic language ("final solution," "evacuation," and "special treatment") was to be identified by Hannah Arendt in her account of the trial in Jerusalem as characteristic of the "banality of evil."

CONTEMPORARY POLITICS AND CULTURE AS A SOURCE OF IMAGINATIVE RHETORIC

The extent to which Plath's work drew on Cold War anxieties becomes clearer when the crystallization of Plath's writing is situated among the debates, rhetoric and issues appearing in the world around her, particularly during her second stay in England when she became increasingly cut off from her place of achievement, America. The Miranda and Caliban/Prospero/Ariel analogy, which is sometimes used to map Plath's experience of exile on a small island with its male dominated world, has clearly led to many fruitful readings of her poetry. Reading Plath this way leads to less emphasis on her relationship with Hughes, and more on the way that the concretization of her language in England was influenced and informed by her fresh reading of institutions, contemporary culture, and international events.

Let me give one, brief example of the way that pinning down cultural meanings to a single, higher cultural seriousness can sometimes fail to do justice to the richness and variety of allusions available to writers. It has already been implied that discussion of Plath's 1962 poem, "Ariel," will always require some reference to *The Tempest* and the released spirit who appears in the play. But, in 1962, "Ariel" was also the name of an Anglo-American telecommunications satellite, damaged and silenced by the radiation caused by atmospheric hydrogen bomb tests. It was also the name of the BBC Staff Magazine and the BBC was an important source of income for Plath during the summer and Autumn of 1962. Finally, the irony in calling her own plodding horse, "Ariel" was undoubtedly Plath's own invention, but it has a parallel in the 1956 science fiction space film *Forbidden Planet*, where the Ariel figure is a portly robot. "Ariel" meant many things in 1962, and the richness of connotation and allusion is one of the delights of language that Plath's poems celebrate. Irony was one means by which the awfulness of the present moment could be endured and it very evident in the last journal entries that have survived, the notes on Devon neighbors made during the spring and summer of 1962.

In treating the horrific with what seemed like comic irreverence, Plath was in tune with her age. The satirical review "Beyond the Fringe" which, in London, featured Peter Cook, Alan Bennett, Jonathan Miller, and Dudley Moore included sketches which ridiculed the naivete of Civil Defence advice to citizens on how to cope once a nuclear bomb has dropped on their region. As a journal entry written sometime after 14 April shows, Plath went to see "Beyond the Fringe" in the spring of 1962 at the beginning of the period in which the comic voice becomes as insistent in the poetry as it had been in the prose. Juxtaposing the "Beyond the Fringe" sketches and Plath's poetry may seem an odd thing to do only if there is a misunderstanding of her seriousness. Plath's writing is serious, but is also more satirical and contemporary in reference than is realized, even though the "Fringe" sketches contain a directness of reference and topicality that Plath sought to avoid.

The possibilities permitted by the use of the ironic voice, which can simultaneously subvert and reinforce the seriousness of the subject, had been explored by Plath when she had written *The Bell Jar* during the previous summer of 1961. With its engineered informality, its drollness and its laconic idioms, it proved to be a significant and intriguing writing voice that was initially reserved for prose. In it we see a version of 1950s America that disguises, but does not make invisible, its parturition in the London of 1961.

2

Writing Novels in Cambridge, London, and Devon: Exchanging White Goddess for WASP

It seemed lively enough, and I was quite proud of the bit about the drops of sweat like insects, only I had the dim impression I'd probably read it somewhere else a long time ago.

BJ: 127

Something was grotesquely wrong. He opened his Shakespeare.

"... O, let him pass! He hates him
That would upon the rack of this tough world
Stretch him out longer."

"The rack," he murmured. "Haydon forgot the rack." And his mind still exercised by the strangeness of the omission, he stared across at the half-open window.

—A. E. Ellis, *The Rack* (1958)

What was there about us, in Belsize, so different from the girls playing bridge and gossiping and studying in the college to which I would return? Those girls, too, sat under bell jars of a sort. . . . How did I know that someday—at college, in Europe, somewhere, anywhere— the bell jar, with its stifling distortions, wouldn't descend again?

BJ: 251–54

TAPPING THE BELL JAR

THE CRYSTALLIZATION OF SYLVIA PLATH'S SENSE OF GLOBAL POLITICS that came about during her second stay in England can be illustrated by contrasting her novel of double masquerade, *The Bell Jar,* with the traces of the novel she began during her first stay. *The Bell Jar,* a novel with an early 1950s setting and published originally under the pseudonym Victoria Lucas, was written in 1961 against the background of the Berlin Crisis and the trial of Adolf Eichmann. At first sight, neither of these contemporary events seems to have any bearing on the narrative, whose

43

setting is the America of 1953. But, appearances can be deceptive. The novel's narrator is masquerading as the 1953 Sylvia Plath, as Lynn in Plath's short story "Platinum Summer"[1] ends up masquerading as her former chestnut-haired self. The narrative events are seen from a distance and the novel's realization and representation of the autobiographical episodes of 1953 are profoundly mediated by Plath's 1961 reading of contemporary institutional and global political structures.

The Bell Jar is, strictly speaking, one of three novels on which Plath worked. It has both a predecessor and a successor, though neither of these other novels has survived. The predecessor, started in Cambridge, England and probably never finished, was apparently destroyed. The successor, started in Devon and also incomplete, has disappeared and may also have been destroyed. Only the novel written in London made its way through to publication.

In a number of letters, Plath tells her mother that she enjoys the spaciousness of novel writing, the point that she had made in the October 1962 interview with Peter Orr. The practice provides welcome relief from the cramped and concentrated economy of poetry. This is not to say that all three of these narrative projects were written at a leisurely place. There is a noticeable contrast between the long period of gestation of the first, and the concentrated, swift writing of the second and third. But, there is more than this. Each is a barometer of the values and ideology in which Plath was immersed, in specific English places. From the fragments that have survived the first novel, started in Cambridge, appears to have had the burden of an imposed mythological and astrological discourse weighing it down. It is an experiment in writing which for Plath remains unsuccessful. *The Bell Jar*, written in London in less than six months, worked for Plath and works for the majority of readers.

It is important to acknowledge this novel as a work emerging from the capital in the early 1960s. It is relevant that this was a time and a place in which there were nuclear disarmament protests on the streets, even though the novel's subject is a young woman entering adulthood in America in the early 1950s. The different country and different time are fully realized not least because of the defamiliarisation caused by distance and difference.

For the purpose of discussion, Plath's first attempt at a novel will be called "Falcon Yard," the second is *The Bell Jar* and the third "Doubletake" (the title Plath gave it in a letter to Mrs. Prouty).[2] The character of the third novel is largely a matter of speculation as nothing appears to have survived, but it is fair to say that the relationship between the first and the second parallels the relationship between Plath's journals and the *Ariel* poems: the relationship between later writing and Cold War discourses is made clearer when earlier writing produced at a time of less political engagement is considered. It is wise to use "clearer," rather than "clear," because the relationship always remains complex. By the time she wrote *The Bell Jar*, Plath may have become more conscious of world politics, but her fear of the label "headline poet," a term she probably associated with the Beat Poets, meant that however much she may have shared Allen Ginsberg's horror of nuclear war, she would never publish anything as blunt, abrupt, and unambiguous as:

> America when will we end the human war?
> Go fuck yourself with your atomic bomb.[3]

Her approach to current events was oblique or tangential, and the social and artistic groups with which she initially identified disapproved of this kind of directness. Plath identified with a very different American cultural tradition, and in 1956 still wanted to write a Jamesian novel, though well aware that James seemed to have written everything that needed to be said on the subject of the American in Europe. Nevertheless, she was determined to write a novel based on her own transatlantic experiences and that is what she started to do.

It may appear ironical that Plath found it impossible to translate satisfactorily into writing her desire to celebrate her meeting with Hughes, but that she was able to suddenly discover a language and voice in 1962 and 1963 that allowed her to articulate what it meant to be split from him. Why should one "performance" work and not another? The answer is complex and not helped by the assumption that the later poems are "about" that split. Important to its formulation is the conjunction of the experience of motherhood and Cold War events in England 1960 to 1963. This grounding in political discourse is a catalyst which significantly alters the writing. The invisible bell jar and the invisible iron curtain are both barriers whose existence is a threat to life. By the time *The Bell Jar* was completed the metaphorical curtain had become manifest as a wall dividing a city. The invisible had become visible, and the ideological barrier could be touched and tapped.

THE BELL JAR AND THE COLD WAR

The narrator of *The Bell Jar*, the older, wiser Esther Greenwood, recounts how she underwent a series of reorientations as she negotiated the events associated with her own breakdown. The world became a strange place; none of the familiar rituals of life (such as washing, getting dressed, talking to people) seem necessary or worth the effort any more. Given her success as an English major and her definition in New York of herself as a poet, the defamiliarization of the ordinary is expressed most strikingly in Esther's recollection of her eventual inability to write or read. Language itself is made strange. First through the unfamiliar language of chemistry symbols, shorthand, German and Russian, and then through the everyday words involved in letter writing and reading. Esther is disorientated by Joyce, dissatisfied by the imititative character of the novel she starts to write, and turns to read the stories of murder and sensation in the scandal sheets. Later, when she attempts to write a letter to Doreen, she is astonished by her own transformed, strange, slanting handwriting, like "loops of string." While in the hospital, she ceases to read, preferring instead to watch movies.

This process of defamiliarization and disintegration can be linked not so much to Plath's past, although the novel is clearly autobiographical, but to a defamiliarization of America and the past that it represented. The voice of *The Bell Jar* is a carefully constructed one, and its ability to disguise the fear glimpsed only briefly ("Promise you'll be there" the narrator says to her mother surrogate, Dr. Norton) can be read as an exercize in transference with the events in the novel serving as a textual parallel to the alienation caused by the anxieties of Cold War Europe. It is the fact of the novel being written among these 1960s Cold War discourses that gives it such power; the mushroom cloud, like the bell jar, can descend at any moment, and this possibility leads to either terror, droll, gallows humor or anger. There is fear in *The Bell Jar,* but it is disguised by the wonderfully mordant humor of the narrator. In the later *Ariel* poems, there is also fear, and humor, and a rich anger.

The novel was written in 1961, several years after the start of "Falcon Yard", but before that project was finally abandoned and destroyed. Plath may have been encouraged to return to the subject of her own institutionalization (explored tentatively in the 1955 short story "Tongues of Stone")[4] by the success of A. E. Ellis's novel *The Rack*, which in "Sylvia Plath and her Journals" Ted Hughes[5] says she was reading during her early 1960 pregnancy. *The Rack* is set in a sanatorium in the French Alps, and deals with the despair that comes from a succession of small, unsuccessful operations for T. B., and although it is in part sardonic, and in part a chronicle of survival, its similarity to *The Bell Jar* ends there. The passion that the central character, Paul Davenant, a Cambridge undergraduate and "sometime captain in the infantry regiment," develops for the seventeen-year-old Belgian patient, Michele, is central to the narrative, and despite the caustic tone the novel's treatment of its institutionalized subject is closer to Thomas Mann's *The Magic Mountain* than it is to *The Bell Jar.* Hughes writes that in reading *The Rack*, propped on her pregnant stomach "in a scruffy hotel near Victoria," with her college days behind her, "it seemed to her she had touched a new nadir."[6]It was not an auspicious return to England.

If *The Bell Jar* appears as an unexpected addition to the family of Plath's writings, it has appropriately long distance ambitions in terms of reaching back in time to disguise the influence of the present. If one ignores the possible influence of *The Rack*, the novel's return to the 1950s appears regressive—whether it is seen as a return to a place and time whose problems were now, with hindsight, seen to have solutions, or as imitative throwback to the style and subject matter of *The Catcher in the Rye*, albeit with a female narrator. It is set in the world of Plath's relatively recent past, but an American past which Plath had completely left behind her. It is a novel of memory, written from a position of exile.

But, this novel could not have been written in the way it was until Plath had developed a multilayered reading of her own past. She created in Victoria/Esther a version of herself, but the names are a clue to the ironizing process by which the narrator is presented and by which she presents herself. Victoria is the name of a Queen of England and Empress of India. It is also the Latin version of Nike, the Greek Goddess of Victory, who appears in the February 1961 poem "Barren Woman" as the "white Nike," one of the children that the "barren" woman had hoped to bear (CP:157). In the Old Testament, Esther is a Jewish heroine, taken in marriage by a Persian king to replace Vashti, who was ousted when she refused to obey the King's demands. By her actions, Esther saves her people from extermination by their enemies. Before she was Queen, however, she was simply another member of the king's harem, and she concealed her Jewish identity. Esther is a Hebrew version of Ishtar, Goddess of fertility, Earth Mother, daughter of Sin, the God of the Moon, whose attributes are love and war. She combines cruelty and kindness, and life and death meet within her. She is the goddess whose name appears as the final word in the October 1961 poem "Last Words."

All of these associations lead the reader in the wrong direction, because the narrator is no goddess, no Queen or Empress, even though the narrative voice has the kind of assurance and detachment that one might expect from such a presence. But in the end there is a kind of triumph, a type of victory in survival. Esther finally shows the independence of Vashti, the Queen whose assertiveness had made her into an symbol of womanhood celebrated in *Villette* and suffragette processions.

Victoria/Esther suffers a series of terrifying experiences—including suicide attempt, sexual assault, and mismanaged electro-convulsive therapy (ECT). Her voice is a device by which the pain and fear is managed, concealing not only the character of the narrator, but the way in which the politics of class, society, and international conflict have been understood. For in this novel, Plath is able to see her former self distantly, as the product of a particular time, class and dominant patriarchal ideology. She was able to view her formative Wellesley experiences with a semi-detachment. She realized in fiction a version of a world that biographers such as Edward Buscher later identified as extremely significant because of its contrast to what she had known before. Her mother's decision to take her children away from the world described in "Ocean 1212W" was aspirational:

> Aurelia's decision to leave Winthrop for Wellesley was far more than a sensible, economic move. It also represented a shift from the lower middle and middle class setting to an upper middle class college town, conceivably a bid to provide her children with the perfect WASP childhood.[7]

The Bell Jar is a novel written in England during one Cold War period and set in the United States during another. The historical and cultural period of the novel's setting is the subject of "Coming Apart in the Atomic Age," one of the most interesting chapters in Pat Macpherson's *Reflecting on The Bell Jar.*[8] Although Macpherson does not say so, there was a well established tradition of naming missiles after characters from mythology, even as early as the Korean War and the name Nike (the Greek version of Victoria) was used in 1953 by the United States military for a missile carrying a nuclear warhead. Plath had probably forgotten this by the time she came to write *The Bell Jar,* but it is well to remember that classical names also had nuclear associations during the 1950s and 1960s.

The novel was produced during the spring and summer of 1961, while Plath and Hughes were living in London, and it was complete by the time they moved to Devon in August. The novel is set during the period of the McCarythyite anti-communist witch-hunts, and begins with the electrocution of the Rosenbergs in 1953, a fact which is linked psychologically and thematically to the traumatic effect of the mismanaged electric-shock treatment administered to the narrator Esther Greenwood. The name of Greenwood was certainly a Plath family name, but it is also similar to the name of the man who had confessed to espionage and then identified Julius Rosenberg as the man who had recruited him. The issue of control, and in particular the control of women by men, institutions and mothers, is an important theme in the novel.

It is also a novel of performance, but the performance, which includes the voice of detached observation (Esther's "I am an observer" has echoes of Isherwood's "I am a camera")[9] and the insights of its narrator Esther/Elly are tightly controlled. Because events are grounded in a new kind of experience, it avoids being contrived, artificial and over-rhetorical, thus avoiding the inauthenticity which had troubled Plath all the time she was trying to write "Falcon Yard."

The autobiographical nature of the events is so detailed that it is no surprise that the novel has been read—and dismissed—as a thinly disguised diary. Esther's experiences not only mirror Plath's, but even the political contextualization is lifted straight from the journals of the period. This is the Rosenberg execution, recorded in her journal on June 19 1953:

> All right, so the headlines blare the two of them are going to be killed at eleven o'clock tonight. So I am sick at the stomach.
>
> .   .   .   .
>
> The tall beautiful catlike girl who wore an original hat to work every day rose to one elbow from where she had been napping on the divan in the conference room, yawned, and said with a beautiful, bored nastiness "I'm so glad they are going to die." She gazed vaguely and very smugly round the room, closed her enormous green eyes and went back to sleep. . . .
>
> .   .   .   .
>
> There is no yelling, no horror, no great rebellion. That is the appalling thing. The execution will take place tonight; it is too bad that it could not be televised . . . so much more realistic and beneficial than the run-of-the mill-crime program.Two real people being executed. No matter. The largest emotional reaction over the United States will be a rather large, democratic, infinitely bored and casual and complacent yawn. J: 80

In the novel, the character who says that she is "so glad they are going to die" is Hilda, and the image used to place her is interesting:

> The night before I'd seen a play where the heroine was possessed by a dybbuk, and when the dybbuk spoke from her mouth its voice sounded so cavernous and deep you couldn't tell whether it was a man or a woman. Well Hilda's voice sounded just like that dybbuk. (BJ: 105)

This was written in 1961. The "dybbuk" comparison reappeared a year later, in a review discussing the complacency of Byron's wife: "How clearly one sees the killing dybbuk of self righteousness in possession."[10]

Another strand, the issue of motherhood, is similarly read along a personal politics/autobiography axis. The effect of the recurrent references to babies is to set up a series of oppositions. The tone and treatment firstly suggest the unaesthetic absurdity of human reproduction, and the gap between romance and reality which leads to a kind of adolescent disgust. As Esther so tactfully tells us, when the Catholic neighbor Dodo displays her fecundity by wheeling her latest in front of Esther's house: "children made me sick" (BJ: 123). But, earlier Esther has admitted that "Dodo interested me, in spite of myself," and the interrogation of the mysteries of maternity (though as she writes, Esther herself has a baby) is usually linked autobiographically to Plath's own recent miscarriage, and textually to a questioning by Esther of her complex feelings about a range of female roles including that of mother, wife, poet, patient, student, journalist, heterosexual lover, and lesbian lover. No less significant in political terms is the horrific humiliation of a woman by male doctors supervising childbirth that she sees at Buddy's medical school.

While acknowledging—as every reader must—the specific personal experience on which Plath is drawing, there is nonetheless some evidence that these two themes (eloctrocution and the control of women's bodies) do not simply reveal a specifically feminist critique of the patriarchy, but one that is partly inspired by geo-political concerns about the arms race. This can be shown through some observations on the reporting of the Cold War events of 1960 and 1961 in contemporary American magazines and the London *The Observer,* and through some remarks on the separate literary discourse to be found in *The Paris Review* (Plath refers to this magazine in the Journal she kept during her appendectomy stay in hospital immediately prior to writing *The Bell Jar*). By drawing attention to the early 1960s reporting of the threat allegedly posed to babies milk by nuclear testing, it can be shown that the Rosenbergs opening provides a metonmyic and invidualized reminder of the arms race and its lethal consequences which is consistent with Plath's individualized but no less felt response to contemporary world events in 1961.

WRITING, POLITICS, AND *THE BELL JAR*

For some critics, the reviewer of *The Collected Poems* in *The New York Review of Books* being but one example, the attempt to equate the death penalty with the hospital treatment carried out on Esther jars on the reader. As with the most angry of the *Ariel* poems, Denis Donoghue argues, the effect is "petulant," the metaphors and analogies too stretched, the comparisons not earned. I think this is an objection which can only be sustained if it is assumed that Plath had little political agenda, and that she was concerned only with her own subjective dilemmas, which is basically Donoghue's charge.[11]

In her study of the writing relationship between Plath and Ted Hughes, Margaret Uroff[12] says that Plath came to political awareness late. Although she had been active in the World Federalist Movement branch at Wellesley High School, this does not seem to have been followed through at Smith, where her work as a student journalist and writer of short stories and poems took her in other directions.

Al Strangeways argues for a stronger acknowledgement of the "depth of [Plath's] intellectual and emotional engagement with political issues,"[13] citing the influence of her teachers Wilbury Crockett and Raymond Chapman, her correspondence in 1950 with Eddie Cohen, the older and more experienced college student from Chicago, and her collaboration with Perry Norton, a friend and high school classmate, on the article for the Christian Science Monitor "Youth's Plea for World Peace," also in 1950. Both Strangeways and Wagner-Martin (1990), therefore, see the anti-war stance of the correspondence and the anti-arms stance of the article as evidence that at 18 her interest in politics was already clear, and that this continuing interest throughout her student years is confirmed by an examination of the many political comments in the unedited *Letters Home*. It is certainly the case that one of the things she most regularly reports on in her accounts of Cambridge (England) is the level of political awareness there and the fact that politics was more immediate, more interesting. In a letter to her mother soon after her arrival at Cambridge, she had written:

> I hope to submit to the little pamphlet magazines here "freelance" and perhaps shall join the Labour Club, as I really want to become informed on politics, and it seems to have an excellent program. I am definitely not a Conservative, and the Liberals are too vague and close to the latter. I shall also investigate the Socialists, and may, just for fun, go to a meeting two of the Communist Party (!) here later on. (LH: 187)

Armstrong and Sinfield (1990) see Plath's article in *Isis* protesting at the treatment of women at Cambridge as symptomatic of a more general political position:

> Her answer to Cambridge's stereotyping of women . . . was characteristic of British progressive thought at the time. This, indeed, became her general political alignment. 1956 was to be the year of Suez and Hungary, and she argued to her mother that soldiers should refuse to fight, that the principles of Christ and Socrates should be followed, that mothers and children had nothing to gain from men fighting. "I wish Warren (her brother) would be a conscientious objector" she wrote. (Armstrong and Sinfield 1980: 77)

Another letter, written at the height of the Suez crisis (LH 1 November 1956), is full of observations on global politics, most notably the arrogance of latent British Imperialism and the eloquence of Gaitskell, the leader of the Labour Party. (Gaitskell died just before Plath, in January 1963, and his death received widespread coverage in the papers that Plath read). She also praises the "superb" editorial in the Manchester *Guardian*. But, the tone is too obviously rhetorical, and whilst wishing to avoid the false dichotomy to which Strangeways rightly objects, in which the student comments are characterized as the expected "emotional" and "proper" female stance against war, there is nevertheless a perceptible difference between the tone of these comments and the language of Plath's 1960s writing.

In a two part article called "Leaves from a Cambridge Notebook" and published in *The Christian Science Monitor* on 5 and 6 March 1956 Plath writes:

> Limiting as (the early specialisation in English schools) may seem to an American one soon discovers that British undergraduates have a remarkable awareness of politics, theater and music—interests not acquired through college courses, but independently.[14]

In that same year, the crushing of the Hungarian uprising and the indifference of the West, made an impact on her, and as a Cambridge student with close links to the newspaper *Varsity* she was eager to take advantage of political journalistic opportunities as they arose. In the article "B and K at Claridges"[15] published in the *Smith Alumnae Quarterly* she describes how she and a friend suddenly found themselves on their way to London as honorary "wives" included in the invitations sent out to two of the (unmarried male) *Varsity* editors. At the reception organized by the Soviet government, she saw Khrushcev and Bulganin, and Plath reports how she found herself in conversation with a Russian army officer. But, the tone is light and not at all analytical, and the close contact with Superpower leaders may not have raised the level of her political consciousness as much as an outsider might think. Plath adopted the rather lofty voice later revealed in the radio program "What Made You Stay,"[16] when, as "Mrs Hughes," a new member of the English faculty at Smith, she was interviewed for *The Sophian*, the college newspaper:

> Political interest runs high at Cambridge, Mrs. Hughes observed. "During the Suez crisis, close friendships were ruined forever because of a difference in opinion! . . . There is a free climate of political ideas in the university. A Communist students group is quite active and there is no feeling of taboo about those who have gone to Moscow." Mrs Hughes remarked "I think the main reason for the greater intensity of their interest in politics as opposed to ours is their greater proximity, both political and geographical, to the events . . . America seemed so peaceful to me when I returned" she concluded.[17]

Richard Larschan suggests that these comments provide less evidence of a political awakening than they do of "dilettantish name-dropping to impress the hometown folks."[18] Earlier it was emphasized that a performative and role-playing element appears in so much of the writing, something overlooked in critical responses which located Plath in the context of the confessional school of writers, so that the repeated "I" of the writing was seen as an unproblematic equivalent of the "I" of Plath's personal conversation. Here, then, Plath is "performing" the role of experienced ex-Smith student, now a woman married to a famous English poet, a woman who has been to one of England's ancient universities and is now much more politically sophisticated than she was as a New England student. This should be read as a kind of careful role playing, calculated to achieve an effect with a particular kind of audience. The prose writing and interviews show Plath's keen desire to respond to the expectations of a particular kind of audience, even when she did not quite judge that need correctly. The appearance of these texts may seem to provide evidence that the political re-education of Plath coincided with her arrival in England, but this "evidence" should be regarded with some scepticism, even though Uroff suggests that Ted Hughes's experience of teaching social studies at a secondary modern school during their first year of marriage—and, her second year at Cambridge—would have furthered a socio- and geo-political awareness. Politics is still largely a spectacle, and the world of politics still part of the Other.

The return to the United States and the plunge into teaching at Smith suspended even this mild process of re-orientation. Though there has always been a tradition of politicians visiting Smith (during Plath's time as a student Senator McCarthy and Adlai Stevenson, for example, visited) such events on an out of city campus always place the politician in the role of celebrity. Plath may have started to view her home country in a slightly different way in the light of her experiences in England. But, she had not become a political animal. Her role was that of poet, Cambridge graduate, and, no less triumphantly, wife of Ted Hughes. In America, as her journals show, she quit the room when the after dinner conversation turned to politics. In a journal entry from 8 March 1958 she recalls an evening in which "there was desultory talk about aborigines, and me going out on the incoming of politics" (J: 203).

But, two years later, she was back in England, and settled in London and about to give birth to her first child at a time of worsening superpower relations. And here an awareness of global politics really does start to become significant for her writing, for her life, and for the life of her baby.

RECONFIGURING THE BODY:
POLITICS AND MOTHERHOOD

When Plath returned to England she was five months pregnant. By the time she started writing *The Bell Jar* in 1961 she had a one-year-old baby and had lost another through a miscarriage. The birth of a child represents a challenge to Cold War despair, because it is predicated on a belief in a long term future. The miscarriage of a baby reinforces Cold War anxieties, for worries about the effect of radioactive particles in the atmosphere added to worries about the effects of chemicals on the food-chain. The body was under challenge from invisible forces, and the most vulnerable were the most likely to be deformed.

As Nancy Chodorow[19] points out, motherhood reconfigures a woman's body in a number of ways, as she experiences pregnancy, lactation, birth, and becomes familiar with the daily process of attending to the baby sick, urine, and feces. Esther's narrative records this presence of the body, initially through Doreen, whose breasts tumble out of her dress, and from whose mouth a jet of brown vomit flies as Esther tries to move her from the corridor.

Following this experience Esther resolves to reject the body. She has bathed to purify herself and she pledges to identify with Betsy and no longer play at being Higginbottom, an anal, body suggestive name. Yet, the very next chapter begins with a description of Esther's love of food and the way that she can eat everything in sight without putting on weight. But, she is punished. The crabmeat at a Ladies Day event gives them all food-poisoning, and Betsy and Esther are sick in the taxi and take to their beds. Throughout this novel there are incidents in which matter such as vomit, blood, and the newborn baby's urine that spurts into the doctor's face, bursts from the inside to the outside of the body. Such incidents suggest an inversion and disorder that is concealed by the ironical tone. Other exposures of the body (the woman about to give birth, legs splayed by the stirrups, Buddy's "turkey" genitals and Doreen's "melon" breasts) anticipate but are quite different from, the images of peeling skin irradiated bodies, reduced to ash or disfigured and distorted, that the reader meets in the 1962 poems.

The body is foregrounded in earthy, direct ways that reflect what the experience of reproduction has taught Esther. The body is objectified and othered, a process that Esther recalls when she describes the posture pictures that were taken at college, when the women students were photographed naked. Esther had been observed half-naked by her neighbour Mrs. Ockenden, and ends up naked on Irwin's bed. Earlier in the novel her dress is ripped to the waist by Marco, and her breasts are bared. The assault reduces her to the women in the scandal sheet, breasts surging over their dresses, legs arranged for the voyeuristic pleasure of the male spectators. As in Plath's journal, the breast is also observed humorously. The nurse whose fat breast smothers Esther like a cloud or pillow (just before the first, abortive electric-shock treatment), and the "immense, steppe-like expanse" of the Slavic woman's wool clad bosom," which Esther observes from Irwin's bathroom are but two examples.

Elsewhere, the body is regarded with more disgust, sometimes concealed by wry detachment. The fat, rude medical student who watches Buddy wrap gauze round Esther's head anticipates Buddy's own fatness, and Esther's: Esther becomes so plump under the insulin treatment that she looks as if she is pregnant. There is a similar kind of fascination with the body in the short stories of Flannery O'Connor: Hulga's artificial leg in "Good Country People" and Tom Shiftlet's stump of an arm in "The Life You Save May Be Your Own"—and the wry, curt speech patterns that are to be found in Southern writing—the short, dry sentence that closes a conversation or theme—characterize Plath's narrative. In O'Connor, the matter-of-fact reporting of the grotesque and bizarre configurations of the human body serves as an ironical commentary on the presence/absence of the spirit. The frequent references to Catholicism in *The Bell Jar*, taken in conjunction with this objectification of the body, have a similar effect of throwing the spiritual into relief.

Motherhood and reproduction, therefore, provide one source of the reconfigurations that are inscribed in *The Bell Jar*, in particular the reconfiguration of the body. But, some of these reconfigurations are completely de-eroticized, and brutal. The mother giving birth is cut to allow the passage of the baby from inside to outside the mother. Later Esther's leg is broken following her skiing accident, and in hospital her legs are flabby with a black stubble covering them. Her head is bruised, and luridly colourful: purple on one side, yellow on another. Her shaved head is sprouting hair like chicken tufts. Earlier when she describes kissing Buddy for the first time their mouths are so chapped it is an insipid experience. Sex is completely de-eroticized in the troubling account of the Southern boy Eric's experience with a prostitute, with her rat-colored skin and stereotyped lips.

Ultimately, the body is reduced to organs and blood. Esther wears the blood smeared on her cheek by the woman-hating Marco openly in the bus, she adopts the identity Higginbottom again, and she describes with morbid fascination the disembowelling that accompanies Japanese hara-kiri. All of this provided ammunition for Holbrook's argument that Plath's writing is an unhealthy celebration of death: it is adolescent, and dangerous for adolescents to read. But, the objectification and defamiliarisation of the body may serve a completely different purpose, and be evidence of a very different process at work on and in the writing. For a better understanding of the significance of the preoccupations and anxieties successfully buried in the text, it is necessary to appreciate the global-political situation of the early sixties, and the fear that this induced.

1960 and 1961, the years in which Plath first first settled in London and then wrote *The Bell Jar* in a spare room belonging to a pair of friends, saw an intensification of the Cold War. The Soviet Union launched Sputnik, the first satellite, and during the late summer of 1961 spectacularly enforced the division of Berlin by erecting the Wall. Both the United States and the Soviet Union began a series of atmospheric H-bomb tests. In England the Campaign for Nuclear Disarmament was founded, with Bertrand Russell and Canon Collins among its leaders. Alan Sinfield[20] points out, however, that a significant number of its leaders were women: Pat Arrowsmith and Peggy Duff were central figures, and a deputation received by Prime Minister Harold Macmillan included: Alix Meynell, Janet Aitken, Diana Collins, Jacquetta Hawkes, Dorothy Hodgkin, Marghanita Laski, Dorothy Needham, Antoinette Pirie, and Mary Stocks. The practice of women spearheading anti-nuclear protest started a tradition that fed directly into later Greenham Common protests. In Britain, two movements, *Women Against the Bomb* and *Voice of Women*, began in response to the Berlin Crisis of 1961.[21]

In a letter to her mother Plath describes her own feelings about nuclear disarmament after witnessing an Easter protest march at close quarters in 1960, the year before she began writing the novel:

> Last Sunday . . . I had an immensely moving experience and attended the arrival of the Easter weekend marchers from the atomic bomb plant at Aldermas[t]on to Trafalgar Square in London. Ted and Dido had left at noon to see Bill Merwin, who was with the over 10 thousand marchers come into Hyde Park, and I left later with the baby to meet a poet-friend of Ted's, Peter Redgrove, and go on to Trafalgar Square with him. He brought a carry-cot, which he is loaning us, and we carried the sleeping baby easily between us, installed the cot on the lawn of the National Gallery overlooking the fountains, pigeons and glittering white buildings. Our corner was uncrowded, a sort of nursery, mothers giving babies bottles on blankets. . . .
>
> I saw the first of the 7-mile-long column appear—red and orange and green banners, "Ban the Bomb!" etc., shining and swaying slowly. Absolute silence. I found myself weeping to see the tan, dusty marchers, knapsacks on their backs—Quakers and Catholics, Africans and whites, Algerians and French—40 percent were London housewives. I felt proud that the baby's first real adventure should be as a protest against the insanity of world-annihilation. Already a certain percentage of unborn children are doomed by fallout and no one knows the cumulative effects of what is already poisoning the air and sea.
>
> I hope, by the way, that neither your nor Warren will vote for Nixon. His record is atrocious from his Californian campaign on—a Machiavelli of the worst order. Could you find out if there is any way I can vote? I never have and feel badly to be deprived of however minute a participation in political affairs. What do you think of Kennedy?/The Sharpesville massacres are causing a great stir of pity and indignation here. (LH: 378)

The usual voice in the *Letters Home* is deliberately upbeat, optimistic, reassuring. The genre of the daughter's letter to mother, particularly when there is shared experience of motherhood, has its own discourse. This particular letter, as printed in *Letters Home,* begins with scenes of sunshine in the kitchen (where there has been cooking) and in Regents Park (where there is newly cut grass and warm earth), all surrounded by news of the new baby. "Nothing is so beautiful as England in April" Plath writes, probably echoing Browning.

Later, the tone changes. The description of the way she sat with baby Frieda at the edge of the Trafalgar Square demonstration spills over into comments on politics, and these remarks tap into a political discourse which is rarely on the surface in Plath's writing, but here is expressed with some rhetorical commitment. Although she is not actually taking part in the march (and neither is Ted Hughes who has gone to watch with a friend) she is moved to tears by it, and expresses the anxieties that were currently circulating in newspapers, on the radio and on television about what H- and A-bomb testing was doing to the atmosphere, and what these weapons threatened to do to civilization.

In Anne Stevenson's biography of Plath,[22] which was thoroughly edited, revised and in places completely rewritten by Olwyn Hughes, there is an attempt to downgrade Plath's political interests—in effect, to depoliticize her. The tension caused by the competing readings of Plath's life are plainly on show in this part of the biography. There is an acknowledgment that "she was fervently opposed to nuclear weapons" and that "no doubt Sylvia did feel strongly about the march." This is immediately qualified by the statement "Nevertheless it appears that the afternoon had not simply been the moving public occasion described in her letter."[23] There then follows Dido Merwin's version of the event, which concludes that Plath may have gone to the march with Peter Redgrove simply out of pique because Hughes had gone with Dido. William and Dido Merwin were the friends who had provided the room in which either Ted or Sylvia could write away from the cramped conditions of the Chalcot Square apartment, where the other remained to look after the baby.

Dido Merwin's version should not be be excluded (though her extraordinarily vitriolic memory of Plath published at the end of *Bitter Fame* has caused most readers to wonder about the impartialilty of her "evidence") but it needs to be noted that in the biographical jottings acquired by Smith College Aurelia Plath noted that both she and her husband were pacificists, and such beliefs would have been communicated by Aurelia to her daughter. But, there is internal, textual evidence that Plath's interest in politics was more than just a performance, firstly in the letter itself and secondly in a collage she produced later that summer.

As an American she feels—for the first time it appears—the need to vote in the forthcoming Presidential election, and the letter which begins with the writer's identification with spring in England soon moves forward to thoughts of the November elections in the United States, and beyond them, to the massacres in South Africa. Her experiences in England, it appears, were nurturing a fear of things that were outside her control, a process that was politicizing her in ways that her American education had not. She wishes to take some kind of action, and admires those who have. The comment that "40 percent were London housewives" sounds very much like a detail gleaned from later reading. There is evidence that this kind of concerned reading was maintained throughout the following months for during the summer—most probably in July—Plath assembled the anti-American, anti-military, and anti-patriarchy collage that is part of the Sylvia Plath Collection.

It is impossible to know if the collage was the product of an idle afternoon or whether it had a more urgent genesis and purpose. Collages of this kind,[24] serving as a commentary on contemporary cultural politics, had been produced by the American Robert Rauschenberg and were not unfamiliar in England. As early as 1952 the sculptor Eduardo Palozzi had shown a series of collages made up from advertisements and other pictures (including *Time* covers), taken from American magazines, at the Institute of Contemporary Arts. In 1956, during the period when Plath was at Cambridge and visited London on a number of occasions, the self-styled Independent Group of architects and artists staged what is often considered the first Pop Art show at the Whitechapel Gallery, and Plath may have seen Richard Hamilton's famous poster-collage "Just what is it that makes today's homes so different, so appealing?." In 1959, a second wave of artists, including David Hockney, Peter Phillips, Allen Jones, and Derek Boshier, encouraged by Peter Blake at the Royal College of Art, produced pop art paintings which drew on American images, from corn flake packets to Marilyn Monroe. Interviewed for a BBC television program "Pop Goes the Easel" in 1962 Derek Boshier said "I'm very interested in the infiltration of the American way of life."

Plath's collage, which Jacqueline Rose discusses in *The Haunting of Sylvia Plath*,[25] is even more revealing than Rose suggests, as an account of the sources, tracked down for the first time, will demonstrate. The picture was assembled from images cut from American magazines recently sent to Plath, and was stuck in her scrapbook. Its significance lies not in its status as an art object, but elsewhere, as textual testimony to the feeling of fear and disgust that Plath was feeling about America's contribution to global tension, allied to a protest about the objectification of women. It is a more developed statement than that to be found on the collages from the undated scrap books discussed by Tracy Brain.[26]

Produced most probably in late June or early July 1960 (allowing for the arrival of the June American magazines in England), the collage was assembled against a background of Eisenhower's unsuccessful tour of supposedly sympathetic Asian countries, the 10th anniversary of the Korean War, and the verbal confrontation between Eisenhower and Khruschcev over Cuba. On 19 June *The Observer* had reported violent anti-American demonstrations in Tokyo, with a picture showing protestors carrying a banner saying "No More Hiroshima." On 26 June the same paper reported a veiled attack on the Kremlin by China in Party statements made in speeches and in the Press, under the subheading "Chinese General Talks of Nuclear War Blackmail." World tension, as reported by anxious liberal papers such as *The Observer,* was increasing, and in Britain, according to figures published in a Gallup Poll, went on increasing until after the Cuban Missile Crisis of October 1962.[27]

Plath's collage is dominated by the the official White House portrait of President Eisenhower printed in many magazines of the period, and has been taken from the 6 June 1960 copy of *Life* (we know this because of what is on the reverse). Eisenhower is in the middle of the picture, and sits exactly as he does in the magazine, except that his left fingers in the collage are holding a hand of cards, taken from an advertisement for Cunard in the 11 June issue of *The New Yorker.* The image of a nuclear bomb carrying jet fighter, bristling with rockets and cut from a General Dynamics advertisement, is pointed phallically at the vagina of the swimsuited woman (cut, bizarrely, from a United States rubber advertisement, also from the same issue—an advertisement which perhaps anticipates the "rubber breasts" of "The Applicant"). The explicitness of the image shows that by now Plath was making the same male sexuality/atomic bomb/death link as Ginsberg in "America." The woman is spread across the left hand side of the page, her feet on a column, and beside her a caption "Every man wants his woman on a pedestal." In his autobiography, Yeats, (a poet Plath admired), records a dream of "a naked woman of incredible beauty, standing upon a pedestal and shooting an arrow at a star."[28] Here the swimsuited beauty is the target for the military "arrows" from the jet. The fighter plane's exhaust trail is made of a loop of Scalextric track, over which two grown men are crouched like excited schoolboys. The "toys for boys" message is explicit, as is the somnambulism of America with the word "sleep" on Eisenhower's lapel and two heads with eye masks on sleeping comfortably with the caption "It's 'his and her time' all over America." The representation of America the eagle, bristling with weapons, but in the care of either stupid or dangerous men, is unambiguous. Behind Eisenhower there is a picture of Vice President Nixon and the American flag, and below the President there is a satellite superimposed on a golf ball (the golf ball, like the "Tums, for acid indigestion" advertisement that sits on Eisenhower's desk, appeared in *Life* and other magazines throughout this summer period).

There are three other significant elements: the caption next to the satellite which says "The worldly new look of the case of the eagle's bugged beak," draws on Cold War anxieties about spying and the imperial role of the United States (America had charged Russia with planting a microphone in an American eagle seal it had presented to one of the United States Embassies), and is clearly linked to the statement in the top left hand corner "America's most famous living preacher whose religious revival campaigns have reached tens of millions of people both in the United States and abroad." This caption in its original context referred to Billy Graham, but in the collage is made to refer to America as a global power, and more specifically to President Eisenhower as a symbol of institutionalized patriarchy. Finally, there is the small picture of a worn-out looking woman in the bottom right hand corner, dwarfed by president, jet fighter, and "model" woman on her pedestal, with the caption "Fatigue build-up . . . America's growing health hazard." All of these have been cut from the 6 June edition of *Life*, which also features an article that chillingly reminded the reader of the past holocaust—the trial of Adolf Eichmann—and, one which suggest a possible nuclear holocaust to come. When Plath wrote in a letter at the end of September that "Frieda is my answer to the H bomb"[29] she was suggesting that an act of human creation was her individual, and individualized, response to those who threatened the world with nuclear destruction and an answer to those whose sense of despair about the future advised against bringing any more children into the world.

Interesting and revealing as the collage is in itself, it also provides evidence of the kind of supposedly ephemeral reading that Plath was doing, and for which there is no such direct evidence in the imaginative prose and poetry, because as Anne Sexton pointed out, poets tend to have their sources not simply hidden in their poems, but "buried."[30] Since we know that Plath looked through the 4 June issue of *The New Yorker* because she has cut the picture of Pioneer V spacecraft from it, we know that she must have seen the full page advertisement for the 7 June issue of *Look*, with its image of the face of a Japanese woman disfigured by the effects of the Hiroshima bomb. It is also extremely likely, since she received *The New Yorker* on a regular basis and has cut out the pedestal and the accompanying phrase "Every woman . . ." from a lingerie advertisement in the 7 May edition, that she saw the 28 May issue, with its two-page photograph of a vast building site in the desert, which the text reveals to be "somewhere in the United States," and which will soon be an almost invulnerable underground launch site for Air Force TITAN Intercontinental Ballistic Missile.[31] Again, this may explain the revisiting of a memory of a journey across the Mojave desert, with its poisonous air, as described in "Sleep in the Mojave Desert," a poem written on 5 July 1960 with a title that recalls the "Sleep" caption on Eisenhower's lapel. The Mojave Desert is—and was—the center for a number of secret military bases with restricted access.

Earlier, it was noted that Plath's girlhood took place against the background of World War II, and some of the tensions and anxieties about the treatment of the Japanese and her own German ancestry at a time when America and Germany were at war are revisited in the short story "Superman and Paula Brown's new Snowsuit" written when she was at Smith in 1955. She had entered adulthood against the background of the arms race. Her high school history assignments scored high grades, but are otherwise unremarkable: they reveal a concerned response to America's role as a global power, and the horrors of war. In February 1946, when she was fourteen, she completed an assignment called "A War to End all Wars" about World War I. The cover is a watercolor by Plath of a girl (presumably herself) at a desk imagining the fighting and slaughter as she reads a book.[32] In the same year she produced a project called "The World and the United States" which is mainly about the attempt to set up the United Nations Organization, and one of the clippings shows a cartoon by Vikki that appeared in the London *Daily News* (possibly a misprint for *Evening News*) showing a child UNO playing a chess game against a group of crafty old "World politics and Nationalism" figures.[33] None of this is remarkable; it was an assignment that her whole class, and probably thousands of other classes were set, in America. The "As" she received for both pieces are testimony to the thoroughness with which she completed both projects, but they provide no evidence of a precocious reading of current events. The pre-college poem "Bitter Strawberries" shows the concerned but undeveloped nature of her response to world events. Originally called "Swords into Plowshares," and published in the *Christian Science Monitor* of 11 August 1950, the poem begins:

> All that morning in the strawberry field
> They talked about the Russians.
> Squatted down between the rows
> We listened
> We heard the head woman say
> "Bomb them off the map."

and the poem continues

> "The draft is passed" the woman said.
> "We ought to have bombed them long ago"

(CP: 299)

A draft version of the poem (LL; dated 10 July 1950), has additional lines in which someone called "Lois" refers to the pictures brought back by her brother showing atrocities involving piles of dead babies and incinerators. Such anti-Communist propaganda clearly has its roots in the discovery of Nazi genocide at the end of World War II as much as Korea, and the belief that what one enemy was capable of could easily be matched by another.

When Plath finally went to Smith and encountered the Smith newspaper, *The Sophian,* the politically aware Hampshire bookshop in Northampton, and took classes in government, it might be thought, that she was ready to absorb political debate and analysis. The journal that Plath began that year does provide examples of an anxiety about world events and the effects of propaganda. Plath's student journal also provides evidence that is relevant to her later dissection of the field of medicine (in *The Bell Jar*) and the arms race (in "Context," the essay she was to write about her relationship to politics in 1962).[34] One particular sequence in the novel chronicles her absolute dread of a science course that she had elected to take, and which she cannot bear. The course assumed monstrous proportions in her imagination and caused her sleepless nights. It succeeded a physics course which she had passed, but which (if Esther Greenwood's account of her physics course is based on this experience) she found terrible. As her Smith College Record shows, this course was called "Phy Sc 193: World of Atoms." But, if there were glances towards the way the outside world was ordered the main focus of attention was her writing, her social life, and her plans for the future. World events did not intrude, but were noted.

Plath's political education continued at Cambridge. In her first year there, she had written to Marcia Stern:

> Cambridge is also intriguing from the point of view of politics: I am getting more and more aware: we have arabs & jews [*sic*] arguing here, south african [*sic*] communists who are going back to fight the totalitarian white government that keeps the colored people in appalling chains.[35]

Plath had watched the reaction to the Suez crisis and the Hungarian uprising with an international perspective that would have been impossible in the United States. At the end of 1956 she writes to Marcia Stern:

> You know, once you're over here, the world looks so small! Cambridge boys went to Budapest during the riots; African trips, Israeli trips, etc. during the summer. . . . [T]he debates raging here since the ghastly bombing of Egypt by A Eden were furious; we have our own Communist cell in Cambridge—most members breaking up over the hungarian [*sic*] crisis.[36]

There is considerable evidence, therefore, that Plath's first period in England had started to make her more aware of global politics, if not in terms of the politics of class and the economic distribution of goods. But, she had yet to be gripped by the kind of fear that she had experienced as an individual on work placement in New York, where in an alien environment she began to appreciate human vulnerability in a way that was clearly very disturbing.

As the Cold War intensified, and as the threat of nuclear war and radiation poisoning became an ever closer reality, she found herself living in an England acutely aware of the presence of satellites, hydrogen bomb tests and the global tension points: Berlin, Turkey, and Cuba. Initially, Berlin and the border with Eastern European countries were the danger zones, and all people living in Europe felt extremely exposed and vulnerable to the grinding of Superpower tectonic plates. Britain in particular was to be an immediate target in the event of any nuclear exchange, home as it was to the American nuclear capability. I think it can be argued that this experience parallels the shock and disorientation of New York, but in a different sphere. In New York, as Esther discovers, the danger is from men who are violent and stand outside the middle class WASP ideology and conventions with which she has grown up. In England, the danger is from military and political leaders who seem prepared to abandon the ideology of peace and security. The discovery of insecurity is mapped in *The Bell Jar,* starting with the meeting with the "waspish" Jay Cee (whose name may suggest a kind of female Christ figure) in which Esther/Ishtar is suddenly made to feel her own limitations. Esther cannot understand why the memory of evading the chemistry class at college should float into her mind during that interview, but the rhetoric of the text makes the reason clear: she has been successful so far partly because she has been a clever role-player and manipulator of others, and now she appears to have been found out. The novel thus explores the management of fear, and the disastrous consequences when that management fails.

On the front page of the Manchester *Guardian* of Tuesday, 19 April 1960, there is a photograph of the CND demonstration in Trafalgar Square, near the headline "Journey's End for 40,000 marchers." As the photograph was taken from behind the speakers standing around the base of Nelson's Column, and looks across the crowd in the direction of the National Gallery, it is likely that one of the heads in the background is Plath's for that is where her letter said she was sitting. She may have seen the picture, although the odds are against it. Plath unfailingly sent her mother multiple copies of every photograph in which she appeared, but, what is more important, is the newspaper context and the rhetoric of the surrounding reporting.

Liberal newspapers such as the *The Guardian* and *The Observer* provide evidence of the kind of Cold War discourse of anxiety that Plath would have absorbed during the early 1960s. In 1961, the year after this demonstration and the year in which *The Bell Jar* was written, *The Observer* reported the Sino-Russian conflict in February, and the mounting pressures in Laos in March. The 1961 Aldermaston march, reported on 2 April had a new concern as shown by the banners condemning Polaris nuclear submarines and missiles. On 9 April there is a major article "The meaning of Polaris missiles in Britain," and then attention shifts to Cuba: first with the mobilization of Cuba after air raids, and then on 23 April the failure of United States sponsored invasion of Cuba at the Bay of Pigs. Though the front page reporting is low key, there is lengthy treatment inside. Further nuclear protests are reported on 30 April, when 826 people are arrested after the Committee of 100 staged a sit-down and lie-down in Whitehall. In May *The Observer* printed a series of articles on "America and the Cold War," while in July Nora Beloff writes about "Exploring the Red Empire." By then, Berlin had become a centre of international tension, and in August the Berlin Wall started to appear, physically dividing the city, and racheting up world tension still further.

Paralleling one kind of present horror was a disturbing reminder of another. The trial of Eichmann, which had been reported all summer, reached a conclusion at the end of August, with a verdict expected in November. During this period the two senses of the word "holocaust" run in tandem, and this is significant for a reading of not only *The Bell Jar,* but also the 1962 *Ariel* poems. It leads towards a recognition that the narrator of *The Bell Jar* is more politically engaged than the narrator's voice may suggest. An acceptance that there is a concealment of this engagement in the persona of the immature version of Esther Greenwood allows for the possibility that this is a novel not exclusively about Plath's treatment of her past which has nothing to say about her reading of her present. There is a very definite link, one that has more to do with stance than subject matter.

Towards the end of 1961, there was widespread alarm about the possible impact of the Russian nuclear bomb tests on the iodine level in the milk being given to children, repeating the anxieties about the effect of the Windscale disaster in 1957. In an October letter to her mother, written from Devon, Plath expressed her anxieties about what was being done to the atmosphere:

Well, I hope the Strontium 90 level doesn't go up too high in milk. I've been very gloomy about the bomb news; of course the Americans have contributed to the poisonous level. (LH: 434)

This remark seems to be a direct response to a newspaper report. On 29 October *The Observer* had carried an article with the subheading "Iodine level in milk may begin to rise this week." The article went on to say:

> It is expected to take some ten days for the radioactivity released into the lower atmosphere to reach Britain. And about three days elapse between contamination of cows' grazing and the appearance of radioactivity in milk. (*The Observer*, 29 October 1961)

We would look in vain for direct evidence of this explict relationship between reading and writing in the occasional poems by Plath and Hughes that appear in the *The Observer* during *The Bell Jar* writing months of 1961. Hughes has six poems on 16 April, Plath has "Morning Star," a poem about the birth of a child, on 21 May. Yet, it is precisely the presence and inscription of childhood that serves as a counter to the talk of nuclear destruction, and in this sense writing about birth becomes a political act at a time when nations seem intent on bringing about mass death.

Clearly, it would be absurd to suggest that *The Bell Jar* is primarily "about" the Cold War. Plath read about world and public events in the various newspapers and journals, but her more deliberate magazine reading was directed at the poetry and short stories printed in publications ranging from *The New Yorker* to the *Paris Review*. The latter, for example, provided some of her hospital reading in March during her appendectomy operation.[37] There she is likely to have been reading volume 25, which carried an interview with Robert Lowell, poems and short stories, one of which was the joint winner of the 1960 *Paris Review Prize for Humor*. All of these can have played some part in her development as a reader and writer. The following issue, 26, carried the other joint winner, and an advertisement for the 3rd *Paris Review Prize for Humor*, and it is possible that this contributed to Plath's decision to write in a humorous vein.

An account of the events in *The Bell Jar* sounds anything but humorous. Its narrator describes her own personal journey towards depression and attempted suicide, and her treatment and eventual "release." Along the way there is a rejection of the mother, an actual suicide, and a series of traumatic sexual encounters. Everything relates to Esther's immediate experience. On a first reading, the Rosenbergs opening seems a rather convenient device to contextualize the events, one that is rather peripheral to the story of Esther Greenwood. The humorous treatment of the events in Esther's life—and, the treatment is and was intended to be extremely humorous—is misleading, perhaps deliberately so. The relevance of the political position of New York as a northeastern city, and of the model of suburban 1950s America are acknowledged even by critics such as Butscher (1976), who was primarily concerned with tracking down the autobiographical sources. But the tendency in criticism has been to move from the historical specificity of the novel's subject matter to considerations of the diegetic relationship within the narrative, the Dostoyevskian doubling and so on. Discussion of the narrative voice needs to acknowledge that the specific ironical tone of voice was nurtured in England. The voice is often compared to the cynical New York form of address we meet in *The Catcher in the Rye*, where Holden Caulfield speaks in a voice that is essentially American, but Plath's cultural experience in England means that there is a difference between her female American version of this voice—the one that we meet in "Superman and Paula Brown's New Snowsuit" written during her last year as a student at Smith—and, the one that we find here in the story narrated by Esther Greenwood.

Plath's ability to confront depression and breakdown through the medium of irony runs parallel with a discourse that was emerging in England through a group of undergraduates who formed The Cambridge Footlights (she had been a member of Footlights during her Cambridge years, but this was a later group), the work of Spike Milligan, and the satire that was to later find a home in the satirical magazine *Private Eye* and the television program *That Was the Week That Was*. Esther's voice is not only older than the voice we hear speaking to the therapist in *The Catcher in the Rye*, it is older than the voice we hear in "Franny" or "Zooey," both of which she is likely to have read in *The New Yorker*.[38]

In Salinger, there is an uncertainty, a sense that the whole edifice may collapse at any moment, that undercuts Caulfield's bravado or Zooey's sermonizing. The fact of the missing, dead brother, whether missing through an accident or suicide, has spoilt the lives of the living in a way far worse than the radio show on which the Glass family used to appear has ruined them. It is manifest in the disturbing reliance Caulfield has on his little sister, or Zooey's mother's refusal to quit her son's bathroom. Esther may have tried to commit suicide, but she does not die. And, though there is a death (Joan hangs herself just as a girl at Smith had done) this death appears too remote to have a permanent effect on Esther. In 1953, it was often remarked that Ethel Rosenberg seemed stronger than her husband. By the time that Esther comes to narrate her experiences, it appears that she has achieved that strength.

Anxieties about the effects of nuclear bombs and a determination to revisit her own past combine to make it possible for Plath to re-imagine 1953 and the bleakest peiod of her life in a way that is ironically much less self-absorbed than in Salinger. The change in title, from the original "Diary of a Suicide"[39] to *The Bell Jar* is indicative of a shift in perception and focus. The first title suggests that the subject is the self: the second the influence of something beyond the individual on that self. A bell jar is a vessel used in a physics and chemistry lab for experiments in which the enclosed material is denied oxygen and condemned to extinction. That definition provides echoes of the effect on the atmosphere of surface nuclear tests, which scientists and governments made possible. The very circumstance of writing the novel in England during a period of middle-class CND protest with which she came to identify and "writing back" to America marks a significant difference between Plath and Salinger as novelists. In America both Salinger and Plath distanced themselves from the protestors associated with the Beat movement: in England Plath was encouraged by her contact with the liberal middle-class protestors in whose circles she began to move to realign herself *with* the protest movement.

By a strange coincidence Salinger started work on *The Catcher in the Rye* in Devon, England when, as part of the American D day forces, he was posted to Tiverton, a town which provided the setting for the short story "For Esme—with Love and Squalor.[40] But Salinger was part of the American Normandy forces about to strike back at the Nazis,and while it can be argued that the authenticity of this experience contrasts with the perceived phoniness of certain aspects of New York life, it was not calclated to breed a questioning of Americanness. U.S. power seemed an unqestionably good thing on D day, the beginning of a popular crusade. After the war Salinger returned to New England and though the rhetoric of his fiction is deeply critical of such things as psychoanalysis, literary criticism, and the professors giving their dry lectures, this rhetoric is not a rejection of the United States as a global power. Zooey says that he was happy to view the world from New York, and sees no need to explore the world. He spends a great deal of time in his bath, listening to a long discourse from his mother.

In *The Bell Jar* Esther also refers to the experience of having a bath, but for her it is a renewing experience, and in this novel there is complete rejection of the mother ("'I hate her', I said")[41] and of older women apart from Dr. Nolan. She also sheds Buddy, the New York experience, and her first lover. Her baby is perhaps a sign that she has recovered, and the original name of the narrator was to have been Frieda Lucas, a fact perhaps linked to Plath's memorable statement that "Frieda is my answer to the H bomb." The novel itself reminds us that the world can be a surreal and alienating and dangerous place, and that the weapon Esther will use to survive is the one that Plath herself uses: the *play* of language.

The link between *The Bell Jar* and the Cold War of 1961 is inscribed in Esther's discovery of supreme male hypocrisy and deceit.The discovery of injustice, lies and unfairness is also a theme of 'Superman and Paula Brown's new Snowsuit,' an earlier prose work written in America during the 1950s Cold War but with a background that is an actual—if somewhat remote to Massachusetts civilians -war. But at that stage she had access to neither the discourse nor the experience of defamiliarisa-tion necessary to read America as an alien place. Most importantly her reading had not induced that level of fear and anxiety that broke through the model of herself that her previous experience had created. It is the sense of fear, the fear of the electro-therapy, that is most striking when one reads this novel alongside the Cold War reporting of the period. That is not to say that Plath had to discover that fear ; there can be no doubt that electo-shock treatment is a terrifying experience. The historical specificity of the discussion of Cold War confrontation and the immi-nence of nuclear war in the early 1960s allowed Plath to read her own history on a broader canvas, so that her individual experiences allow an interrogation of the larger, controlling forces. To compare *The Bell Jar* with *Candide* (as does Butscher) seems inappropriate because the man-ner of telling in each case is so different, but both texts offer devastating critiques of philosophical and political positions. Esther is not naive in her own suburban and early college world, but lifted out of that into New York, into the United Nations and Russian translators, into the competi-tive marketplace of publishing and into mental hospital and sexual poli-tics, she is unprepared. The unmasking of her role-playing deceptions is as damaging to her as the discovery of the deceptions of others. And, the discovery of her own inadequacy occurs at the heart of the forum for global political discussion, as she sits with Constantin:

> in one of those hushed plushed auditoriums in the UN, next to a stern mus-cular Russian girl with no make-up who was a simultaneous interpreter like Constantin. . . . For the first time in my life, sitting there in the sound-proof heart of the UN building between Constantin who could play tennis as well as simultaneously interpret, and the Russian girl who knew so many idioms, I felt dreadfully inadequate. The trouble was, I had been inadequate all along, I simply hadn't thought about it. (BJ: 77–80)

Both the people and the situation confront Esther with their "otherness." Constantin is Russian—a representative of the country that Americans were encouraged to see as the enemy. So, too, is the girl, whose stern-ness, muscles and lack of make-up offer an alternative construction of womanhood to the one into which Esther has been indoctrinated. Sitting in the sound-proof auditorium Esther lists the things that are still un-known to her, and it is a long list.

Throughout Plath's years in England, the process of cultural defamil-iarization caused her to start reading America as a nation differently. In a similar way, her return to Smith as a teacher caused her to adjust her view of the specific and local case of the English Department there. United States rhetoric about the evils of communism, about the need for nuclear deterrence, and about the ideal suburban family was far less persuasive when heard from a distance. As a student she had begun to express dissatisfaction with this rhetoric, but, as the Journal for that period shows, the journal voice had simultaneously bought into it. She wanted (and achieved) the prestige of Smith, of publication as a writer, of marriage to a significant, handsome published poet, of combined motherhood and creativity. But, experience had taught Plath that these were all very different from the myths that had been constructed and passed down to her. In *The Bell Jar*, Esther says that she found out what a hypocrite Buddy was on the day that she saw the baby being born. The narrator is, thus, disabused of two naive beliefs on the same day. She learns that men construct stories to deceive women, and that some women collaborate in this deception. Buddy's revelation that he has already slept with a woman is an important symbol of his deceit, and the childbirth scene is similarly reported by Esther as an act of deception; the woman is drugged so that she will not know the pain and, therefore, "go straight home and start another baby."

This woman has her legs held in stirrups. Esther has two metal plates strapped to the side of her head. Ethel Rosenberg, as journalists reported in 1953, had to be given extra charges of electricity because she was still alive following a dose that had been sufficient to electrocute her husband. The dominant argument in America was that drugs and electricity were the necessary agents by which society was to be controlled. The Rosenbergs seemed to threaten America's nuclear supremacy in the arms race, and so they had to be executed. The sentence expressing Hilda's delight at the prospect of their death contains a sentiment Plath finds so appalling that she rewrote the first page of chapter 9, to ensure that the words not only appeared as the first sentence in the chapter, but were repeated further down the page in italics.

The well established reading of *The Bell Jar* as a novel of alienation can thus be interpreted as a process of both political and psychological alienation. As Geyer-Ryan says: "In Sylvia Plath's *The Bell Jar*, the mental crisis of Esther Greenwood makes itself felt for the first time in the bizarre alienation of New York, which is transformed into an environment of abomination."[42]

Furthermore, the alienation of New York can be mapped against the alienation of London: both cities ostensibly had much to offer an ambitious writer but the immediate lessons they taught were uncomfortable ones. In New York, Esther discovers the predatory nature and violence of men, the tensions of the city and the troubling aspects of global politics represented by the man from the United Nations and the execution of the Rosenbergs. To be plunged back into suburbia and to live the same life is impossible. She can never "go home again." In London that feeling of alienation from America (the *Alma Mater*) means that the United

States, as much as London, is the place in relation to which she feels abject, abandoned. London can be exciting but it is also gloomy, deprived,
and depressing. In the 1960–61 period, Plath is further alienated from
her "home" by Cold War politics. America, rather than the Soviet Union,
was the target for much of the protest, partly because America seemed
to be using Britain as a military base and partly because American capitalism was seen to have a vested interest in perpetuating the arms race.

The increasing sureness with which Plath was able to question Cold
War rhetoric and the nuclear arms race in 1960, and her identification of
this race in her collage as a race orchestrated by men, allowed her to write
about her own American experience of eight years earlier in a new way.
A political awareness informs the novel as significantly as does Plath's
reading of the more acknowledged sources, such as *The Catcher in the
Rye* and Shirley Jackson's *The Bird's Nest*, both discussed by Wagner-
Martin (1987). The influence of Lowell's *Life Studies* which includes
"Memories of West Street and Lepke" is also discernible:

> *These are the tranquilized Fifties*
>
> .   .   .   .
>
> *I was so out of things I 'd never heard*
> *of the Jehovah's Witnesses*
> *'Are you a CO?' I asked a fellow jailbird.*
> *'No,' he answered, 'I'm a J.W.'*
> *He taught me the 'hospital tuck,'*
> *and pointed out the T-shirted back*
> *of Murder Incorporated's Czar Lepke*
>
> .   .   .   .
>
> *Flabby, bald, lobotomized,*
> *he drifted in a sheepish calm,*
> *where no agonizing reappraisal*
> *jarred his concentration on the electric chair—*
> *hanging like an oasis in the air*
> *of lost connections. . . .*[43]

As Mazzaro explains:

> As that poem had seen his own breakdown, shock treatment, and recovery in
> terms of the electrocution of Czar Louis Lepke of Murder Incorporated,
> Plath's heroine sets her own breakdown, shock treatment and recovery against
> the electrocution of Ethel and Julius Rosenberg.[44]

Plath's global political concerns as a student had been almost entirely
Emersonian and solipsistic, but the voice heard in the 1960s writing is

not. Again, such a statement may seem to require a resistant reading of
The Bell Jar, where Esther's reaction to the discovery of her own inadequacy is what begins the slide towards depression, apathy and the contemplation of suicide: an apparently self-centered, self-preoccupied response. Esther's mother tries to change her outlook by encouraging her
to work in a hospital where she will see that other people are worse off.
Esther says it did not work.

A contrary argument, however, is present in the text. It is linked directly to the future of the babies that women bring into the world:

> I leafed nervously through an issue of *Baby Talk*. The fat, bright faces of ba-
> bies beamed up at me, page after page—bald babies, chocolate-coloured ba-
> bies, Eisenhower faced babies, babies rolling over for the first time, babies
> reaching for their rattles, babies eating their first spoonful of solid food, ba-
> bies doing all the little tricky things it takes to grow up, step by step, into an
> anxious and unsettling world. (BJ: 234)

This is the second reference to Eisenhower. Earlier, Esther had been
looking at the same kinds of magazine that Plath used in constructing her
collage the previous summer:

> On a low coffee table, with circular and semi-circular stains bitten into the
> dark veneer, lay a few wilted numbers of *Time* and *Life*. I dipped to the mid-
> dle of the nearest magazine. The face of Eisenhower beamed up at me, bald
> and blank as the face of a foetus in a bottle. (BJ: 93)

If the reference to Eisenhower is linked to the previous scene when Esther looked at the foetuses in jars at Buddy's training hospital, and to the
central portrait of Eisenhower that appears in the collage, then it easier
to see this as a novel which can be read politically. As Marion Harris
points out:

> If this novel goes less deeply into psychotic experiences than Hannah Green's
> *I Never Promised You a Rose Garden* or Janet Frame's *Faces in the Water* it
> also does a much more complete job of relating the heroine's madness to her
> social world.[45]

Babies and Presidents are synonymous: powerful men want women to
bear children, but in the bullying nature of their control they are children
themselves.

Occasionally, the voice of the concerned, adult Esther, one whose
voice sounds more like the more reflective woman approaching thirty
that Plath was when she wrote the novel, interrupts the cynical voice of
her younger incarnation. The mature, wearisome and anxious-sounding
sensitivity of a remark such as "babies doing all the little tricky things it

takes to grow up, step-by-step, into an anxious and unsettling world" shows a concern for others that contrasts with the dismissive treatment of Joan and Esther's mother, for example. It is the voice, perhaps, that can only be conveyed by someone who has both given birth to and lost a baby at a time when there were increasing suspicions about the damage that fall-out was doing to pregnant women, to their unborn babies, and to the milk being drunk by those just born. These glimpses of an experiment in another voice and performance anticipates the anxieties revealed in a poem such as "Thalidomide" and the polyphonic representation of the nightmarish, apocalyptic, contemporary world that Plath was to conjure up in her 1962 *Ariel* poems, several of which were written during the Cuban Missile Crisis itself.

The politicization of Sylvia Plath was considerably furthered, two months after completing *The Bell Jar*, when she read the 28 October edition of the liberal New York magazine, *The Nation*. The whole issue was devoted to an analysis of the arms race, and the way that America was setting the pace. Calling his analysis "Juggernaut: The Warfare State," Fred J Cook, the sole writer, divides up his argument into eight sections, with titles such as "Growth of militarism," "There is nothing like a bomb," "The Warfare State," and "Face of the Radical Right." The analysis is preceded by a short "Introduction by the Editors" who conclude with these words:

> The problem . . . is not merely to beat back the power of the military-industrial complex; it is to convince the American people that they have created a Juggernaut—the Warfare State—that is moving inexorably toward that very holocaust it was designed to avoid.[46]

When Plath read this article, alongside another about the rush to buy fall-out shelters in America, she was very disturbed by it. In a letter to her mother in December written on Pearl Harbor Day she explained:

> The reason I haven't written for so long is probably quite silly, but I got so awfully depressed two weeks ago by reading two issues of *The Nation*—"Juggernaut, the Warfare State"—all about the terrifying marriage of big business and the military in America and the forces of the John Birch Society, etc.; and then another article about the repulsive shelter craze for fallout, all very factual, documented, and true, that I simply couldn't sleep for night with all the warlike talk in the papers, such as Kennedy saying Khrushchev [*sic*] would "have no place to hide" and the armed forces manuals indoctrinating soldiers about the "inevitable" war with our "implacable foe" . . . I began to wonder if there was any point in trying to bring up children in such a mad self-destructive world. The sad thing is the power for destruction is real and universal, and the profession of generals, who, on retirement, become board heads of the missile plants (*to which*) they have been feeding orders. I am also horrified at

the U.S. selling missiles (without warheads) to Germany, awarding former German officers medals. As the reporter for the liberal Frankfurt paper says, coming back to America from his native Germany, it is as if he hadn't been away. Well I got so discouraged about all this that I didn't feel like writing anybody anything. Ted has been very comforting and so had Frieda. One of the most distressing features about all this is the public announcements of Americans arming against each other—the citizens of Nevada announcing they will turn out bombed and ill people from Los Angeles into the desert (all this official), and ministers and priests preaching that is is all right to shoot neighbours who come into one's bomb shelters. Thank goodness there is none of this idiotic shelter business in England. I just wish England had the sense to be neutral, for it is quite obvious that she would be "obliterated" in any nuclear war, and for this reason I am very much behind the nuclear disarmers here. (LH: 437)

This letter is some indication of the depth of feeling that the arms race could induce in Plath, her worries about the future of her children, and her sense that Britain would be obliterated in a missile exchange. It also demonstrates her belief that her own country—America—was the principal villain, and the sense of betrayal that a country that had provided her with so much (she is constantly writing to thank her mother for American babyclothes, American magazines, American toys, and American recipes) is now threatening to take it all away. What is also interesting is the mixture of ideas at play here. The discourse of the Cold War intermingles with the discourse of the war against Nazi Germany, as shown by the references to German generals. The conclusion of *The Nation* editorial itself illustrates how one discourse can be appropriated by another. Jacqueline Rose has pointed out that the word holocaust was originally used in connection with Hiroshima and Nagasaki, and then applied retrospectively to the extermination of Jews.

The exchange between her political reading and her writing is shown by an article she wrote that winter. Plath responded eagerly when she was invited by the editors of the *London Magazine* to state what it was that informed her poetry. The position statement that was later reprinted in *Johnny Panic and the Bible of Dreams* as "Context," begins as follows:

The issues of our time which preoccupy me at the moment are the incalculable genetic effects of fallout and a documentary article on the terrifying, mad, omnipotent marriage of big business and the military in America: "Juggernaut, the Warfare State," by Fred J Cook in a recent Nation.[47]

The statement is preceded by Hughes's own explanation of what he as a poet values, and the contrast is noticeable: "The poet's only hope is to be infinitely sensitive to what his gift is, and this in itself seems to be another gift that few poets possess."[48]

Hughes's account avoids any reference to contemporary events, refer-
ring instead to Yeats, Wordsworth, Coleridge, Blake, Damon, and Plato.
The difference is emphasized in another (unpublished) letter written by
Plath to her mother ten days after the one quoted above. In it, she ad-
vises her mother not to worry too much about Hughes's "metaphysical
interpretation" of his play "The Harvesting," offering her own more political reading: the play is one "which I think reads perfectly as a symbolic
invasion of private lives and dreams by mechanical war-law and inhumanity such as is behind the warfare laboratory in Maryland."[49]

There is, thus, a clear body of evidence to show that Plath's thinking
was strongly informed by feelings about the Cold War and the global
arms industry. The letter following the CND demonstration in Easter,
the collage satirizing the American war machine in 1960, the response to
the Cook article in 1961, and her own statement in "Context" in early
1962 all indicate a writer who is engaged with the ideas of politics. At the
end of the winter of 1962 Plath met Elizabeth Compton, and according
to Linda Wagner-Martin:

> When Elizabeth said she was a member of the Liberal Party, Sylvia jumped
> up and said 'Thank God, a committed woman!' Their conversation ranged
> from armament and American big business to Sylvia's plan for expanding her
> family and garden.[50]

Plath's belief that English churches would not resort to the bellicose tone
of American preachers turned out to be misplaced. In a letter to Aurelia,
dated March 12, Plath tells her mother of the plans to have the children
baptized on Sunday, 25 March.

> Although I honestly dislike, or rather scorn, the rector. I told you about his
> ghastly H Bomb sermon, didn't I, where he said this was the happy prospect
> of the Second Coming and how lucky we Christians were compared to the stu-
> pid pacifists and humanists and "educated pagans" who feared being inciner-
> ated, etc. etc. I have not been to church since. I felt it was a sin to support
> such insanity even by my presence. (LH: 449)

And, in case this emphasis on the pervasiveness of tension, the culture of
anxiety, and the high profile of the Campaign for Nuclear Disarment in
England is thought to be exaggerated, here is an extract from "The
Kennedy Tapes," which recorded the conversations that took place in
The White House during the Cuban Missile Crisis of that same year,
while Plath was producing her *Ariel* poems:

> President Kennedy: The British Press are not even with us today.
> Bundy: Even today we got the *Manchester Guardian* saying we're wrong.
>   (Tuesday, 23 October, 1962 10 A.M. Cabinet Room)[51]

The President was alert to the anti-American feeling expressed in *The Guardian* editorial, while the transatlantic feeling of tension was noted by one of his advisors: "The reaction among students here was qualitatively different from anything I've ever witnessed . . . these kids were literally scared for their lives."[52]

But, that is to move forward one year. In 1961, the tension was not quite so extreme, but it was palpable. Judith Cook, a thirty-four year old woman who belonged to the Quaker community in Cornwall and was the mother of three children recalled the following year how one night:

> we watched a programme that showed the Russian and American tanks facing each other in Berlin, and the commentator interviewed an American colonel who reckoned they'd be using nuclear weapons by next Tuesday. I was horrified. I sat down and wrote a letter to *The Guardian*—from the viewpoint of an anxious mother . . . [to] express my fears and feeling of powerlessness. (*The Guardian* 7 March 1962)

Cook's letter clearly struck a chord. She received a thousand letters in four days, and responded by founding the "Voice of Women" for mothers who were prepared to campaign for peace.

POLITICS, PARENTHOOD, AND VOICE

Eight years after the publication of *The Bell Jar,* there was a powerful reminder of one particular circumstance connecting the more reflective Esther to the execution of the Rosenbergs, the event which provides the opening reference in Plath's narrative. The circumstance is the apparently unremarkable phenomenon of parenthood.

In 1971, E. L. Doctorow's novel, *The Book of Daniel,* was published. Doctorow's novel is narrated by Daniel Isaacson whose parents have been executed for treason, and by analogy it reminds readers that not only were the Rosenbergs Jewish, not only were they accused of betraying (atomic) secrets at a time of Cold War tension, not only were they executed despite considerable public protest, but they left behind two young children. Esther Greenwood, the narrator of *The Bell Jar,* whose name is not unlike Ethel Rosenberg's maiden name (Ethel Greenglass), has survived her own "electrocution" and she too has a baby. She is in that sense a survivor.

On the other hand, the bell jar may descend at any moment "in Europe, somewhere, anywhere" (BJ 254) as Esther concedes, only one page before she listens to the "brag of her heart" which says "I am, I am, I am" (BJ 256). Both "brag" and the earlier doubt seem to undercut this confidence. In an extract from her 1949 "Diary Supplement" (LH: 40) the writing voice says "I am I. I am powerful, but to what extent? I am I." The confidence is there—in the same extract she calls herself "The girl who wanted to be God"—but, it is qualified. And, for the mature narrator of *The Bell Jar* confidence can be a boast, a performance, necessary to survival. What, then, is to be made of the worry about the return of the bell jar? It is possible to retain the reading of the narrator as a stronger, more confident person if the bell jar that could descend in Europe is taken to be as much a reference to external events—perhaps even nuclear war— as it is to interior depression. In this reading fear of failure is replaced by distrust of those who manage (or rather, mismanage) the world.

Plath's apparent dismissal of her own novel has diverted attention from the importance of its genesis in time and place, as if a quickly written novel can escape the specificities of its origins. Plath described her novel as a "potboiler," but this is a misleadingly—perhaps, deliberately misleadingly—casual term. The activity of writing was never perfunctory, never a mere diversion for Plath. She wanted success—in *The New Yorker*, in the field of poetry, in the field of fiction—for reasons of career and survival. She had two children, and even before Hughes had left her they had no regular, reliable source of income on which they could depend. Writing was a job, and a source of income to replace teaching. Even if the novel is viewed as a piece of crafted fiction, in the *New Yorker* polished style, (as discussed by Sinfield), exploring the New York/college boy and girl world as presented by J. D. Salinger, but through a female lens, the economics of novel writing as a profession do have a bearing on its form and its entry into the market place and these are important considerations when assessing this book. *The Bell Jar* is mediated by market concerns, but I do not think a purely imitative book would have had the success it has had. It has survived its period more successfully than Salinger's novels. Discussion of its politics should not be confined to its subject of the 1950s, nor should discussion of its style and voice be dictated by its resemblance to Salinger's novels.

As a novel written from a distance, as an example of "writing back" (in time and in place) it differs significantly from the Salinger texts. Zooey makes it clear that he sees no reason to leave New York, that he is suspicious of the phoniness that accompanies European culture, that he and all the Glass family are on some kind of religious quest. The beauty of Plath's Esther is that she does not take herself that seriously. Although she is monstrously dismissive of nearly all the adults around her (as are Caulfield and Zooey) she does not suffer from the latter's substantial egoism. She has that sense of self-irony; if she switches off the pose we sense there will still be something there. In the case of Holden Caulfield, and Zooey Glass, they are the pose, and yet seem to be unaware of it. Several years earlier, when the "Falcon Yard" novel had become bogged down and she was searching for inspiration, Plath knew that she could write in the Salinger voice, but saw the first person narrator as a limitation:

> I could write a terrific novel. The tone is the problem. . . . I need a master, several masters. . . . Joyce Cary I like. I have that fresh, brazen, colloquial voice. Or J. D. Salinger. But that needs an "I" speaker, which is so limiting. (J: 156)

By 1961, she had discovered how to successfully work within this "limitation."

The Bell Jar is a more mature book, a book that comes out of exile (in England), political engagement (Plath has learned to complement the mysticism encouraged by Hughes with a day-to-day practicality that comes from motherhood), and from a sense of the future that having a child engenders. It is a book which questions a number of things that are directly linked to the global and gender politics of 1961. It questions marriage, it questions science and the control of women's bodies by men, and it questions the self-centeredness of breakdowns by presenting Esther's breakdown ironically. The comic absurdity of both life and death are products of twentieth-century Europe, and in some senses *The Bell Jar* is closer to Beckett than it is to Salinger, closer to Kafka and Hamsun than it is to American fiction. Even though the world it describes is quintessentially American, the treatment is not.

Venus and Astrology, Witch, Wooer, and White Goddess: The Heavy Burden of the Cambridge Novel

In Love with Myth: Eschewing Politics

The distinctive voice and argument of *The Bell Jar* is thrown into relief when it is compared with what evidence remains of Plath's earlier attempt at a novel. If *The Bell Jar* is a distinctively American novel written in a small room in London, the earlier "Falcon Yard" drafts reflect more obviously the specific cultural and intellectual environment from which they emerged.

The first troublesome, attempted novel was begun in Cambridge in 1957, during Plath's second year there, and the sense of the global and the political seems absent, even though part of the narrative is set in England, France, Germany and Italy—countries on the front line in the event of a Cold War military exchange. She was to miss the accident at the Windscale nuclear reactor which released radio active material into the surrounding countryside and contaminated the milk. By then, she had moved with Hughes to Northampton in Massachusetts, to take up a teaching post at her old college. But, the Cambridge environment insulated many from the significance of this dangerous incident: the Sylvia Plath who became concerned about radioactive contamination of the environment was no longer a young student but a writer and young mother living in London.

In March 1957, Plath tells her mother that the novel is tentatively to be called "Hill of Leopards," and is to be about an American girl "finding her soul in a year (or rather nine Fulbright months) at Cambridge and on the Continent" (LH: 311)

When Plath digs out these writings in 1958 while teaching at Smith, there is some joy, but the main feeling is one of despair. She regards the novel episodes as sentimental and vain, but resolves:

> Will try now writing over each chapter as a story with definite motion and climax, building up minor characters so they become actors, not just observed, like wallpaper by the girl's eye. . . . Work on a chapter at a time: "Friday night in Falcon Yard." twenty pages each.[53]

She is determined to succeed in prose. On 14 January she notes that with poems, if they are bad, they are bad. With prose there is always the possibility that it can be saved: " . . . I'll try if the prose isn't too bad. . . . Prose is never quite hopeless" (J: 185).

By 20 January it is all prose: "Working over the kernel chapter of my novel, to crouch it and clench it together in a story. Friday night in Falcon Yard" (J: 185).

Plath then proceeds to outline the characters and plot, which are autobiographical and Jamesian: an American woman in Europe.

> A girl wedded to the statue of a dream, cinderella in her ring of flames, mail-clad in her unassaultable ego, meets a man who with a kiss breaks her statue, makes man-sleepings weaker than kisses, and changes forever the rhythm of her ways. (J: 185)

The image of the woman in her "ring of flames" parallels Plath's description of a scene from the silent French film *The Temptation of St. Joan* which she had seen at the Museum of Modern Art in 1955.[54] It also anticipates the image of the "horizon of faggots" that appears in the 1961 poem "Wuthering Heights," with the mail-clad figure suggesting Joan of Arc burnt as a witch and too convinced of her own rightness to recant.[55]

Plath is strengthened and invigorated by the Falcon Yard writing: "Prose sustains me. I can mess it, mush it, rewrite it, pick it up any times. . . . So I will try reworking summer stuff: The Falcon Yard chapter" (J: 186).

By 13 May she records that thirty-five pages of "Falcon Yard" have been sent to *New World Writing*.

But, this is very brittle writing, because after a row with Hughes, she does not say anything more about her novel until 9 July, when she notes that "[p]rose writing has become a phobia to me" (J: 247). As she was all-too-well aware, the story of the young American girl entering Europe and being unprepared for the way it will challenge her had been well worked before: "The damnable thing is that Henry James has done it all, with his endowed and innocent Isabel Archer."[56]

We do not know what the thirty-five pages that were sent away con-tained,[57] but we do have a version of the central "Falcon Yard" encounter in the form of the short story "Stone Boy with Dolphin" that was included in *Johnny Panic and the Bible of Dreams* (JP: 297). In this story, the name of the central character is Dody Ventura, and a number of people that her 20 January journal entry mentions ("Get in minor characters, round them out. Mrs Guinea, Miss Minchell. Hamish") make an appearance. Mrs. Guinea is the Scottish housekeeper who provides linen for Dody's college room, and who thinks beer and men are ugly words. Miss Minchell is the college secretary who acts as supervisor and who the women have to outwit if they are to get back to their rooms after hours. Hamish is the hapless student who Dody uses as an escort to the Falcon Yard party, where she meets the writer from London called Leonard. She bites him on the cheek. He takes her hairband, the symbol, perhaps, of her "mail-clad ego." She leaves with Hamish, climbs over the wall into Queen's College, begins to sober up, and then creeps back to her own room. She is wet, and her clothes are torn. She undresses, and opening her window exposes her naked body to the cold winter air, to be in imag-inary contact with the garden statue of the boy with the dolphin that has become her talisman, and which she has hitherto kept clear of snow.

Apart from this, very little of the "Falcon Yard" manuscript appears to have been preserved from the flames. In the collection of Plath manu-scripts held at Smith College there is a single typed page, numbered 25, with the title "Venus in the Seventh" at the head of the page. It has sur-vived because it was used as a piece of paper on which Plath made notes about *The Bell Jar* to reassure the English publishers who were con-cerned about litigation. The *Bell Jar* notes concern the meeting with Dr. Gordon and Esther's experience at the hospital. The other side of this sheet, the page 25 of "Venus in the Seventh," consists of a typed de-scription of a scene in which a woman (the woman who elsewhere in Plath's notes for this period is called Judith Greenwood) called Jess and a man called Winthrop have arrived in Munich on a cold, snowy night and are seeking a hotel. The evidence suggests that this is taken from a chapter which explores the heroine's relationships with a number of un-satisfactory men, before the traumatic meeting in Falcon Yard. In astro-logical terms "Venus in the Seventh" suggests female eroticism in the

sphere of relationships, and the incident seems to be based on the visit
to Munich that she made with Gordon Lameyer. On the day that she and
Hughes learn that he has won the *Harper's* prize for *Hawk in the Rain*,
she notes in her journal:

> Scene for tomorrow: precise description of departure from Paris in spring
> with Gordon: . . . grim train ride; elegant meal; flavorless life; snow in Munich;
> frightening surgical hotel. (J: 154)

Plath is clearly unhappy with what she then produces, because on 4
March she says that what she has written on her three-pages-a-day stint
is "atrocious:"

> *It's hopeless to "get life" if you don't keep notebooks.* I am angry now because,
> except for snow, I forget what the trip from France to Munich was like. (J: 155)

The page that has survived is interesting for several reasons. The most
obvious is that it provides a fragmentary glimpse of the larger project, despite the claim in *Bitter Fame* that no trace of this novel survives in her
papers.[58] The second reason is that we have an interesting record of the
genesis of this page. In March 1956 Plath was spending Easter in Paris,
going out with a series of men, but thinking of ways of seeing Hughes
again. They had met in Cambridge, she had spent one night at his London flat, and then she had gone to Paris.

One of the people she describes in her Paris diary is Tony Gray, who
is presented as a "Tennis, anyone?" Oxford stereotype. They have brief,
platonic contact, and when she sees him again in October (by which time
she has married Hughes), "pale, blond and shrunken" at the railway station, terrible memories of that Easter come flooding back. They provide
a "Novel idea," as she goes on to explain:

> The springtime of horror, drowning, where three men menaced and no choice
> was worth making. . . . The German train shuttling to Munich. . . . Darkened
> room. . . . Pale lithe bodies. (J: 150)

On the next page of the journal the novel is referred to again, and there
are notes on Gordon and the journey from Paris to Munich and then to
Italy.

This is the scene that the surviving page seems to describe, for where
the journal has the "German train shuttling to Munich" the "Venus of the
Seventh" page has the "chittering train wheels . . . the train chuffing. Munich. . . ," a phrase which anticipates the line in "Daddy" (1962) where
the controlling male is equated with the German language "chuffing me
off like a Jew.")[59]

The third reason for this being an interesting page is the reason for its survival. The set of notes on the reverse is headed "Doctor Gordon," a character whom Plath reassures the publisher is "fictional," though the "botched shock treatment is real." Gordon was the name of the man who accompanied Plath to Munich, and is presumably the basis for the character called "Winthrop," (Winthrop being Plath's former home and a Puritan Governor).

There is a fourth reason why this sole page is interesting. Its title points the reader away from politics to myth and provides some clue as to why the writing that Plath was producing was not proving as satisfactory as she hoped. The astrological title "Venus in the Seventh" signifies that this chapter is to deal with the goddess of love in relationships. In fact, it seems as if it was to be an exploration of Judith/Jess/Sadie character's sexual odyssey before she is united with the actual man she seeks. It is a rather self-conscious allusion, and the evidence of the title, combined with the metaphorical burden that vases, falcons, and characters' names were being required to carry, suggests that Plath—influenced no doubt by Hughes's own interests—was rather too conscious of allegory and the need to create a depth of symbolism which the actual material just could not sustain. In the "Stone Boy with Dolphin" story Dody mentally lists the planets as she prepares for the moment of the seismic meeting: "Mercury. Venus. Earth. Mars. I'll get there." The cosmology seems superfluous, or rather it is not successfully integrated into the writing

Plath is able to identify the difficulty in a precise way:

Free now, of a sudden, from classes, papers. Half the year over and spring to come, I turn, selfish, to my own writing. Reading a glut of *Sat Eve Post* stories till my eyes ached. These past days I realized the gap in my writing and theirs. My world is flat thin pasteboard, theirs full of babies, odd old dowagers, queer jobs and job lingo instead of set pieces ending in "I love you." To live, to gossip, to work worlds in words. I can do it. If I sweat enough. (J: 186)

But, there were other reasons, which she was only to acknowledge later, for the writing being unsatisfactory. The importation of astrological allusions parallels Ted Hughes's own interest in the subject. In the rendering of the Falcon Yard meeting, which he describes in the poem "St Botolph's," he says:

Our magazine was merely an overture
To the night and party. I had predicted
Disastrous expense: a planetary
Certainty, according to Prospero's book
Jupiter and the full moon conjunct
Opposed Venus. Disastrous expense

According to that book. Especially for me.
The conjunction combust my natal Sun.
Venus pinned exact on my mid-heaven.
For a wait-and-see astrologer—so what?[60]

Plath's journals contains one other sketch that was intended for the novel. Called "Fish and Chips" it was written on 11 March 1957 and describes a couple going in to buy fish and chips, with the man reluctant to enter the shop because he has a gun in his pocket. The couple are not named. Plath's Journal entry for 11 March says simply that this is to be from the "Cambridge-spring part of the book." As with "Venus in the Seventh," it is a plain, effective piece of writing, uncertain only in voice (and point of view).

We can never know how much of this was reworked in America, but there is evidence that she was still working on the novel in 1959 and that she was still trying to incorporate mediaeval imagery. She had a new name for her main female character:

A discovery, a name: SADIE PEREGRINE. . . . Suddenly she became the heroine of my novel *Falcon Yard.* Oh, the irony. Oh, the character. In the first place, S P, my initials. Just thought of this. Then, Peregrine Falcon. Oh, oh. Let nobody have thought of this. And Sadie: sadistic. (J: 309)

A name that Plath had "in the beginning of my Silver Puserver story" now replaces the former Judith and Jess. It is a name that Jacqueline Rose finds revealing, or to be more precise it is a constuction of an identity that is revealing. It is yet another of those identities and voices with which Plath experimented throughout her life.

The book was never completed, and there is some distance between the aspirations Plath had for the symbolic role of the characters—the woman was to be simultaneously the blonde "bitch" and the "White Goddess" (J: 168)—and, the plainness of the writing. The project had just been carried back across the Atlantic: the bitch/Goddess comment is made at Cape Cod, a few days after Plath recorded her conception of the powerful central image that would inform the novel:

Novel: *Falcon Yard:* central image: *love, a falcon,* striking once and for all: blood sacrifice: falcon yard, central chapter of book: the irrefutable meeting and experience. *Emblem:* lord & lady riding smiling with falcon on wrist. Get impersonal into Judith, create other characters who act in their own right & not just as projections of her. . . . (J: 163)

Plath worked on this novel at various times over a number of years, mainly from 1957 to 1959. Plath appears to have been reluctant to abandon it and it appears to have been brought back across the Atlantic to England. According to notes made by Aurelia Plath for *Letters Home* the rough draft of the novel was burnt page by page before her very eyes on 10 July 1962, following the discovery of Hughes's infidelity.[61] Aurelia Plath's understanding was that it was a story based on experiences in Cambridge, Plath's marriage and life with Hughes in the United States, and that it would end with the decision to return to England and the birth of the first child. In an interview published in *Bostonia,* Aurelia Plath said:

> Unfortunately she burned this second novel when she discovered that her marriage was threatened. You see, the hero of that book was her husband. It was to be given in rough draft form as a birthday gift. I watched her tear the manuscript into shreds and deposit each section in the fire. She burned lots else at the time.[62]

Aurelia was eager to establish a special relationship between this novel and its companion. In a draft letter to Olwyn Hughes, dated 22 June 1968, discussing *The Bell Jar* (which Olwyn, acting for Ted, the children and her own publishing house wanted to bring out in America), Aurelia described the composition of *The Bell Jar* and the intended sequel:

> The work was, in part, lifted from diaries she kept during her 6-month illness in 1953. . . . The companion book which was to follow this—and I have this all spelled out in letters from her—was to be the triumph of the healed central figure of the first volume and in this the caricatured characters of the first volume were to assume their true identities. (MRBR)

Aurelia's remark partly represents her own sense of pain caused by the representation of the mother—and her friends—in *The Bell Jar.* It also invites the question: where are these "diaries"? Only a fragment from this period is in the public domain—the few pages referred to earlier. Whatever has become of them, it is a reminder of the fragmentary and partial nature of the prose texts that survive.

The Missing Novel: Betrayal, a Doubletake, and the Proof of Imperfection

The success of *The Collected Poems* in 1981 (for which Plath was posthumously awarded the Pulitzer Prize), combined with the fact that from her last eighteen months the creative writing that has survived is the poetry, has ensured that we primarily think of the later Plath as Sylvia Plath *the poet.* Yet, during this time in England she produced a considerable body of prose and knew that if she was going to make a living from writing it was going to be from short stories, novels and reviews. Some of the prose writing—the reviews, a few prose sketches and short essays, and the letters—from this period has survived, but much has not. The journals have never been published, and nor has whatever work she had done on another novel, one which was going to be quite different in subject matter from the abandoned "Falcon Yard," but whose tone and content remain largely a matter of guess work.

It is worth acknowledging the existence of this writing, however, for a number of reasons. It may reappear, and if it does it will be extremely interesting to see the voice that Plath has used and the extent to which it is a controlled performance. Did it draw in the wider political world, or was it purely a domestic drama? Even its disappearance affects our reading of the poems; that reading is more partial than it would be had we the other writing to put alongside it. From the glimpses of its character that have survived the erasure of this prose work does not appear to be the erasure of a style of political writing of the kind found in Hughes's 17 August 1962 gift to his wife, Joseph Heller's *Catch 22*. It is a shame that nothing survives to indicate whether or not Plath read Heller's novel, (though a tea-stain on page 177 of her copy suggests that someone had been reading it), as the satirical tone seems to find an echo in the poetry of this period, and may have been evident in the prose. One effect of the disappearance of this prose has been to give the 1962 poems an isolated prominence that Plath presumably did not fully intend (unless she would have gone on to destoy her own prose work) and so it is important to mark its existence.

The evidence that there was a third, unfinished novel is considerable. It comes from both Plath's own comments and the comments of those who knew her. In a letter in the possession of Susan O'Neill-Roe's mother, Susan's stepfather, Alan, writes of his belief that the manuscript of this novel made its way to her London apartment in 1963.[63] In a letter to Douglas Claverdon written in mid-November[64] Plath wrote that she hoped to be living in London in the New Year *finishing* her second novel. What is unclear is just how much she had written, and what happened to it. In an essay published in *World of Books* in 1962 (called "A Comparison") Plath compares the experience of writing poetry with that of writing a novel, suggesting she saw herself as doing both. The piece had been written for a BBC Home Service radio programme which was broadcast in July, and her week-to-week calendar has the small reminder "novel" written at the top of the week beginning 1 July. In a letter written to her mother during the final phase of the Ariel cycle of poems, she wrote: "I am doing a poem a morning, great things, and as soon as the nurse settles, shall try to this terrific second [*third*] novel that I'm dying to do" (LH: 473).

In the Introduction to *Johnny Panic and the Bible of Dreams* Ted Hughes wrote that she had typed 130 pages, which disappeared around 1970 (*JP*: 11). This seems to contradict Anne Stevenson's comment[65] that Ted Hughes remembers only one or two draft chapters, unless of course, they were extremely long. Judith Kroll records in her study of Plath's poetry (Kroll 1976) that she had seen an outline, and that these notes referred to two recently screened films, *Jules at Jim* and *Last Year at Marienbad*, the first of which deals with an ever-changing triangle of relationships, and the second with a mysterious beautiful woman and the subject of adultery. All the accounts suggest that the theme of the novel was to be a relationship that turned out to be a mismatch, or as Hayman describes it (giving the novel the name "Double Exposure," the name used by Hughes), a marriage flawed with deceit. The title of the novel was constantly changing, it appears, because at one stage it was to be called, curiously, "Interminable Loaf," although this is a possibly ironical reference to the Cambridge novel, which despite years of cooking failed to rise. This seems unlikely, however, as Plath had inserted a note to herself in her week by week diary for Friday, 10 August 1962 "Start Int. Loaf!!!" and in a letter to Olive Higgins Prouty dated 20 November 1962 Plath offers to dedicate her next novel to her benefactor:

> I hope to really get into my second novel this winter & finish it as soon as I get to London & can count on a mother's help. It is to be called "Doubletake," meaning that the second look you take at something reveals a deeper, double meaning. This is what was *going* to be the "Interminable Loaf"—it is semi-autobiographical about a wife whose husband turns out to be a deserter and philanderer although she had thought he was wonderful & perfect. (Letter to OHP, 20 November 1962, MRBR)

Aurelia Plath, who donated this letter to the Smith Collection, added the following annotation: "Proposed dedication mentioned in L(etters) H(ome). It would be her *third* novel, counting the burned ms as # 2" (MRBR).

The odd title may actually be an allusion to Plath's relationship with her mother, if Aurelia is the subject of the poem "The Rival" as is often assumed. This poem originally had two additional verses, the first of which began: "Compared to you, I am corruptible as a loaf of bread" (CP: 291) It has always been puzzling that her mother should have been quite such a rival, but the shoal of letters mentioned in the poem suggests this reading.

Olwyn Hughes seems to have seen the "third" novel, because in a letter to Aurelia she writes (discounting the unfinished "Falcon Yard" from

her calculations, as had Plath): "Her second novel was about Devon . . .
and is part written" (Olwyn Hughes to Aurelia Plath, 2 July 1968, (MRBR)

PLACE, NOVELS, AND JOURNALS

Cambridge, London, and North Tawton represent very different versions of England. It is impossible to draw any conclusions about the missing novel, but the romance and history of Cambridge seems to have informed "Falcon Yard," to be replaced by a harder, acidic metropolitan
prose produced in London. London and New York (which is where *The
Bell Jar* begins) are big cities not dominated by the college culture which
characterized Northampton in Massachusetts and Cambridge in England. In returning in her imagination to create the world of *The Bell Jar*
Plath was looking backwards (a decision unsurprising in one who feels
herself to be in exile), but through the fresh eyes of a central Londoner
living in an area that meant that she was no longer isolated from the daily
lives of ordinary people. She was a writer in a city, not a student in a university town, or a student or teacher making a cultural day visit to the
capital. This had also been her experience in Boston, and out of that experience came her best short story, "Johnny Panic and the Bible of
Dreams." In London, this sharpening of urban awareness (which had
seemed to overwhelm her when she went to New York on her *Mademoiselle* assignment) yielded an even more effective cutting edge as
Plath became aware of the significance of national politics for ordinary
people on low incomes who lived in cold houses through her (grateful)
experience of the National Health Service (NHS). Witnessing at first
hand—and reading about—the Campaign for Nuclear Disarmament encouraged a fresh insight into international politics. Functioning as a
mother she experienced a new, practical identity which set her apart
from the male artists around her. She carried the lessons of these experience out of London in 1961, not back to America (which she now re-
assessed), not back to Cambridge (whose attitude to American she had
always found so irritating), but to a small, isolated West Country town on
the edge of Dartmoor. Before considering the importance of these re-
alignments for her Devon writing in the form of the 1962 poems, it is important to look closely at the journals written in the 1950s for evidence
of the earlier influence and reading of politics and place that they reveal.
For Plath's achievements as a writer in England were not the outcome
of her formation in that country, but of her reformation.

3

Winthrop to Winkleigh: Performance, Politics, and Place

INSIDE HOME AMERICA: GENDER POLITICS AND MASQUERADE, GLOBAL POLITICS AND PERFORMANCE

> The carriage wheels screaked past again. Somebody seemed to be wheeling a baby back and forth under my window.
> I slipped out of bed and on to the rug, and quietly, on my hands and knees, crawled over to see who it was. . . . With great care, I raised my eyes to the level of the window sill.
>
> —*The Bell Jar*

BECAUSE SOME OF THE LATER VOLUMES ARE LOST, SYLVIA PLATH'S journals effectively stop before 1960. The so called journals written after this date are largely sketches of people in either the London hospital in which she stayed or in the Devon neighbourhood in which she lived. They are rightly included as Appendices in the version of *The Journals of Sylvia Plath* published in 2000. Her notes from 1960 onwards do not provide many insights into what she was thinking about the wider world; instead, they largely record what she was seeing.

With the journals proper it is a very different matter, for they do provide a wealth of evidence about her perception of the world of of the 1950s. Unsurprisingly it is a distinctively American world. America is the powerful home so that the international scene is glimpsed when it breaks through the dominant preoccupations of home, school and college. But, however much competition for Plath's attention there may have been, when world events come into focus, they are discussed with passion.

Global politics are a twentieth-century phenomenon, made possible by global technology, global economics and global discussion of issues such as security and human rights. The journals not only show that Plath was interested in all of these things, but that her view of the world underwent a slow but gradual change. There is a noticeable contrast between the political stance taken in the 1960s extant writing and the stance taken in the bulk of the journal writing which precedes it. In essence the difference is between the primary concern with the politics of gender and identity that informed Plath's reading of national and global politics during her student years in America and Cambridge University, and the very different reading of international politics that came to her in England. In between was a difficult period in Northampton and Boston, where the immersion in social activities of teaching and hospital work had to be kept in check at home where the model of writing, poetry and art with which Hughes and Plath identified meant that her daily work was viewed as a distraction. These battles for an understanding of the relationship of art to politics are acted out most clearly in the 1950s journals, and they are far from the "true voice" of the unmediated Plath that is sometimes claimed.

The 1950s Journals, no less than the Journal sketches of 1961 and 1962, are to be regarded as performances and experiments in improvisation. There is much introspection in these journals, but it is a would-be successful writer's introspection, where every problem could lead to a story or poem. They also trace the formation of political attitudes which are inextricably linked to the politics and culture of 1950s New England. Finally, they can be regarded as rehearsals for the later, more concretized writing produced in England, where the very fact of being cut off from so much of the culture that had shaped her identity forced Plath to engage directly with the new and different debates surrounding her in Cambridge, London and North Devon.

These three approaches to Plath's work need to be amplified. The student journals and the letters will be read in the light of theories of masquerade and performance to show that it is possible to assess Plath's politicization (or lack of it) more fairly if the extent of role playing and experiment in the writing is properly acknowledged. Secondly, by assessing the relationship between place and politics it will be shown that Plath's move from Winthrop to Wellesley and then to Northampton are moves further into the interior in both a figurative and literal sense, which contributed to her identification with a role—that of writer—that itself represented a problematical political act. Finally, a consideration of the character of the political discussion in the 1950s journals prepares for a reading of the poems and other writing from 1960 onwards that shows that this later work contains an awareness of global politics that is far more intense and concretized—though more camouflaged—than anything contained in the Smith journals, the poems and the short stories written by Plath in America.

MASQUERADE AND MASK:
THE POLITICS OF AMERICAN OPTIMISM

As a mid-twentieth century American Plath grew up at a time when the United States' rise to globalism meant that in the war against Germany and Japan it had been able to demonstrate its imperial strength in campaigns all over the world. Plath also grew up in the part of America—New England—where many of the American ruling class were educated, and she eventually mixed with boys who went to Harvard and Yale. As a young girl, Plath endorsed the full range of American ideals, reassured by peace and prosperity at home and influence abroad. Anne Stevenson sums up the evidence of Plath's childhood outlook on the world thus:

> Almost all Sylvia's childhood writings reflect the Horatio Alger ethic of the era: happiness is the right of everyone, to be be achieved through hard work; success is the reward for work; and fame and money are the measure of success. It was a philosophy Sylvia would have imbibed at school as well as at home. A few weeks before her death in London in 1963, she wittily lampooned the conformist ideology in a piece for *Punch,* "America! America!", but her childhood letters suggest not the slightest irony. (Stevenson 1989: 8)

Later, as a student, Plath questioned some of the values of her WASP background (complicated already by the fact that there were German and Catholic members in her family), but she was not drawn to alternative political positions which would have provided a sustained critique of American imperialism. The English and American literature she favored provided a broad, liberal critique of behaviour that turned attention towards the "self" rather than the social or political group.

The student journal written at Smith does frequently question the culture that surrounded the writer, but these questions are themselves largely articulated within frames determined by that culture. In her 1983 essay, "The Puzzle of Sylvia Plath," and in her 1991, *Reflecting on the Bell Jar,* Patricia Macpherson offers a marxist-feminist reading of the socio-political environment in which Sylvia Plath grew to maturity. Macpherson argues that the dominant ideology of "self-fulfilment" and the "ethic of enterprise" was influential in shaping the identity of Plath's mother, Aurelia, and that this in turn structured Sylvia's ideology, writing and ambitions. In this ideology success in education and parental self-sacrifice are axiomatic, and opportunity becomes not "a choice but a moral and psychological imperative."[1] Her father Otto's life was a model of "struggle, opportunity seized and outstanding achievement"[2] while for Aurelia this success was to be achieved vicariously: her role was to be a good wife and mother. This she was, by all accounts, but owing to her own struggle and self-sacrifice, a crushing weight of expectation was imposed on the daughter. This helps explain the over-eager tone of *Letters Home.*

If the letters to her mother sent from her first day at Smith College constitute evidence of one kind of textual performance, Plath's ability to perform according to expectations was not new. It had been observed while she was still a high school student by her English teacher Wilbury Crockett. Quoting Crockett, Edward Butscher notes: "Although only a teenager, she was already "very adept at role playing."[3]

Before she left high school, Plath clearly identified her future career as "Writer" and in so doing was promising to resist what Betty Friedan came to call "The Feminine Mystique."[4] This was "the powerful and repressive self-image propagated after the Second World War by male experts, magazine editors, academics and advertisers. Taught to live only only for their husband and children, women were prevented from developing a strong and satisfying sense of personal identity and self worth."[5]

However, Plath's high school aim of becoming a writer did not really challenge 1950s constructions of femininity. Her teenage image conformed perfectly with that construction: pretty, polite, hard-working, church-going, interested in clothes, drawing, cooking, and boyfriends. In both writing and behavior, there was a strong desire to be orthodox, and Plath was initially resigned to the fact that because of the way she had been socially constructed she was forced to suppress other forms of desire, though she resented the sexual unfairness of it:

> I have too much conscience injected in me to break customs without disasterous [sic] effects; I can only lean enviously against the boundary and hate, hate the boys who can dispel sexual hunger freely, without misgiving, and be whole, while I drag out from date to date in soggy desire, always unfulfilled. The whole thing sickens me. (JPI: 20)

In her 1929 essay, "Womanliness as Masquerade," Joan Riviere argues that what culture calls "pure womanliness" is indistinguishable from masquerade. It is an act of concealment by which women disguise their "masculine" strivings. In other words, women perform as "women" to divert the male gaze from the supposed transgressive nature of their ambitions:

> Womanliness therefore could be assumed and worn as a mask, both to hide the possession of masculinity and to avert the reprisals expected if she was found to possess it—much as a thief will turn out his pockets and ask to be searched to prove that he has not the stolen goods.[6]

Interest in this essay has increased as studies of women's writing have shifted from a discussion of gender as "sexual difference" to the notion of gender as a construction, something which is learnt, taught, textual-ized and subject to constant interrogation and modification. In turn, there has been a reaction to this model of unfixed, unstable identity. However sound it may be theoretically it provides a rather slippery and imprecise platform from which dispossessed women can build. For practical purposes women—and, men too—may need to acquire and identify with a more fixed identity in order to be able to successfully operate in the world. This characteristic cloaking of identity can be traced in the representation of gender—in all art forms.

Plath grew to adulthood in eastern Massachusetts during the late 1940s and early 1950s, a period which saw the end of the world war with the Axis powers and the beginning of the Cold War with its new set of foes. Along with much of the rest of the United States, New England was dominated by a culture which largely sought to resituate women as either glamour objects or mothers, so that men returning from the War could reassert their roles as breadwinners and heads of households. Plath had lost her father at the beginning of the War (he had not been a soldier and had died of an embolism in the lung) and her mother had been the breadwinner. Yet, while she demanded of her mother that she did not remarry, marriage remained one of the important goals for this 1950s Smith College student.

The journal writings may be less dense and more clearly referential than the imaginative texts, but it is clear they contain a significant element of performance and masquerade, and the journals are best regarded as experiments in writing. They return again and again to the problem of being a woman and a writer, but it is limiting to read them *only* in terms of gender. As Marx and Foucault have suggested, through the process of acculturation a person acquires his/her subjectivity and learns what it is to be a member of a class, a power group, as he or she acquires an ideology. Economics, social practices, self-regulation, reward and punishment, and peer influences all combine to shape a "person." The individual experiments with roles, with identities, with behaviors and performances. S(he) learns what it is to be a (wo)man, a daughter/son, a middle class white American or an exiled expatriot. Experiments in behavior have their parallel in experiments inscribed in early writing or "juvenilia."

Plath's numerous biographers—most notably Wagner-Martin,[7] Stevenson,[8] Hayman,[9] and Alexander[10]—document from differing perspectives the paradox of Plath's childhood and teenage years. In one respect Plath's early experiences were orthodox, conventional and narrow. Middle class, suburban Massachusetts in the late 1940s and early 1950s was largely conservative, comfortable and not infreqently smug. (Plath was to meet smugness and conservatism in England, too, but owing to the bankruptcy of war, less comfort.) This is the description of the America of the period given by Plath's roommate, Nancy Hunter Steiner:

The generation to which we both belonged spent its formative years listening to radio newscasts from the battlefronts of the Second World War—the one that would end all wars. Those years were a time of new opportunities, new fortunes, and new dimensions for the American Dream. We watched as our mothers went off to work in unprecedented numbers, as the nation achieved unparalleled prosperity, and as the people of this country united in unquestioning devotion to a single national cause. . . . We had been encouraged since childhood to believe that all would soon be well in the best of possible places and we had no reason, now, to abandon our optimism. We packed our cashmere sweaters and our unshakable convictions in a set of brand-new luggage and we were on our way.[11]

This is such a dominant reading of white America in the early 1950s that the reader suspects that there are other concealed narratives waiting to be told. It is an enduring, unchanging narrative, fixed in early television and subsequently recreated, recycled, and parodied. Yet the clichéd picture of a mid-twentieth-century American life circumscribed by shiny cars, refrigerators, plentiful food, and a moral code which prohibited sex before marriage and sought to prepare women for the roles of wife and mother is borne out by Plath's college journal entries. The voice of the teenage Sylvia agonizes over the pull of sexual desire drawing her into the potentially disastrous forbidden zone, which in the absence of contraception was likely to result in unwanted pregnancy and social disgrace. When, at times of disappointment and shattered self-esteem she gave expression to feelings of frustration and thwarted ambition the writer is aware of overdoing the performance and aware of the absurdity of a well fed, academically successful and frequently dated young woman—or girl as she prefers to describe herself—complaining in this fashion. This itself becomes incorporated in the performance, providing opportunities for further self-recriminations—and, further writing. Even her relationship with her dates is grist for her experiments in language. Here, she is commenting on her current contact with a boy called Bob: "How can he know I am justifying my life, my keen emotion, my feeling, but turning it into print?" (JPI: 22)

In one sense, the worries about achievement, about marrying the right man, about being a success, and about being popular, are hugely conventional and performed, and part of the rites of passage of many young American women of that period and social group. The writing may be better than most, but the journal is of a kind kept by many intelligent, introspective students. In Plath's case, the uncertainty caused by conflicting responses to events is reflected in the record of shifting mood swings, from wretched hopelessness to exultation. A despairing entry will be followed by commonplace comments about the clean habits of the boy who is going to take her to the Yale Junior Prom—he does not smoke or drink—a remark itself offering a revealing glimpse of the conventional Puritanism that served as a psychological and physical restraint on women much more than men. Plath's college journals were private notebooks, and for any reader there is a sense of invasiveness at broaching the seemingly personal reflections of a sensitive young student.

On the other hand, Plath's ambitions as a writer, and her background contain elements which were at odds with the dominant conventionality that makes such a journal typical. The former encourages the reader to approach the Journal as a series of experiments in writing. The latter marks her apart from the priviliged Smith women. Plath brought to Smith a hybridity of cultural experience that meant that she would always view the privileged, wealthy Vassar woman as "Other."

The biographical details are well known. Plath's father had died just after she was eight, and when she, her mother, her brother, and her grandparents had moved from Winthrop to the house on Elmwood Road lack of space meant that she had to share a bedroom with her mother. The combination of this claustrophic proximity to the mother (the house by middle-class American standards is relatively small) and the absence of a father during those impressionable years from ten to seventeen clearly made their mark. The voice of the journal is quite aware of this: it wonders if she needs the company of men so desperately because she is seeking some kind of compensation for what has been lost. In *The Bell Jar* Esther Greenwood remembers running across the sand with her father in the year before he died, and "how strange it had never occurred to me before that I was only purely happy until I was nine years old" (BJ: 98). Furthermore, Plath's father's German background and her mother's Austrian roots had a particular significance as she grew up against the background of the Second World War, something she draws on in her later short stories "The Shadow" and "Superman and Paula Brown's New Snowsuit."

In 1945, when Plath was thirteen, Nazi Germany was defeated, and the atrocities of the concentration camps, which institutionalised an ideology promoted by a leader who shared her maternal grandparents' nationality, were revealed in radio reports and newsreel footage. Hiroshima, Nagasaki, and, in the immediate post war years, the Cold War continued to add to the feeling of horror, despair and insecurity. Throughout the period of this college journal, the Korean War was being fought, and the volume provides a sporadic commentary on such world events. These were times of considerable international tension, yet the American journal writing is rather perfunctory when it comes to international politics, and almost silent on national political issues.

Nevertheless, the anxieties brought about by the 1940s had been internalized, and were to surface in the poetry and short stories written in

Ameria, most notably the short stories based on childhood reminiscences of wartime. Both "Superman and Paula Brown's New Snowsuit" (1955) and "The Shadow" (1959) glance back to confusing schooldays inhabited by characters from comic books, an awareness of a world of war and prison camps, and the injustice and prejudice of other children. The immediate global politics of the 1950s are well hidden, but surface elsewhere when she has a non-American reader. On Christmas Eve 1950, she sent a letter to the penpal she had started writing to at school, Hans-Joachim Neupert. In the letter she concludes that the atom bomb will never rid the world of evil, and that democracy will not survive a nuclear war. But, as an eighteen-year-old the fears voiced are principally—and understandably, given that the Second War War was so recent—for her own unlived life:

> Of course there are dances and parties on weekends, but this warscare bothers me so much that I can never completely forget myself in artificial gaiety. Always in the background there is the fear that I will never be able to live in peace and love for the rest of my life with my friends and my family. Many feel the way I do—and would sacrifice much for peace. But then there are those fools who think the only thing to do is to have a war to end the Communist threat. I don't see how anyone can believe the the A-bomb would cure us of evils. Surely democracy and freedom would mean little in a world of rubble and radioactive rays. (Letter from SP to Hans-Joachim Neupert, MRBR)

Two years later, Plath was writing to him again, revealing the conservative nature of her domestic politics, or her unwillingness to criticize the President to someone from Europe. On 21 March 1952 she wrote:

> The country is all excited about the coming elections . . . and Eisenhower seems to be a favorite. . . . The one thing I don't like in his program is that he favours Universal Military training. You know what a pacifist I am! (SP to Hans-Joachim Neupert, MRBR)

These letters also represent a dialog, an experiment with voice, and a conscious positioning, (in this case, rather self-conscious) that is characteristic of so much of the writing. Like all writing it is dialogic, but in Plath's case there is a pronounced sense of answering, of replying to points made in arguments conducted in the writings and conversations of others, points which are then internalized. Initially tentative, later answers are more passionate as Plath writes back from England to smothering institutional America addressed via rare but significant moments of anger in her letters to her mother, and the long letter to this period that is *The Bell Jar.*

In this early letter to Neupert, it may appear strange that she does not mention the Democratic candidate Adlai Stevenson, but this is a letter to Germany, to a German pen-friend, and she is part German-American.

This is a dialog with an audience that is also her own listening self. She is writing back to herself as much as she is writing back to her pen-friend. She is experimenting with voices and opinions as part of an apprenticeship in writing identity. Later, in England, she hopes that her mother will not vote Republican—here, the questioning of Republicanism is very tentative.

As a student at Smith College Plath was at an institution that was ambitious for its women, and there were opportunities for students to question and resist the dominant cultural norms. Comfortable and insular in some ways, it had, nevertheless, been the base for Betty Friedan's radicalism. It was not difficult for a student to keep in touch with world events and to take the first steps towards conscious politicization. Even though she had much less money to spend than several of her contemporaries (relying on scholarships for financial support) free copies of the *New York Times* were delivered to the common rooms in the women's student houses such as Haven House, the one in which Plath was a resident. Such newspaper,s would supplement the limited political coverage provided by the weekly college newspaper *The Sophian.*

Northampton was also the home of The Hampshire Bookshop, which promoted international political awareness. Run by Marion Dodd, a Smith alumna, it provided books for both students and the town and took a sailing ship as its motif, echoing Emily Dickinson statement that "There is no frigate like a book." In 1954, Plath sent Gordon Lameyer a Valentine with a message to say that she had been to a talk given by Esther Forbes at the Hampshire Bookshop: she was clearly aware of its program and character.[12]

Early entries in the college journal, written in a great fat volume intended for Lawnotes and purchased from the Harvard Co-operative Society, occasionally record a response to wider global issues. Unsurprisingly, given Plath's age and the remoteness of these events (for non-military families) from day to day life in America itself, they do not dominate the Journal, but instead creep into entries as undercurrents of anxiety, as yet unfocused:[13]

> This is my first snow at Smith. It is like any other snow, but from a different window, and there lies the singular charm of it. . . . The house across the street is melting and crumbling into whiteness. . . . Now there is a stippling of white caught on the edge of things, and I wonder what would happen to us all if the planes came, and the bombs. . . . I can only hazard. In the back of my mind there are bombs falling, women and children screaming, but I can't describe it now. I don't know how it will be. But I do know that nothing will matter much—I mean whether or not I went to House Dance or to a party at New Year's. It is amusing to wonder whether dreams would matter at all, or "freedom" or "democracy." I think not; I think there would only be the wondering

what to eat and where to sleep and how to build out of the wreckage of life and mankind. . . . (JPI: 31–32)

The scene starts softly, in a writerly poetic manner. But then, as if dissatisfied with this performance and the impression it is making, Plath undercuts it with a serious, adult reference to the political world of global war. This switch is another example of role playing, serving to check the self-indulgence of the snow writing and Plath is alert enough to concede that this gentle experience at Smith would matter not at all if war intruded. The writer is performing, trying out subjects and styles, toying with her themes. If there were real bombs there would be no time for introspection and theorizing. But, the writing is never false, it is always passionate and if the passion is for life in its most broad and most immediate sense—the pleasures of eating, of sexual desire, of constantly rediscovering the beauty of nature and art—the writing never conveys the impression of being dishonest or insincere.

That said, in this 1950s writing the fear of international war does not seem to be very real, even though the Korean War was in progress. How, then, is it possible to explain that Plath was later to convey a much younger narrator's fear of the brutality of war? In "Superman and Paula Brown's New Snowsuit" (published in the Smith *Spring Review* of 1955), the narrator is in her fifth grade and World War II is in its first year. Her mother allows her to go and see *Snow White,* not realizing that the second feature is a war picture:

> The movie was about Japanese prisoners who were being tortured by having no food or water. Our war games and the radio programs were all made up, but this was real, this really happened. I blocked my ears to shut out the groans of the thirsty, starving men, but I could not tear my eyes away from the screen. (JP: 163)

The figures invade the writer's dreams, anticipating the images of death and atrocities that haunt the sequence of poems from the winter and early Spring of 1962.

FEAR AND DESIRE: DISPLACED MOTHERLAND AND FATHERLAND

It is clear that Plath's writing voice became harder and more concentrated when she had experienced real fear as an adult, reinforced by a sense that she was on her own. In her first twenty years she had experienced bereavement but the first real experience of fear seems to occur in New York when for the first time she had the opportunity to break out from the protected environment. The previous winter her leg had been encased in plaster following a skiing accident, and this constraint had been frustrating and unnerving. Not only could she not get around, she carried a badge of abnormality. She had been on theater trips and dates to Boston and New York before, so this was by no means her first experience of metropolitan life, but the context of the *Mademoiselle* excursions was very different. She was among strangers. The process of defamiliarization caused by a leg in plaster was multiplied by encounters with violent and predatory New York men, and carried even further by the defamiliarization brought about by depression. In a letter to her brother, she uses the imagery of smashed fruit, deformity and diseased nature to convey this experience of re-education, expressed as misanthropic disgust:

> [T]he world has split open before my gaping eyes and spilt out its guts like a cracked water-melon. . . . [the effect of] getting lost in the subway and seeing deformed men with short arms that curled like pink, boneless snakes around a begging cup stagger through the car, thinking to myself all the time that Central Park Zoo was only different in that there were bars on the windows—oh, God, it is unbelievable to think of all of this at once—my mind will split open. . . . Smith seems like a simple, enchanting, bucolic existence compared to the dry, humid, breathless wasteland of the cliffdwellers, where the people are, as D. H. Lawrence wrote of his society, "dead brilliant galls on the tree of life." (LH: 117–20)

The presence—and importance—of the representation of fear in Plath's writing has long been recognised. It is the theme of the 1958 short story "Johnny Panic and the Bible of Dreams" with its refrain:

> The only thing to love is Fear itself.
> Love of Fear is the beginning of wisdom.
> The only thing to love is Fear itself.
> May Fear and Fear and Fear be everywhere.
>
> (JP: 33)

This chant forms part of the ritualized punishment of the narrator, who has been illicitly reading hospital records of psychiatric patients' nightmares. The conclusion of the nightmare punishment is enforced electric shock treatment, and this story is an earlier example of Plath's willingness to visit in prose fiction the experience which would later be so central to *The Bell Jar.*

The experience of fear leads to the discovery of new kinds of discourse which contributes to the reshaping of subjectivity. This is strikingly illustrated by the contrast between the 1955 short story "Tongues of Stone"

(JP: 267) and *The Bell Jar* (1963). Both explore similar events—the institutionalization of the depressed female protagonist, her temporary belief that she is blind, the breaking of glass to obtain sinister shards, but,
the narrative voice is flat and distant in the short story, while the first person narrator of *The Bell Jar* can view events with a sharpness and irony
that is largely absent in the earlier experiment.[14]

POLITICAL COMMENTARY AND PERFORMANCE

The entry that began with the description of the first snow at Smith continues in an increasingly didactic voice:

> Yet, while America dies like the great Roman Empire died, while the legions
> fail and the barbarians overrun our tender, steak-juicy, butter-creamy, million-
> dollar stupendous land, somewhere there will be the people that never mat-
> tered much in our scheme of things anyway. In India, perhaps, or Africa, they
> will rise. It will be long before everyone is wiped out. . . . And so I will belong
> to a dark age, and historians will say "We have a few documents to show how
> the common people lived at this time. Records lead us to believe that a ma-
> jority were killed. But there were glorious men." And school children will sigh
> and learn the names of Truman and Senator McCarthy. Oh, it is hard for me
> to reconcile myself to this. But maybe this is why I am a girl—so I can live
> more safely than the boys I have known and envied, so I can bear children,
> and instill in them the biting eating desire to learn and love life which I will
> never quite fulfill, because there isn't time, because there isn't time at all, but
> instead the quick desperate fear, the ticking clock and the snow which comes
> too suddenly upon the summer. . . . Now I am living on the edge. We all are
> on the brink, and it takes a lot of nerve, a lot of energy, to teeter on the edge,
> looking over, looking down into the windy blackness. . . . (JPI: 32)

This is broad brush political commentary, suggestive of liberal humanist
readings from literature and history rather than midnight discussions of
Lenin, Trotsky and global capitalism. The entry does reveal, however,
Plath's fondness for the parapet image (applied by Tony Tanner to Ro-
jack's walking in Norman Mailer's 1965 novel *An American Dream*, but
equally applicable to Plath)[15] which anticipates the title of Plath's final
poem "Edge." It is not true to say that Plath discovers a completely "new"
language when she comes to write the *Ariel* poems; certain elements of
the imaginative rhetoric of that productive period in England can be
found in the archaeology of the earlier writing.

   If one accepts the argument that this writing is a kind of performance,
a trying on of linguistic clothes and attitudes, it should not be surprising
that in the journals examples of "committed" political observation are

soon followed by entries which return to the preoccupation with suitable dates and the difficult decisions about what to do during the summer. It would be surprising if they were not filled with such entries and the fact that as Plath becomes an older student the preoccupation with notions of self and art gradually seems to eclipse this nascent wider awareness of the world of global politics suggests that Plath's experiences in America were not politicizing her in any profound or fundamental way. But, this gradual disappearance is misleading, for these very global, political concerns continue to be undercurrents that re-emerge more sharply and spectacularly in the poetry and prose written in England between 1960 and the beginning of 1963.

Plath was conscious of the need for the greater political awareness that would arise from a wider range of experience, and for now speculative writing (writing about herself as spectacle) has to be a substitute for such experience:

> Entry 121 September 1951: I envy the man his physical freedom to lead a double life—his career and his sexual and family life. . . . I will not submit to having my life fingered by my husband, enclosed by the larger circle of his activity. . . . I must be in contact with a wide variety of lives if I am not to become submerged in the routine of my own economic strata and class. I will *not* have my range of acquaintance circumscribed by my mate's profession. (J: 35)

Society and "self" continue to be the subject for spectacle in later entries in this journal. Several years later she was continuing to feel that she was "too close to the bourgeois society of suburbia" (8 January 1959, J: 288), and a month earlier, following a conversation with her therapist Ruth Beuscher, she had tried to identify her sense of unease and incipient anger. It was not directed at herself, she concluded, but at her mother and those who tried to construct her in ways that she found inimical:

> *Who am I angry at?* Myself. No, not yourself. Who is it? It is my mother and all the mothers I have known who have wanted me to be what I have not felt like really being from my heart and at the society which seems to want us to be what we do not want to be from our hearts. I am angry at these people and images. (Journal Notes 12 December 1958, published J: 271 with "my mother" omitted)

These instances of political and social observation are evident in the early writings of the 1950s but vanish as quickly as they appear, overtaken by a voracious appetite for personal success. Plath's politics in her college days always remain the servant of her philosophy of individualism that is very specific to her time and place, and her youth (full-time education stretching out the period of youth). The tensions between organized pol-

itics and individualism, complicated by the issue of gender (which suppressed individual aspirations for women) are acted out in the world-
weary list of things the young adult woman is forced to confront as part
of the American rite of passage. Some of these asterisked items—marked
in the Journal in this way by Plath—reveal what to her had been a painful
experience of the American class system, though she had yet to become
politicized in economic terms:

> *To go to college fraternity parties where a boy buries his face in your neck or
> tries to rape you if he isn't satisfied with burying his finger in the flesh of your
> breast. . . . *To be aware that you must compete somehow, and yet that wealth
> and beauty are not in your realm *To learn that a boy will make a careless re-
> mark about "your side of town" as he drives you to a roadhouse in his father's
> latest chromium plated convertible *To learn that you might have been more
> of an "artist" than you are if you had been born into a family of wealthy intel-
> lectuals. (J: 21)

Later, her marriage provided a fresh curb on the urge to become socially
active: in the Boston journal entry of 8 January referred to earlier, she
complains that Hughes refuses any church and that she has no community of which she can be a part. The longing for society hardly constitutes
evidence of political concern, however and even as a politically alert
woman alive at the time of the Bay of Pigs invasion, a woman able to dis-
sect America's excesses and flaws, Plath was never attracted to anything
approaching hard left Marxism. The journal voice recognised that she
valued the trappings of western culture rather too much to be committed to a cause. The self-analyzing voice acknowledges the passing of innocent idealism in an entry made as early as 1953:

> (I am no longer the crackpot idealist who will eat redbeans in a tenement all
> her life): I like theater, books, concerts, paintings, travel—all of which costs
> more than intangible dreams can buy. (JPI: 173)

The voice seeks the role of artist, with the individuual standing in opposition to the mass of people, "all the stinking people in the world" who so
disgusted her when she went to the Yankee Stadium in New York City
(LH: 117). It is interested in a kind of aristocracy, not revolution, as the
continuation of the first year (then called "freshman") list of the tasks involved in becoming wiser, makes clear:

> *To learn that you can't be a revolutionary *To learn that while you dream and
> believe in utopia you will scratch and scrabble for your daily bread in your
> hometown and be damn glad if there's butter on it *To learn that money makes
> life smooth in some ways, and to feel how tight and threadbare life is if you
> have too little. . . . *To yearn for an organism of the opposite sex to compre-

hend and heighten your thoughts and instincts, and to realize that most American males worship woman as a sex machine with rounded breasts and a convenient opening in the vagina, as a painted doll who shouldn't have a thought in her pretty head other than cooking a steak dinner and comforting him in bed after a hard 9–5 day at a routine business job. . . . *To study the futility of war, and read the UN charter, and then to hear the announcer on the radio blithely announce "the stars and stripes march" for our courageous fighting forces *To know that there is a mental hospital on the hill in back of the college, and to have seen the little shoddy man walk out of the gate, his face a mongoloid study of slobbering foolishness, and to have seen him somberly drop an eyelid in a wink at you, while eyes and mouth remained wide open and fleshily ignorant of their existence in his face.

(Journal 1950–53, pp. 64–65; first and last sections [political references] originally unpublished. MRBR Middle section published J: 21)

The self-dramatizing, performative style suggests an uncertainty over identity, not surprising in a young American woman who has entered a privileged Eastern college without the advantages of birth and money enjoyed by many of her contemporaries. The comments about men suggest the frustration experienced by women of fierce intelligence knowing that they will be judged by appearance and their success in dating boys. The protest at war suffers from its position in the list, and the indiscriminate way in which it is presented as one more complaint against the world. The worry about the inmate of the State mental hospital hints at anxieties about madness and rape, and a breakdown of order.

It is perhaps significant that the event which clearly contributed to a change Plath's young adult outlook is the experience of New York during her *Mademoiselle* assignment. She wished to be a commercially successful writer, and perhaps imagined that it would be like a twentieth-century equivalent of Jo's discovery of publishing, culture, politics, and city life in *Little Women*. But, if *The Bell Jar* is drawing on actual experiences, Plath is shocked by the promiscuity, the competition, the shallowness, the tawdryness of city life: it is a first really unnerving glimpse of the possibility of lawlessness. Neither Wellesley nor Smith had prepared her for New York in 1953, even though she stays in an all-women hotel and has a busy schedule arranged for her. She is the victim of sexual predators, she learns that the world is dangerous. These bar and clubland men do not "worship" the vagina, they simply wish to penetrate and use it. The imminent execution of the Rosenbergs preys on her mind. This is not the world of theatres, books, concerts, and paintings. It is the world that it is to be encrypted into the 1960 collage, and the 1961 writing of *The Bell Jar*.

Far from being strengthened by the experience of New York, Plath discovered that it increased her sense of vulnerablity. Excursions out of the all-women world of the hotel into the world of Manhattan and the United Nations were very different from excursions from the female worlds of her Wellesley home or Smith College to dates with Amherst, Harvard or Yale boys who played largely by the rules and kept within the tacit boundaries of middle-class America. She almost certainly wrote about about these New York experiences in journals which have disappeared. There is some evidence that both *The Bell Jar* and the short story "Tongues of Stone" draw on a single journal source, because they use, for example, similar "Lazarus" images (deleted from the published version of *The Bell Jar*).

But, although the New York experience, the subsequent depression, abortive electric shock treatment, suicide attempt and hospitalization did not immediately translate itself into a more assured writing voice—there was a process of recovery to be undergone first—it was eventually to galvanize the the writing in its criticism of the organization of the world that she knew.

The early writing shows that process of Plath's political subject-formation went something like this. First a period in which, as a school student she espoused a sincere but unrooted pacifism and anti-war rhetoric. This was followed by a period in which her idealism faded as she began to identify with the model of the artist, the writer, and the aesthete. Still a student, this constuction of identity is made more complicated by questions of gender and sexuality, and she passes through periods when she accuses herself of penis envy and of having an inferiority complex. All of this points to the influence of her reading on her behavior and writing, not just for the ideas and theories that the reading supplies (Freud being an obvious influence in 1953), but for explanations and models which are variously encouraging and depressing. Finally, there is the reorientation caused by the 1953 experiences, which Plath survives, and as a result she recognizes the need to take the "voyage out" if her writing and experience were to to develop.

CROSSING THE WATER: SEEING ENGLAND THROUGH AMERICAN EYES

Plath's experience of New York had been too short and shocking to allow her to immediately review, reassess, and re-evaluate Wellesley and Smith, but her writing shows that process had started. Her criticism of society was now rooted in a more substantial experience, but she still lacked a political template that provided a set of categories with which she could analyse those elements of society and world politics which annoyed her. But, a change was in process.

This can be glimpsed in a telling letter written to her mother in February 1955 during her final year at Smith when her next move was undecided. She is toying with the idea of teaching in Morocco, and in countering her mother's objections constructs a paragraph which revives the rhetoric of her former idealism and belief in world service. The letter seems to be principally a means of persuading and reassuring her mother by means of demonstrating to her that she wishes to "counteract McCarthy and much adverse opinion about the United States by living a life of honesty and love amidst these people for a short time" (LH 1975: 163). This leads to the neo-colonialist tone of this part of the letter, and while the desire to show the world a better image of America hardly constitutes a radical critique of her own society, it does demonstrate a sensitivity to its flaws.

The arrival of the Fulbright scholarship put paid to these Moroccan plans, but Plath carried this broad, unfocused impatience with society to England, where she complained of its innate conservatism: "England is so stuffy, cliquey, and plain bad, bad . . . [omissions?] (LH: 293).

She made a similar complaint about England's politics, its class system, its literary cliques and small-minded critics in a letter to her mother written on 19 March, but much earlier than that, in January 1956 after she had been in England for only one term and had spent some of the vacation in France, she compared the two countries. England came out second-best: "I must admit that my heart is with the French! The contrast coming back to England was really painful . . . [more omissions]" (LH: 205)

But, here, the voice reveals the kind of judgment that hints at the legacy of Plath's Wellesley upbringing: "Could hardly understand the harsh Cockney of London, the bored, impersonal, dissatisfied faces of the working class, the cold walls between people in train compartments" (ibid.).

On 1 April 1958, she writes in her journal:

Grumpy with Ted who sometimes strikes my finicky nerves as coarse—scratching, nose-picking, with unwashed, unkempt hair and a dogmatic grumpiness—all unnecessary and unpleasant, about which I am nagging if I say anything. (JPI: 360)

This is followed by a positively Nietzschian observation on 6 April:

I am, at bottom, simple, credulous, feminine and loving to be mastered, cared for—but I will kill with my mind, my ice-eye, anyone who is weak, false, sickly in soul—and so I have done. (JPI: 361)

Before 1960 and the birth of her first child, Plath's political statements are detached, transient and insufficiently realised. As Richard Larschan has pointed out[16] she never got "round to voting before the age of 28, even though eligible in 1956 when her Smith College Commencement Keynote Speaker, Adlai Stevenson, was running for President; and she was living in Boston when John F. Kennedy ran for the US Senate in 1958." Perhaps, as Linda Wagner-Martin has observed, [17] this can be explained by her institutionalization in the fall of 1953, and her years spent in England. Absentee ballots were not easy to acquire.

CULTURAL HYBRIDITY, BODY, AND PLACE: WELLESLEY TO WINKLEIGH

By locating Plath in the New England culture in which she had been shaped as a child and young woman so as to identify her complex roots, it is possible to gain a better insight into Plath's post-1960 writing in and from England. Like any other young woman of her generation she interiorized the cultural values of her time, but unlike many of those women she also moved away from that culture in terms of time *and* place. It was not the Fulbright scholarship to Cambridge that was the significant cultural move. Smith and Newnham colleges were different in that Smith's location was deliberately separate and distant from male colleges, but both Smith and Newnham recruited privileged women, and the women students entered the same social circle as the the men from the old, prestigious men's colleges that surrounded them. A much more important cultural and experiental shift was the move from America to London, followed shortly by motherhood and a further move to a small, spare Devon town.

To illustrate the cultural disjunction involved in this move, and the significance of place, and the survial of Smith girl values in a world remote from Smith, let me cite an apparently unremarkable event that took place in late 1962, less than a week after the completion of the poem "Lady Lazarus," when Plath was living alone with her children in the small, isolated town of North Tawton. Plath's marriage was over, and the Cuban Missile Crisis less than a fortnight past. The visit to the almost fairyland sounding Winkleigh was a sign of an attempt to break free from these traumas, and to return to a once familiar world.

There is something very attenuating about the cultural and ethnographic journey that Plath made out of 1950s Massachusetts to 1960s Devon. In one sense the movement forward in time was effectively nullified by the exchange of place. Plath always felt that England was a claustropobic, deadening society, and in her final months in the countryside the Court Green experience paralleled that of a sanatorioum. She was alone among strangers, recovering from a shock, in a pleasant but strange place. London had the attractions of a major (though ravaged) city and although at Court Green, her North Tawton home, there was the superficial consolation of history, tradition and initial local status as "lady of the manor" appearances were very misleading. North Devon was not the Home Counties. The village north of North Tawton was no Jane Austen village, no Rodmell or Rye. Winkleigh, where on Saturday, 3 November she visited the hairdressers in the village square, was a town even more cut off from the rush of twentieth-century life than its neighbor North Tawton. Even now Winkleigh feels as if it is frozen in the 1950s and in 1962 it would have appeared poorer and more backward.

The visit to the hairdressers is recorded in a number of different, but miniscule ways. The appointment appears on her week-by-wall diary, and the outcome is described in a letter to her mother written on 7 November (LH: 478). The new hairstyle is captured in the photographs taken by Susan O'Neill Roe and sent to her mother. All of these suggest vigour, energy, and an enthusiasm for reinvention. "My haircut gives me such confidence, truck drivers whistle and so on, it's amazing." (ibid.) The concern with fashionable image ("I had my fringe cut just before I came up to London in the most fashionable style," is a reawakening of and a return to the identity cultivated at Smith and Cambridge. It is the beginning of an attempt to retrace steps—first to London, and then to the wider publication on an international stage. It is also an action which appears to defy politics and history. And, it is a deliberatively performative act which has strange consequences. In restyling her appearance the writer has used a familiar enough event to defamiliarize herself—in a word cut for some reason from the published letter Plath describes the effect as "weird."

The difference between Winkleigh in North Devon in November 1962 and Wellesley at the edge of Boston November 1952 is made more pronounced by the fact that the signficant restyling of her hair is an episode which repeats, though much less strikingly, the moment when she dyed her hair blonde in the spring of 1954 in the year following her 1953 suicide attempt. The new image was what her mother describes as "'trying out' a more daring, adventuresome personality" (LH 1975: 138), an experience that was to be the subject of a short story "Platinum Summer." Here, the experiment in masquerade is doubly complicated. Initially, in the rhetoric of the narrative, it allows the best of two worlds: "Men approached thinking Lynn was the worldly platinum-blonde type of woman only to find out she was something quite different" (LL: 1955).

Then, when Lynn discovers she is attracting the wrong kind of men and that her beloved Eric would like her to return to her natural color, she dyes her hair that color, thus masquerading as her former self, whilst remaining aware that she has it in her power to release or conceal the "phosphorescent" self.

But, the change in place and status in England meant that Plath was occupying an historical moment and geographical location which did not provide quite the same easy possibility of an equivalent fashionable rein-vention of herself as newly configured woman. She was living deep in the country, where poetry—and beauty parlors, fashion, style and the kind of movie mogul met by Lynn in 'The Platinum Summer'—were not the common currency. They were, in fact, almost completely absent.

Yet, neither are these small North Devon towns and villages old and remote in the romantic sense which a reading of Thomas Hardy, or Lau-rie Lee might encourage: they are (and were) poor, unpretty, and neg-lected. They are off the beaten track in the way that it is difficult for even the rest of the English—who have an idea of the West Country that is mixture of Arthurian legends, cider orchards and smugglers' coves—to appreciate. Her favorite novelists were Woolf and Lawrence, but North Tawton provided neither the satisfaction of urban sophistication of a Bloomsbury kind nor the consolation of the kind of English upper mid-dle class literary life provided for Lawrence by Lady Ottoline Morrell.

Plath resisted the sense of isolation as much as possible, and seemed to derive genuine satisfaction from the sense of history and roots that the English countryside seemed to offer. Her letters show that she had visi-tors and went visiting, that she could get out to London, and that she cor-responded frequently. And even at the end of her stay in Devon, when the damp, cold grey winter has started to set in, she was still resistant (and Smith/Wellesleyian) enough to want to reinvent herself with a new hair-style that corresponded to the images of young French women in Euro-pean films and fashion. The style was similar to that of the the French singer Françoise Hardy, as photographed by Traeger for the January 1963 *Elle* magazine. If contemporary art was interested in the Americanization of England Plath's adoption of an art-college chic cut represents the out-ward Europeanization of an American, albeit in a farming community where sophistication was another word for frivolity.

The concept of hybridity is used in the discussion of post-colonialism to indicate the condition by which the colonized identity comes to imi-tate or adopt the values and norms of the colonial power. This results in the emergence of a hybrid culture which endures colonisation by dis-sembling and subverts it through masking and mimicry. Hybridity sur-vives the withdrawal of the colonial power; there is no return to the pre-colonial condition.

The term is used by Tracy Brain in her discussion of what she calls Plath's Midatlanticism (Brain 1998: 24). Culturally, Plath was neither American nor English. Her accent sounded English to Americans, but deep southern American to her English neighors. Such occupation of the uncertain territory of estrangement is traceable in *The Bell Jar,* where the concept of cultural hybridity is central, argues Brain (Brain 1998: 17–30).

Plath drew attention to her own hybridity in her interview with Peter Orr in 1962, in which she challenged his assumption that she was a general American by drawing attention to her German and Austrian background.

In both 1954 and 1962 Plath experienced loss—loss of esteem from the facial scar (the "scarlet letter") that was a legacy of her 1953 suicide attempt, loss of esteem from the discovery of her rival in 1962. If this were an attempt to read the life, both moments of remodelling involving identification with dominant models of femininity could be read as examples of womanly masquerade, accompanied by a parallel challenge to other women, be they mother, or female contemporaries. It is a moment of mimicry. In England she is the colonial subject, because that is the way Americans were treated, and that is the way she had come to feel that she was being treated in her marriage. A sense of cultural alienation, loss and theft is conveyed at the beginning of "Ocean 1212–W," the memoir of her childhood written for the BBC Home Service around this time: her "vison of the sea" is now the clearest thing she owns, "exile that I am" (JP:117)

If the term hybridity is only partially applicable, (because Plath was not ethnically oppressed in the way that colonized indigenous people were) then the discourse of psychoanalysis provides a more specifically gendered theory of interpretation for the evidence of display in the writing and the actions. As Angela Moorjani expresses it:

> Th[e] matric castration anxiety goes hand in hand with envy of the mother's childbearing capacity, rivalry with women, and the need for exaggerated display of feminity, a kind of womanly masquerade, or female homeovestism, which, moreover, accompanied by dread of the nonmatric (partial) male and the devaluation of maleness. Female fetishistic homeovestism (the flaunting of womanliness to prove one has the matrix) . . . make[s] restitution in fantasy for imaginary losses.[18]

Recording visits to the hairdressers may seem so unremarkable as to be banal, and especially irrelevant in a study which has announced its intention to avoid reading the texts as records of the life, but, in Plath's writing the fear of the bald madonnas, the stitched mannequin heads and the detritus of hair and skin that the reader encounters *are* notable.[19] In her chapter "The Body of the Writing" Jacqueline Rose[20] discusses the relationship between the body of which Plath writes, the body politic, and the body of work that is the writing. On the day after her visit to Winkleigh she wrote the poem "The Couriers," in which she eschews the institution of marriage and looks outwards with new eyes:

> A ring of gold with the sun in it?
> Lies, Lies and a grief

(CP: 247)

The poem, with its references to the Alps and the grey skies of Britain, locates the speaker in Europe, but it suggests no firmness of identity or discovery of a new home. The very opposite is true: the voice in Plath's later poetry knows there is no possibility of home. Instead, the journey from Winthrop to Winkleigh involved an interaction with a series of significantly different places on different sides of the Atlantic, each of which called forth a different response, a reformulation of identity and a readjustment of her political position.

Transatlantic Writing: Nation, Dream, Exile, and Class

The specificity of place is important to a discussion of Plath's writing and politics because political ideologies, and assumptions about the way life should be organised and conducted, are realized very differently in separate decades *and* in separate places. Ideologies resist universalisation and are always tied to a particular institution or region because they are always filtered through the culture of a particular group in a particular place. In Plath's early life in America that process of political filtration supplied by family and school meant that the overt political presence or respect for the importance of union, party or pressure group was largely sifted out by the normative values and social ambitions of the aspirant class with which Plath was expected to identify. Apart from her various schools, an accommodating, liberal Unitarian church also provided a site for collective activity, but its teaching could be interpreted in a way that was not too demanding of its members. Unitarianism, out of which Transcendentalism had grown, is known for its meditative tolerance rather than its strictness.

The space that might otherwise have been occupied by religious or strongly held political beliefs (whether conservative or progressive) was occupied instead by dreams of individual career (and marital) success and literary achievement. Although by this standard Plath's move from one place in Massachusetts to another, and then from America to England and from one part of England to another, may appear to represent a journey that has significance for her real political development only after 1960, the mere fact that other preoccupations—family, career success and the arts—were dominant in the American years is itself a reflection of a political position, one which privileges the individual above the collective. That Plath willingly embraced much of what it meant to be a 1950s American makes her later interrogation of its values all the more interesting. As a schoolgirl, Sylvia Plath did belong to groups such as the Girl Scouts, the school orchestra, the United World Federalists, and various Church groups; this was the accepted means by which the individual showed his or her roundedness through demonstation of an ability to be a team player, sociable and well-liked. Such groups reinforced the dominant culture and did not question it in any significant way. The extent of Plath's political reorientation in England is thrown more sharply into focus if the evidence of this earlier formative and shaping influence of place and community is placed alongside.

Dreaming of Winthrop: Massachusetts Writing, the Move to the Interior, and the Problem of Detachment

At the end of 1962, looking back from an unpleasantly cold midwinter London a month after her thirtieth birthday, Plath wrote a reminiscence of her childhood home, "Ocean 1212 W," for the BBC radio series "Writers on Themselves." Though presented as autobiography and not fiction, like *The Bell Jar* "Ocean 1212W" is a prose exploration of an earlier time, its setting is Massachusetts and it was written from the distance of the other side of the Atlantic Ocean. There the similarity ends. The voice of the first person "I" has little of Esther Greenwood's dry cynicism. The essay is wistful and nostalgic in tone. Its subject is the child's relation to the sea, the sea as a breathing, sometimes generous and sometimes dangerous mother, the sea which in the 1958 poem "Full Fathom Five" (CP: 92) was associated with "father-sea-god muse" (J: 243). In her correspondence Plath called it her "sea script." It was Leonie Cohn at the BBC who suggested the title by which it is known.[21]

The speaker of "Ocean 1212W" tells us that the nearness of the sea everywhere in Britain, offers no help in conjuring up that former vision of a seaside childhood. As the letter-writer Plath said to Richard Murphy in August 1962[22] "I am sick of the bloody British sea."

Such bluntness is absent in "Ocean 1212W" written a few months later, except when the birth of the rival baby brother is announced and there is a glimpse of Esther's voice:

> It would be—a baby
> A baby.
> I hated babies. . . .

(JP: 120)

This baby is the first disturbance in this maritime Eden. The death of Plath's father is mentioned only in passing (in the final paragraph), but is anticipated in the final image of the sea. In the Autumn of 1939, there is a terrible, violent storm which provides the narrator with her last distinctive memory of the ocean of childhood.

England offered a superficial similarity to Massachusetts—the shared place names, the language, the importance of the sea to its history—but, its landscape and history ("Ocean 1212 W" begins with the words "My childhood landscape") made the England of 1962 a place that Plath found it difficult to link with that memory of a securer past. In England, the speaker of "Ocean 1212W" reports, she gets out of her car and sniffs the sea air:

> But that is not it, that is not it at all.
> The geography is all wrong in the first place.
>
> (JP: 118)

The formative influence of geography on our perception and structuring of the world—the geopolitics of place—is acknowledged by Plath here and at the end of "Ocean 1212W," where she speaks of the first nine years of her life being sealed off "like a ship in a bottle" when her father died and her family moved inland. Unlike the bell jar image in her novel, this glass vessel encloses a happy child, though one who can never escape from her sealed prison. The strongly conveyed sense of separation and exile is reinforced by two ironic contrasts. The happy associations of the telephone number that provides the title contrasts with the December 1962 reality, where Plath could not get a telephone installed in her London flat and was, thus, cut off from her American family in a way that she had not been in Devon. And, had Plath been a nine year old in England, the country of which she later had such hopeful dreams, she would have found herself on an island which evacuated its city children and which in 1940 and 1941 was in the middle of the terrible assault of the German blitz. The Autumn of 1939 saw the invasion of Poland and Britain's declaration of war, a different kind of storm, and the incidence of death and bereavement on an international scale.

LANDSCAPE AND THE SPECTACLE OF PLACE: DREAMING OF ENGLAND

In her study of Plath's poetry Robyn Marsack makes the following claim:

> It is particularly noticeable to British readers that her sense of history is not grounded in place, that she has no familial sense of where she lives—unsurprisingly, since she lived apart from her family and was occupied in creating her own out of nowhere, in a way. This lack of rootedness was both a stimulus and a real loss: correspondingly, it did nothing to shore up her already fragile identity.[23]

Although Plath's time in England 1960–63 was apparently very rootless, Marsack's comment does not seem to take account of the limited movement in place during her early childhood (from one side of Boston to another) and the length of time she spent in one house in Wellesley, nor, in its later claim that the poetry lacks specificity, exploring a psychological rather than a geographical landscape, does it seem to do justice to the precise location of the yew tree, elm, Withins, bee meeting and many other "events" that appear in the later poems. Nevertheless, Marsack reminds readers of the importance of emotional deracination as a feature of Plath's short life and the relationship between identity, belonging and not-belonging, that should inform a discussion of her writing. The simultaneous need to escape while avoiding the exacting price of exile, is a tension explored in much twentieth-century writing, as Terry Eagleton and others have discussed.[24] Each geographical move carries a political meaning as it represents a psychological reaching out for the better community or group. At the same time each move also evokes a partial sense of loss, though this also signifies a new understanding. The dull suburbia of Wellesley had to be escaped, as did the teaching community at Smith. Because Boston did not satisfy Hughes it could not satisfy Plath. England beckoned a second time, but this time the place of dream was to become the place of exile. The disenchantment is never complete—she discovers in her garden in Devon an enjoyment of the closeness to nature that parallels the one recalled in "Ocean 1212 W." But, the England of the imagination is very different from the geopolitical reality of England, as her two experiences of that country were to reveal.

DREAM, EXILE, ALIENATION

There is a long utopian tradition in literature and myth of projecting a political fantasy onto a real landscape in the hope that some version of the imaginary model can be realized in a future time. William Morris does this with *News from Nowhere*, Charlotte Perkins Gilman does it with *Herland*.

In an interview that was broadcast in September 1962,[25] Plath says that she arrived in England with an English major's reading of London. In other words she had a specifically literary anticipation of what she had come to see. This dream of England is traceable to 1952, ten years earlier, when she records a meeting with her English teacher from high school days, who had been an important influence on her decision to major in English at Smith:

Entry 152 Today was good. Mr. Crockett for two and one half hours in the afternoon, and after long talking in his green pine garden over sherry I got the flash of insight—the after-college objective. It is a frightening and wonderful thing: a year of graduate study in England, Cambridge or Oxford. . . . I will go to Paris, to Austria during vacation. England will be the jumping off place— I will bicycle all over England on weekends. . . . Today a dream was planted: a name: England. A desire: study abroad. (J: 57)

Plath soon became disenchanted with some aspects of England. In 1956, in her second term at Cambridge she had written an article for the Oxford students' magazine *Isis,* dissecting the awkwardness and pomposity of Oxbridge men, and the way that women were seen largely as sexual fodder.[26] Some of the disillusionment was also evident in the the the second year in letters to close friends, but in between were patches of great brightness and optimism. The tone changes as the circumstances change. Initially she wrote her friend Marcia Stern a very optimistic letter, at the beginning of her first Spring and soon after she had met Hughes: "I must admit I'm slightly concerned at my total lack of desire to come back home ever!" (Letter to Marcia Stern, 21 March 1956, MRBR).

But, by the end of the year the reality of the experience of domestic life as a married woman subsisting on a low shared income in wintry England cause her earlier homesickness to return:

> If only you could imagine how grim England is in winter! . . . Nothing ever gets dry or clean; no iceboxes (one really doesn't need them) & everything falls apart in your hands—carpet sweepers, plumbing pipes, wiring. Oh God Bless America, land of the Cookiesheet, Central Heating & Frozen Orange Juice! I can't wait to get home. Ted is staunchly British, but I am hoping that he will see the enormous difference in America & want to settle there eventually. England is no place to bring up children—bad teeth, lousy dentists, careless overworked Mds. It is, really, a dead country. (Letter to Marcia Stern, 15 December 1956, MRBR)

Plath was alone with Hughes, and was missing the kind of female network that existed at Smith, a women's college. Newnham was a women's college too, but following her marriage she was now living out (special permission had to be granted for her to continue her studies after her marriage), and she is dismissive of the English women with whom she does have some contact. They are not like American college women: "I miss woman-talk. The English women are pathetic. Either blue-stocking cows or butterflies with frivolous hectic accents" (Letter to Marcia Stern, 15 December 1956, MRBR).

The Cambridge journal voice is set on returning to her home country, which was beginning to represent all that England lacked:

> [I]ronically, one of the most practical reasons for my longing to be back in america is what I formerly scorned: iceboxes, wash machines, hot water, stoves that do more than burn the top & leave the bottom soggy. I know now that if

I want to keep on being a triple-threat woman: wife, writer & teacher (to be swapped later for motherhood, I hope) I can't be a drudge, the way house-wives are forced to be here. [M]y whole range of cooking is very limited by the fact I have no icebox & my stove doesn't cook deep things & the heat will be one minute 200, the next 500. [A]nd it is impossible to get these old fur-nished apts. anywhere near clean: walking on the rug sends up clouds of desert dust, even after furious beating, & so on. [C]oal stoves silt everything up, & medical care is so bad, not to mention dental care, that everybody by the age of 20 has several front teeth out (it's such a bother to fill them) or rotted away. [N]o promising jobs, starvation wages. [A]h me. I am becoming an american jingo. (Letter to Marcia Stern, 9 April 1957, MRBR)

During this first experience of England, Plath was learning to see herself as an American. In America her contact with the more privileged women at Smith had taught her what it meant to be middle American and she was now beginning to realized how much this experience had shaped her expectations and values. The powerful model of suburban materialism and comfort celebrated in *The Ladies Home Journal* emerged from a dis-course that one part of her never found it possible to relinquish.

DREAMING OF EXILE:
RESURRECTING THE "DEAD COUNTRY"

Plath's eagerness to return to America was accompanied by high hopes of converting Hughes to a love of the things in the United States, which she had discovered she both enjoyed and valued. But, these hopes were in vain. He was restless in Smith and Northampton, where they had gone to teach. After seven months back in America Plath, too, was beginning to react, wondering if even a move to the city of Boston will solve their dissatisfaction:

I dislike apartments, suburbs. I want to walk directly out my front door onto earth and into air free from exhaust. . . . And America wears me, wearies me. I am sick of the Cape, sick of Wellesley; all America seems one line of cars, moving with people jammed in them, from one gas-station to one diner and on. I must periodically refresh myself in this crass, crude, energetic, de-manding and competitive new-country bath, but I am, in my deep soul, hap-piest on the moors—my deepest soul-scape, in the hills by the Spanish Mediterranean, in the old, history crusted and still gracious, spacious cities: Paris, Rome. (J: 202–203)

England beckoned once again: she was determined to love it this time. In a letter to Lynne Lawner dated 4 September 1958, with the summer drawing to a close in Boston, Plath expresses her complex feelings about leaving Massachusetts:

The little voyeuse in me, or whatever it is, says, oh, go live in England. . . .
From this side of the Atlantic I again experience the weight of water between
me and Europe that I am sure convinces some people Europe is a figment of
a cracked brain. . . . Ted is very homesick, and I am in many ways more akin
to the English temper than the American, but not in so many as to make me
deny that I will feel a good bit in exile. (Letter to Lynne Lawner, 4 September 1958, MRBR)

Yet, as the late 1959 departure date approaches, the voice is cheerful and
optimistic, the gloom of England either forgotten or suppressed, the
prophecy of the imagined detail of square and park remarkably accurate:

Nov 4 Pleasant dream of return to London: renting a room with the bed in a
garden of daffodils, waking to soil smells and bright yellow flowers. Nov 11 I
am excited about England. When I think of living in America, I just can't imagine where: hate suburbs, country too lonely, city too expensive and full of dog
turds. I can imagine living in London, in a quiet square, taking children to the
fine Parks. Moving to country right outside, still being near. . . . Nov 14 [A]
sense of joy and eagerness at living in England. Partly, too, because of the recent hospitality my poems, and my story, have found there. (J: 325–30)

The changing, contradictory, and ambivalent feelings about England
found in these journal entries reveal a clash of competing geopolitical
perspectives. The discourse of American optimism and hope for the future, combined with a New England belief that old England is the place
of tradition and Massachusetts roots collides with the experience of England whose geopolitical position is post-war, post-affluence, and post-
expansionist. The experience of austerity, blitz, bomb shelters, and smiling in the face of adversity is a defining moment in twentieth-century
British history. It was recent in memory, and out of it came a post war
identity that made a virtue of denial, shortages and the ability to defy the
threat coming from Europe. This acceptance, in speech, writing and behavior, of insularity and bareness is something with which Plath's journal
voice is unfamiliar. It is something that is uncomfortable and disorientating to an American, and it is a discourse most pronounced in London,
which had borne the brunt of the blitz. It is to London that she now
moved, leaving America behind for ever.

ANOTHER ENGLAND: THE DEFAMILIARIZATION
OF PLACE AND CLASS

The feeling of exile indeed accompanied Plath to England. In his essay,
"Sylvia Plath and Her Journals," Ted Hughes recalls Plath in this way:

With her last college days well behind her, and only writing and maternity ahead, the December London of 1959 gave her a bad shock—the cars seemed smaller and blacker and dingier than ever, sizzling through black wet streets. The clothes on the people seemed even grubbier than she remembered. And when she lay on a bed in the basement room in a scruffy hotel near Victoria, a week or two later, with *The Rack* by A. E. Ellis, propped open on her pregnant stomach, it seemed to her she had touched a new nadir.[27]

"Only writing and maternity ahead" is a strange expression, given Plath's ambitions (though Hughes goes on to acknowledge the writing achievements of the following three years). More immediately, the stimulus of her first baby and the flat in Chalcot Square were sufficient to allow a convincing performance of the optimistic voice. She was convinced that she would not want to go back to America: "I think I shall be a very happy exile & have absolutely no desire to return to the land of milk & honey & spin-dryers" (Letter to Lynne Lawner, 18 February 1960, MRBR).

The reference to material comforts suggests that the feeling of withdrawal had already returned, however, and as a young mother the absence of electrical goods taken for granted in America was very burdensome.

The move out of London, like so many of the moves undertaken by Plath, was undertaken willingly. There were the nearby moors of Dartmoor and Exmoor, and she was also carried along by Hughes's desire to escape London. But, the retreat to the country proved disastrous. Court Green has the romance of the country cottage, but North Tawton was not a beautiful village; that it is off the tourist route proved part of its attraction for Hughes when he returned to live there after Plath's death.[28] Her sense of bewilderment is conveyed in this Journal entry, written in 1962, but looking back to the previous New Year. This was the period immediately preceding the birth of their second child and the New Year period which produced the sequence of drafts discussed in the next chapter:

A curious desperate sense of being locked in among these people, a cream [*sic*], longing toward London, the big world. Why are we here? Ted & I very excited. Our first social event in North Tawton. Our last, so far. (JPI: 631)

The circle into which she was drawn in North Tawton, was partly one whose narrowness and complacency is revealed in the short story whose title "Mothers" points towards its subject, that archetype of English middle-class conservatism The Mothers' Union (JP 106). The American Esther of the story discovers that the church around which the Union is built happily supports married mothers but exiles divorcees. The North Tawton villagers, as described in the sketches that appear in the published journals, come from an older generation, some of whom—Percy and Rose

B, for example—have retired from London. They were different from the suburban Bostonite families of Wellesley, and by the time she wrote these sketches Plath must have felt more acutely than ever the difference that came with being regarded as—and of being—an American.

THE POLITICS OF CLASS

The issue of class, and the disovery of the economic roots of class, could have played an important part of Plath's education in England, but circumstances were not propitious. At Cambridge, Plath continued to meet a privileged group of people, many of whom had been educated in public (that is private) schools in England. Although this was quite different from the privilege of Yale, Stanford, and Smith, it was for her a recognizable world. Young English men may have been gauche and awkward with women, they may have been poorer specimens physically, but they took money for granted and had the social graces that Smith College and her mother had led her to value.

Yet, Plath's own class position fell between two worlds. She was not a "Society Girl" of the kind personified in *The Bell Jar* by Mrs. Savage, the ex-Vassar Girl at Belsize who had "loused up [her daughters'] debutante party by signing herself into the asylum." Even Joan has a fur coat. Plath did not have time to learn to play bridge. She was too busy aiming for the much needed "A" grades. She was not a debutante, and never entertained the idea of marrying a wealthy man who would have provided a passport into that world.

Hughes came from a working class background, but this was disguised by his presence in the context of Cambridge and his chosen profession as a poet. Poets and writers are honorary members of the middle class, unless they are radical in their politics, and this Hughes was not. As a countryman who valued rural England Hughes was conservative by nature, even though he had no ambition to enter establishment society (he became Poet Laureate on his own terms, avoiding involvement in public life) and wrote approvingly of Wesker's socialist plays.

Elizabeth Sigmund, who as Elizabeth Compton befriended Plath during her Court Green days, has said that she thinks Plath misread the complicated and deeply ingrained class system in England. When asked if Hughes ever suffered from an inferiority complex (a question which itself revealed something of Compton's class perceptions) Plath is alleged to have dismissed such a thought because Hughes had lunched with the Duke of Edinburgh.[29] Judith Kroll, in her desciption of Plath in *Notable Women of America: The Modern Period,* emphasises the class difference, and suggests that Hughes resented being "reformed."[30] The Boston journals certainly reveal evidence of tension caused by the conflict between Hughes's traditional working-class expectation that his wife should darn his socks and sew on his buttons and Plath's desire to assert herself as an independent woman who wished to construct marriage on the equal terms that she imagined all artists believed in.

> Both of us must feel partly that the other isn't. . . . "earning bread and butter" in any reliable way. I'm not "sewing on buttons and darning socks" by the hearthside. He hasn't even got us a hearth; I haven't even sewed a button. (JPI: 445)

Plath's ironic comment—her wit, even in the most difficult situations, particularly in the most difficult situations, is sometimes overlooked— suggests that she is hoping that things will change. In England, however, 1950s working class literary rebellion was sadly unreconstructed when it came to relations between the sexes: the misogyny of Osborne's *Look Back in Anger* went largely unremarked in post-Britain, where married working women had gone back to being homemakers in ways that they had not in the United States.

Comments establishing a shared family reading of class are glimpsed in the letters between daughter and mother. In one sense Plath's letters— and, her mother's too, for that matter—should be regarded with some watchfulness, as some particular kind of filial performance, but equally Plath's can be seen as a revelation of a reading of society that in moments of homesickness and depression defaults to the reading conditioned by her upbringing:

> Ted's cousin Vicky drove us to Whitby, a British seaside resort, for a day and a night. We took the baby, who is a very good traveler. . . . There is something depressingly mucky about English seaside resorts. Of course, the weather is hardly ever sheer fair, so most people are in woolen suits and coats and tinted plastic raincoats. The sand is muddy and dirty. The working class is also dirty, strewing candy papers, gum and cigarette wrappers.
>
> My favorite beach is Nauset, and my heart aches for it. I don't know, but there is something *clean* about New England sand, no matter how crowded. (27 August 1960, LH 391)

That her mother was one of the principal sources of this class attitude is made clear from the tone of this letter sent to Plath some two years later. Aurelia is advising her daughter on a poetry reading she is going to give in a new town called Stevenage. Aurelia had seen a program about this town on American television, showing how Stevenage has been built partly to re-house former dockers who have been moved out of a slum area of London:

I should think one would have to select rather simple poems with which individuals of such an audience could identify—background explanation would not only be helpful but essential. (Aurelia Plath to Sylvia Plath, 4 December 1962, MRBR)

But, as Richard Larschan has pointed out[31] the advice may stem from Aurelia's teaching experience, and signal the very sensitivity to the needs of audience that Sylvia might otherwise have lacked. To be fair, Plath did not allow herself to fall into the trap of equating the dirt which she seems to revolt her, with ignorance. She had found Boston dirty in 1959:

Boston is filthy: a drift of weekly soot on the windows, the windows smeared with greasy cooking exhalations. (JPI: 456)

The voice is like that of the slightly disgusted narrator of *1984*. Yet, when she came face-to-face with working class schoolboys, the ones taught by Hughes during her second year at Cambridge, she could see that society had made them into what they were, just as she could see that society had made her into what she was. She attended a performance in which these forty "teddy boys" presented a series of little Elizabethan plays produced by Hughes: ". . . and my heart bled for them: adorable, clever, huggable darlings they seemed and the deadly jobs that await them, and their family backgrounds etc. is terrifying!" (Letter to Marcia Stern 9 April 1957: MRBR)

This evidence of a shift in social commentary contrasts with the voice of the dissatisfied American who in her earlier years in England found fault with the dentistry and health provision. England shows her the conditions in which ordinary working class people live, and she is immediately sympathetic to their needs. This shift in perception is arrested when she moves back to Northampton and then begins therapy with Dr. Ruth Beuscher. In seeking to resolve her feelings of guilt through an understanding of her relationship with her husband and mother she was being encouraged to turn inwards. Her journals from the Boston period are full of speculative self-analysis.

England provided experiences which countered this fierce individualism. She began to rely heavily on the NHS herself, starting with the birth of Frieda in London in 1960 when a NHS midwife came to deliver the baby at her Chalcot Square flat. Plath could write with real warmth and humor, even when in that most demanding of English institutions, the hospital ward. Plath's journals during the period of her appendectomy operation—22 February to 6 March 1961—give a very warm picture of the women in hospital. The tone is quite different from the acid detachment of *The Bell Jar*, which was started around this time. One of the functions of Plath's writing—whether prose or poetry—was to permit anger to be expressed in a controlled, channelled way. In the process of crafting and creating her texts the targets for the satire are sometimes surrogates for a diverse range of quite complex and complicated feelings of anger and frustration.

Yet, once again, she found herself wrenched out of a society and community with which she was beginning to develop ties. Plath's growing sense of alienation and isolation is what becomes manifest through the descriptions of Devon people in the parts of her Journal for this period that have survived, although in the prose Plath usually holds back the extent of the scorn shown in such poems as "Eavesdropper" (CP: 260), preferring here to use the material for novel-rehearsals. The jealousy that emerges as the wide-eyed, pretty 16-year-old Tyrer daughter clearly has an effect on Ted is channelled into some amusing writing:

> Nicola & Ted standing at opposite sides of the path under the bare laburnum like kids back from the date, she posed & coy. I came out, sniffing the baby like a restorative. I just brought back some of daddy's records, she said. May I come over Friday and listen to your German linguaphone records? I have a better idea, I said, and rushed in and took out the records & booklet & thrust them into her hands. "This way you can study them to your heart's content all the rest of your vacation." She had asked Ted if the secretary in his "Secretary" poem was a real person. So hopes begin. For some time I seriously considered smashing our old & ridiculous box victrola with an axe. Then this need passed, & I grew a little wiser. (JPI: 641)

But, eventually, the bitterness is expressed more directly, and there are comments about these "potato people" who surround her. On 18 October 1962, she writes to her brother Warren:

> By next fall I hope to have earned and written my way to a flat in London where my starved mind can thrive and grow. My God, Warren, imagine yourself on an endless potato farm, forever deprived of your computers, friends, relatives and only potato people in sight. I am an intellectual at heart. (LH: 472)

As always, she is more charitable in the comments she sends to her mother, but the general sentiments are the same:

> I dearly love the people I know in town, but they are no life. I am itching for museums, language study, intellectual and artistic friends. I am well liked here, in spite of my weirdness, I think, though, of course, everybody eventually comes round to "Where is Mr Hughes?" (LH: 473)

Plath's social position in Court Green was complex. Before the break-up of her marriage and her autumn in Devon as a single parent the unattractive isolation and feeling of exile was balanced by the status of the house in the village; it was not large, but a house of some prestige, being the place in which Courts were said to have taken place, and next to the site of the wrestling green (wrestling is a traditional West Country sport, and is still practiced in Cornwall). If the stories about villagers coming to request the right to harvest the daffodils are true, this could have encouraged Plath to see herself as the the lady of the manor, in a small remote town which had no real manor. In the radio broadcast "What made you stay" she performs this role as if she is trying to emulate an expatriate American woman in a Henry James novel. In this performance, Plath becomes more English than the English, and she speaks in a highly mannered imitation of a certain construction of ruling-class English, in the manner that might be expected of the Lady. Yet, as visitors to England soon discover, rural houses of real status were traditonally set in their own parklands in the country, and were not to be found in small farming towns like North Tawton. Even this proved to be a chimera.

Plath became politicised in England partly through her contact with the NHS and the Campaign for Nuclear Disarmament in London, partly through her reading of newspapers and contact with health visitors and liberals. This process did not come to an end when she moved to Devon. She was still entitled to NHS support and she continued to have newspapers and radio which kept her in touch with both the world of global politics and the world of arts. Most of all, she continued to write, even during the last months of her second pregnancy, even on the days surrounding the birth. Giving birth itself becomes a political act; she was never entirely satisfied with the identity of wife or mother, even when she fleetingly claims in a letter or journal entry that she is. A close look at the actual process of writing itself, which remained her source of strength throughout her time in England, provides the detailed manuscript record of the very specific, material ways in which Plath's winter writing in this Devon house is simultaneously informed by motherhood, global politics, and the recently completed text of *The Bell Jar*.

4

Revising and Revising:
The Bell Jar Manuscripts, Two January 1962
Poems, "Elm," and *Ariel*

TRACES OF GLOBAL POLITICS:
CASE STUDY IN THE PROCESS OF COMPOSITION

THE CLAIM THAT SIGNIFICANT ELEMENTS IN SYLVIA PLATH'S POETRY and fiction have their genesis in the specific influences of the immediate period and place is unremarkable until we add to it the claim that during the process of composition these influences are disguised. Such claims are best explored by studying manuscript drafts, particularly those written in London and Devon in the second half of 1961 and the first half of 1962. A close examination of the process of composition reveals much about the density of the post-1960s writing and the complex evolutionary changes that both prose and poetry underwent.

One purpose of these case studies is to demonstrate what might be described as the systematic and painstaking "collage" method used by Plath. Arguing that poetry is constructed from the available discourses is not an attempt to reduce art to simple "borrowing": the process demonstrated here of revising, disguising, reshaping, discarding, and creating a verbal collage and then dismantling it, is informed, and not governed by the available discourses. These discourses, however, are absorbed, internalized and buried in the subconscious. The politics of poem and novel are, thus elements whose place and importance in the art can be assessed by a close observation of the process of composition.

The first set of manuscripts takes us back to the composition of *The Bell Jar* and throws light on the composing stages through which the novel passed. The second set is linked directly to the first (being the versos in many instances) and although it includes poems which were never published, this set of drafts provides a link with the spring and autumn poetry of 1962. In other words the *Ariel* poems can be shown to have longer antecedents than might otherwise be thought. This changes our reading of the *context* of these later poems by releasing them from the sole association with sexual politics, allowing that parts of them are informed by images formed during a period when the concern with international politics was more manifest.

Although no handwritten version of *The Bell Jar* survives—and, there may never have been one—the existence of early drafts, corrected by Plath, together with two copies of the final manuscript have been known about ever since they were purchased by Smith College. The drafts have attracted particular attention, not so much in their own right but in relationship to the poems written on the reverse, as Plath recycled the pink Smith memo paper which she had largely smuggled out of Smith College during her teaching year there. The recycling may simply have been an act of convenience and economy, but critics (such as Susan Van Dyne and Jacqueline Rose) have made a strong case for seeing this reuse as a deliberate act of inscription.[1] At times, there does seem to be a significant relationship between what is on one side of the paper and what is on the other. If such a relationship is accidental, it is uncanny.

Not so well examined is the number of typed versions known to exist. There is evidence, of the existence of a version that comes between the pink memo version and the final manuscript. This version was 289 pages long, it was typed on white typing paper, and survives in the form of large sections of the final manuscript. Substantial sections of it have disappeared, however, while the reverse sides of other parts have been re-used for discarded poems written in January 1962. Its existence is partially acknowledged in the cataloguing at Smith, but its actual scale and significance has, as far as I can tell, never before been fully appreciated. Both *The Bell Jar* pages and the poems written on the reverse reveal much that is of interest about the evolution of Plath's writing, its interaction with contemporary newspaper discourse, and the voice and imagery that we meet in the *Ariel* poems of autumn 1962.

THE MATERIALITY OF THE WRITING:
KNOWN AND DISCUSSED VERSIONS OF *THE BELL JAR*

Two typed drafts of *The Bell Jar* on pink Smith memo paper are kept in the Mortimer Rare Book Room at Smith College. The second draft (Draft B in the Smith Collection) has been clearly labelled as such by Plath. Many of Smith's *Ariel* poems are on the reverse of these pages—that is, on the reverse of pages from both drafts.

Draft A is incomplete and has a main character called Frieda. It starts in chapter 3 with the food poisoning episode and ends in chapter 9 with the encounter with Marco, the woman-hater. It is a typed manuscript much revised by Plath with black ink: these alterations have been incorporated in Draft B.

Draft B also has some gaps in the sequence, notably the events described on pages 193—212 in the final manuscript. Also missing are the final fifty or sixty pages of the novel, which describe Esther's stay in hospital, her electric shock treatment there, her loss of virginity and her release. This version generally—but not consistently— has the name Frieda crossed out and replaced with Victoria (both versions have the surname "Lucas"). Plath has also replaced the earlier title, "Diary of a Suicide," with the new title "The Bell Jar." Sentences appear in this version which are cut from the published version. One example is from a passage in which Victoria describes how she can renew herself by taking a bath, a ritual which takes on a baptismal significance. In Draft B the following comparison, cut from the published version, is made: "I remember in some play the gypsy's daughter who is a whore is supposed to turn into a virgin on each new moon. . . ."[2]

Within a folder containing photocopies of these recycled drafts, Smith also have a single sheet labelled Draft C. This, I think, is half a page of chapter 9, page 106, of the final manuscript, abandoned and rewritten, apparently, when Plath had the idea that the sentence she was in the middle of writing ("I'm so glad they have been electrocuted") would make a good opening sentence for this chapter. She was so pleased with this sentence, that it is repeated, in italics, in its original position, in the published novel.

Cataloged under "Fever," however, is a set of drafts of an unpublished poem, drafts that are extremely interesting in their own right. The catalogue indicates that these are written on the backs of *The Bell Jar* manuscript C, and this is indeed a version of the novel which is different from drafts A and B.

Also kept at Smith is the manuscript submitted to the publishers in England and it is complete in the sense that it matches the published version. At the top of each page Plath has typed "THE BELL JAR" in the top left hand corner, and "Plath" and a page number in the top right hand corner. Many of these typed numbers have been crossed out in pen and replaced by lower numbers, suggesting that material has been cut. At some stage the name, Victoria Lucas, has been replaced by the name Esther Greenwood (in response to the publisher's request that the pseudonym Plath was using as author was different from the name of the main character). Another name changed is Virginia, who becomes Elaine (the character in the novel that Victoria/Esther begins to write during the disastrous summer at home that climaxes in her attempted suicide). A carbon copy of this typed manuscript is also held at Smith College.

The Smith Collection also contains additional pages, on white typing paper, on the reverse of the (draft?) poems "New Year on Dartmoor" and "Waking in Winter." These *Bell Jar* pages are numbered 205 and 207 ("New Year on Dartmoor") and 197, 200, 201, 203, 204 ("Waking in Winter"). These are interesting manuscripts, throwing light as they do on the process of composition of both novel and poems.

Assuming that Plath was working from a pad of typed paper turned over to expose the blank sides, then—as is the case with the pink Smith paper—she would be working from the end of a manuscript to the beginning. In other words the page numbers would be dropping with each successive piece of work, and this would imply that "Waking in Winter" follows "New Year on Dartmoor." Images in the former would seem to suggest a midwinter setting in Devon—and not a December setting in London, which is what the 1960 date given to it in *The Collected Poems* would indicate. All the evidence suggests that it is an early 1962 poem.

The reversed sides of the same version of *The Bell Jar* has been used for the progressive drafts of "Fever" which uses pages of white typing paper numbered 196 ("Fever" Copy 1), 186 and 279 (Copy 2), 289, (Copy 3), 280, 270 and 271 (Copy 4), 269 (Copy 5) and 268 (Copy 6). Altogether there are sixteen pages (ranging from 186 to 289) of this version, but with many omissions.

SIGNIFICANCE OF THE PROSE MANUSCRIPT EVIDENCE

The appearance of typescript C was initially very misleading. At first it seemed to suggest that a whole manuscript was missing. If pages 186 onward exist, what happened to the previous 185 and the many gaps from 186 to 289? For a brief time, I wondered if they had been burnt along with Hughes's letters because Plath had written "Falcon Yard," the unfinished novel celebrating the relationship with Hughes, on the reverse. This "novel" was started before *The Bell Jar* but worked on subsequently, and only a few fragments survive. It seemed a possibility.

After closer examination it became clear that I had misread the evidence, and that the bulk of the manuscript had not disappeared after all. The majority of it had been used by Plath as the final manuscript, except that when there were pages she wished to cut at this final stage, there had been fresh retyping to mask the editing. This explains why some of the pages of the final manuscript have not been renumbered, even though they follow some which have. The renumbered pages all complement Typescript C. Typescript C is almost certainly, therefore, a set of pages that have been removed from a 289 page long manuscript. They have subsequently been reused for draft poems. However, the extant pages do not account for the full quantity of material that has been cut. If 16 pages survive, then the equivalent of another nine are missing. One of these—a page numbered 254 to be precise—has been discovered among the Hughes papers held at Emory University. The existence of these abandoned pages demonstrates how much pruning went into this so called "pot-boiler" of a novel.

Another reason why these manuscript pages are significant concerns the way that they have been reused. They provide evidence to support a redating of "Waking in Winter" and further evidence that Plath was writing poems on the back of *The Bell Jar* long before the *Ariel* sequence. This is confirmed by the development of the October 1961 manuscript of "The Babysitters" held at the Lilly Library, which has been written on the verso of pages 136, 271, 270, 279, and 269 of the discussed version of *The Bell Jar* (presumably, in some cases, on carbon copies of the pages held at Smith). All of this does not make invalid the much discussed relationship between those September/ October 1962 poems and the text on the reverse of the paper, but it does show us that there was a much earlier precedent for recycling the manuscript of this novel.

Finally, the passages edited out of this version provide further evidence of a theme (Lazarus/rebirth) that connects *The Bell Jar* to the "Ariel poems," and a subject (Joan/Jane and lesbianism) that exercised Plath enough to rewrite and make cuts from this draft.

Setting the Record Straight: The Drafts of "New Year on Dartmoor," "Fever," and "Waking in Winter"

On the reverse of the white typescript *Bell Jar* pages are drafts that never became poems published in Plath's lifetime. Three of these drafts are included in *The Collected Poems* (CP) but are identified in misleading ways. In *The Collected Poems* the first and last of these poems are separated by twenty-five pages. "Waking in Winter" appears as the final poem listed under the heading "1960," while "New Year on Dartmoor" appears as the first poem of 1962. "Fever" is not included in *The Collected Poems,* except as a footnote for the 20 October poem "Fever 103°," as if it is an early attempt at that poem.

The first hint that all may not be as it should be is in the notes provided by Hughes. For "Waking in Winter" he explains: "This poem has been extracted from a tangle of heavily corrected manuscript lines, and must be regarded as unfinished" (CP: 290) while about "New Year on Dartmoor" he says, "A fragment extracted from a tangle of corrected manuscipt, this poem must be regarded as unfinished" (CP: 292).

If the manuscript evidence argues for a 1962 date for both poems, one must then ask how close are they, and which one came first. I think it can be shown that there is no doubt that "Waking in Winter" was written first, and that it is an earlier version of "Fever." Not only that, but taken as a sequence these drafts represent writing that is intended to—and does indeed—document the last month of pregnancy, the birth of the child, and its first outing. They also chart a process by which the earlier nightmares of the speaker, expressed in images drawn from the violence of international politics retreat and dissolve in the miraculous freshness of new life.

THE LONG ROOTS OF "ELM,": "WAKING IN WINTER"/"FEVER," AND "NEW YEAR ON DARTMOOR"

The evolving titles of these midwinter drafts are themselves instructive. The sequence begins with the title "Woman as Landscape"[3] and then becomes "The Ninth Month".[4] Copies three and four of the catalogued series carry the title "Waking in Winter." The next draft of this poem is called "Fever in Winter".[5] This then becomes "Fever 103°",[6] a title to be used in a quite different poem (but, one written in a similarly stressful situation) from the *Ariel* period. Finally there are further drafts[7] all with the title "Fever."

The evidence that "Waking in Winter"/"Fever" should be regarded as one poem and not two, and the justification for suggesting the above sequence, is as follows. First, there is at least one image that runs consistently from Copy 2 of "Waking in Winter" to Copy 6 of "Fever." The speaker's sleep has been haunted by dreams of atrocities, an "assembly line of cut throats" and dreams of "destruction and annihilation." Hughes's poem "Dream Life"[8] describes the source of these dreams as historical images of death camps rather than present horrors. Yet, the slight variations in the drafts are instructive, juxtaposing as they do these atrocities with "newsprint," as in the last version of "Fever," for example, where such a scene "broods in the newsprint . . . a refuse of atrocities." This is different from, though given additional significance by, the potential suicide's throat-cutting, made explicit in Anne Sexton's "You Doctor Martin" (which was published in Sexton's *To Bedlam and Part Way Back* in 1960 and which Plath would have read) and the removal of sharp instruments in the hospital in *The Bell Jar.* Plath was responding more immediately, this suggests, to the disturbing news from Algeria and the Congo, news that came throughout December and early January. A photograph of Baluba mothers carrying wounded babies appeared in *The Observer* on 17 December 1961,[9] while in the New Year reports appeared in *The Times* and other newspapers describing the violence and anarchy in Algeria, where "[m]achine gun raids from cars, stealthy throat-cutting, shots fired in broad daylight, lynching and sporadic communal clashes have all become . . . a part of the daily scene."[10]

It was around this time that the article published in the *London Magazine* in February 1962 was written. Invited to comment on the relationship between her poetry and contemporary events, Plath wrote that her poems were "[n]ot about the testaments of tortured Algerians, but about the night thoughts of a tired surgeon."[11]

Even so, Plath certainly voices concern elsewhere about world events. Throughout the autumn of 1961, there was widespread alarm about the possible impact of the Russian nuclear bomb tests on the iodine level in the milk given to children, and this was compounded soon after the birth of Plath's son by the news that the United States was planning "H-tests on British island."[12] Earlier, in an October letter to her mother, Plath had expressed her anxieties about what was being done to the atmosphere[13] and as already indicated, there is reason to believe that this was a a direct response to a newspaper report in *The Observer* on 29 October.[14]

World tension was increased when the Soviet Union exploded a 50-megaton nuclear bomb on 30 October: the equivalent of fifty million tons of TNT, this single explosion exceeded the sum total of all the explosions in the Second World War. It was—and, still is— the largest nuclear bomb ever tested in the atmosphere. By contrast (and, perhaps, too, by way of escape) "The Babysitters," the poem Plath had written on the 29 October was a wistful reminiscence of happy days looking after children in the innocent world of Marblehead, Massachusetts ten years before—appears to be the last until the birth of her son in January 1962, a writing silence of two months.

There is further evidence of Plath's anxieties about the pollution of the atmosphere in her *New Statesman* review "General Jodpur's Conversion." The subject is a children's book in which a general who has wanted to excel as a military leader undergoes a change of heart when he is thrown by his runaway horse and finds himself unseated in a field of beautiful flowers:

> It is also—in these days when more and more poisons are fisting themselves in the upper atmosphere—a uniquely meaningful book for parents—a sort of Age of Anxiety wish fulfilment.[15]

The second attempt at "Fever 103°"[16] contains the line "crying destruction, destruction, annihilation, ash" so that even though in the essay "Context" she could quite rightly claim that her poems "do not turn out to be about Hiroshima, but about a child forming itself finger by finger in the dark."[17] Plath is actually describing the finished piece rather than the complex genesis of the poem. These midwinter abandoned drafts, then provide a glimpse of this genesis, and at the same time anticipate a number of the images which appear in the more well-known autumn 1962 poems. Plath's personal situation was then remarkably different, but the global discourse into which she was tapping (before, during and immediately after the Cuban Missile Crisis) was if anything more nightmarish.

The poem "Elm," started on 12 April, is an interesting bridge between the midwinter poems and the poems of September and October of 1962. Although Anne Stevenson acknowledges this link between the two periods of writing[18] when she says that the voice that the reader hears in "Elm" is the voice of the *Ariel* poems, she unhelpfully asserts that this is a new voice (the unique *Ariel* voice) and that it reflects a move away from the outward world to the world of the interior self:

> Ted Hughes's work turned outward to the natural world beyond the self as Sylvia Plath's never could. Her entire development as a writer had consisted of steps, in a halting progress, that often made it difficult for her to live, toward the revelation at the core of her being.[19]

This reading creates the kind of simplistic binary opposition that is very suspect. For "Elm" emerges not just from the contemplation of her own position in April, but from the situation and drafts that Plath had been exploring in midwinter. In draft 4C Plath has included the lines:

> I too have suffered the atrocity of sunsets
> Scorched to the root
> My red filaments burn and stand, like a hand of wires[20]

And, this survives in the published version (with the word "too" deleted). One of the midwinter drafts ("Fever in Winter") begins: "The elm is a clot of burnt nerves,"[21] while a later version ("Fever") has, "The nerves sizzle in my hands, little red,burnt trees."[22]

Images common to these midwinter drafts and "Elm" are of atrocity, filaments, snakes, hooks, shrieking, tin, wires, wind and bad dreams. At each reworking, as if assembling a collage, Plath draws on a bank of startling, striking phrases to construct a poem that may indeed be read against her own immediate autobiographical experiences, but is in fact much richer, much more allusive than such a narrow reading allows. An abandoned pair of lines is suggestive of the world of nuclear weapons: the Creator of this world suffers from amnesia:

> He has forgotten the white men that shine like radium,
> Engineering another vision, engineering themselves back.
> He, like a phoenix, shall subside in fire.[23]

The gradual evolution of the poetry provides evidence of another strand. Contrasting with the images of destruction is the presence of new human life. For the, second, very contrasting theme that runs through the mid-winter drafts is a narrative of childbirth. The early drafts of "Waking in Winter" celebrate the final month of pregnancy, with the woman "as land-scape," a woman who colours all those around her just as the red soil around her colours the cows and sheep. Then, suddenly, the birth itself arrives in the text. In Copy 2 of "Fever" the speaker had described the boiled medical instruments, the mask of the nurse and purple afterbirth that will be buried "on the back hill." In Copy 4, Plath interrupts the poem she is writing to compose a separate poem on the actual moment of birth. The baby appears like a "rocket" after the the two have battled over his arrival, their first "fight." It is a remarkable, direct description of childbirth:

> You stuck & would not come.
> The pain grew back & contained me like the mouth of a flower,
> Black, blood-sweet.
> So we fought our first fight.
>
> It was so quiet
>
> You came in spite of it, a rocket
> Sailing, in a wall of water, on to the sheet.
> Head, shoulders, feet, dragging three shrieks
> After you like ripped silk. Blue, irrefutable
> As a totem.[24]

Surrounding this text are accounts of other moments. It is now 4 A.M. and the "baby is sleeping," a phrase which appears in Copy 4 of "Fever" and is retained until the end. The peaceful image of the sleeping baby is the poem's gentle answer to the discord imposed by the outside world, and offers some hope that if the crisis can be withstood, harmony will prevail.

Annihilation and childbirth are the two competing and contrasting dialectical strands that run consistently through all pages, suggesting that these texts should be regarded as a single, evolving piece of writing. It is true that sometimes Plath does cut out a separate, independent poem from the middle of a piece of writing, and that sometimes a fresh title indicates a fresh concept. There are experiments with bee images in these poems, with disturbing thoughts "hiving" through the speaker's mind, and of "Sleepy bees (that) rest in my brain / Stirring their lithe legs and dreaming of flowers," but there is no break in the continuity. For cataloging purposes, the archivists at Smith assumed a break occurred at the end of the final page of writing that has the title "Waking in Winter." This has the opening line: "I can taste the tin of the sky."[25]

The "tin" image reappears in the first line of "Fever" however, providing further evidence of continuity: "The elm is a clot of burnt nerves, the sky is tin."[26]

If this continuity is accepted, then the "elm," the red soil and the birth of a midwinter baby confirm that these are both Devon writings, and that "Waking in Winter" does not date from London, 1960. It is from January 1962 (or possibly December 1961), and is an interesting beginning to a sequence of writings. That sequence may be regarded as continuing into "New Year on Dartmoor," a poem which describes the baby"s first experience of frosty moorland.

The draft title of "New Year on Dartmoor" was "The Bald Truth about: Frost on Dartmoor in the New Year" and the poem describes the white, unreal scene for which the new born baby is totally unprepared. The description "New Year" may seem a little odd for a date of 17 January (at the very earliest), but it is still the first month on the calendar, and the year in that sense is still new. In any case, the emphasis in the poem is on the baby's "new year."

The draft title echoes that of an earlier free exercise in poetry "The Bald Truth about: the Grass at Wuthering Heights" written in September of the previous year, soon after Plath and Hughes had moved to Devon, and one of a series of draft pages that were to lead eventually to the published poem "Wuthering Heights."

There are other questions raised by these drafts such as whether "New Year on Dartmoor" should be regarded as just one further episode in a long narrative sequence that began with the ninth month of pregnancy. Although all of these writings were abandoned, and never intended for publication, the next piece of writing that Plath produced was "Three Women," a long exploration of gender and maternity, so perhaps Plath entertained the thought of some kind of linked episodes here.

Another question raised by the lines which juxtapose her present winter nightmares with memories of an American summer is whether the present anxiety infected even the past, or whether it liberated an expression of contempt for that past.

> All night I have dreamed of destruction, annihilations—
> An assembly line of cut-throats, and you and I
> Inching off in the gray Chevrolet, drinking the green
> Poison of stilled lawns, the little clapboard gravestones,
> Noiseless, on rubber wheels, on the way to the sea resort.[27]

The grey Chevrolet recalls the car driven by Esther's mother in *The Bell Jar*, and the summer holiday taken by Plath and Hughes when Aurelia Plath let them use her car. More interesting is the reappearance of the "cut throats" image in a draft of "Little Fugue" written on 2 April:

And you, during the Great War
In the California delicattesen

Lopping the sausages!
They color my nightmares sleep
Red, mottled, like cut throats
The quiet throats of Jews[28]

Tim Kendall [29]discusses this draft to illustrate Plath's complex attitude to Jewishness, a concept which she sometimes embraces and with which she sometimes identifies, but which she just as frequently objectifies and "others." Here the Jewish allusion was eventually removed by Plath, but it encourages Kendall to trace a link between these lines about the father to nightmare images of scenes from the Jewish holocaust. This may be their function here, but the image of cut throats can be linked to another, more contemporary Algerian source, as shown earlier. Under pressure of extreme stress Plath was able to expel the concentrated language that was to become the poem in ways that parallel the "freedom" achieved by the abject, whereby expulsion can paradoxically confer power. Contemporary and past sources were frequently juxtaposed, with the contemporary becoming increasingly disguised and buried as the draft was revised and reworked.

POETRY AND *THE BELL JAR:*
Re-visiting the *Ariel* Relationship

Given the precedent of the *Ariel* poems, it seems logical that a lower number on a recycled typescript of *The Bell Jar* would suggest a later date. But, this assumes that the paper supply was still in the order in which it had been used to type the novel, and we cannot be certain about that. In fact, a closer examination of the sequence of pages that form the first two chapters of Draft B of *The Bell Jar* suggest otherwise. Two parts of the poem "Cut" for example, obviously written one after the other (they are a continuation of the same poem) appear on chapter 1 page 2 and chapter 2 page 1 (a circled number 10 appears at the head of this page but this seems to refer to the number of typed pages in this chapter) of Draft B. Over fifteen sequential pages separate them.

Even more challenging to the belief that the pages were consistently used in the original sequence in reverse is the case of "The Tour." Draft 5 of "The Tour" has page 1 on the reverse of chapter 1 page 8 of *The Bell Jar*, and page 2 on chapter 1, page 1. Even if Plath were in the habit of sifting through the pages to find a particularly relevant backing sheet to start a poem, there is no reason why the second, continuation page of a poem should be on another unconnected *Bell Jar* page—unless this page followed the other in the reshuffled pile. It seems quite lucky that paper in a "scrap" pile is likely to be mixed up, particularly if there are young children in the house.

Finally, "The Tour" draft 5, page 1 is dated 25 October, and as already mentioned it is on the reverse of chapter 1, page 8 of *The Bell Jar*. Draft 1 of the long poem "Nick and the Candlestick" is on pages 7, 6, 5, and 4 of Draft B of *The Bell Jar*—but, is dated 24 October. That is, it was written before "The Tour" and therefore page 8 must have been underneath page 7—only possible if these two pages were face up, or if they had switched position. In either case it seems to prove that the pile of paper was not an undisturbed one before Plath drew on it.

I have emphasized these points only to qualify the picture of Plath writing her way back through this novel, so that the peeling off of sheets becomes like the systematic countdown of a rocket. It was not like that. If occasionally there was deliberate selection, there was also much randomness.

Perhaps more important is the evidence of a direct interface between the discourses of the newspaper reporting of global events and the discourse of poetry. It also confirms the significance of Ted Hughes's observation that "(her) attitude to her verse was artisan-like: if she couldn't get a table out of the material, she was quite happy to get a chair, or even a toy. The end product for her was not so much a successful poem, as something that had temporarily exhausted her ingenuity."[30] That does not seem to fully take account of Plath's zealous pursuit of publication, but it does provide an accurate insight into the processes of composition evident in these drafts. The continuity of the themes is easily overlooked. Even in this chapter, I have skated over the March poem for three voices "Three Women," which actually continues to experiment with many of the images that run through the drafts and poems from January to April and beyond. Some of these points are taken up in the discussion of "Three Women" in the final section of chapter 8.

In the early critical responses to Plath's poetry much was made of the suicide, which this was read back into the writing, with the poetry and prose being duly interpreted as unhealthy celebrations of death. The writing that I have been discussing documents the period immediately before, during and after the month of childbirth—remarkable in itself. Furthermore, the evidence of even the small fragments of writing represented by these manuscripts, which variously illustrate the scrupulous control of the irony in *The Bell Jar*, the concentration of anger sparked by newspaper reports of atrocities, and the celebration of the wonder of birth and new life, indicates how much there is in the texts which bespeaks Plath's humor, her celebatory spirit and her responsiveness to international politics and events. Attention to the detail of Plath's writing shows that the art she produced looks well beyond her own life.

5

Women and Politics on the Wireless:
Sylvia Plath, Laura Riding, and the BBC

Poets will not only hide influences. They will bury them!
  —Anne Sexton, "The Bar Fly Ought to Sing" (1966)

I think I would like to call myself "The girl who wanted to be God."
Yet if I were not in this body, where *would* I be?

LH: 40

LAURA RIDING, POETRY, AND POLITICS

SYLVIA PLATH HAD HIGH REGARD FOR BBC RADIO, NOT LEAST BE-cause it supported poets by broadcasting readings, interviews and discussions on the Third Programme and the Home Service wavelengths. Both were "serious" radio services which contrasted with the revealingly labelled "Light Programme," also run by the BBC. Just before she died, Plath had agreed to appear in three discussion programs to be recorded in May 1963. Each program would have earned her 30 guineas, at a time when the average weekly wage for women was seven guineas. It was an important source of income.

The BBC had a monopoly of sound broadcasting in England and provided programmes and a service of a kind that was then quite unfamiliar in the United States. Its style and content was very specific to a pre-commercial era, coming as it did from an institution that had its own coat of arms and Royal Charter. The summary of the news that appeared at the beginning and end of each evening was delivered in a ringing Home Counties, Received Pronunciation accent and would include reports of world events consistent with an institution that had "And Nation shall speak Peace unto Nation" as its motto. The news broadcasts reflected the world perspective of a country that still remembered its former role as an imperial power. The BBC had always sought to stand slightly detached from the culture of which it was (and is) itself an important expression. Between 1960 and 1963, BBC radio still bore the marks of the mission

133

of its first Director General, John (later Lord) Reith, to maintain high standards, to provide high culture and to consolidate the reputation for trustworthy news reporting that it had earned during the World War II.

In two short stories, "Superman and Paula Brown's New Snowsuit" and "The Shadow," Plath had described the formative influence of radio drama on the imagination of the child. As an adult woman with two young children of her own she continued to find stimulus in the imaginative work read on the radio: the demands of young children often make listening easier than reading. Moreover, the Home Service broadcasts provided important moments of release from the insularity and isolation of the Devon village in which Plath found herself. In July 1962, George MacBeth, then a producer at the BBC radio Talks Department, responded to her request by sending Plath four scripts of short stories by Reginald Ottley, an English born Australian known best for his children's stories.[1] The stories read on the radio (Plath had most likely heard the story broadcast on the Home Service on the 20 June "Death Rides to the Edge") provide further evidence of the wide range of narratives and language that Plath found interesting. Ottley drew on his experience as a cattlehand in Australia, though some of his stories of outdoor life and animals are set on the Pacific islands. "Death Rides to the Edge" is a Lawrentian tale of an incident involved in rounding up cattle, during which a young rider fights to control a frightened horse on the edge of a ridge in a violent rainstorm.

In the specific arts field of poetry broadcasts, there was another important aspect to the readings that Plath heard. It is extremely likely that in England the opportunity to hear *women* reading poetry on the radio was instrumental in shaping her own decision to write "Three Women" as a poem for three voices and in her increasing preference for a poetry that should be read aloud and heard. During 1962, Plath would have had the opportunity to hear Elizabeth Jennings, Stevie Smith and her own work, usually read by herself, on the wireless (as the radio was still known), a medium in which broadcast politics, news and the arts were constantly juxtaposed. When George MacBeth, whose own work increasingly focused on poetry in performance, required a voice to read a poem by an American woman poet, he turned to Plath, as he did when she recorded a Carolyn Kizer poem in July for Donald Hall's round-up of American poetry[2] Carolyn Kizer was a little older than Plath and had studied under Roethke, a poet also admired by Plath. Since 1959 Kizer had edited *Poetry Northwest*, the magazine she founded in Washington State. In 1961, her collection, *The Ungrateful Garden*, had been published and this included poems about motherhood ("A Widow in Wintertime"), poems addressed to her lover ("Addressing the Cover") and separate sections dedicated to her mother, and to her father. In one of the later poems, a woman who is in some kind of institution cries out to her mother "Mother! My madness hates you!" There are witty poems, and serious political ones: "The Death of a Public Servant" observes the death of a Canadian Civil Servant driven to suicide by the allegation that he was a communist. Kizer's feminism provides a model which explores politics, motherhood, and marriage.

Readings such as this, and readings of her own poetry not only earned Plath money, they elicited correspondence that was forwarded to her. There is evidence in the BBC Written Archive that following the broadcast of "Three Women," first transmitted on the Third Programme on 19 August 1962 and repeated on 13 September of that year, Plath received letters from listeners as far away as Australia, suggesting that the programme might also have been broadcast on the World Service of the BBC. But, as well as writing and performing poetry for radio, Plath listened to it.

On 2 April 1962, ten days before she started "Elm," Sylvia Plath began writing the poem that was to become "Little Fugue." The first, handwritten draft is headed "On listening to Laura Riding," and underneath the heading Plath has written "The lights are humming—How my small room rides" ('Little Fugue'—Draft, p. 1 MRBR). It is one among many examples of the direct interaction between Plath's immediate reading (or listening) and her writing. On 1 April (which also happened to be her daughter Frieda's second birthday) the BBC Third Programme had broadcast a selection of Riding's poems at nine o'clock in the evening. These poems were read by Olive Gregg, but introduced by the author herself. An examination of the relationship between the words spoken by Riding and the words written by Plath will serve to illustrate the dialogue between Plath's writing and the intellectual and ideological environment which mass communications provided. More specifically it will show not only Plath's interaction with BBC radio, but her response to the ideas of a powerful woman who had renounced poetry.

Laura Riding was a writer whose life and poetry paralleled Plath's in many important ways, but differed significantly in others. A New England American who was wedded to the idea that poetry is a supreme art, she had been the one influential woman among the group of Nashville poets known as the Southern Fugitives, and had rebutted the charge of poetic obscurity with a degree of self-belief and conviction that Plath often lacked. Laura Riding had lived in Europe with the poet Robert Graves, whose subsequent theory of the Triple Muses and the White Goddess came to be much admired by Ted Hughes. *The White Goddess* was an account of myth and writing that Graves completed after his affair with Riding was over, and during the interval Graves had moved to Devon, the same county in which Plath was now living (he had been in the audience when Plath read "Insomniac" at an award ceremony the previous October).[3] When he came to work on *The White Goddess*, however, Graves still viewed Laura Riding with considerable respect and affection, regarding her as the first of his Muses. Riding had not been embarrassed to present herself to the world as a god, and Graves had gone along with this, accepting that she was an incarnation of Isis, who herself represented the matriarchal rule of the White Goddess. When Plath moved home in England, she took her large Isis print with her, and it appears behind her in one of the photographs of the period.

It is clear why the mythic references in Plath's poetry have provided such rich material for critics. Isis's attributes of magic, fertility and motherhood, her status as object of a mystery cult, her subsequent reputation as the inventor of writing and language, her ultimate status as universal goddess, the bringer of civilization and the universal mother, and her origins as daughter of Earth and Sky seems to correspond very closely to the imagery and rhetoric of many of Plath's 1960–63 poems. For example, according to separate versions of the legend, Isis is either a Muse whose head-dress or horns enclose the disc of the sun, or in the myth of The Golden Ass of Apuleius the goddess appears to the hero Lucius with "snakes coiled round her head encircling the disk of the moon." Read "Ariel," "The Moon and the Yew Tree," "Elm," or even "Edge" alongside this information and these poems seem to be offering some kind of commentary on or argument with the Isis myth. This is part of the challenge of Plath's work: several aspects of Plath's reading can be convincingly represented as central to her writing.

Thus, for example, Laura Riding's poetry, prose and experience seems to find echoes in Plath's own output. Riding had written poems about the female child falling in love with her father ("Postponement of Self"), the psychological walls between former lovers ("To a Loveless Lover"), the questionable categories of gender ("Care in Calling") and of tigers, moons, mirrors, mouths and spiders. Riding was Jewish; she had attempted suicide by jumping out of a window. She survived this attempt, as did her self-belief. In her post-suicide attempt period she came to believe that bodies had had their day, and that the corporeal was something from which human beings should strive to escape. Her own body had been badly injured in the fall.

The varied male literary influences on Plath—Lawrence, Auden, Yeats, De Quincey are just a few of the many that critics and biographers have regarded as important—are unsurprising in a writer who had spent six years majoring in English. The influence of powerful women writers—Emily Brontë, Emily Dickinson, Virginia Woolf, Marianne Moore, Anne Sexton, and Stevie Smith—has also been recognized, as has Plath's admiration for strong, independent women such as Dorothea Krook, her tutor at Cambridge. Laura Riding certainly fitted into the category of powerful, independent women but her known identification with Isis and Lillith, figures from mythology, can be misleading, for that is not the Laura Riding that Plath heard in the radio broadcast.

Many of Riding's images and themes have parallels in the later Plath poems. Two of these images, however—the transcendent white Goddess that rides "Ariel," and the perfection of the dead woman in "Edge"— initially attracted comment and speculation in those early readings of the poems which emphasised the influence of Hughes and Graves (rather than Riding), or else in later readings which see the moon/goddess discussion as an explicit exploration of gender and the experience of writing as a woman.

There was another important side to Laura Riding, however, brought out in the radio interview, and this was a reminder of the marked difference between the way in which she and Graves responded to world events. Both believed that the consequence of the historical shift from the worship of female deities to male gods was disastrous. For Graves this regrettable development had to be challenged through art, not politics. Graves's biographer (and nephew) describes Graves's reading of this theological shift, thus:

> While working on *The White Goddess* he had become increasingly convinced that in turning, as it were, from the worship of the Triple Goddess to that of Zeus, in replacing feminine with masculine control, society had made a disastrous mistake. To worship the Goddess was to keep in natural balance with one's surroundings. To worship a male God, on the other hand, was to unleash a terrible destructive power upon the world in the form of the "restless and arbitrary male will." Before publication of *The White Goddess,* Graves would add several paragraphs in which he described how the western world had "come to be governed by the unholy triumvirate of Pluto god of wealth, Apollo god of Science and Mercury god of thieves."[4]

The *White Goddess* [5] was written against the background of the close of the Second World War, from June 1945 to January 1946, a period which included the dropping of the atomic bomb on Hiroshima on 6 August 1945. But, Graves's feeling of despair about the human race did not translate into political action: instead it is buried or displaced in this analysis of myth and religion.[6]

Laura Riding, on the other hand, had responded to the international conflicts of the 1930s in a quite different way. In 1936 and early 1937 she drew up a "Letter on International Affairs," which was sent to four hundred people. Written against the background of the Spanish Civil War, the letter asks the carefully selected men and women to whom it was sent to work towards the salvation of the world from the current peril and muddle. Its argument that that the voice of women—the specifically female voice—has been drowned but should be heard, matches the argument that Plath was to make implicit in the *The Bell Jar*, a novel which at first sight seems largely divorced from politics and international affairs, and also in many of the poems written by Plath in England between 1960 and 1963.

Having asked her readers "What shall we do?" (about the world situation) Laura Riding writes:

> Let us first consider who "we" are—we the "inside" people. First of all we are the women. Women are those of us who are most characteristically, most natively, "inside" people . . . with us, on the inside of things, we have had the poets and the painters and all those men who have been able to treat the outer mechanism of life as subsidiary to its inner realities—who have discovered the inside importances.[7]

Riding's "Letter" argues that there has been a fracture between the affairs of the "outer" world—the world of international politics—and the world of the personal, the "inner" world. This reading of events corresponds in several ways to the one Plath acquired during her time in England, and in some ways the circumstances of the two poets *were* similar. Like Riding, Plath wrote her poetry against a background of world tension. Like Riding, she did not feel that she personally should—or, could—enter the world of international politics as an active player, but she wished to influence those who could. Like Riding, she was living with a poet who distanced himself from even this modest level of political engagement. Richard Percival Graves's account of Robert Graves's response to Riding's open "Letter" suggests that in this respect Graves and Hughes shared a similar reaction to their partners' concerns about world events. In its emphasis on the destructive power of the masculine principle, Graves initially agreed with Riding's analysis.

> However, it was one of Graves's most fundamental beliefs that it was not a poet's job to become involved in politics; and in one of his most interesting poems at this time, "The Fallen Town of Siloam," there is an implied, though perhaps subconscious, criticism of Riding's determined efforts to bring about social and political change: "It behoved us indeed, as poets," Graves wrote,
>
> > To be silent in Siloam, to foretell
> > No visible calamity.
>
> He felt happier when Riding concentrated on her literary work: they were both looking over their poems for possible collected editions; and on 13 March Graves noted in his diary with a mixture of relief and sorrow that Laura had written 'her first poem in months': "To Juan Marroig in Prison".[8]

If Graves and Riding differed on this matter, however, in a way that parallels differences between Hughes and Plath, there are also significant differences between the two women poets. Unlike Riding, Plath did not have the confidence that she could exert that much influence on the world through direct action, and ostensibly her political concern never allowed her to be more than a political spectator. For, unlike Riding (who was childless, and at that time was living with an adoring Graves in London), Plath had two very young children, and in 1962, at the time of writing "Little Fugue," was experiencing an increasingly isolated and lonely life in a small town in Devon. It is in that small rural community that on 1 April in her room at Court Green she listened on the BBC Third Programme to Riding introducing a reading of her poems with some remarks about the nature of poetry.

Plath's poem, "Little Fugue," dated the next day, begins with some meditations on the yew tree that grows in the nearby churchyard—the same yew that she had written about in "The Moon and the Yew Tree" the previous October, and which she could see from her Devon house. After completing seven lines, the last of which is "O I am of a graveyard mind" Plath writes a new heading "Yew Tree in March," suggesting that she is drawing on earlier notes or memories. The fugue is beginning, and the draft title suggests that the dominant theme will be Gravesian.

As the musings unwind the meditation on the yew tree and the clouds gives way to to a very specific memory of a blind pianist at her table on a ship, feeling for his food. This man could hear the tumult of the deaf Beethoven. Suddenly this little thought causes the poem to leap from this remembered detail to the Gross Fugue of the noisy yew hedge, and the image of mouths stopped by the many feet of the yew, like organ pipes. The noises of the dark yew transmute into the voice of her father, and she imagines him lopping sausages in the California delicatessen during the Great War. Then the poem presents images of a world like a flickering movie screen, with flickering shapes of villain and lover, the bad man and the good man.

The poem then jumps to the present and two lines are written and then rejected:

> Today it is poison in the rain,
> The grained faces of [word crossed out] Orientals.
> ("Little Fugue" Draft 1: MRBR)

The crossed out word is important, as it indicates that act of concealment to which Anne Sexton referred in the epigraph to this section. It also suggests that themes that were exercised in her writing during 1960 and 1961 had not gone away. As Plath's pregnancy advanced and as her second child was born, Plath had appeared to be silent between "The Babysitters" in October 1961 and the long verse poem for voices "Three Women" of March 1962, As we saw earlier, Plath had been far from silent, however, and her anxieties about the effects atmospheric nuclear bomb tests were having on milk and babies fed into her writing. As we have seen, they fed especially into a series of abandoned drafts written during January 1962, the month in which her son Nicholas was born, and they feed into the poem here.

The "poison in the rain" sounds like radioactivity. And, the word crossed out and replaced by "Orientals" looks as if it could be "Hiroshima." It has been crossed out so energetically that it is impossible to say with absolute certainty what the original word was. But, the shape of the first six letters certainly suggests "Hirosh-," and this would be supported by the replacement word "Orientals," and the reference to the poison in the rain. The archivist who cataloged all the Plath papers at Smith thinks the word is "Hiroshima."

If this is the case, then it reveals much about Plath's writing in 1962, her response to contemporary events (radioactivity in the atmosphere), and the process by which contemporaneity is first distanced historically (1961/62 nuclear tests represented by the 1945 Hiroshima atom bomb) and then concealed altogether as these lines are omitted from the typed version of the final text. It is fair to conclude, therefore, that in England from 1960 onwards Plath came to regard Graves's grammar of mythology with gradually increasing detachment and irony, and that serious contemporary political issues, world events that parallel those that engaged Laura Riding, come to occupy some of the vacated poetic and intellectual hinterland. Such a specifically historicist reading of Plath's writing contrasts with the vast majority of the Plath criticism that has greeted her work, from the publication of *Colossus* to the present day.

Laura Riding, High Art, and the Abandonment of Poetry

There is a long tradition in Plath criticism of trying to establish a defining moment or experience which caused her to discover her "true voice." Longer poems such as "Poem for a Birthday" (1959) or "Three Women" (1962) have separately been considered as watersheds, whilst the same claim has been made for "The Moon and the Yew Tree" (1961) or "Elm" or "The Rabbit Catcher" (both 1962). When discussions of the changes in direction taken by Plath's writing considers writers other than Ted Hughes and those mentioned earlier, Robert Lowell usually features as an important influence. It is Lowell who is credited (by Robyn Marsack,[9] for example) with showing Plath an example of how poetry *could* be, if it were less concerned with the formalism of "high art" and more concerned with a direct exploration of a specifically post-1945 experience of pain, anxiety and breakdown. Plath acknowledged this influence in a later radio broadcast: Lowell's work is cited as an example of a vibrant kind of American poetry that takes more risks than the poetry then being written in England.

But, Riding, in the introduction to the program that was broadcast on 1 April 1962, also had some challenging things to say about poetry, things which were more radical than anything that Lowell had said. In her opening statement she says that in writing the poems published in 1938 she had explored "the possibility of using words in poetry with the true voice and the true mind of oneself." That quest had ended in her decision to renounce poetry altogether: .

> I had fervently believed that in poetry the way so to use words might be found—which had nowhere, yet, been found, completely. But after 1938 I began to see poetry differently, even to see it as a harmful ingredient of our linguistic life. My view of poetry, which led me to suppress my poems, has not changed.[10]

It is no wonder that Plath has written "How my small room rides" as the lights hum, and she reflects on these provocative remarks. In her comments, Laura Riding was challenging a view of writing that Plath had developed during and after her Smith College years, a view shared and reinforced by Hughes. Implicit in this view is the Romantic belief that through poetry writing gains access to a higher truth. Riding had come to reject that view, on the grounds, she argued, that art is always artifice, and leads to a separation from what she regarded as truth and reality:

> The equivalence between poetry and truth that I had tried to establish was inconsistent with the relation they have to each other as—the one—*art* and—the other—*the reality*. I came close to achieving, in my poems, trueness of intonation and direct presence of mind in word. But, what I achieved in this direction was ever sucked into the whorl of poetic artifice, with its overpowering necessities of patterned rhythm and harmonic sound-play, which work distortions upon the natural proprieties of tone and word.[11]

Riding knew that her remarks would cause offence, especially where there is "esteem of poetry," and in a comment that must have sounded as if it was being addressed directly to Plath, she acknowledges that "esteem of poetry and self-esteem tend to become intertwined—as I have reason to know."[12] But, the shortcomings of poetry are in its divisiveness. Practitioners must believe in the superiority of poetic language, and this leads to a separation in culture and people:

> I have learned, for instance, that poets, to be poets, must function as if they were people who were on the inside track of linguistic expression, people endowed with the highest language-powers; that, in functioning so, they not only block the discovery that everyone is on this inside track, but confuse themselves and others as to the value of their linguistic performances; that the novelties of expression achieved in poetry leave ordinary speech, and its literary counterpart, prose, sunk in their essential monotony and unaspiringness; that there is no vital connection between the verbal successes of poetry and our actual speaking needs—they are no more than dramatic effects produced with words.[13]

This challenge to the profession of poetry, to the serious practice of an art that had acquired a highly privileged status was not new, but it was unusual in coming from such a serious practitioner as Riding. In the Preface to her *Collected Poems* of 1938, she had delivered a powerful and passionate defence of poetry and now, in this broadcast, Third Programme listeners were treated to a startling reassessment of the role of the poet in society.

Laura Riding is one of a triangle of woman poets—and this category had been important for Plath, ever since her mother had introduced her to the work of Emily Dickinson (to whose white dress there is perhaps an allusion at the end of "Little Fugue")—that offered Plath alternative writing models and strategies. Together with Anne Sexton and Stevie Smith, Riding offered a series of challenges to the model of poetry to which Hughes subscribed. Sexton, who sent Plath a copy of *"All My Pretty Ones"* later that summer, took Lowell's "confessional" style in a consciously gendered direction. Sexton's poetry moves further inwards, and explores the most intimate and specific of female experiences, such as menstruation and the ownership of breasts. Smith's writing—poetry and prose—led to an exchange of letters between the two writers—and, offered a move towards the eccentric, the humorous and the absurd which Plath had experimented with in "The Tour." Riding's comments offered another model, one which made the radical and drastic suggestion that poetry needed to be given up altogether ("[F]or the practice of the style of truth to become a thing of the present, poetry must become a thing of the past"). Clearly, Riding's comments did not lead to an abrupt change in Plath's practice—she continued to write both poetry and prose—but, Riding's evocation of *the reality* as an absolute totality that stands in opposition to the values of art did indeed stimulate Plath into a response in her immediate, subsequent writing.

For example, on the first page of the first draft of "Little Fugue," Plath speculates on the relationship between poetry and "truth," and the yew tree which Hughes had set as a subject for poetry becomes the vehicle for that speculation:

> The yew's black fingers agitate
> It is a tree of poems, of dead men;
> A churchyard person, always sorry.
> There is no truth in this.
> How it flings up, like black blood.
> This I consider. There is no truth,
> Only the
>
> (Little Fugue, Draft 1 p. 1, MRBR)

The draft is abandoned there, but there are sufficient images (poems "of dead men," "There is no truth in this," "This I considered. There is no truth.") to suggest a meditation on the argument contained in the program she had heard. The broadcast was a starting point, a point of departure. I actually think it is more, as the challenge is taken up, and the argument *with* Riding is explored (ironically in verse) throughout the poem, though the title "Little Fugue" suggests a meshing of several themes, rather than a preoccupation with just one. The process of change is cumulative.

An ink line is drawn under the first attempted draft, and the next version begins with the punning title "Yew Alone" (As Rose[14] points out, this is just one of the many linguistic tricks with which the poem plays: you/yew, eye/I, morning/mourning in the poem's exploration of language, memory and amnesia). The image of the tree may have been suggested by the sixth poem that was read in the broadcast, Riding's "Intelligent Prayer," which begins with the lines:

> A star by world-connivance seems part of the hill.
> A tree not by mere folly stands up creature-like.
> Such painstaking acts of intelligence widely accost.
> It is a compliment to nature to perceive them.[15]

The "creature-like" tree is there to be perceived: nature invites such observations. But, orders are something else. To be "assigned" the tree as an exercise (as Hughes says she was when she wrote "The Moon and the Yew Tree" [CP: 291]) involves a different context for communication, and a resistance.

As Jacqueline Rose has pointed out,[16] "Little Fugue," among other things, is a discussion of the failure to communicate, and she reads it as a forerunner of "Daddy," where the speaker says "I never could talk to you." In both poems the father appears in concrete, specific detail and this has no precedent in the selection of Riding poems read on the radio. It is possible, however, that the fifth Riding poem read, "Autobiography of the Present," with its images of bees, would have brought the memory of the father back into Plath's mind.

The failure to communicate with the father ("There was a silence! / Great silence of another order / . . . . Do you say nothing?" CP: 188), or the ability to communicate in different ways that are brought about by obstacles to communication, was suggested during the broadcast programme. The second Riding poem read was "The Map of Places," and seventh "The Wind, the Clock, the We," Their sea and ship images may have reminded Plath of the blind pianist on the ship on the Atlantic crossing, a man who could hear Beethoven, the deaf composer of the *Grosse Fuge*. Images of both deafness and blindness were presented during the reading. The first poem read in the programme was "Lucrece and Nara," and this contains the lines:

> Unnoticed as a single raindrop
> Broke each dawn until
> Blindness as the same day fell.
> 'How is the opalescence of my white hand, Nara?
> Is it still pearly-cool?'[17]

The tentative questioning of uncertain people—in this case, lovers—conveys a feeling of sensual disorientation.

"World's End," the fourth poem read, begins with an image of the changed senses, as the ear and eye decline, but also become more pure:

> The tympanum is worn thin.
> The iris is become transparent.
> The sense has overlasted.
> Sense itself is transparent.[18]

Yet, if that last line suggests progress, the title of the poem and the later references to loss suggest Plath's sense of being of a "graveyard mind," a phrase which appears on the first page of the drafts of "Little Fugue" (MRBR: Draft 1, p. 1). On the other hand, the transformation of senses suggested in Riding's poem would help explain the "I see your voice" which puzzles Rose: Riding's "The Wind, the Clock, the We" speaks of the "voiceless language" of wind and clock. The wind itself, which appears as the subject of another Riding poem read during the broadcast ("The Why of the Wind") and which is linked to cold, winter and fever, survives as a presence in the opening lines of the published version of "Little Fugue," where it shakes the tree and drives the clouds across the sky.

The Riding program serves to demonstrate the process by which Plath's writing was influenced by the discourses she heard through the mass media in England in the early 1960s. It is a subtle, complex process. Whether the print or radio reporting concerned arts or politics, in those circumstances where the ideas and images had a particular resonance or challenged the certainties of the present, they took root in Plath's mind. Some of these images were then nursed, and fostered by Plath's imagination produced radical shoots in bizarre and wonderfully inventive ways, as other memories, associations and ideas were grafted onto the idea. The poem gradually took shape, like the child in Plath's comment, growing finger by finger. There was no single origin. Even in the case of "Little Fugue" it is possible that the ink line drawn under the comment "On Listening to Laura Riding" is there to suggest separation from the writing that follows. But, I do not believe that the links I have proposed in this particular instance can all be coincidences, and the fact that the epigraph "On Listening to Laura Riding" was not crossed out or destroyed by Plath has the effect of suggesting deliberate connection. Louis Simpson went so far as to suggest that this broadcast was instrumental in producing the burst of creative energy that followed.[19]

"Little Fugue" is not a political poem in the sense that it seeks to address the wider global politics in the manner of Laura Riding during her letter writing campaign of 1937. Yet, in fusing references to history (the Great War, German orders, the history of her father), to impediments to communication (silence, blindness, deafness) and to the immediate presence of "reality," to use Riding's term (the nearby yew tree, the morning arrangements, the writer's fingers and baby) the poem does address this outer world in a manner and voice that is very different from the voice of the student Plath of the early 1950s. And, this is only partly explained by the obvious fact that time has passed, that the 1960s are a different decade, and that Plath is older and more mature. All of these are relevant, but it is the change of place, the relocation from Massachusetts to England, and the view of America from the outside, as a more politicised writer and mother, that contributes significantly to this alteration.

"What made you stay?": Sylvia Plath, a Wireless Performance, and Virginia Woolf

Later in that same month of April 1962, Plath was interviewed at Court Green, for a BBC radio series featuring four Americans who had decided to settle in England. The program, called "What made you stay?" has been mentioned in passing several times already. It was broadcast in September of that year, and revealed a voice quite unlike that to be heard in

"Elm" or the major poems in the *Ariel* sequence, which Plath was soon to unleash. The recorded voice that we hear, of the contented wife and mother who happens also to be a published poet, is as carefully constructed as any of Plath's other voices of maturity. The tone of modulated assurance, conveying the familiarity of residence, ownership and social position, has the hauteur of a Virginia Woolf character.[20] Plath plays the part to the hilt. It is a striking performance. She is the "lady of the manor" in her country house, assured and almost regal. A number of listeners wrote in to the BBC and their letters were forwarded to Plath at her Devon address.[21]

Several years earlier, on her first stay in England, Sylvia Plath had taken up a Fulbright Scholarship at Newnham College, the women's college at Cambridge where Virginia Woolf had delivered as a visiting speaker one of the two addresses that were to be later published as "A Room of One's Own." At Newnham, Plath bought and read a number of Woolf novels including *The Voyage Out,* and in the corner of the notes outlining the sequence of events in *The Bell Jar* there is a coda suggesting that Plath's novel was going to be rounded off with some scenes taken from the Harvard Summer School period of 1959: it was going to conclude with a section described as "Going to Europe: Voyage Out."[22] This sequence, if it was ever written, was omitted from the novel Plath eventually submitted to her English publisher, but it may have provided the opening for the unfinished novel that we know only from the title of one of the episodes "Falcon Yard."

The point of "The Voyage Out" reference is that it alludes to a novel in which a young woman travels with great hope to a small distant island, but during the voyage experiences a nightmarish vision of goblin and tunnel, partly induced by an unexpected sexual advance. Virginia Woolf's early novel is an exploration of many things, including exile and defamiliarization, consciousness, and politics (Mr. Dalloway, who is also on the voyage, is a politician). The original draft of the novel incorporated several kinds of writing, including early experiments in the style known as stream of consciousness.

Were it not for the fact that Plath eventually found the English novelist's work wanting, it would be tempting to read Plath as a latter day American Virginia Woolf, interested in technique and the significance of the female voice whilst possessing a sense of her own ability and superior consciousness that intermittently gives way to depression (and finally to suicide). This is ground explored by several critics and it is not surprising that discussion of the diversity of literary influences on Plath remains one of the continuities of Plath criticism. It is easy to see her as a predominantly literary writer.[23] She read widely and it is all too tempting to glimpse the influence of other writers in her work. One wonders whether it is a coincidence that the "couch/carpet" juxtaposition in Louis Simpson's "Summer Storm" appears in Plath's "Monologue at 3 am," or that the description of the ride on Jamie Lockhart's horse "Orion" in Eudora Welty's *The Robber Bridegroom* includes a striking number of words used by Plath in "Ariel." Does the wit and mordant humour owe more to Dorothy Parker than it does to Salinger? Such speculative possibilities are minor additions to the very substantial weight of detective work done by critics such as Wagner-Martin, Brain, and Strangeways. They lead us into fertile territory, but away from politics.

But, not entirely. For, of considerable relevance to the present study, is Plath's abiding interest in the literary heritage. It is her changing view of that heritage and its institutionalization through criticism that forms part of an interrogation of the forces whose power and institutionalisation she increasingly came to reassess. Plath's questioning of the literary heritage gradually fuses with her interest in international politics: the one allows her to interrogate the role of institutions in the other. Literature may question politics, but politics also questions literature, and in a period of Cold War tension resistance replaces transcendence as the more urgent and necessary strategy for dealing with life. This questioning of institutions was gradual and at first very tentative, and it can be traced back to some formative moments which mark the beginnings of this process of "writing back."

6

Institutions and the Formation of Political Judgment: Arenas, Ruins, Hospitals, and Other Troubling Places

WRITING BACK

THE EXPRESSION "WRITING BACK" INDICATES THAT THERE IS SOMEONE or something to write back to, and usually suggests correspondence. Lovers and relatives write back to one another: so do pen friends. It is not normally an expression applied to the process of producing a poem, a short story or a novel. Yet, it is a phrase applicable to much of Sylvia Plath's writing, because in addition to the literal writing back to her own high school pen friend, her writing back from Smith to boyfriends and to all the friends who sent her letters at Cambridge, and the stream of letters she sent to her mother, Plath's poetry, fiction and journals and short stories also represent a particular species of reply—a response to institutions, structures and individuals who provoked a passionate or coolly ironic reaction. Plath's writing is a dialectic, in which she carries on an often intense argument, sometimes with herself, sometimes with *a* history, sometimes with *her* history and sometimes with individuals and institutions who seek to construct and constrain her. Often, she is writing back to a form of behavior or an expression of an idea which she is eager to capture in some appropriate form, or in response to disturbing political events about which she has read. In all this, there is a powerful sense of replying to the feared or loathed "Other," the part of the world which seeks to threaten or engulf the speaker. The provocation may be unseen, it is often off-stage, and the poetry is in medias res. But, the unheard and the unseen can be traced in the written, and the question can be constructed from the answer.

The passionate replies to individuals—whether father, mother, husband, or child—are well documented. Moreover, it has been long understood that the specific addressee—"Daddy," for example—may stand for a whole range of people, for a principle or pressure that is merely ex-

148

pressed through the individual. Similarly Plath interrogates the forces operating in society through responses to specific places—whether a ruin such as Top Withens, also known as Withins, in Yorkshire, or a churchyard yew tree or surgeon's theater. The institutions such as schools, hospitals, psychiatric wards, and church, with which she had most contact, begin to be viewed as agencies of political control. Part of her response is to escape through romantic actions, so that the horseriding on Dartmoor is the equivalent of the shoreline adventures described in "Ocean 1212W." Both involve contact with nature in territory that seems to exist outside institutional structures. But, Plath does not retreat from the political world in the way that Hughes and Graves can be said to have done: in the last months of her life she returned to London to grapple with the city and all its challenges. At the same time she held on to her country house. She did not want to choose between them.

The issue of choice, the first of three related issues to be explored here, is an expression of Plath's interest in the division of the world into opposing principles which are sometimes complementary and sometimes antagonistic. Plath's exploration of dualism in character and plot has been well documented—it was after all the theme of her Dostoyevski thesis. Both dualism and choice appear as themes in *The Bell Jar,* but a particular kind of choice, between the world of grace and beauty and the world of animality and danger, precedes and postdates the writing of the novel.

The relationship between place and institution is the second issue and it can be shown by examining the evolution of a piece of writing inspired by a visit to Haworth, the home of the Brontës. A different kind of dialectic operates here, as Plath begins a dialogue with the literary past evoked by one particular building. The dialogue is taken up in successive years in several pieces of writing. The pieces, all of which relate to a visit to the ruin at Top Withens, supposedly the "real" Wuthering Heights, provide evidence of Plath's exploration of heritage and literary Romanticism, and the tradition of writing established by nineteenth-century English women novelists. The political ideology of literary Romanticism had been cherished by Plath right up until the questioning of the spiritual that took place following the birth of her children. From 1960 onwards, her art and ideology shifts from an emphasis on the world of spirit to an emphasis on the world of the material, through which the spiritual is mediated. It is not surprising that a Romantic, Transcendental view should have dominated her thinking for so long. With the exception of 1959, when she had worked in a hospital in Boston, Plath had spent the whole of the 1950s as an English Literature specialist, either as a student or as a teacher. Subject English has its own very specific dominant ideology and political assumptions.[1]

As the Top Withens pieces evolve an argument with place, ghosts and materiality develops as the writer reaches for the spirit that she is convinced must be hidden in the tree, building, or place. Hidden behind these particular writing is the Brontë novel, in which ghosts may lurk, violence is meted out on the weak, and the handsome man howls like a wolf. Contemporary events seem absent, yet in engaging with a canonical work of English Literature Plath reveals her resistance to the straitjacket that such literary heritage can impose. Her writings refuse to be primarily about the novel, or about Emily Brontë. Instead, they engage with contemporary problems, even if this engagement still leans on the literary heritage for its support. She visited the Brontë museum as a tourist and climbed to the ruin with other tourists. Literature was already being packaged.

In all of the writing completed in England there is a distinction to be made between the various kinds of "writing back" that Plath was undertaking. When writing about America, as she did in *The Bell Jar,* Plath is writing back into her past in terms of both time and place. In the initial writing in and about England, Plath also delves back into a past, but this time it is the past of literary history, myth and tradition.

Discussion of a third issue provides a means of moving closer to an understanding of Plath's response to her reading of the nuclear war threat and the resistance to it in England in the early 1960s. The issue is the relationship between fear and institutional control. Here it is helpful to review the impact of earlier institutions such as the mental hospital behind Smith on Plath's understanding of the feared Other and the realization of terror and political control. Plath spent long stretches of time in medical institutions, whether the infirmary at Smith where she was treated for her sinus problems, the mental institutions in and around Boston at the time of her breakdown, the hospital in which she worked in Boston, or the hospital in London where she had her appendectomy operation. These all feature in her writing, whether in the form of journal entry, novel episode or poem.

The specificity of the built environment is as important as the specificity of politics—politics is always mediated through discourses and institutions operating in a particular place, often in particular buildings at a particular time. It is clear that Plath was increasingly willing to enter into a relationship with these specificities, as she addressed the issue of choice: first through its conquences, then through an understanding of the complex factors which governed it. Initially she had defined the problem as "what to choose?." In England this was to be replaced by "Who or what is determining those choices?." One answer was her history and childhood: the other was the juggernaut of the multi-national military weapons industry.

THE DOORS AT THE END OF THE ARENA

Is it a tiger this year, the roar at the door?
—"Years" 16 November 1962

In her early Journal of 1950–53, Plath makes at least three separate allusions to the phrase "the lady or the tiger?." This refers to an immensely popular nineteenth-century short story of that name written by Frank R. Stockton and published in 1882.[2] The story concerns a tyrannical but whimsical King who left the punishment of those charged with crimes to chance. Those accused—always men—would be taken to the arena, and told to choose one of two doors. Behind one was a beautiful lady: those who chose this door would immediately be married to her in an extravagant public ceremony before the gathered crowds. A life of pleasure was then promised. If, however, the person chose the other door, then a ferocious tiger would appear, and the chooser's fate was to be devoured by the beast—again, as public spectacle.

Such were the choices of a young courtier who had fallen in love with the King's daughter (and she with him) with the difference that the daughter knew what was behind each door and was able to signal unobtrusively to her lover to go to the door on his right. The narrative is left unresolved, with the narrator suspending the action as the daughter makes her signal, leaving readers with the question, "Which one do you think she indicated?" Although the story is about men making decisions about their own fate, it ends with a woman being able to make that choice for her man.

The issue of choice is a recurrent theme in Plath's writings. In his *Poetics*, Aristotle argues that in circumstances when the protagonist has to make a choice not knowing the consequence, then true heroic character is revealed. Plath seemed to hate making choices of this heroic kind because it entailed such high risks; she did not share the philosophical attitude of Frost's speaker in "The Road not Taken." She was immensely practical, but also worried about missing out on the snowy woods. In her teenage years, where, in the sexual politics of the class to which she aspired, women were judged by the successes of their marriage, this was expressed in the decisions that had to be made about men: whom should she marry, whom should she reject? The consequences of making the wrong decision were dire, because so much was invested in the choice.

For the female reader, who is required to identify with the male subject, Stockton's story is a paradigm of the transgressive act involved in writing. In psychoanalytical terms, if the female reader of this story imagines herself as the phallic woman—that is, the woman who identifies with the protagonists and not with the female onlooker—then the feeling of helplessness is compounded by the consequences of enforced (and un-welcome) choice. It is a moment of suspended powerlessness, and in psy-choanaltyic theory the rage against imaginary loss of the phallus is trans-ferred into phallic fetishism, with surgery, limbs, eyes, or other body parts as the surrogates for phallic loss.[3] In Plath's 1960s writing, these very im-ages suggest the dismembering of body and identity. What if the imag-ined chooser selected the tiger and not the lady? The answer is destruc-tion and carnage.

What is interesting about the Stockton story is the dualistic world it constructs. There is either pleasure or pain, or in extreme cases, such as the decision the daughter has to make, there is only the choice between two kinds of pain. The story is told with all the detachment of a legend, or in the style of Saki, as if there is some delight to be taken in life's cru-elty and little ironies. It is easy to imagine Plath reading her own life in these terms: having believed that she had chosen to marry the lady, she discovers that the lady and the tiger are one and the same. In Hughes's radio play *Difficulties of a Bridegroom,* first broadcast in January 1963, the animal self of the protagonist Sullivan that rebels against the bride's attempts to turn him into an abstraction, is represented as a roaring tiger.[4]

There is another way in which a reading of the Stockton story can be applied to Plath's own career as a writer. In one sense it can be said that she made a journey away from the "lady" that could have been her post Smith destiny—a 1930s photograph displayed in the College's Bass build-ing shows women science students examining astronomical telescopes out of doors in their *mink coats.* This gives some indication of the role of Smith as a kind of finishing school where young ladies then progressed into society. At Smith, Plath was outwardly determined to be recognized as that lady. She did not adopt the Bohemian look of jeans and bare feet. She wore a hat and white gloves, she was religiously clean and well groomed, she worried about her reputation. But, during her years in England, in Devon and in London, she began to abandon some of these traits with greater confidence, in her life and in her writing, especially in North Tawton even when she briefly enjoyed the role of "lady of the manor." The visit to the Winkleigh hairdressers is an atavistic attempt to retrieve the lady, after the tiger (or lioness, panther or leopard—perhaps the species of wild cat is less important than the image of ferocity) had been released among the lines of the *Ariel* poems.

The tiger lurking in the Smith journals, where she dissects human frailty with a scorn that for a long time was considered unpublishable, is let loose in *The Bell Jar* in ways that prepared the ground for the the voice of the *Ariel* poems. This, I think, is in part because the world at large was becoming increasingly ferocious, as the Cold War became colder and a nuclear war seemed about to destroy the world she knew. The predatory

"Other" is more than any one person, it is the power of history, institutions, governments and the military complex to shape and destroy life. By the time she had moved to England in 1960, Plath was ready to accept that there cannot be an "outside" from which artistic insight is immune; the world of global and national politics permeates everything, including "transcendent" poetry.

The process begins with the interrogation of the separation of worlds. The questioning of the general categories themselves—lady, tiger—is anticipated in her pre-1960 writing. In 1958 she noted in her journal:

> A Rousseau poem: a green-leaved world. With the naked lady on her red velvet couch in the jungle's middle: how close to this I come. (JPI: 347)

In the poem inspired by the painting—the poem is called "Yadwigha, on a Red Couch, Among Lilies" (1958) and the painting is Henri Rousseau's "The Dream" (1910)— the wild beasts which are clearly lions (although lions do not live in the jungle) become tigers, as if to emphasise the conjunction of lady and tiger that was part of her personal mythology. Yet, the woman is naked, calm yet seemingly vulnerable: the openness of the scene increases the eroticization. Yadwigha is the name of the Polish model who, when she posed for the painting, was Rousseau's lover:

> Yadwigha, the literalists once wondered how you
> Came to be lying on this baroque couch
> Upholstered in red velvet, under the eye
> Of uncaged tigers and a tropical moon.
>
> (CP: 85)

The sensuality of these categories also entered her daily life. She records the presence of her own "tigress" perfume in February 1958[5] and sewed red velvet curtains at her flat in Fitzroy Road. They also find a place in the poetry written in England. The speaker in "Last Words" (21 October 1961) imagines being buried in an Egyptian sarcophagus with "tigery stripes." Images from that "dream" inform the writing *and* the "real" world. One of the cats that she acquires for Frieda is given the name "Tiger."

What is clear is the insight these continuities give to her writing *method*. Sylvia Plath would regularly use the knowledge, the memories, the experiences and the notes that she had assembled in one culture while she was actually in another. Put simply, she was *writing back* in both a literal and figurative sense—writing back into her past, but writing back to the present world of England and writing back to this new "Other."

More specifically, when she was in America after her first visit to England, the series of writings exploring the walk to Top Withens engage with that past from the distance of past and place, but draw on notes made at the time in England. We have already seen this process in action when she moved to England and wrote a novel about her breakdown and suicide attempt in America, drawing on her journals. Although there is a recognisable "I" in both interrogations of the past, the "I" should not distract us from the wider interrogation of the meaning of history, and in the case of the Top Withens writing, an interrogation of literary history.

THE RUINS OF LITERATURE

The Process of Composition: "Withens," reading and a Dialectic with Heritage

Story: two—Moor-setting—walk to Haworth, to Wuthering Heights—physical, rich, heavy-booted detail. (JPI: 302)

The Brontë sisters command a central place in the canon of nineteenth-century novels, and Emily Brontë's *Wuthering Heights* appeals to the Romantic, escapist strand in all writers and readers. The Brontë influence on women writers is a large issue, and on twentieth-century American women writers the dual influence of nineteenth-century literary Romanticism and twentieth-century exile is a complex matter. Virginia Woolf, whom Plath greatly admired, had commented on the significance of the woman writer of the nineteenth-century for the woman writer of the twentieth, and by visiting Yorkshire, Plath was tracing the footsteps of two contrasting but linked predecessors.

As Strangeways points out,[6] Virginia Woolf's first published work[7] was an account of a visit she made to Haworth in 1904. Published in *The Guardian* on 21 December 1904 the essay is a meditation on a visit to the Brontë's former home and its meaning for her as a woman from a new century. Woolf's piece is discussed by Gilbert and Gubar[8] in *The War of the Words* where they note the powerful fascination of the "deadness" of the writers that Woolf admired, and the dangerous tendency of ghosts to haunt and inhibit the living.

By looking at the prose descriptions of the walk to Top Withens, the remains of the building that supposedly once inspired Emily Brontë's description of the house Wuthering Heights, it is possible to see how a piece of unpolished prose feeds eventually into a personal, mythological and political poem which explores the meaning of being a woman writer amidst the ghosts of the female literary heritage. At the same time Plath was making notes in her carbon-copy notebook for a short story, which also appears to have come out of this visit to Yorkshire and the meeting with Hughes's mother.[9] This story, published in *Gemini* in 1957 and collected in *Johnny Panic and the Bible of Dreams* is discussed by Strangeways[10] as further evidence of Plath's exploration of the power of the past to haunt the present. It is a theme which informs the 1957 poem of the same name, even though the subject is entirely different. The poem "All the Dead Dears" describes a tomb in a museum at Cambridge containing the body of a woman, a mouse and a shrew, the woman's leg having been gnawed at by one or both of the little creatures. The fascination with these figures, the story which their corpses tell, and the intrusion of that distant past into the now, is the issue that the poem explores.

The short story, on the other hand, is put together by a number of members of a Yorkshire family in a way that is reminiscent of the storytelling method of *Ethan Frome,* and it is principally Mrs. Nellie Meehan's story. In her original notes Plath made it clear that the story was to have a "Wuthering Heights background," going on to say that it will "present vivid influences of ghosts on woman who <u>almost</u> has second sight".[11] Nellie, like Nellie Dean, provides that background, as the story relates the suicide of a carpenter called Lucas who hanged himself on a beam through which he had drilled a hole for his daughter to fasten her swing. On the night of his death Nellie is visited by an apparition; the ghost of her sister whose appearance explains what was to be have been the opening sentence (it becomes the second sentence in the published version) "I saw an angel once".[12] Before the apparition there is the sound of knocking, itself reminiscent of the banging that "wakens" Lockwood at Wuthering Heights.

The actual visit to Haworth and Withens first appears in the "Journals" as a written sketch in the carbonated notebook of 1956–58 on the undated page 31. It is likely to have been started during the period spent in Yorkshire following the post-wedding visit to Spain—that is, in or around August or September 1956. It is certainly after 26 August, and on 2 September Plath wrote to her mother to say that she had started a sketch of Wuthering Heights after an excursion to Haworth with Ted and his uncle. On the 11 September, Plath wrote to her mother "Read *Wuthering Heights* again here and really felt it this time more than ever" while on 28 September she mentions a long ten mile walk to the house and the wonderful contents of the Brontë museum [LH: 269–73]). On page 31 of the carbon copy book there is a detailed "inventory" of the contents of the Brontë parsonage in Haworth. The notes continue on to page 32, and on to the second page 32 (there are two pages for each number) Having explored the Brontë home, Plath then walked out to Top Withens, and it is probably on this occasion that she completed the pen drawing of "Wuthering Heights." The original is presumably still in the possession of the Hughes family, and if there is a number close to "32" in the corner of the drawing, it would suggest it was completed at this time.

The account of the visit—that is the written sketch itself—does not appear until page 43, and has been written in Cambridge, presumably at their new address of Eltisley Avenue. The evidence suggests that this is some months after the visit, as the date "October 9" occurs prior to page 35. Under the heading "Withens," Plath describes the parsonage "redolent with ghosts," Charlotte's bridal gown and the small luminous books. After about 10 lines the description takes the reader on the journey through the moorland landscape up to the house, which is small, lasting and has pebbles on the roof.

Nearly a year passes before the visit becomes the subject of a brief, passing note in the journal entry for 12 September 1957 that coincides with her return to Northampton to teach at Smith. The walk to the Heights is recalled along with sea crossings and sickness. Plath then plunges into teaching, and according to her own standards produces relatively little published work during the following academic year.

This sketch, produced in Yorkshire, is then consulted (apparently) in Boston some 18 months after this, in April 1959, as Plath prepares an article for *The Christian Science Monitor*. This is to be a commercial, practical piece of journalism: writing is her career. On 23 April she notes in her journal: "I think: a *Wuthering Heights* article for red-shoe money" (J: 300).

She starts work and gives it the title "A Walk to the Withens." On 25 Saturday April she writes in her journal:

> Clear day, dragged up as usual early, but exhausted, too much so to write, so worked on polishing up essay on Withens (Yorkshire) only to be stopped in title from final typing by not knowing spelling Withens or Withins. (J: 301)

But, on 3 May she notes "I have Walk to Withens written and ready." The piece was despatched, accepted, and published in *The Christian Science Monitor* on 6 June.

The subject itself was not exhausted, however. Three completed poems—two by Plath and one by Hughes— look back to this visit, Ted Hughes's being a response to Plath's account of the scene. Plath's poems are "Two Views of Withens" (1957) and "Wuthering Heights" (1961), while Hughes replies with his own poem "Wuthering Heights," published much later in *Birthday Letters* in 1998. Plath's "Wuthering Heights" was written in September 1961, soon after they had moved to Court Green in North Tawton, where the nearby moors are likely to have brought back memories of Yorkshire.

Plath's pieces need to be considered as a series of texts, each one a reworking of its predecessor. Each is certainly a new text in its own right, but one which clearly and deliberately draws on what has gone before,

and they provide written evidence of an evolutionary process that is repeated in the last year and a half of her life. It is her characteristic working method.

The original 1956 sketch says that there are two ways to get to the
house, both tiresome. Plath describes the grasses and sheep that are
passed on the way that is usually taken by the public, and then the arrival
at the abandoned ruin, inhospitable, with two trees on the lee side of the
hill, and a name scrawled on a rock. *The Christian Science* article starts
by saying that there are as many ways to the Withens as there are com-
pass points, and that she has only tried two of them. She describes in detail setting out with a group of people, some of whom turn back along the
way, but eventually they arrive: "Now, distanced in space and time, I remember Withens as I found it then—a surprisingly small house of black
stone. . . ."[13] Both prose texts refer to the possibility of ghosts, but in
slightly different ways: "The furious ghosts nowhere but in the heads of
the visitors and the yellow-eyed shag sheep" (Notebook, October(?)
1956, J: 148–49). The spirit of place is expressed much more positively
in the published article:

> And yet, so strong were my impressions of the book, I felt at Withens the pres-
> ence which endows places long loved and lived in with a radiance subject to
> no alteration or ruining by wind and rain. Withens stands, and stands alone,
> ringed by the moors.[14]

Yet, this is not the reworking of memory that it may seem. At the end of
the journal sketch, immediately following the comment on the ghosts and
sheep Plath has noted the following: "House of love lasts as long as love
in human mind" (J: 149). What is clear from the published article is that
the reference to "two ways" to the house in the original sketch is there
because Plath has visited the ruin on two separate occasions, something
that is not entirely clear from her letters to her mother, where it sounds
as if the same visit is being described twice. The second visit is described
in *The Christian Science Monitor:* a journey made with Hughes from a
different direction some weeks after the first. They appear to get lost, but
eventually after crossing hill after hill they stumble upon it. The journey
is the subject of this part of the piece, the building simply a relief and a
chance to return to have high tea in Haworth before sundown.

In the first of the two poems, "Two Views of Withens" (CP: 71), written in Massachusetts in 1957, there is also a reference to kindly ghosts
and the House of Eros. But, in the poem actually called "Wuthering
Heights" Plath has moved beyond the house, beyond nineteenth century
literature, beyond the specific visit. The numerous drafts—the Lilly Library has sixteen pages of drafts—reveal an exploration of a number of

themes. The title "Withins" appears in what appears to be the earliest draft, which already has the line that will be used as the opening of the finished poem "Wuthering Heights." The speaker stands like a witch, with the horizon "ringing me like faggots" (LL).

The second page has much of what will be the second stanza of the completed poem: "There is no life higher than the grasstops" (LL).

The fourth, fifth, and sixth (there is no third) explore the missing souls, the people who once lived in this house, the ghosts of the departed and the few syllables of conversation that have survived in the sounds of the moor. The seventh page replaces the title "Withins" with "Wuthering Heights." The speaker is on the edge of the world, and aware of a world beyond earth. At this point the poem suddenly draws on an image not from history but from its own time: "It is like being mailed into space" (LL).

This image, although apparently cosmic and universal, is very specifically of its time. 1961 was the year in which human space flight began: Yuri Gagarin had orbited the earth in April, and Alan Shepard had been sent up in a rocket in May. In this poem, as in much of Plath's writing, the contemporary discourse of international politics overlaps with the literary and mythological discourses of individual self-expression. The poem is not ahistorical, nor is it only look back into the literary past. It is certainly addressing the past, the effect of memory and the presence of ghosts. But, it is filtered through a mind that is also rich with discourses and issues of the present, and all these elements fuse into the final, completed, complex text. Contemporary images are filtered into the text so that they lose their more obvious political specificity and do not disrupt the overall rhetoric of the poem.[15]

The process of composition continued over many more drafts, in which as many things were added as removed. The writing reveals evidence of restraint. The writer is still uncertain about her response, perhaps because she is still uncertain about what that response should be. Plath was operating under restraints during most of life (sometimes cultural restraints, sometimes physical ones). It is the removal of that element of institutional and cultural restraint that released the untrammelled voice of the later poems, a voice so seemingly unrestrained that it divides readers, and has critics such as Alice Miller[16] reaching for the diagnostic instruments of psychoanalysis.

Psychoanalytic readings have made an important contribution to our understanding of Plath's poetry and prose and they are not at odds with an argument that Plath responded in her writing to public and international events. There is a strong possibility that a person's predisposition to engage with public life and politics, or to profess indifference to them, can be traced to upbringing. The influence of mother and father is a rich field for those wishing to apply psychoanalytical theory to her work.

Slightly less rich, but no less interesting, is the formative role of specific buildings (and the institutions they represent) suggested by Plath's exploration of "Wuthering Heights" with its genesis in Withens and the visit to the Haworth Parsonage. In Plath's case the psychological impact of buildings can be taken closer to home—literally.

HOMES, INSTITUTIONS, AND THE MIND

Anyone who has seen the Brontë house in Haworth, knowing the personal circumstances of the Brontë family, cannot fail to be struck by its closeness to the graveyard, which seems to march towards the Parsonage garden as if the dead wish to colonise the space occupied by the living. As Terry Eagleton[17] has argued, Emily Brontë's *Wuthering Heights* may have a great deal to do with the Irish Famine, the economics of new money and the developed bourgeois discourses of law and property, but Emily's readiness to tap into other, Romantic/Gothic literary discourses of the supernatural, ghosts and the man/beast is not totally divorced from the psychological impact of reading what she did, living exactly where she did and the extreme closeness of her relationship with her sisters and brothers. "Nelly, I am Heathcliff" is clearly more than a statement of love, it is a statement about merged human identity and the issue of cultural hybridity.

Similarly, anyone who has visited the places in America lived in by Plath, knowing the circumstances of her life, cannot fail to acknowledge the peculiar psychological effect that even the outwardly ordinary world of suburbia or the outwardly comfortable world of Smith College can have on an individual if the ordinariness of buildings disguises a claustrophobic relationship. Plath's bedroom at her home in Wellesley is surprisingly roomy, until you remember that she shared this room with her mother from about the age of ten onwards. In the nineteenth-century many poor working class children shared single rooms with their parents, but for a suburban bedroom to be occupied by a mother and daughter (Plath's grandparents had the other bedroom) during a young, sensitive girl's most formative years is something rather different. It is a conjunction as close as a marriage, but without the element of initial agreement involved in the marital relationship. That this closeness had a marked effect on Plath, as haunting as the death of her father, is clear from her poems, journals and *The Bell Jar.*

But, not immediately. In starting at Smith, Plath was branching out independently, free of her mother for the first time, though she still would not have had a private room. For three years all seemed to be well. Semesters and vacations alike passed enjoyably. Her unusual adolescent experience seemed to have had no long-term psychological effect on her.

Yet, in the summer of 1953, she made an attempt at suicide. The voice of the scrap of journal that survives from this period suggests that she felt inadequate and trapped in the house once more with her mother, still sharing a bedroom at the age of twenty. She was then institutionalized and eventually returned to Smith the following January, having received electric shock treatment the previous autumn in a private mental hospital.

Up on the hill behind the Smith campus there still stands the enormous former State Mental Hospital, now closed except for an administrative block. It is an ominous building, wing after wing of high late Victorian architecture, surmounted by surveillance towers on the roofs. It is a bizarre coincidence and juxtaposition, that just up the road from the Smith athletics track, and the Smith riding stables, should have been this institution that seemed to be reminding the women of Smith that lurking behind the veil of "normality" was this other world, peopled by the "other." For so much of the patriarchal assault on women's attempts to achieve independence through education and the vote had characterized ambitious women as mad neurotics, unwomanly females, and abnormal Harpies. During Plath's time at Smith, it was a slightly nervous joke among students that "you would end up there." The sounding of the warning horn when someone went missing was an unsettling noise for those in the immediate vicinity.

Built in 1858, as the Northampton Lunatic Hospital, it operated a pioneering program whose progressive approach, the brainchild of the Superintendent Pliny Erle (1864–85), involved the recovery of mental health through work. It reached its zenith during the time Plath was at Smith; by 1955, the hospital was home to nearly 2,500 patients.[18]

For the more disturbed patients between 1930 and the 1950s, the treatment was hydrotherapy or wet packs. Hydrotherapy involved lowering patients in canvas slings into tubs of warm flowing water for three-hour stints, while wet packs (for those for whom hydrotherapy was deemed insufficient) involved packing patients in wet sheets, usually for three-hour periods but around the clock in more extreme cases. In the 1950s, this was replaced by electroconvulsive therapy and in 1955 ECT treatment was at its peak.

Plath, as was noted earlier, marked her disturbed awareness of the existence of the hospital in her Journal list of things she had learnt in her first year, and here the political sits alongside the psychological in such a very striking way, that it is worth quoting from it again:

*To study the futility of war, and read the UN charter, and then to hear the announcer on the radio blithely announce "the stars and stripes march" for our courageous fighting forces °To know that there is a mental hospital on the hill in back of the college. . . . (JPI: 36)

This, was written long *before* her breakdown, during her first year at Smith, but a letter written in hospital after her suicide attempt (but not given to her mother at the time) shows the dark shadow that this institution cast:

> Pretty soon, the only doubt in my mind was the precise time and method of committing suicide. The only alternative I could see was an eternity of hell for the rest of my life in a mental hospital, and I was going to make use of my last ounce of free choice and choose a quick, clean ending. I figured that in the long run it would be more merciful and inexpensive to my family; instead of an indefinite and expensive incarceration of a favorite daughter in the cell of a State San, instead of the misery and disillusion of sixty odd years of mental vacuum, of physical squalor, I would spare them all by ending everything at the height of my so-called career while there were still illusion left among my profs, still poems to be published in *Harper's.* still a memory at least that would be worthwhile. (LH: 129; letter dated 28 Decemember 1953).

She recovered and returned to Smith College to complete her course, and the years that followed in Cambridge and Northampton again and then in London seem to have been more confident years. She was not so disturbed by potentially troubling buildings. In London, the nearby zoo may have had its troubling elements,[19] but, for Plath, it was mainly a source of delight for the young parents and Frieda. The Devon house may have bordered the graveyard, and Plath felt it to be very miserable in winter, but the delights of the Spring daffodils, the fruit trees and the bees were significant compensations. It was cold in winter, but no Haworth Parsonage. Even her stay in the St. Pancras hospital seems to have been a not unpleasant experience: she writes cheerfully about the other patients, the sense of rest and recovery as someone else has to look after the baby for a change, and the bright young nurses.

"This Earth Our Hospital": Politics, Abjection, and the Looming "Other"

It would be a mistake, therefore, to generalize about the psychological impact of these institutional buildings and their former inhabitants; it is sufficient to say that she was often disturbed but also inspired by them. The four psychiatric units—Valley Head Hospital (where she underwent ECT treatment prior to her suicide attempt) Massachusetts General Hospital, McLean (the one in which she underwent further treatment in the autumn of 1953) and the psychiatric clinic at Massachusetts Hospital in Boston where she worked as a secretary in 1958 were clearly ominous, sometimes terrifying places. Plath drew on these experiences for the short stories "Johnny Panic and the Bible of Dreams," "The Daughters of Blossom Street" (originally to be called "This Earth Our Hospital") and the best chapters in *The Bell Jar.*

The political effect of these institutions and the Wellesley house in which she felt confined was to reinforce that reading of human behavior as a highly individualistic, inwardly driven phenomenon, best understood through introspection. The ostensible collectivity of Haven House at Smith did not seem to resist this tendency; the women were encouraged by the college culture to be competitive in their struggle for academic and dating success. This process can be contrasted with the experience of the National Health Hospital in London, where there was a real sense of collectivity. The patients were from all over the country, from all classes, and the service was an example of socialism in action. This had an impact on her reading of society. In the 1962 interview with Peter Orr, in which she says "I'm rather a political person," she also says that she prefers the company of doctors and midwives, people who are "practical" and not "narcissistic" like writers.[20] Yet, the "The Surgeon at 2 a.m." of September 1961 remains the agent of sinister forces.

POLITICS AND PSYCHOLOGY

What is apparent in the later writing is a growing sense of "Other," and I do not think it is easy to separate in Plath's writing the psychological from the political, or either of these from the sense of place. The Other may be absent parents, husband, America, the Soviet Union or institutions. What they all have in common is a tendency to control, or threaten the writer's (imagined) autonomy.

As Foucault has shown,[21] governance, sexuality, politics, and psychology are inextricably intermingled in social practices. The concept of the "Other" may have its roots in clinical psychiatry and may have originally tended to focus on the individual's relation to specific individuals, but it is now seen to have a much broader application than this. In her chapter "The Psychoanalyzing of Sylvia," Al Strangeways[22] concentrates on the significant number of attempts to interpret Plath's poetry psychoanalytically, either through classic Freudian readings of the dominance of the father and the Electra complex (which Plath herself was encouraged to believe by Ruth Beuscher, her therapist) or through Melanie Klein's theories, which pay much more attention to the importance of the mother at the centre of the psycho-drama. Other significant psychoanalytical readings have drawn on R. D Laing, D. W. Winnicot and the critic Nancy Chodorow, whose *Feminism and Psychoanalytic Theory* [23] has influenced Jacqueline Rose and other feminist critics who take more account of more recent cultural theory.

For Rose, a post-structuralist, psycho-analytic reading is concerned only with the writing, and may say nothing about the person. Drawing on Lacan as much as Freud, the focus is on the chance signifiers in the text and not the individual, for the text is to be regarded as a thing apart from the writer through which it is mediated. The Sylvia Plath who shared her mother's room and commented on the "mental hospital on the hill" is to be separated from the speaker inscribed and constructed in "her" texts, which are in this reading to be seen as independent of her. This approach is at the very opposite end of the spectrum to that adopted most blatantly by David Holbrook[24] and more subtly and impressively by Stephen Gould Axelrod,[25] who see a direct connection between the writing and the childhood experience of psychic disruption played out on an adult field.

Perhaps the critics who have been most strongly influenced by Lacanian theory are Julia Kristeva, Luce Irigaray, and Hélèn Cixous, and their work too has been used in readings of Plath. Strangeways discusses the influence of Kristeva's reading of abjection theory on critics such as Rose. She considers the consequence of critical readings which place emphasis on the primitive feelings of rejection, leading to a casting off of symbols of identity, whether acted out in language or other forms of performative behavior. In Strangeways' view they still repeat attempts to relate the writing to the woman behind the writing, repeating in another form the mistaken attempts to make links between representations of maternity and the woman's actual mother explored by Lynda Bundtzen in her more biographical reading.[26]

The weakness of readings that try to locate Plath in a tradition of *l'écriture féminine* is that they tend to be both ahistorical and reductively essentialist. In writing the body the woman once again becomes identified with the body, and not a cerebral, socially responsive individual at all. Plath's writing is so multilayered that it appears to simultaneously endorse and reject this kind of reading: it encourages such a reading through its fascination with the body, the body parts, and the female bodily functions, including childbirth (which Plath constantly contrasts with the sterility and barrenness of othered women) but it rejects it in trying to shed, remove and peel away the parts as if in some attempt to get back to an noncorporeal essence which is pure, and ungendered.

This involves a return to the concept of the abject, which is a means by which the self secures for itself an identity by expressing its horror—and terror of the bodily world that surrounds it, as is symbolically—and most dominantly represented by the presence of the mother. It accommodates this terror by performing it, and Strangeways discusses at length Plath's 1959 "Poem for a Birthday," which many see as transitional, experimental, fragmentary, biographical and a performance of the Abject: it is her most consciously psychoanalytical. Plath's interest in and knowledge of psychoanalytic theory came not only from her experience with Ruth Beuscher, but through her own interest in Jung, her knowledge of Freudian readings of Lawrence and Hamlet, and her interest in the writing of Eric Fromm, a copy of whose *Escape from Freedom* she owned. The subject of the divided self, later given tremendous attention through R. D. Laing's *The Divided Self* of 1960, had been the subject of her college thesis, and the doubling motif in *The Bell Jar* was clearly a legacy of this. In an interview broadcast in the *Voices and Visions* series[27] Aurelia Plath said that the only book that Sylvia really read during the weeks before her suicide attempt was Freud's *Abnormal Psychology,* most of whose symptoms she became convinced she possessed. The contemporary discourses of psychoanalysis were clearly absorbed by Plath during her American years, and they constitute one of the dominant discourses that influenced her writing during this period. But nothing operates in isolation. Fantasies may operate at an individual level, but they are always shaped by material forces.

7

"The issues of our Time:" *The Observer,*
Poetry, and "Thalidomide"

THE NEWSPAPER, MULTINATIONAL DRUG COMPANIES
AND A HEADLINE POEM: CASE STUDY
IN THE PROCESS OF COMPOSITION

To ANTICIPATE THE APPROACH TO BE TAKEN TO THE POEMS OF THE second half of 1962, the poems rather loosely known as Sylvia Plath's *Ariel* poems, it is instructive to focus on one that is usually mentioned in passing, partly because it does not seem to be in keeping with its more famous predecessors. A close examination of "Thalidomide" however, reveals much about Plath's approach to writing, the text's interaction with contemporary political issues and discourse, and the mediation of her writing since her death.

In the autumn of 1962, Plath wrote a poem she originally called "Half-Moon." A complex response to the discovery that a tranquilizing drug that had been prescribed for pregnant women was causing deformities in the babies they subsequently bore, she eventually gave it the more explicit title, "Thalidomide." The poem was not published in her lifetime, but appeared in *Winter Trees* in 1971, and again, of course, in *The Collected Poems* ten years later.

The poem, however, has a rather more interesting publishing history than this. On 14 January 1963, Plath sent "Lady Lazarus" and possibly nine other poems ("Death and Co.," "The Swarm," "The Other," "Getting There," "Little Fugue," "Childless Woman," "The Jailer," "Thalidomide," and "Daddy") to *Encounter.* These were published in *Encounter* posthumously on 21 October 1963 (exactly one year after the period of Plath's most furious and fertile writing activity). In 1965, a limited edition (150 copies) of a selection of Plath's work, *Uncollected Poems,* was published by a small press called Turret Books, run by Edward Lucie Smith and Bernard Stone. Lucie Smith had worked in the same office as Assia Wevill, with whom Hughes was continuing a relationship in 1965, and so publisher and copyright holder were linked both personally and professionally. The Plath poems included in this slim book, printed by Villiers Publishers Ltd., were "Blackberrying," "Wuthering Heights" (Plath's pen and ink drawing of Top Withens appears on the cover of *Uncollected Poems*), "A Life," "Crossing the Water," "Private Ground," "An Appearance" "Finisterre," "Insomniac," " I am Vertical," "Candles," and "Parliament Hill Fields." A copy of a draft version of "Half-Moon" appeared as the center pages, illustrating all the alterations that characterize a work in progress. Curiously, nowhere does it appear to explain that this draft was to evolve into the poem called "Thalidomide" that had already been published in *Encounter*.

For those seeking evidence that the publishing history of Plath's work is a record of the silencing, erasure, and colonizing of texts that patriarchal supervision produces, there is much to fasten on to here. The galley proofs have as a running heading the name of *Sylvia Rath,* corrected by Hughes on all occasions but the last (the heading above the proofs of "Candles" and "Parliament Hill Fields"). The mistake may at first appear to be some awful in-house bad taste joke, but is more likely to be a simple misreading, for there is other evidence of editorial clumsiness or misunderstanding. The typesetters have tried to produce a printed version of "Half-Moon" but have given up half way through the manuscript from which they are working, for after the word "dragging" a whole line of question marks appears, signalling defeat. Hughes has put a line through the whole page of this incomplete galley proof.

Draft 3 of "Thalidomide" forms part of the Plath collection held by the Mortimer Rare Book and Manuscript Library at Smith College, and matches exactly the page that appears in the middle of *Uncollected Poems*. Exactly, that is, except in one striking respect, a difference which ironically seems to confirm that it was the text used in that publication. On the sheet of pink "Smith College" memorandum paper which Plath favored for so much of her writing, an editor or typesetter has circled words which are difficult to read in the middle of the poem, and has scrawled in the top right-hand corner "Please type or rewrite legibly. . . . Century." In the card catalogue at Smith the entry for this draft notes "Marks made by editor (according to T. H.) have been whited out." Indeed they have, though quite an unsightly—and, one has to say, symbolic mess do they leave on the pink manuscript. Yet, there is nothing sinister here.

The simple and most likely explanation is that the typed versions of the poems were passed to the printers, and somehow the manuscript was included with them. Even so, as a professional writer, Plath never sent draft copies to publishers, and the apparent colonizing of a page of her writing never intended to be seen by the gaze of professional publishers, its invasion by inscriptions and the whiting out of these inscriptions, is somehow very troubling. That it survives to trouble, however, is itself worth noting. If Plath's writing is colonized by editors this is only a more obvious example of what Foucault has identified as a discursive practice that operates throughout society—as texts are appropriated by critics, governments, and other agencies through which power and culture is mediated. Plath colonized her own texts repeatedly—recycling and redeploying images and phrases in the way that was pointed out in the discussion of the January 1962 poems.

Although Sylvia Plath intended "Thalidomide" to be included in her *Ariel* sequence the poem has not received a great deal of critical attention. It seems unrepresentative of that series in being a response to a specific social problem, and it is not part of the rush of poems that were written during October, the poems that included "Daddy," "Ariel," and "Medusa." Susan Van Dyne[1] reads it as one of a series of poems exploring the issue of maternity, and the potential conflict that exists for a professional woman writer between the production of children and the production of language. What if the love of language—the need to articulate experience—should result in a diminution of love for one's own infants? The perils involved in choice-making were very real to Plath, and are described in *The Bell Jar*, when Esther imagines the figs on the tree turning rotten as she tries to decide which one to choose. The problem is that if you choose one thing, it is invariably at the expense of others.

But although "Thalidomide" clearly does explore some of these questions, the title indicates that it is addressing a specific issue of the early 1960s. An analysis of this poem develops further the argument that Plath's poetry and prose overlap with the contemporary rhetoric of the Cold War and the discourse associated with the threat of global nuclear warfare. The poem is a response to a specific news item relating to the deforming effects of a medicine produced by a multinational drug company. Plath did not wish to write headline poetry, but was responsive to headlines.

"Thalidimode" may seem a rather odd—and easy—way of illustrating this process. After all, Ted Hughes, in his footnote in *Collected Poems*, explains that "By the time this poem was written, the connection between the tranquilizing drug, thalidomide, and the 1960–61 crop of deformed babies was established." Susan Van Dyne says of the poem:

> Maternal feeling spurs this poem of social conscience; Plath forces herself to conceive what the medical establishment in Britain was denying, the monstrous consequences of a drug administered to pregnant women.[2]

Plath had recorded her fear of bearing a deformed child in a journal entry made at Cambridge:

Yet. I have a fear, too, of bearing a deformed child, a cretin, growing dark and ugly in my belly, like that old corruption I always feared would break out from behind the bubbles of my eyes. (Journal entry, 19 February 1956 in "Cambridge Notes," JPI: 200)

But, if the poem explores the "fears of finding one's children unlovable"[3] it is also a response to the threat to children posed by the multinational companies, whether makers of weapons or makers of drugs, and the colonization of women, their bodies and the products of their bodies by male science and power. Radiation and Thalidomide both do terrible things to unborn babies, but whereas the poem "Thalidomide" announces its contemporary concern, the parallel concern about radiation is disguised in the other poetry of this period. Both Strangeways and Rose comment on Plath's tendency to treat historical events as myth, and this is misleading if it is taken to mean that Plath neutralized politics in this way, or was not interested in it, or saw history as fable. Her 1961 worry about the effects on babies of Strontium 90 in milk should be read as a concern that feeds directly into a more metaphorical use of the image of radiation in her poems. The connection was part of the surrounding discourse throughout 1962, and there is nothing abstract or neutral about it. In its "Science and the Citizen" column, the July 1962 issue of *Scientific American* reported on two recent radiaton reports:

> As to genetic effects, "the number of gross physical or mental defects" caused by fallout in the next generation is placed at 110. For all future generations the number is 3000. . . . In the case of another constituent of fallout, the widely discussed strontium 90, the Advisory Committee report says that "there are no countermeasures". . . .[4]

"Thalidomide," however, is a much more specific, historicizable response to contemporary events than even the title suggests, with its reference to a drug taken by pregnant women. The poem was started on 4 November. On that day, the London *Observer* published an "Observer Inquiry" called "The Thalidomide Babies" which included graphic pictures showing the malformation of arms and legs caused by the drug. The leading top left-hand corner photograph shows an Afro-Caribbean child without any arms and with disproportionately large feet, and the page includes other photographs of infants without arms or legs.[5]

The early drafts of this poem show how disturbed Plath has been by these images—and there seems little doubt that it is these particular images to which she is responding.[6] They appear to be half-people, and their "amputations crawl & appal [*sic*] / Spidery, unsafe" (MRBR). She rejects them as loathsome, and in a phrase scratched out likens them to "that abortion" at the zoo, the bird-eating spider, hair-legged and big as a man's hand.[7] All night she labors to "carpenter" a place in her heart for the "thing I am given," whether it is beautiful or awful. On the second page of the first draft, as the moon—half-moon, half-child?—creates a smoky light in her room the image is reflected from a cracked mirror, and then fades, "flees and aborts like dropped mercury."

By the time of draft three, the one that appeared in *Uncollected Poems,* Plath has excised the more horrific comparisons, and the poem gives more space to feelings of compassion. The "dark amputations" of the child still "crawl and appal," but it is now less realized as a monster and has become instead a "shadow" with "awful, indelible buds / Knuckles at shoulder-blades / And the flower faces / That shove into being." The nature imagery of "buds" and "flower faces" softens the harshness of the "awful . . . knuckles at shoulder-blades." But, the poem still ends with a sense of rejection, the cracked mirror and the image aborting "like dropped mercury." The front page of *The Observer* for 4 November includes a report headed "Thalidomide mother on trial" which describes how a twenty-four-year-old mother from Belgium had been charged with the premeditated murder of her thalidomide baby, Corinne. The baby, without arms or collarbone, and "with embryonic hands growing directly from the shoulders," was one week old when she died in a "mercy-killing."

The daily reality of the body sometimes seemed to trouble Plath. In the copy of *Mrs. Dalloway* she had added to her own library during her time in Cambridge she had underlined the paragraph which begins:

How Shakespeare loathed humanity—the putting on of clothes, the getting of children, the sordidity of the mouth and the belly.[8]

Throughout her life, Plath was greatly disturbed not simply by the misshapen body, but by apparently trivial things such as other people's hairpins, the existence of unwashed hair and dandruff, and the close proximity of men who were shorter than her (though this did not prevent her from having a relationship with Richard Sassoon). Sometimes, two elements combined to unnerve her, as in her journal description of the "little shoddy man" from the mental hospital behind Smith College, "his face a mongoloid study of slobbering foolishness." She may have feared "perfection" when it found expression as cold, soulless, barrenness and blankness, but she found it equally hard to warm to the imperfect.

There is evidence of this dread of the supposedly "abnormal" in a number of her poems. In the 1957 poem, "The Disquieting Muses," Plath asks how it is that she has become haunted by the sinister figures who do not seem to inhabit her mother's world. They are the gift of some "disfigured and unsightly cousin" not invited to her Christening. The de Chirico painting from which the title it taken is a surreal, disturbing picture of three "ladies" with heads "like darning eggs." The tall, front figure is "Mouthless, eyeless, with stitched bald head" (CP: 75).

The dread of featurelessness appears in so many poems written in England from 1960 onwards, and suggest a dialogue between life (represented by a child) and the killing coldness of the intellect. The cool, reasoning, abstract philosophers in "Magi" have blank oval faces without nose or eye, as they gaze down on the child in the cot. The lifelessness of science and cold surgery is frequently conveyed by these images of anonymity. In "Face Lift" the woman's face has been "sagged on a darning egg." The speaker in "Tulips" says "I have no face" as she becomes flat and shadowy, while the body under the surgeon's hands in "The Surgeon at 2 a. m." also "has no face." The moon in "Barren Woman" is blank-faced, while in "Candles" and " The Moon and the Yew Tree" it is "bald."

Images of baldness appear so often as to suggest a nightmarish vision of either vulnerable exposed bodies or complete dehumanization. In "Love Letter" the "bald eye" of the unborn baby suggests the former, while the same expression (in "Whitsun") used of adults suggests something more sinister and robotic—the world conjured up in "Brasilia." In "A Life" the "bald, hospital saucer" resembles the moon: "Parliament Hill Fields," a written meditation on miscarriage, is on a "bald hill." The desolation of that poem may seem to contrast with the "bald cry" of the baby in the celebratory "Morning Song," but given the significance of the word for Plath it suggests the vulberability of exposure. The "Insomnia" has "bald slots" of his eyes. The "Barren Woman" imagines herself mother of "several bald-eyed Apollos." These are contradictory images, for the exposure of the unprotected or undeveloped evokes pity, whereas the blankness of the featureless evokes terror.

In de Chirico's painting, the lower portions of the Muses' torsos turn into fluted columns, like Doric pillars. They anticipate the images of sterile, or dead, blank perfection that Plath describes in "The Munich Mannequins" and even "Edge," though where the Muses and Mannequins are grotesque in their baldness, angularity and lifelessness, the lifelessness of the dead statue-like woman in "Edge" is accepted (though perhaps ironically) as a thing of beauty, perhaps because she has borne children.

The importance of bearing "perfect" children is discussed by Pamela Annas[9] in her study of the mirror in Plath's work. Annas discusses the feelings expressed by the First Voice in "Three Women" the poem for three voices inspired by a Bergman film and set in and around a maternity ward. This speaker has given birth to a child in a way that the verse celebrates, but she then retreats into a rather troubling complacency:

I do not believe in those terrible children
Who injure my sleep with their white eyes, their fingerless hands
They are not mine. They do not belong to me.

I shall meditate upon normality
I shall meditate upon my little son

("Three Women," in CP: 185–86)

Annas reads this as the voice of 1950s America, happy to have fought the war in Europe and Asia but unwilling to confront the horrors of the concentration camps and the effects of the atomic bombs on the survivors of Hiroshima and Nagasaki. Strangeways reports how Raymond Chapman, Plath's history teacher at high school, tried to jolt his students out of their complacency by having blow-up photographs of the inmates of Bergen-Belsen, Dachau, Auschwitz, and Buchenwald displayed in the classroom. Plath reveals her own horror of war disfigurement in "Berck-Plage" (1962) and it is tempting to trace the discomfort with these images to the Puritan suspicion that disfigurement is the Devil's mark. In speaking of the wishes for her son, the First Voice in "Three Women" says:

I do not will him to be exceptional
It is the exception that interests the devil.

(CP: 186)

By "exceptional" the speaker may mean outstandingly bright, rather than ill-formed, but the same conformity is implicit. Certainly, as Annas points out, 1950s white America expressed many of its post-war fears about impurity, fuelled by anxieties about Communism, in the comic-book and cinema images of lurid monsters from outer space. Strangeways points out that in the years leading up to the writing of the *Ariel* sequence there had been a number of popular films addressing issues relating to the Holocaust: *The Diary of Anne Frank* (1959), *Exodus* (1960) and *Judgement at Nuremberg* (1961), but these, too, approached the horror in an indirect fashion.

There is clear evidence in "Thalidomide" that Plath carried on the debates about her own life and fears through the language of poetry and imaginative prose by drawing on the discourses and images of the wider political world in which she lived, and this may have been more direct process than is sometimes realized. Throughout her adult writing career, she was exploring what it is to be a woman. What is specific to her writing in England is not just that she is interrogating what it is to be a woman who is also a mother and a poet, and one who has been deserted by her partner, but that as she does so she draws on the discourses in which these issues were being represented in many different guises all around her. The writing ends up being about something far more allusive than simply her own life or state of mind. The poems and the prose not only explore the performativity of behavior and gender[10] and the relationship between language and experience, they are also informed by the contemporary social and political discourses that were specific to England from 1960–63. The two have a symbiotic relationship. Not only was this inevitable, but Plath was consciously moving away from the world of the transcendental and the esoteric, and viewing much more sceptically that rich field of myth and archetype which her imagery has often led critics to discuss. In "Years," a poem written two weeks after "Thalidomide," Plath seems to explicitly turn her back on the mystical and the magical in which she had once immersed herself. In a line later crossed out, she had written "What I love is being" and this line was to be preceded by "Eternity bores me / I never wanted it." The world of the present is what engages her and it is a mistake to read the work too teleologically, whether that ending is identified as the flight of the queen bee or the "perfection" of death.

Plath engaged with contemporary issues in her writing, in her reading, in her support for pacifism and the Campaign for Nuclear Disarmament, and in the hopes and fears she had for her children. Their existence was a political statement, their future a political investment. She had made the link between motherhood and the very real, present nightmare world of the destructive application of science when she had written in her journal "The whole experience of birth and baby seems much deeper, much closer to the bone, than love or marriage. . . . Frieda is my answer to the H bomb." But, she did not write protest poetry, and it is not being suggested that we read her poems for a hidden political agenda. In the "Context" essay she says that she is not a newspaper headline poet ; instead, she prefers to approach current issues in a "sidelong fashion." Even when a specific of contemporary issue is announced as it is in a poem such as "Thalidomide," Plath does not write about it in an obvious polemical way. Her poems are not "about" these subjects, but as she herself hinted, neither are they not about them:

> My poems do not turn out to be about Hiroshima, but about a child forming itself, finger by finger, in the dark.[11]

This article begins "The issues of our time which preoccupy me at the moment are the incalculable genetic effects of fallout and a documentary article on the terrifying, mad, omnipotent marriage of big business and the military in America." In the reassessment of Plath's work along the lines that Strangeways and others have proposed, the specificity of "Thalidomide" may turn out to be less unusual than we once might have thought.

8

The Language of Apocalypse: The *Ariel* Poems and the Discourse of Warfare

> The whole experience of birth and baby seem much deeper, much closer to the bone, than love and marriage . . . Frieda is my answer to the H-bomb
> > —Letter to Lynne Lawner, 30 September 1960

> I am nobody; I have nothing to do with explosions.
> I have given my name and my day-clothes up to the nurses
> And my history to the anesthetist and my body to surgeons.
> > "Tulips," 18 March 1961

> Don't talk to me about the world needing cheerful stuff! What the person out of Belsen—physical or psychological—wants is nobody saying the birdies still go tweet-tweet, but the full knowledge that somebody else has been there and knows the *worst,* just what it was like.
> > —21 October 1962

THREE MINUTES FROM ARMAGEDDON

1962, THE YEAR IN WHICH SYLVIA PLATH WAS HEARD ON BBC RADIO using the voice of New England aristocracy (self-assured, theatrically-distinguished, and quite at home in Old England), was to be both the most turbulent and terrible year Plath had so far experienced, and one that was to produce the writing for which she is best known. In January 1962, her second child, Nicholas, had been born, and the combination of the unfamiliar hardship of an old Devon house, the demands of two young children, the isolation from friends and family and the cold, dark winter, so lowered her resistance that the spring saw no mitigation from the colds and flu that seemed her regular companions. Astonishingly, she continued to write poems, and seems to have kept a journal and embarked on a novel. As if that were not enough, the summer saw the collapse of the marriage to Hughes, and in September she was left to manage the house and the children by herself. The unbearable sense of disappointment and betrayal served only to drive Plath to produce yet

173

further writing, writing this time of a white hot, coruscating intensity. The sequence of poems which she intended to be published under the name *Ariel* date from this period, poems which have absorbed language, ideas, images, politics, memories, knowledge, beliefs, and feelings with the concentrated intensity of a black hole.

The dominant reading of Plath, influenced inevitably by the harrowing biographical details, has seen this process in narrower, more personal terms, viewing the poems as a transmutation of rage and pained personal experience into expressions of feeling and thought which transcend the particular. This kind of reading has been offered most subtly by Susan Van Dyne[1] and sees expression in Linda Wagner-Martin:

> In the midst of this emotional storm, Sylvia finished "The Applicant" and wrote "Daddy," poems that are clear testimony to the power of art to transform. The fury that she had managed to keep more or less in check all summer burst loose, and more fiery poems appeared—"The Jailer," "Purdah," "Ariel," "Lady Lazarus." Some of Sylvia's finest poetry poured out in the weeks following Ted's departure.[2]

The legitimacy of this reading of the 1962 poetry may not need to be queried, but its air of finality is certainly questionable. The link between the breach in the marriage and the production of Plath's most powerful poetry tends to segregate these late 1962 poems from their predecessors. If we look for continuity, hower, we will find it: the "Fever" of January 1962, though unfinished, has the intensity and some of the imagery of the October 1962 "Fever 103°" and since the context for the earlier poem is the moment of childbirth, well before the marital separation, the rage-at-betrayal explanation will not do. An examination of the radio poem for three voices, "Three Women" reveals further evidence of continuity between the spring and autumn writing of 1962.

As always, it is necessary to add to the dominant readings a sense of the historical moment: by considering texts and discourses that are contemporary with Plath's writing, it may be possible to discover sites of intersection, for just as the writing contributes to the historical moment so the historical moment informs the writing. Once again, discussion is theoretically grounded in a New Historicist belief that all writing is a rewriting, and that we can only tell stories having already heard stories.

But, it is always necessary to concede that the contact between discourses may be more tangential than symbiotic. In the case of Edith Wharton, for example, the fact that she travelled through England at the time of social unrest, strikes and the suffragette movement in the years leading up to the World War I appears to have had no great impact on her fiction, which concentrates largely on the world she knows and the class to which she belonged. This class was largely immune from these events, and it would be hard to argue that Wharton's novels of 1910–13 are a barometer of contemporary national or global politics. It took the actual outbreak of war itself for the two worlds to collide, and from 1914 until 1917 war and the subject of writing become one for Wharton. The situation in 1962, however, was very different: there was not just a shared feeling that there could be a war, but that it could be a last conflict which destroyed everyone and everything.

THE LANGUAGE OF THE COLD WAR

Plath's world was not directly invaded by war, but anxieties about what war meant were on a different scale to anything that had been known before. It is a change described by Al Alvarez, *The Observer's* Poetry editor and a friend, reader and adviser to Plath, in his Introduction to *The New Poetry:*

> What, I suggest, has happened in the last half-century is that we are gradually being made to realise that all our lives, even those of the most genteel and enislanded, are influenced profoundly by forces which have nothing to do with gentility, decency and politeness. Theologians would call these forces evil, psychologists, perhaps, libido. Either way they are forces of disintegration which destroy the old standards of civilization. Their public forms are those of the two world wars, of the concentration camps, of genocide and the threat of nuclear war. . . . I am not suggesting that modern English poetry, to be really modern, must be concerned with psychoanalysis, with the concentration camps or with the hydrogen bomb, or with any other of the modern horrors. I am not suggesting that it *must* be anything.[3]

Nuclear weapons were not the only expression of Cold War rivalry. A reorientation in global perception was also occurring as humans began to enter Space. On 12 April 1961, Yuri Gagarin had become the first man to orbit the earth. Alan Shepard entered space at the beginning of the next month, and, in February 1962, John Glenn became the first American to complete an orbital flight. In August of that year, when Plath's 13 August poem about burning Hughes's letters inevitably draws attention towards the breakdown of the marriage, two Soviet flights, launched on the 11 and 12 of August, marked the first group flight. And on 3 October, Sigma 7, commanded by Walter M. Schirra, was launched. All of these were major news stories, usually covered on the front pages of newspapers.

The overlap between spaceflight, exploration, technological rivalry, and military dominance was sometimes graphically illustrated. On 26

April the "unmanned" satellite Ariel was launched. As a joint United Kingdom–United States project it was the first international co-operative satellite. But, on 6 May *The Observer* reports under the headline "Ariel will have to dodge US Bomb test" that the high altitude bomb tests planned by the Americans could disable communication satellites such as Ariel. This was emphasised by Bernard Lovell's article "American Roulette 500 miles Up" about the potential disasters being caused by atmospheric testing. In the same issue, the first of a series of articles by John Davy appeared under the general heading of "Our Nuclear Future: the Unthinkable War." This was followed up on 13 May with part 2: "What if Deterrence Fails" and a week later by part 3 "Mastering the Bomb." Similar articles appeared each Sunday throughout June, July, and August.

In the essay printed as "Context" in February 1962, Plath had explained the relationship between her writing and contemporary events:

> The issues of our time which preoccupy me at the moment are the incalculable genetic effects of fallout and a documentary article on the terrifying, mad, omnipotent marriage of big American business and the military in America: "Juggernaut, the Warfare State" by Fred J Cook in a recent *Nation*. Does this influence the kind of poetry I write? Yes, but in a sidelong fashion. I am not gifted with the logic of Jeremiah, though I may be sleepless enough before any vision of apocalypse. My poems do not turn out to be about Hiroshima, but about a child forming itself finger by finger in the dark. They are not about the terrors of mass extinction, but about the bleakness of a moon over the yew tree in a neighbouring graveyard. Not about the testaments of tortured Algerians, but about the night thoughts of a tired surgeon. (JP: 92)

Later in that year, on 2 September 1962 there was a reminder of these issues that Plath almost certainly would have read. In a London *Observer* feature article headed "Arms and America: Juggernaut or Jellyfish?" the journalist Nora Beloff gives her response to the subject of the *Nation* article:

> The left wing *Nation* has devoted a special number to analysing the size and power . . . (of the military industrial complex) . . . and has suggested that it has become a juggernaut leading the country to war. But noting its singular absence of direction, Dr T Schelling, specialist on military matters at Harvard, has retorted "No, not a juggernaut, a jellyfish."[4]

The pervasiveness of this language of war, military conflict, destuction cannot be overestimated. The American magazines such as *Life* and *Time* for this period are remarkable for the advertizements which display the abundance associated with the good life, but also for the anxieties about

Communism and the "Red" threat that inform the rhetoric of so many of the articles. Stories about spying, about Polaris missiles, about the nuclear capability of Russia, about the need for America to arm itself and be strong appear in nearly every issue during this period. The need for vigilance, for spy planes and spy satellites is emphasised in drawings and diagrams straight out of H. G. Wells. The sense of tension, of paranoia and trepidation is vividly illustrated by these publications, and it seems likely that if Aurelia was sending these magazines in 1960, she continued sending them in 1961 and 1962. Plath may have simply bought editions in England: her letter to George Macbeth at the BBC showed that she read *Time*.

In England the media were not quite so jingoistic, but the mood of alarm was still communicated in newspaper articles on a weekly basis. It is certain that Plath read *The Observer*, and it will be discussed as the most demonstrable source of a separate political discourse relevant to a reading of her poetry.

The year 1962 was a period of extreme Cold War tension, as the reports in *The Observer* remind us. The Berlin confrontation, Russian anxieties about American nuclear weapons in Turkey, American fear of communism in general, and the military build up in Cuba—all of these contributed to global uncertainty throughout the Spring and Summer. The arms race continued at a frightening rate, and the image of the mushroom cloud was a chilling reminder of the awesome power of nuclear weapons.

If Plath had been totally immured in Devon it is just possible that she would have been immune to these developments in ways that she clearly had not been in London. But, we know that she visited the capital on a regular basis, that she went into Exeter on an even more regular basis, and that she was in contact with friends and the "outside" world through the visits of these friends to Court Green, through the media of the telephone and the radio. It is inconceivable that she would have remained ignorant of, and unaffected by, the international news. There is a photograph of her sitting in front of the radio (LH: 484) and if she listened to the broadcasts she marked on her week-by-week calendar she would probably have also heard the news. She read newspapers. As early as 1956, she had written to her mother that *The Manchester Guardian* was her "favourite British newspaper" (LH: 282). She also contributed to, and read *The New Statesman* and *The Observer*. Of the two, I intend to say more about the London Sunday newspaper because of the evidence of an inter-relationship suggested by "Thalidomide." But, first a few comments on the weekly left–wing journal, *The New Statesman*, to which Plath was an occasional contributor throughout 1962.

"THE SWARM" AND *THE NEW STATESMAN:*
Plath and Political History

Plath contributed reviews to, and presumably read, *The New Statesman,* a weekly current affairs magazine whose politics are left of center. Occasionally there is a direct link between the reading she was doing for her reviews, and her poetry.

On 7 October she wrote "The Swarm," the fourth poem in the bee sequence. The bees have formed a black cloud, seventy feet up, and they have to be brought to earth by the firing of guns. They fall into a straw hat and the beekeeper is pleased. Early on, the poem announces its theme of jealousy, but one subject it addresses (one among many) is power and control. The bees are controlled, returned to the "prison" of the hive, like Napoleon after Waterloo being exiled to Elba.

> It is you the knives are out for
> At Waterloo, Waterloo, Napoleon
>
> (CP: 216)

The falling bees are the red tatter of his army, the army of the man who has exercised so much power and even in defeat seems pleased with everything.

Earlier in the year in her review of *"Josephine"* by Hubert Cole,[5] Plath had described Napoleon as the "godhead of France." In "The Swarm" the ball of bees hears the "Pom! Pom!" of the gun. It is so dumb it thinks the bullets are the sound of thunder or

> the voice of God
> Condoning the beak, the claw, the grin of the dog
>
> (CP:)

In the inverview with Peter Orr recorded on 30 October 1962[6] Plath says that she has become fascinated by history:

> I am very interested in Napoleon, at the present. I'm interested in battles, wars, in Gallipoli, the First World War and so on, and I think that as I age I am becoming more and more historical. I certainly wasn't at all in my early twenties.

In other *New Statesman* reviews, her comments on books serve also as a commentary on her own situation, and this is significant not so much for biography as for what it reveals about the synthesising process in her work and the movement from the particular to the general. For example, in the review headed "Oregonian Original"[7] there are remarks on patriarchal dominance and violence that correspond to the poetry Plath was writing at this time. Plath describes a moment in *The Wonderful Button* by Evan Hunter, when the subjects see the world afresh:

"Why the king is just a person," they whisper. And they begin to smile seeing themselves (just persons,too) as kings.[8]

In her review of "Punch and Judy Carry On" she writes:

A more familiar homunculus is the humped and hook-nosed Punch of Punch and Judy, a veteran wife beater, [who] scrams like the bully and coward he is when Judy lands a few smacks.[9]

In "The Swarm" Napoleon has the hump of Elba on his short back, while in "Cut" (24 October) the thumb is a little man, a "homunculus." Hughes's poem "Tutorial" has as its subject a fusty scholarly presence, described as "the homunculi." The poem appeared in the 2 November issue of the *New Statesman* In a later review (her last), a review of *Lord Byron's Wife* by Malcolm Elwin, Plath describes Annabella's response to Byron's betrayal in terms that suggest once again her impatience with humorlessness, however fraught the circumstances:

And the "Suffering Angel" could write: "I have escaped from the greatest Villain that ever existed." Something of the Grand Guignol shows in these extremes of white and black. Byron himself had only praise for "Dearest Bell," excused his morbidities by a press of money troubles and liver trouble, and begged her back. But a sudden muzz of camp followers and rhetoric had swallowed Annabella. One is snowbound in the end, if not brainwashed, by the humourless rhetoric of past wrongs which she was to sustain until her death. Amid these "Justifications" with their Saharas of jargon, Byron's few letters refresh like water. Annabella's refusal to grant her spouse an interview (she never saw Byron again), let alone try to make a second go of it, seems due less to his cruelty, adultery, incest and the rest than to the "formidable apparition" of that consistency Byron had observed in her before their marriage—a consistency fixed by the ego-screws of pride and need to be forever, like Milton's God, tediously in the right.[10]

This is an uncannily accurate anticipation of a reading of Plath's life taken by the more notorious final chapters of Ann Stevenson's biography. The point is worth making not simply to show that Plath was ahead of the biographers, but to suggest once again that to reduce the poems to the rhetorical protest of autobiography is to charge Plath with a practice that she clearly found reprehensible. Towards the end of this review she writes:

To the bitter end Augusta [Byron's sister] acted the hectic if unsuccessful Pandarus. Her portrait of Annabella after the separation cuts oddly across the latter's pompous letters:

She is positively reduced to a Skeleton—pale as ashes—a deep hollow tone of voice and a calm in her manner quite supernatural

How clearly one sees the killing dybbuk of self-righteousness in possession! And what better luck this cherished, sympathetic sister might have had as Byron's wife.[11]

Plath undoubtedly saw parallels in her own position vis-à-vis Hughes and the Byron marriage which resulted in separation after only a year, and was characterised by the bride's jealousy of her husband's sister, the "redheaded sister" who appears in Plath's "Amnesiac." Even Arabella's mother elicits what can be taken to an allusive reference to Plath's own mother, but as always it is sugared with self-referential wit:

Mr Elwin begins, as might many a shrewd marriage counsellor, with a meticulous investigation of the bride's mother. Judith Milbanke was certainly formidable enough for *anyone's* mother-in-law.[12]

But this had not prevented her from telling her mother on 29 November how pleased she was to be asked to review this book by a friend who was a literary editor.

The *New Statesman* was not the journal to convey the tension of the biggest Cold War confrontation of Plath's lifetime, the Cuban Missile Crisis of October 1962. The issue of 26 October, which was also the middle of the *Ariel* writing period, contains an article by Bertrand Russell, "Can Nuclear War be Prevented?" but also a poem "Edwin" by Edwin Morgan on the recent death of Marilyn Monroe. Monroe, who in America had appeared in Plath's dreams, had constructed herself and performed as the woman that men demanded, but it had not brought her happiness. Plath, like many women of her generation, was becoming increasingly aware of the significance of that. Cold war events, such as the Missile Crisis, were threatening to deny women the opportunity to learn from this lesson. The voice of the *Ariel* poems protests that it shall not be so.

INTERNATIONAL CRISIS, *THE OBSERVER*, AND THE *ARIEL* POEMS

For three days the Cuban Missile Crisis of October 1962 commanded the attention of every person over the age of five in Britain and made their normal daily preoccupations suddenly less important. It would be surprising if Plath was immune to such a feeling of national and international tension, both before and during the Missile Crisis week itself and it is fascinating to trace where the cold shadow of media reports of nuclear confrontation seems to have fallen across many of the poems. On 25 May Plath wrote a poem about the barrier between two people. Originally called "Walls," with disturbing images of a red wall and a red fist (not necessarily Red fist and wall), it initially contained a line "a terror of scorching death" crossed out in Draft 1. The poem eventually evolved into "Apprehensions," with its white, grey red and black walls, and its images of suffering, death and bereavement: crosses, pietas, bleeding, and sourness. The image of the red fist, opening and closing, survived the various revisions, and the images of blackness, of featurelessness and of birds that characterize so many of Plath's poems can, no doubt, be taken as direct reminiscences of Hughes the husband, of the recurring Disquieting Muses and of the sinister hawks of Hughes's poetry. But, this surreal, nightmare landscape, with its "terror of scorching death," can be read as the child of more than marital apprehension: it is also consistent with the fears raised by contemporary newspaper reports. The Berlin Wall, constructed a year before during the month Plath completed *The Bell Jar,* remained a fault line threatening a global earthquake throughout 1962, and the sealed border had seen American and Russian tanks lined up and confronting one another almost gun barrel to gun barrel. Both superpowers knew that a single incident would lead to more than a conventional exchange of weapons: missiles were on the alert. *The Observer* on 6 May and again on 13 May featured unnerving stories about the increased threat of nuclear war and its consequences. The 6 May issue contains the first of a series of three articles by John Davy carrying the collective title "Our Nuclear Future" and is called "The Unthinkable War" The same issue also carries a report on concerns about the possible consequences of American high altitude nuclear explosions. Under the headline "Ariel will have to dodge US bomb test" the paper reports that the high altitude bomb tests planned by the Americans could disable communication satellites, such as Ariel, a fear which turned out to be fully justified.

The tension continued throughout the summer with reports of atmospheric hydrogen bomb tests. On 2 September, the Sunday morning reader of *The Observer* was greeted with a photograph of Khruschev but the alarming news came from the United States. Under the heading "Rainbow Bomb Surprise" the correspondent in Washington reported that the new radiation belt from the recent American high altitude nuclear explosion was stronger than expected and might persist for many years. An announcement from the United States Defense Department had confirmed that the radiation completely stopped transmissions from the Anglo-American satellite, Ariel.

In any discussion of Plath's *Ariel* sequence of poems, or of the poem 'Ariel' itself, it is usual to acknowledge that "Ariel" was the name of the horse on which Plath used to go riding on the moors. It was not a fast horse, but the sound of its hoofbeats on the ground had a certain resonance for Plath, as she makes clear in the draft for "Years":

> The piston, in motion puts me in my ecstasy [last five words deleted]
> My soul dies before it
> And the hooves of horses
> Their merciless churn on the black macadam [last words deleted]
>
>   ("Years," Draft 1 MRBR)

Discussions of "Ariel" have also acknowledged the obvious allusion to the enslaved spirit eventually freed by Prospero. Sometimes critics draw attention to a T. S. Eliot connection. Eliot, a poet studied closely by Plath when she took a special course at Smith, wrote a series of poems exploring religious belief and spirituality, published in pamphlets called "Ariel." Al Strangeways also notes the similarities between "Ariel" and D. H. Lawrence's "The Woman Who Rode Away" even though, as Strangeways concedes, Plath's view of woman differed so greatly (though not completely) from his. In the earlier discussion of Plath's magazine collage, the Yeats dream referred to by Guttenberg[13] of "a naked woman of incredible beauty, standing upon a pedestal and shooting an arrow at a star" clearly seems to have some resonance for this poem, and one can see why a reading of a poem such as this, as of "Fever 103°" can legitimately concentrate on its eroticism, though the reading of "Fever 103°" as a masturbatory poem seems a little off-mark when we remember that its sister draft "Fever" emerged from the act of parturition. Finally, the allusion that seems furthest from the world of satellites, and the one that Plath underlined in her own dictionary, is the one that proves to be most germane. "Ariel" is a Hebrew word meaning "lioness of God," and it is the meaning that was emphasized by Judith Kroll[14] in her early and influential reading of Plath.

Kroll quotes from a number of sources to show that "Ariel" is also a cryptic name for Jerusalem, as it also means "altar of God." The destruction of Jerusalem foretold in the Bible becomes the fire that burns sacrificially on the altar. So the religious reading takes Kroll to the understanding that Ariel equals the holocaust. It is true that Plath often seizes the imagery of the holocaust—that is the Jewish holocaust—to represent what is sometimes read as a rather over-worked parallel between her own personal suffering and the genocide practised on the Jewish people, or, to be more generous, the tendency towards mass dehumanization. But, what the existence of another contemporary meaning of Ariel, that of a communications satellite damaged by nuclear radiation, allows us to consider is the possibility that this poem has a contemporary association that has gone unremarked. And, if this is true of one poem, it may be true of others. It therefore becomes interesting to read the poems of 1962 with one eye open on contemporary Cold War discourse.

RESURRECTING LANGUAGE: POETRY, EICHMANN, AND THE CUBAN MISSILE CRISIS

The Cuban Missile Crisis of October 1962, which climaxed in a week during which millions of people were not only one step away from nuclear extinction but *felt* that they were, does not synchronize with the personal trauma experienced by Plath during the summer and autumn of 1962. Quite obviously, Plath discovered the relationship between Assia Wevill and Hughes several months before the Americans discovered the existence of the missiles in Cuba. But, the global tension reached its peak almost exactly when Plath's own writing became most sharply pronounced, as if the madness of the world accelerated and induced her own feelings about the madness and destructive tendencies of the men and women around her. Nowhere does she make this explicit connection herself. The letters to friends from this period say nothing about the world crisis, only her own, and if the current study was concerned with the issue of biography it would be quite reasonable to claim that she was far too preoccupied with her personal problems to even notice what was happening in the world. Yet, a contemporary comment shows that silence on this subject was a sign of its terrible reality. In December 1962 an insurance salesman wrote to the CND magazine *Sanity:*

> I have over 700 families on my books and the thing that struck me most about the Cuban affair was the fact that when the crisis was at its height, nobody dared mention it. My policy-holders, normally talkative, looked worried out of their lives, but paid their premiums like automatons, and studiously avoided any mention of the thing that was obviously uppermost in their minds.[15]

Without benefit of the text of the journal she was keeping, or the novel she was writing, we rely on the poems and the letters for evidence that Plath's writing was informed by the public reporting of Cold War events. The letters document the desperate practical predicament faced by a person abandoned to look after two children in a remote part of a country that is not even her own, but say little about the wider world. The poems, too, may appear to be concerned with matters other than world events. But, so many of them are about predatory, destructive people, men and women, old and young, single and married: the unfaithful lover and "other woman" are by no means the only, or even the main target. The tone is often so scathing that it suggests an anger not just with an individual, but with the whole of humankind, a kind of Swiftian misanthropic disgust best expressed in the satirical voice she had come to practice in *The Bell Jar*, where the theme of betrayal runs through the novel, as Esther is let down by her mother, but also and more significantly by Buddy, and all the other men that she encounters. In December 1961, when she had finished this novel and moved to Devon, she wrote to her mother:

> I began to wonder if there was any point in trying to bring up children in such a mad self-destructive world. The sad thing is that the power of destruction is real and universal. (LH: 438).

The poems of September and early October, including the "bee sequence," all written before the Missile Crisis, seem remote from the world of day to day events, and seem the most "transcendent" of all Plath's poetry. There is a real beehive, and these poems seem rooted in these specific "realities" of beekeeping, but like the bees themselves, they take flight from the particular 'event' that appears to be their source. "Daddy" and "Medusa" are slightly different, drawing in one case on the other horror discourse of the late twentieth century, that of the Nazi concentration camps and their victims, and in the other on the analogy of the perceived corrupting discourse of Catholicism. These poems, too, have an intertextual relationship with the contents of contemporary newspapers and journals, however, though in slightly different ways from the one discussed so far.

Plath's poem "Daddy," without doubt the most well-known and the most ferocious of the autumn 1962 poems, has troubled readers for three main reasons. One is the apparent similarity in tone and style between this poem and a poem by Anne Sexton, "My Friend, My Friend" published in the Antioch Review of summer 1959.[16] Now it is always possibile to make out a case for one writer being influenced by another through selective quotation: in "Daddy" Plath's line "Bit my pretty red heart in two," seems to echo Dorothy Parker's pained complaint in "A Very Short Song" that when she was young someone "Broke my brittle heart in two." But, the Sexton similarities are more sustained than a single coincidence of lines. The opening two stanzas of the Sexton poem suggest something of the authorial voice of Plath's poem, the imagery and the rhythm:

> Who will forgive me for the things I do:
> With no special legend or God to refer to,
> With my calm white pedigree, my yankee kin,
> I think it would be better to be a Jew
>
> I forgive you for what you did not do.
> I am impossibly guilty. Unlike you,
> My friend, I cannot blame my origin,
> With no special legend or God to refer to.

Plath takes a similar exploration of Jewishness much further in her poem, and appropriates the imagery of the holocaust. Critics have questioned Plath's sense of proportion in drawing parallels between her own personal oppression and the genocide carried out by the Nazis. Without wishing to justify this act of cultural theft (for George Steiner, it was a "subtle larceny"),[17] it is worth remembering that the Nazi past was also the Nazi present, as the Eichmann trial brought forth witnesses who had been in the camps and who testified to the horror. Plath herself seemed to have a horror of Germany. The only visit, to Munich, had been a personal disaster, and her inability to learn the language of her grandparents seems almost willful. It is, perhaps, all too tempting to read this identification with Jews as a compensatory device for a fear of the very opposite: that of being a lover of Nazis. Her father and the Nazis were both German and both had been destroyed. She had loved her father, and been denied the chance to see him as a man who was *not* a Nazi.

From Journal Cambridge March 8 1956

I rail and rage against the taking of my father, whom I have never known. . . . I lust for the knowing of him; I looked at Redpath at that wonderful coffee session at the Anchor, and practically ripped him up to beg him to be my father; to live with the rich, chastened, wise mind of an older man. I must beware, beware of marrying for that. Perhaps a young man with a brilliant father. I could wed both. (JPI: 230)

January 3rd 1959 Notebook

All my life I have been "stood up" emotionally by the people I loved most: daddy dying and leaving me, mother somehow not there. (JPI: 455)

She had been denied (because he had not lived) the direct experience of his non-complicity, of his difference. She has not seen her father rejecting the tyranny that came out of Germany. What survives is the photograph of man with a postage-stamp moustache, and the memory of a man who delegated the care of his children to his wife. His image becomes

confused with the ideology that his nation has spawned. Consequently,
Plath indentifies with his/their victims.

Furthermore, the two holocausts—the holocaust of Hiroshima and the
holocaust of the camps, which had registered on her consciousness during her most impressionable years, had returned with the simultaneous
reappearance of Eichmann and the threat of nuclear warfare. And, the
Nazis were not just in Germany, or in the past—there were reminders of
their presence in England, too. On 1 July, *The Observer* ran a feature on
Fascism in England, showing that it did not disappear with the English
Fascist leader, Mosley.

The discourse that surrounded the trial of Eichmann, especially the
work of Hannah Arendt, contains arguments which find parallels in poems such as "Daddy." In *Eichmann in Jerusalem,* which had been serialized in *The New Yorker,* Arendt described the pedestrian, banal bureau-
cratic language of the evidence, which combined horror with comic
absurdity:

> The German text of the taped police examination, conducted from May 29,
> 1960, to January 19, 1961, each page corrected and approved by Eichmann,
> constitutes a veritable gold mine for a psychologist—provided he is wise
> enough to understand that the horrible can not only be ludicrous but outright
> funny.[18]

Eichmann insisted on using stock phrases, and Judge Landau clearly felt
that this was a cunning strategy to disguise the truth. Eichmann could
think of no other way of expressing himself:

> Dimly aware of a defect that must have plagued him even in school—it
> amounted to a mild case of aphasia—he apologized, saying "Officialese
> [*Amtssprache*] is my only language." But the point here is that officialese be-
> came his language because he was genuinely incapable of uttering a single
> sentence that was not a cliché. . . . The longer one listened to him, the more
> obvious it became that his inability to speak was closely linked to his inability
> to think. . . . from the standpoint of somebody else. No communication was
> possible with him, not because he lied but because he was surrounded by the
> most reliable of all safeguards against the words and the presence of others,
> and hence against reality as such.[19]

The dehumanization that accompanies the impoverishment of language
is something that the voice in many of the *Ariel* poems—not only
"Daddy" and "Lady Lazarus," but the de-personalized German dummies
in "The Munich Mannequins" and the dismantled woman in "The Applicant"—both dreads and activates. The language itself is often deliberately clichéd, colloquial, peppered with stock slogans, or shrill with the

excitement of what Eichmann called "winged words".[20] And, in her earlier study of state power, *The Origins of Totalitarianism*,[21] Arendt had provided a justification for writers to speak on behalf those who had actually suffered the consequences of ethnic genocide:

> If it is true that the concentration camps are the most consequential institution of totalitarian rule, "dwelling on horrors" would seem to be indispensable for the understanding of totalitarianism. . . . Only the fearful imagination of those who have been aroused by such report but have not actually been smitten in their own flesh, of those who are consequently free from the bestial, desperate terror which, when confronted by real, present, horror, inexorably paralyzes everything that is not mere reaction, can afford to keep thinking about horrors.[22]

Arendt goes on to make the point that the confrontation with horror, whether real or imagined, will not change the personality. Such a claim encourages a different reading of "Lady Lazarus" or "Ariel":

> A change of personality of any sort whatsoever can no more be induced by thinking about horrors than the real experience of horror. The reduction of a man to a bundle of reactions separates him as radically as mental disease from everything within him that is personality or character. When, like Lazarus, he rises from the dead, he finds his personality and character unchanged, just as he had left it.[23]

Such a comment also endorses the ending of a draft version of "Daddy," which concludes with the reassurance of the final line of the penultimate verse in the published version. "Daddy, you can lie back now." Plath's change/addition is a significant change, in that it emphasises the revenge of the victims rather than the release of the dead man's soul.

Another characteristic of this poem that troubles readers is the childlike terminology. Why is a thirty-year-old woman speaking as if she is a little girl? The response that patriarchy has tended to infantalize women, so that they remain dependent "girls," an argument that informs Edith Wharton's most successful novels, has not been accepted as a satisfactory defence. Yet, if we look at contemporary discourses again, using the Sunday newspaper that we know Plath read, it is noticable that two days after she had written this poem an advertisement appeared for *The Standard Life Assurance Company* showing a little girl in front of rows of kittens. She is pulling gently at her mother's arm and saying, in very big letters "Better see what Daddy says. . . ." The text continues, in smaller type: "Appeal-judge, decision-maker is Daddy. That is the way your family likes it, for they have loads of faith in you. Not just for the kitten-size things. . . ."

There seems no doubt that Plath wrote her first draft of "Daddy" two days before, on 12 October, and that the title "Daddy" was there from the start. This was not the first appearance of this advertisement, however; it had appeared on Sunday, 27 May in *The Observer,* and together with a companion advertizement in which a small boy is appealing to his Daddy to retire (from batting in the cricket match they are playing) the advertizements appeared at intervals throughout the summer and autumn of 1962. It is quite possible that it appeared in the *Radio Times* or some other periodical that Plath saw during that week: that Plath had an eye for the iconography of advertizements is clear from her 1960 Eisenhower collage.

Seen alongside the poem the advertizement does seem significant. Some kittens had been acquired for Frieda: they make an appearance in the poem "Lesbos." But, it would be wrong to regard this as any kind of key that "unlocked the poem": the poem "Medusa" originally had the title "Mum:Medusa." and there is evidence that Plath called her own father "daddy" because that is the word used by the girl in the story "Superman and Paula Brown's New Snowsuit" and in Plath's own journals as we have seen. The voice that is heard, therefore, is partly contrived and partly inherited.

The contrivance of voice is a major weapon in Plath's poetic armory, something that was considered earlier in the discussion of Geyer-Ryan's arguments regarding the satirising of women's speech. In her study of the relationship between Plath and Emily Dickinson, Gayle Wurst[24] advances the argument that Plath simultaneously admired Dickinson's poetry and was impatient with the 1950s image of Dickinson as the child-woman in awe of "The Master," the childless woman who in Ted Hughes's terms found an outlet for her passion in her writing. The reconstruction of Dickinson, which was being effected by new readings of her work, helps to explain Plath's delight at being considered by Al Alvarez the one American woman poet who along with Dickinson will be remembered, as it does her decision to call her own second child Emily if it had been a girl—a reference to the two Emilys (Brontë and Dickinson) and her father Otto Emil Plath. Wurst considers the relationship to be complex, reminding us that Dickinson's father was an Edward, as was Hughes, suggesting that there is some kind of conflation of father/Master/husband. Whatever the case, it is clear that the poem did not exorcise the father element in this triangle, for as Wurst again points out, the loss of the father is what gives the sweet memories of the sea at Winthrop their poignancy in *"Ocean 1212W,"* written some two months later.[25]

In the *Paris Review* that Plath struggled to read in hospital in March 1961, a poem called "Men of War" describes a host of jellyfish that have been washed up on the shore and in the harbor. The etymological link between Aurelia's name and the jellyfish suggested by the tentacles/ snakes around Medusa's head has not gone unnoticed. But, once again, it is useful to resist the call of the biographical, whilst not denying that this is a poem which at many points touches on a relationship between an actual woman and an actual mother: allusions to the Atlantic, the land-spit geography, and the "paralyzing of the kicking lovers" would make such a denial look rather strange. If however, the stinging, paralyzing force can be the mother of the short story "Mothers," or "The Disquiet-ing Muses," or the Holy Mother of the Catholic Church—which it clearly is at some points—then there seems no reason why it cannot also be the Mother Country America, which threatens to sting and kill more power-fully than the bees, so that all in England are "overexposed like an X Ray." The men-of-war can be female warriors, or sexless like the stinging bees. The baggage and guilt associated with America the nuclear superpower is transferred onto the Mother figure, partly because the father is absent (or has just been dealt with in "Daddy") and partly because the guilt about rejecting the father that she loves (he bit her "pretty red heart in two") leads to an more violent abjection of the mother. Geyer-Ryan places the Medusa of mythology alongside other women who have spo-ken out, and who have suffered the fate of demonization:

> Full female voices, such as those of the Sphinx, the Sirens and Sappho, or a sight which repels male sexuality, such as that of Medusa, are banished by the cultural discourse in the shadowy world of the abnormal and the inhuman.[26]

Yet, the poem ends with a tantalizing ambiguity "There is nothing be-tween us" (CP: 224).

The speaker is simultaneously asserting absolute difference and ab-solute identification, and this can be read as woman to mother (woman who is now also a mother herself) or citizen to home country. Plath and America are now divorced in the same way that she is divorced from her father and mother, and "divorced" from her husband. The speaker can-not identify with a country—a military jellyfish of the kind she read about in *The Observer* on 2 September—that is prepared to risk nuclear war with Russia. But, equally, she cannot deny her complicity: she is that identity. The only way to escape is to shake off all identities, and that is what nuclear war is likely to do whether people wished it or not.

POETRY, BETRAYAL, AND ARMAGEDDON

Even though the discovery that Hughes was having an affair occurred in July, while Kennedy did not tell the world about the missile sites until 22

October, it is possible to draw parallels between the suspicion about the exact nature of the Russian presence in Cuba and the suspicions of personal betrayal that Plath chronicles in "Crossing the Water," "Apprehensions," and "The Rabbit Catcher." As "events" these feelings occur in July, and are immediately translated into poems, but as speech acts/language events the climax is delayed. Even though Plath and Hughes had effectively separated in late August, the realization of separation sank in during September and October after he had been told to quit the house, and is whipped to a fury by a combination of anxieties about approaching winter darkness and cold, Plath's thirtieth birthday on 27 October, recognition of future isolation, loneliness, failure, and entrapment—and, the most neglected piece in this complex jig-saw, the world crisis.

Agents had sent reports to Washington about the sighting of Russian troops and weapons as soon as they had started to arrive in Cuba, but these had been ignored, largely because the CIA did not think it possible that the Soviet Union would do such a thing. But, their reports proved to be remarkably accurate. The Crisis effectively began in England on 22 October, when President Kennedy announced at 7 P.M. the blockade of Cuba, and showed on television the U2 photographs of the missile sites. If we track the developments over the next few days, which would have been reported on the radio news (We know that Plath listened to the radio because she marked certain programs in her week to week wall calendar, and there is a reference to a wireless talking to "itself like an elderly relative" in "The Detective" of 1 October.) we can consider the extent to which there is evidence to support such a reading. Although the time difference—six or five hours, depending on the time of year—would normally mean that a seven o'clock broadcast would not have registered in England until the next day, Plath's inability to sleep during this period, and her early (4 A.M.) rising meant that she was living an unusual relationship to American time that was neither British nor American, but would have been alert to early morning broadcasts that marked the end of the American day.

In early October, during the period preceding the crisis itself, Plath wrote a series of poems that are frequently regarded as very specific personal responses to individuals, poems that were triggered by thoughts of Hughes, her dead father Otto, her mother Aurelia and her West Country neighbours. From the 10 October to 21 October (the day of Kennedy's broadcast) Plath wrote "A Secret" (10 October), "The Applicant" (11 October), "Daddy" (12 October),"Eavesdropper" (started on 15 October, but later modified on the last day of the year) "Medusa" (16 October), "The Jailer" (17 October), "Lesbos" (18 October), "Stopped Dead" (19 October), "Fever 103°" (20 October) and "Lyonesse" and "Amnesiac," both written on Sunday 21 October, the day before Kennedy's announcement. The usual grouping relates some of these to relatives ("Daddy," "Medusa," "Stopped Dead"), has some inspired by experiences with friends or neighbours ("Eavesdropper," "Lesbos") with the remainder being associated with strong feelings about Hughes's controlling personality and adultery ("A Secret," "The Applicant," "The Jailer," "Fever 103°," and "Amnesiac," as well as "Daddy"). Nearly all of these poems are written on the backs of pages of Hughes's "The Calm," a play written by him at the time of Plath's miscarriage.

No one in the West seems to have anticipated the seriousness of the Cuban Missile Crisis, and it would be wrong to read history backwards. Early October was not a time of unbearable global tension. Yet, as was argued earlier, this was a Cold War period in which the potential for intercontinental nuclear war was rarely absent from the news. One thing that characterizes these poems is the obsession with deformity and the recurring images of flaking, peeling and bleeding, suggesting the horror of the loss of skin and mutation that is associated with the effects of radiation and nuclear bombs or male control. In "A Secret" there is the "dwarf baby" with the "big blue head" (reminiscent of the blue baby whose birth Esther witnesses at Buddy's Medical School in *The Bell Jar*), in "The Applicant" "the glass eye, . . . rubber breasts or a rubber crotch" and a kind of radiation suit that is "waterproof, shatterproof, proof // Against fire and bombs through the roof // Believe me they'll bury you in it." In these early and mid-October poems the feverishness of real illness and high temperature is translated into what can be read as images of asphixiation and irradiation in a nuclear holocaust:

> Such yellow sullen smokes
> Make their own element. They will not rise,
>
> But trundle round the globe
> Choking the aged and the meek,
> The weak
>
> Hothouse baby in its crib,
> The ghastly orchid
> Hanging its hanging garden in the air,
>
> Devilish leopard!
> Radiation turned it white
> And killed it in an hour.
>
> Greasing the bodies of adulterers
> Like Hiroshima ash and eating in.
> The sin. The sin.
>
> (Fever 103°, CP: 231)

The image of the speaker's head as a Japanese lantern complements the image of the peeling skin in "Amnesia" written on the next day, Sunday, 21 October. They reach a kind of climax—a rather strained, artificial climax many critics have alleged—in "Cut," written on the 24 October, which many would regard as the tensest day of all.

The poem that is central to the argument being advanced here is "Lady Lazarus," one of those poems that has been criticised for being self-congratulatory, self-centred and petulant. It was started on the 23 October, the first of the most anxious days in the crisis when Khrushcev said "no" to Kennedy's demand that ships should stop to be searched. It continued through a series of drafts until the 29 October, the day which effectively saw the crisis resolved as Khrushcev announced that the missiles would be crated up and returned to Russia. Famously, Al Alvarez persuaded Plath to delete the line that is the most direct allusion to nuclear warfare—"I may be Japanese"—advice which he later regretted giving.

For Susan Van Dyne and others "Lady Lazarus" is a poem celebrating female survival and resurrection. It is written on the back of that section of *The Bell Jar* which describes the caviar meal at the *Ladies Day* headquarters and ends with the purifying bath—the tub that originally turned the whore into the virgin, like the gypsy's daughter who turns into a virgin each new moon. In an early draft of the poem Plath had written these lines, before crossing out the second of the two:

> And there is a charge, a very large charge
> For a night in my bed
>> ("Lady Lazarus," Draft 1, MRBR)

Another deletion presents the speaker's family as an all female one:

> Now I have two girls
> They are already beautiful
> And are they proud
> Of their mum's profession?
> Yes!
>> ("Lady Lazarus" Draft 1, MRBR)

A third deletion takes the reader closer to the conflation of personal fevers and global incineration:

> I burn & turn & have no need of
>> ("Lady Lazarus," Draft 1, Deletion, MRBR).

Much later, in the fifth page of Draft 1, there is the following line that survives in the finished version:

> I turn & burn
>
> (MRBR).

Throughout the poem, there is much that could be characterized as Cold War discourse. The speaker is reduced to a skeleton, reduced to bone—all human flesh has fallen off. Plath is actually thin, of course, but the imagery seems to go well beyond the specific personal instance:

> I am your valuable,
> The pure gold baby
>
> That melts to a shriek.
> I turn and burn.
> Do not think I underestimate your great concern.
>
> Ash, ash—
> You poke and stir.
> Flesh, bone, there is nothing there—
>
> .   .   .   .
>
> Out of the ash
> I rise with my red hair
> And I eat men like air.
>
> (CP: 246–47)

This imagery draws on the Nazi concentration camp ovens as much as it does the nuclear holocaust of Hiroshima and Nagasaki, which in the published version, following Alvarez's advice, has become suppressed. It is multi-allusive with the roast turning on the spit, which in "Mary's Song" is the lamb/Lamb and the Jews being burned as heretics, and the once more repeated allusions to gold ash, and holocaust. And the red hair, that echoes the "red-haired sister he never dared to touch" of "Amnesia," written two days before. Like "Medusa," which seems to be drawing largely on the imagery of Catholicism but has metaphorical glimpses of radiation with its "Overexposed like an X-ray," so this poem contains traces of the real apocalypse which seemed about to be enacted on earth.

Although *The Collected Poems* suggest otherwise—because of the point at which Plath actually dated her finished poems—she began work on the poem that was to become "Nick and the Candlestick" on the 24 October. The poem conveys that sense of great anxiety for her child in the face of terrible power:

> Let the stars
> Plummet to their dark address,

> Let the mercuric
> Atoms that cripple drip
> Into the terrible well,
>
> You are the one
> Solid the spaces lean on, envious
> You are the baby in the barn.
>
> (CP: 241–42)

Baby Nicholas is the speaker's, and perhaps humankind's savior, and his survival is crucial. The poem was finished and dated on the 29 October. The date is again important, for on Sunday, 28 October *The Observer* had a front page picture of young, elementary children in Florida crouching down in the recommended position of "Duck and Cover," resting their heads on their schooldesks in preparation for a nuclear attack. As the discussion of "Thalidomide" has shown, Plath was not immune to such photographs. And, tension was still very high. A front page article suggested that the Cubans expected an invasion at any moment, while the main headline read: "Kennedy: no deal until the missiles are made useless."

This was originally part of a longer poem which included the lines that form "By Candlelight," the gentle poem that is dated 24 October. Both poems express concern and love for a child. Children are the catalyst in Plath's politicization. Through looking at their world, she experienced the need to look beyond her own—but does this amount to politicization?

On the same day Plath wrote "Cut." The personal incident may appear to have nothing at all do with the Cold War. She has simply, but very painfully, cut her finger while peeling or chopping an onion. It is a thoroughly individual, domestic, specifically personal incident. It is a gendered moment: a woman is preparing food, and the blood that flows is emblematic female blood.

With the emphasis I am giving to these poems this personal accident is made to carry a great deal of political baggage, and for some readers this is too much for such a slight incident. This impatience and dissatisfaction is understandable if we uncouple the poem from its moment of writing. But, if it is acknowledged that 24 October was an exceptional day—and for all of those in North America, Europe and Russia who were aware of the news it was an extremely memorable day—then what may appear to be an ephemeral, unimportant moment actually becomes a very human example of the world's jittery nerves and accidental tendency towards self-destruction. The slip of the knife is indicative of the tension that is being felt across the world, which in Plath's case is magnified by the pressure of being trapped in the countryside and abandoned in marriage. The blood pumped "straight from the heart" becomes a metaphor for all death, all destruction, including self-destruction, an idea taken further by the conceit of the roughly bandaged thumb:

> Saboteur,
> Kamikaze man—
>
> The stain on your
> Gauze Ku Klux Klan
> Babushka
> Darkens and tarnishes. . . .

(CP: 235–36)

Is this just a comical moment, after all? Yes and no. The injured thumb as "trepanned veteran," wounded soldier and Homunculus, with the drops of blood as Redcoats may have the wry tone of a metaphysical poem by John Donne, but the tone is a rhetorical device to achieve a specific goal, and as with the rhetoric of *The Bell Jar*, does not indicate an indifference to the subject. The thumb in its bandage reminds her of Kamikazi pilots, the material reminds her of the hoods of the Ku Klux Klan, both male agents of death. But the bandage is also a headscarf, a Russian headscarf, so America and Russia are conflated in this image, with America threatening the (female) Russian. "Babushka," according to Plath's own dictionary, comes from the Polish word for "old woman," and is the root of the word "babble." So this is a very gendered poems about male violence; and, it can be argued, female language. Most extraordinarily, the poem is written on the back of chapter 1, page 2 of *The Bell Jar*, and takes us right back to the Rosenbergs. It is almost too perfect, as if the poems have been rearranged and dated to create the kind of marvellous red herring that scholars will follow until they are exhausted. On a day that many thought could be the final day of the world (though behind the scenes negotiations between Kennedy and Khrushcev were continuing), Plath has worked her way almost to the very end of her pink Smith Memo paper, and the very beginning of the draft of the novel. These contextual frames provide "Cut" with a cultural significance that possibly the poem itself does not invite. Yet, it is impossible to read the reference to the "thin, papery feeling," which links onion and thumb, without thinking of other allusions to the peeling of skin, and the shedding process whereby the speaker sheds layers of being as an onion is stripped of its layers of skin.

The poem is dedicated to the nurse, Susan O'Neill-Roe, whom Plath found such a source of support during this period. Together with the midwife Winifred Davies, she is the kind of practical, organized woman for whom Plath had developed such a high regard, and to whom she makes reference in her interview with Peter Orr six days later. Such women are contrasted with self-centered men of the artistic kind and, by implication, military leaders of the life-destroying kind.

"Ariel" is another poem which, like "Lady Lazarus," is written across a period of several days, starting with 17 October and finishing on Plath's birthday, 27 October. From the first there is an image of great energy, force and power emerging from an explosive moment:

> One white melt, upflung
> to the lover, the plunging
> Hooves
>
> (Draft 1: MRBR)

The lover is expunged, but the explosion survives. In the process, the woman rides and sheds her past, her skins, her clothes, her constructions. For Susan Van Dyne, it is an act of bodily exhibition and of transgression:

> White
> Godiva, I unpeel—
>
> (CP: 239)

The poem can be read in a variety ways: its eroticism suggests a celebration of sexual pleasure, "foaming to wheat," driving on to extinction, the sexual "little death," oblivion and suicide. But, it is more militant than that with its images of the power of the lioness, the arrow piercing the red eye. And, though the martial imagery is specifically female, (lioness, Godiva) it becomes increasingly phallic: the flying arrow, swimming like a sperm, driving towards its end. And, if we take the Ariel reference also to encompass the contemporary anxiety about atmospheric tests, the arrow becomes the kind of ballistic missile that will destroy itself and civilization when it creates the cauldron of the nuclear explosion. In the collage of 1960 the cold, murderous, rapacious aim of the nuclear bomber is plainly displayed, and the summer reporting of the damage done to to the solar cells of the Ariel satellite by the intensification of radiation caused by atmospheric nuclear tests may all be part of the discourse that informs this poems, as may even a memory of John Hersey's much read account of Hiroshima:

> There were many dead in the gardens. At a beautiful moon bridge, he passed a naked living woman who seemed to have been burned from head to toe and was red all over.[27]

On the Monday following the day on which the Missile Crisis started to ease, Plath went to London for a few days, primarily to record her poems for a radio broadcast. According to her diary she travelled up to London on Monday 29 October, and visited Alvarez and met the BBC producer on the same day. The recording may have been made then, or the following day when the broadcast took place. Astonishingly, Plath read poems that she had only just finished, for "Lady Lazarus" is dated 29 October. As the meeting with the BBC man was scheduled for lunchtime she must either have finished them very early in the morning, continuing her practice of rising at 4 A.M. (although Susan the nanny was staying overnight) or have revised them on the train.

A poem that looks as if it was written in London, but is clearly dated 27 October, is "Poppies in October." Few critics draw attention to the fact that although rogue flowers do sometimes survive into the autumn, these poppies are probably the poppies that decorate wreaths and are worn on lapels in the period leading up to Remembrance Sunday. Their significance as a reminder of war at a time when the world seemed to be on the brink of another war, should not be overlooked, but once again the poem resists a simple, martial reading. The red poppies contrast with the grey sky, and it may appear as if they are to be read simply as late flowers. Yet, the "red heart blooming through the coat" suggests remembrance poppies, which, "cry open in a forest of frost, in a dawn of cornflowers." ("Poppies in October," CP: 240). Their sudden appearance is an unexpected gift, and contrasts with the reminders of ordinary mortality, the woman (in an earlier draft of the poem, a man) taken away in the (originally "the white decorous hearse / Which once shut will roll her for ever into the diminishing grey architectural perspective . . . ") ambulance, and the dull eyes of the men in bowlers. It is this allusion to bowlers which seems to take the poem out of a Devon context, although bowlers would be worn by British Legion men on parade, or perhaps men on their way to work in the bank. The poem was dedicated to Helder and Suzette Macedo, her friends from London, and ended with an exclamation mark. Plath's wishes have been ignored in *Collected Poems*, which includes neither the dedication nor the final punctuation. It was one of those poems recorded on the 30 October 1962, but not broadcast until after her death.

In this program, "The Poet Speaks," Plath was interviewed by Peter Orr. At one point, Orr asks her if she has a keen and great sense of the historic, and as we saw earlier, she replies:

I am not a historian, but I find myself being more and more fascinated by history and now I find myself reading more and more about history. I am very interested in Napoleon, at the present: I'm very interested in battles, in wars, in Gallipoli, the First World War and so on, I think that as I age I become more and more historical. I certainly wasn't at all in my twenties.[28]

Orr follows up with a question about the source of her poems, and, again, the reply is instructive. Plath says that her poems are rooted in personal "sensuous and emotional experiences," but with this qualification:

> I think that personal experience is very important, but certainly it shouldn't be shut-box and mirror-looking, narcissistic experience. I believe it should be *relevant* [italics in orginal], and relevant to the larger things, the bigger things such as Hiroshima and Dachau and so on.[29]

This remark has the effect of taking readers to the past which is what it is intended to do. Because she was such a self-disciplined writer she knew that she was using the material of the present to take the writing well beyond the here and now. For the same reason that she does not mention her immediate personal circumstances, she does not mention current events. Both are there, and she knew it was impossible to escape them. Instead, she would *use* them, as she had been using them before her break-up with Hughes.

Performance, Continuity, "Three Women," and the Late Poems

Plath's writing addresses the anxious interrogation of identity that takes place in a nuclear age. At a time in England when radio and newspapers brought both work and immediate news for poets such as Plath, it should not be surprising that this interaction is inscribed in the texts she produced. It should also not be surprising that some of the distinctive characteristics and concerns of the *Ariel* poems of the last quarter of 1962 are mirrored in those that precede them and those that follow, for Cold War anxieties dominated public concern during the years Plath spent in England. The high tension of the Cuban Missile Crisis was simply a more extreme form of the anxiety that existed in the preceding three years, and it took some time for that tension to ease.

"Three Women" is a "Poem for Three Voices." It is a poem for radio written in the Spring of 1962, and was broadcast on the BBC Third Programme in August of that year. The three women represent three of the multiple voices that Plath experimented with throughout her writing career: that they are three women in a maternity ward gives them a special significance. As well as being explorations of identity, they are usually read as specific explorations of female identity, motherhood, and fertility. The immediate inspiration was a Bergman film, most probably *Brink of Life* (1957), as the close parallels in this account of this "chamber play" film suggest:

The plot centers on three women in a maternity ward during a critical period of forty-eight hours. The sense of a *Kammerspiel* world is reinforced by the first shot, which shows the ward's door opening to admit Cecilia, who is in labor. The film will end with the youngest woman, Hjordis, resolutely going out of the door, departing for an uncertain future. The women's pasts are revealed through dialogue. In addition, each actress is given one hyperdramatic scene. The first, and perhaps most impressive, present Cecilia's reaction to the death of ber baby. Characteristically, Bergman dwells on this display of shame, anguish, and physical pain. In a drugged haze, cradled by a maternal nurse, Cecilia recalls her worries about the delivery, accuses herself of failing as a wife and mother, and alternates among sobs, cries of agony, and bitter laugher.[30]

Plath's long poem is also a continuation of the writing process discussed in chapter 4, tracing a continuity of imagery from "Waking in Winter" in January 1962 to "Elm" in April. "Three Women" was written in March, and contains many reworkings of the images that appear in the January 1962 draft poems. It also contains ideas that are repeated in different forms throughout the summer and autumn poetry, and are traceable in even the final poems of 1963.

The Second Voice speaks of several of the things that were recorded in the January drafts: she says, "I dream of massacres / I am a garden of black and red agonies" and refers to "destructions," the "bare trees, a depriviation" and the way that "a dead sun stains the newsprint." The First Voice says that "[t]he rain is corrosive" and that as a mother she too is the "center of an atrocity." The birth of her son fills her with wonder, and is rendered in terms very reminiscent of the January draft:

> Who is he, this blue, furious boy,
> Shiny and strange, as if he had hurtled from a star?
> He is looking so angrily!
> He flew into the room, a shriek at his heel.
>
> (CP: 181)

"Three Women" is interesting for a number of reasons. For the understandable reason that the "double" was the theme of Plath's Dostoyevsky thesis at Smith, and appears as an organizing device in *The Bell Jar*, it has been tempting for critics to read Plath in terms of a binary, a self and an alter ego, or more pathologically, as a split-personality expressed in text. The identities here are divided into three, and help lead the reader away from the more simplistic doublings—towards, I hope, a reading that acknowledges the multiple identities and voices that the writing deploys quite deliberately and quite consciously. This is more performance than madness.

As well as taking us back to the writing of 1960 and 1961, the "Poem for Three Voices" also takes us forward to the later poems of 1962 and early 1963. For example, the First Voice says that she "does not believe in those terrible children / Who injure my sleep with their white eyes, their fingerless hands" in a way that anticipates the November 1962 poem "Thalidomide" discussed earlier.

More significant is the link between the childlessness of the second woman (Second Voice) and global patriarchal politics that formed the epigraph to the the introductory chapter of this book. The woman who has lost her child through miscarriage is the woman who is controlled by men, the flat men who are responsible for destruction, bulldozers, guillotines and the "white chambers of shrieks." This linking of barrenness and politics allows a different reading of those poems addressing childlessness; instead of straightforward examples of anger directed towards women who have no children, perhaps these are also poems directed at a global system which is poisoning the world and causing women to abort, or be infertile. It is this woman who feels diseased with death, it is this woman who is haunted by terrible dreams.

The release of these dreams into poetry is an important stage in Plath's writing career. Elizabeth Bronfen (1998: p. 100) discusses what she calls the "rhetoric of deception" which Plath confronts in her 1962 poetry. The deception appears in the way that humanity—and, America in particular—has pretended that the world has not been changed by the fact of the concentration camps and the explosion of the atomic bomb. An awareness of this pretence explains Plath's need to conceal her identity as the author of *The Bell Jar*. Bronfen argues that the desperate need to believe that things are as they always were leads to the kind of suppression addressed in Plath's 1956 short story "The Wishing Box" (JP: 48). Agnes Higgins envies the ease with which her husband Harold recalls and recounts his marvellously rich dreams. Her own dreams are rarer, dark and terrible and have always been so since the more carefree days of childhood when she dreamed of fairies and of flying with Superman over Alabama.

The conjunction of terror and humour anticipated in this mischievous black comedy of a newly-married couple is one of the reasons it is legitimate to ask the question, raised by Bronfen, "What if the voice of Ariel—though, without doubt, Plath's most astonishing poetic achievement—were no more real than the other voices?" (Bronfen 1998: 33). What, one might add, if the world situation was so dangerous that the rhetoric of normal discourse was no longer possible? In this case what Steiner regards as the overdone Gothic effects of the late poems, which are as arty and histrionic in his view as Picasso's *Guernica* (Steiner 1965: 330) may perhaps be controlled statements of politics simultaneously performed and disguised as expressions of personal and global anger.

The Institution of the Family and the Final Unfinished Messages

I AM THAT I AM
—(Exodus 3.14)

I see . . . human embryos bobbing around in laboratory bottles like so many unfinished messages from the great I Am
—"Johnny Panic and the Bible of Dreams," 1958

No poet of shadow to crawl into,
And his blood beating the old tattoo
I am, I am, I am.
—"Suicide off Egg Rock," 1959

I am, I am, I am
—*The Bell Jar*

Continuity and the Process of Composition

When I began this study of Plath's relationship to politics and place, I had not read Ted Hughes's close analysis of Plath's "Sheep in Fog" (Hughes 1994), a late poem first completed on 2 December 1962 and then revised on 28 January 1963. Hughes's essay, written from a unique position, represents his own very thoughtful study of the process of composition, and the detail of the analysis travels in a very different direction from the one taken here. The confidence of some of the interpretations which such a close, informed position seems to permit—there is an absolute assuredness about the detection of the poem's "real meanings"—is likely to divide readers, yet, ironically, Hughes's general belief that there is a set of invisible ideas informing the evolving text endorses, rather than runs counter to, the argument that political discourses which are apparently avoided in the poems nevertheless inform and influence their language and rhetoric.

The actual application of Hughes's approach, however, hightlights important differences in emphasis. First, Hughes considers that there is a significant change in the tone of the poems written during the *Ariel* period, and the final 1963 poems. Secondly, he is insistent that the "hidden" ideas that inform the poem are drawn from myth, and not politics. In this particular case he seems to be on firm ground. Whether or not his specific identification of the stories of Phaeton and Icarus as inspirations for some of the imagery is correct (it is open to debate, to say the least), "Sheep in Fog" certainly resists a global political reading, unless the revised title is taken to include an allusion to the *Scientific American* description of the "Follow the Leader"[31] sheeplike condition of humankind, blundering in a Cold War fog. That seems unlikely.

Hughes sees it as signficant that apart from a revision on 31 December, of "Eavesdropper," no poems were written between 2 December and 28 January. He does not mention, however, that this interruption coincided exactly with Plath's move to London and the associated furnishing of a new flat. She had been writing under very trying practical circumstances before, it is true, but the housemove offers a possible explanation for the silence, and should be mentioned. The essay's apparent disregard for the historical specificity of the moment of writing allows a reading that emphasises Plath, the myth maker.

In his reading Hughes argues that "Sheep in Fog" is an important transitional poem. In its 2 December form it is the last of the Autumn poems, and in its revised 28 January form it marks the beginning of a new series, intended, Hughes says, for a separate collection. Using the drafts, which are numbered and can therefore be sequenced, (the third handwritten page is dated (2 December 1962) and the typescript dated and placed (2 December, Court Green), Hughes discusses the evolution of the poem in terms of its transformation from a poem of specific detail[32] that in its 2 December form ends unsatisfactorily, to a poem of mythic resonance that in the 28 January form ends on a more internally consistent note of resignation or loss. He argues convincingly that by the end of January "the rage, which was also a kind of joy, has evaporated. What remains is mourning."[33]

The poem, originally called "Fog Sheep," describes a morning horse ride in winter in a misty, hilly rural landscape. The ride contasts with that in "Ariel"—here the horse is slow, and the mood subdued:

> People or stars
> Regard me sadly, I disappoint them.[34]

The steady clop of the horse's shoes on the macadam (in an explanatory note quoted in *Collected Poems* [CP: 295] Plath says the horse was walking slowly down a macadam hill) creates a mournful, tolling sound: "Hooves, dolorous bells—" (CP: 262).

Hughes goes on to say that the upbeat ending to the 2 December version jars with the gloomy preceding lines. It is as if Plath willed the poem to end positively against her better judgment. In the original ending the sheep of the title make an appearance, providing closure with a final, comforting set of images:

> Patriarchs till now immobile
> In heavenly wools
> Row off as stones or clouds with the facies of babies.[35]

Images of babies, heaven and benign patriarchs signify positives in Plath's work, Hughes argues, and she wrenches the poem round to this positive conclusion because the productive period of *Ariel* had yielded a series of poems that celebrated achievement. This forced ending, which she knew did not work, was nevertheless an attempt to sustain that mood and rhetoric.

So far the argument is persuasive, and it continues to be so as Hughes traces the next stage in the process of composition. This poem, Plath acknowledges when she re-examines "Fog Sheep" on 28 January, with its "dolorous bells" is essentially about a feeling of failure and the December ending she has written is not right. She changes the title to "Sheep in Fog," but removes the reference to the sheep in the last three lines, replacing them with lines responding more directly to the preceding accumulation of bleak images:

> They threaten
> To let me through to a heaven
> Starless and fatherless, a dark water.[36]

Hughes then goes back to the first draft and its abandoned images of "ribs, spokes, a scrapped chariot" and its later revision. For Hughes, this is a key image, for the chariot is no less than Phaeton's chariot, destroyed when Phaeton took his father Apollo's horses too near to the sun and they fell to the earth. The imaginative leap is supported by its deliberate contrast to the success of "Ariel," where the speaker flies on her horse into the sun, the "red Eye / The cauldron of the morning." In the earlier discussion of "Little Fugue" (chapter 5) I noted Plath's willingness to play with homophones such as Eye/I and morning/mourning, and this playfulness is evident in "Ariel." The mood of the poem "Ariel" is exuberant, and the rush of the mood sweeps past the potentially troubling word "suicidal."

By 2 December, Plath had exhausted her own drive towards optimism. Psychologically, Hughes argues, she had fallen to earth, and the poem "Sheep in Fog" uses the myth of Phaeton as a narrative model through which she can give wider substance and resonance to that process. The horse is no longer a flying creature, and the chariot image completes the sense of disaster. The fallen Phaeton becomes the speaker transformed into his chariot: "I am a scrapped chariot."[37] There are then two more leaps of the poetic imagination. The crashing of Phaeton's chariot is replaced with the idea of the fallen Icarus—Hughes introduces biographical detail here by saying that Plath kept a picture of Icarus in her student flat and was particularly fond of Auden's poem about Brueghel's painting of Icarus plunging unnoticed into the sea. This remains an unwritten idea, but appears at the next stage of the first draft in the phrase likening the blackening morning to "a dead man left out," which in the final version of the poem becomes "A flower left out."

Hughes is confident that this subtextual myth is the key not only to this poem, but all subsequent Plath poems. The absence of direct textual evidence for this is seen as part of the argument's (and the poem's) strength:

> The "melting" of the Phaeton myth behind Ariel into the "Icarus myth" behind this (and the last eleven poems) is done with beautiful, extremely powerful effect, yet without overt mention of either. And one can see how any mention of either would have killed the suggestive power of the mythic ideas. . . . [H]aving seen these drafts we do not respect the poem less. We understand it far better, because we have learned the peculiar meaning of its hieroglyphs. These drafts are not an incident adjunct to the poem, they are a complementary revelation, and a log-book of its real meanings.[38]

It is doubtful that this confidence is justified and that these myths *are* the key to the poem's "real meanings." In the way that Hughes presents the argument, it does not allow for possibility that the complexity of poetic discourse might be dense enough to include, or to be drawing on, more immediate and specific events. The significance and the specificity of the word "rust" is important to the discussion here.

A closer look at the first draft shows that the speaker and the horse are of the same colour, and that the colour of rust is pervasive. The reddish soil of Devon, which presumably splatters horse and rider, becomes an image of universal decay:

> And the world the color of rust—
> The world rusts around us
> Ribs, spokes, a scrapped chariot.[39]

This last line also seems to take its image from a very specific piece of agricultural machinery, of the kind that is often found at the edges of farms or fields. The iron seat, the ribs of something like a harrow, and the spokes of the wheel all, in their rusting condition (and the preceding line indicates that they provide evidence of the rusting world), suggestive of a very material, solid object. There seems no reason why Phaeton's chariot should be made of iron, and the adjective "scrapped" suggests the unwanted material of the scrapyard rather than something that has fallen from the heavens. And, to be pedantic, in the legend of Phaeton the boy is cast down by Zeus's thunderbolt to save the earth and the stars from the scorching of the sun, but the chariot and horses must survive for time and the sunrise to continue.

But, even if Hughes's reading assumes that Plath's poetic license permits a reworking of the myths to include a crashed chariot (the darkening morning indicating a sunless sky, and the final line suggestive of the dark water into which Phaeton plunges and dies, would then make more sense), what these references to Phaeton and Icarus take us away from— not deliberately, because I am sure Hughes had better things to do with his time than to pore over back copies of *The Observer*—are the specific gender and father images in the poem, and its possible intertexuality. The absent father with which the 28 January poem ends is not just Otto, nor is it the Helios or Apollo which the child Phaeton goes to seek out, it is the absent father of Plath's children, and there are a number of contemporary textual reminders of this absence in other poems by Plath.

The poem "Totem," written on the same day as the revised "Sheep in Fog" addresses among other things the argument with Catholicism, and transubstantiation: let us eat the dead hare "like Christ," the poem proposes. The hare, skinned, is like an abortion, and the catalog of later animal images—the hood of the cobra, the spider—is present here. The images may also serve as a commentary on the radio play "Difficulties of a Bridgroom," broadcast on the 21 January, in which a hare is sold to buy two roses for the man's lover. Although probably inspired by the Rosicrucian tale of *The Chemical Wedding* those close to Hughes would recognize Assia Wevill in the lover figure.

In the poem "Child" also written on 28 January, there are images that parallel some of those in "Sheep in Fog." The child in question should be a

> Pool in which images
> Should be grand and classical
>
> Not this troublous
> Wringing of hands, this dark
> Ceiling without a star.

(CP: 265)

The starlessness, the fatherlessness and the dark water, therefore have a specificity (parent-child) which pulls the reading in another direction from that of Freudian or mythic God/Father/Male principle. From looking through *The Observer* on 6 January Plath would have noticed three poems by Ted Hughes, the first of which, "Water," begins: "On moors where people get lost and die of air."[40]

More significantly, perhaps, on 27 January, the day before "Sheep in Fog" was revised and "Child," "Totem," and "Munich Mannequins" were written, Hughes's "Full Moon and Little Frieda" was printed in *The Observer,* and though this is a positive poem celebrating the child's delight at the sight of the moon, it too has its dark water, its "dark river of blood," its "many boulders" and its pail tempting "a first star to a tremor." The 27 January copy of *The Observer* was also the one in which the "Operation Safety Catch" advertizement appeared, the text closing with its own hint at starlessness: "One Moment in Annihilation's Waste. / One Moment, of the Well of Life to taste— / The Stars are setting and the Caravan / Starts for the Dawn of Nothing—Oh, make haste!"[41]

The reason for questioning Hughes's interpretation is not on the grounds of its plausibilty, but because of its finality and closure. As a reading it supports the commonly held view that there were sudden sea-changes in Plath's writing. Many of the so-called decisive breaks prove to be subtle shifts rather than moments of metamorphosis, where, it is argued, Plath's writing changes significantly from one kind to another. There are continuities that always undermine such a model of change, as the earlier discussion of "Three Women" has shown. A few further examples from the other final poems of 1963 provide more evidence of this process of continuity.

On the 1 February Plath wrote "Words." This, too, picks up the imagery of echoes and horses that were worked into "Sheep in Fog." They become ways of describing the destructive effects of empty words:

> Axes
> After whose stroke the wood rings,
> And the echoes!
> Echoes traveling
> Off from the center like horses.
>
> . . . .
>
> Words dry and riderless,
> The indefatigable hoof-taps.
> While
> From the bottom of the pool, fixed stars
> Govern a life.
>
> ("Words," CP: 270)

The last three lines, with their suggestion of the underwater, astrological influence of the sunken, fallen stars, offer a new working of the ideas contained in the revised ending of "Sheep in Fog." They provide a significant variation on the dark water/starless heaven of the 28 January lines, and suggests a continuity consistent with the claim that January 28th represents a fresh beginning. Yet, these parts of "Words" also redeploy an imaged found in "Elm," where there is also a congruence of horse, hooves and echoes:

> Love is a shadow.
> How you lie and cry after it
> Listen: these are its hooves: it has gone off, like a horse.
>
> All night I shall gallop thus, impetuously,
> Till your head is a stone, your pillow a little turf,
> Echoing, echoing.
>
> ("Elm," (CP: 192)

"The Munich Mannequins," another 28 January poem, are barren and stand surrounded by snow in the German morgue city between Paris and Rome. Plath had used the image of dress shop dummies in a 1960 poem recalling the passengers on a transatlantic voyage to England:

> Midnight in the mid-Atlantic. On deck.
> Wrapped up in themselves as in thick veiling
> And mute as mannequins in a dress shop,
> Some few passengers keep track
> Of the old star-map on the ceiling.
>
> ("On Deck," CP: 142)

Used in this way the image does not have the troubling associations evoked by the figures in "The Disquieting Muses." That association was to return, however. In "Three Women," the poem for radio written in March 1962, the Second Voice says:

> It is a world of snow now. I am not at home.
> How white these sheets are. The faces have no features.
> They are bald and impossible, like the faces of my children,
> Those little sick ones that elude my arms
>
> ("Three Women," CP: 178)

In the examination of "Thalidomide" attention was drawn to the way that the images of baldness and featurelessness signal a continuing dread of dehumanization. This parallels those accounts of mass destruction and the melting of human features caused by nuclear bomb explosions, an imagery quite specific to the Cold War period. The emergence of this imagery also coincides with Plath's first pregnancy, with early allusions to wires, torture, electrocution, and bald and dismembered figures appearing in the final section of "Poem for a Birthday" written in November 1959, just before sailing for England:

> The grafters are cheerful,
> Heating the pincers, hoisting the delicate hammers.
> A current agitates the wires
> Volt upon volt. Catgut stitches my fissures.

A workman walks by carrying a pink torso.
The storerooms are full of hearts.
This is the city of spare parts.

My swaddled legs and arms smell sweet as rubber.
Here they can doctor heads, or any limb.
On Fridays the little children come

To trade their hooks for hands.
Dead men leave eyes for others.
Love is the uniform of my bald nurse.

("Stones," CP: 137)

These lines show that there is continuing preoccupation with the body, first noted in the the earlier discussion of the Smith student Journal, but now modified by the addition of a second body, that of a child, that is annexed to the the writer. The first poem written in England in 1960 was "You're," addressed to the baby growing in the womb. The new human being, a blank sheet "with your own face on," and "jumpy as a Mexican bean" contrasts with the anonymity and lifelessness of the "Body" and of the dead children in what appears to be Plath's final poem, written three years later:

The woman is perfected.
Her dead
Body. . . .
Each dead child coiled. . . .

("Edge," CP: 272)

Looking back to the earlier writing, rather than forward to Plath's suicide, allows a slightly different reading of this poem. "Edge" was originally "Nuns in Snow" and the problem with Van Dyne's reading of a leakage from "Wintering," is that the bees that die in the snow are not mothers. And could not the perfection of death be ironical, as it is in "The Munich Mannequins?" If we look backwards to the cluster of poems written early in the previous October rather than forward to the suicide, the poem takes on a rather more complex meaning. The title is anticipated in "A Birthday Present" with its question "It is shimmering, has it breasts, has it edges?," while "The Detective" has mocking images of the ossifying body hung out like dried fruit, with the breasts most desiccated:

These were harder, two white stones.

. . . .

There was no absence of lips, there were two children,

(CP: 209)

The image of children reappears in "The Bee Meeting," where the barren body of hawthorn has etherized its children. Set against these still, disturbing images of atrophy is the rallying call of "Stings"

> They thought death was worth it, but I
> Have a self to recover, a queen.
> Is she dead, is she sleeping?
>
> (CP: 215)

The marble statue figure in "Edge," which is suggested by the reference to the "illusion of a Greek necessity" and her toga, is implied in another earlier poem "The Other," describing the barren woman with her "womb of marble," with its reference to "White Nike." Though the dead woman in "Edge" has dead children (so not a nun?) these children could be the unborn, the aborted or the miscarried: that is what they are in "Three Women," where the Second Voice says:

> I did not look. But still the face was there,
> The face of the unborn one that loved its perfections.
> The face of the dead one that could only be perfect
> In its easy peace, could only keep holy so.
>
> (CP: 178)

In fact, it is babies themselves that are likened to nuns, in "Three Women." The First Voice is describing the new-born children in their cots, with their names tied to their wrists:

> I think they are made of water; they have no expression.
> Their features are sleeping, like light on quiet water.
> They are the real monks and nuns in their identical garments.
>
> (CP: 183)

Earlier, in the 1961 poem "Tulips" the nun image is used to signify purity, although the context suggests that is ironical, since the speaker has just been swabbed by the nurses in preparation for a hospital anaesthetic and operation:

> I watched my teaset, my bureau of linen, my books
> Sink out of sight, and water went over my head
> I am a nun now, I have never been so pure.
>
> (CP: 161)

The experience is pleasant, and the speaker imagines that this sense of peacefulness is:

> . . . what the dead close on, finally: I imagine them
> Shutting their mouths on it, like a Communion tablet.
>
> (CP: 161)

And yet, according to the speaker in "Barren" to be "nun-hearted" is to be infertile, and she imagines herself a museum without statues, but with a marble courtyard, and "grand with pillars, porticoes, rotundas." If "Edge" is seem as a continuation of earlier, pre-*Ariel* writing, its theme becomes the imperfection of humankind, with the perfection of death rendered ironically. Perfection involves the artifical arrangement of the body—it is "unnatural." This is made most clear in "The Surgeon at 2 a.m.," who, having completed his operation, says:

> It is a statue the orderlies are wheeling off.
> I have perfected it.
> I am left with an arm or a leg,
> A set of teeth, or stones
> To rattle in a bottle and take home. . . .
>
> (CP: 171)

The woman in "Edge" is, thus, not a prefiguring of Plath herself. The subject is the woman who has rejected life by rejecting motherhood, the woman whose performance of beauty is cold and unhuman. Death may have the seductive aura of *les fleurs du mal,* but it also has the barrenness of the moon and the milkless pitcher. "Edge" and "breast" were linked in "A Birthday Present" (". . . has it breasts, has it edges?") and may be so here.

Earlier it was argued that the Second Voice in "Three Women" brings together issues of infertility and global politics. This voice also introduces another argument that informs the later writing—the argument with established religion, and the men who would be jealous gods:

> (They) would have the whole world flat because they are.
> I see the father conversing with the Son.
> Such flatness cannot but be holy.
> 'Let us make a heaven,' they say.
> 'Let us flatten and launder the grossness from these souls.'
>
> ("Three Women," CP: 179)

The oppressiveness of the powerful, whether church or state, confronts Plath's willingness to believe in the possibility of individual transcendence, of the individual's transformation through soaring flight of the kind described at the end of "Stings" in language that anticipates the triumphant tone of the ascension that concludes "Ariel." The release offered by the spiritual, with its images of transcendence and salvation, offered a seductive appeal even when Plath was witnessing the power of material, institutional and political forces to shape the life of the individual.

Plath's dialogue with religion cannot be ignored, for the concerns with the global nuclear threat reinforced by the pressures of single parenthood pushed Plath during the last six months of writing in the direction of her Aunt's religion, a religion that both repelled and attracted her. Catholicism had also been her mother's religion, so such conflicting feelings were not so surprising. Perhaps Catholicism offered something which Unitarianism and Anglicanism coud not provide. Plath's engagement with it, through correspondence with an American Augustinian priest studying in Oxford, is another strand in her debate with the world of institutions, and provides further evidence of continuity in the writing where some see only rupture.

9

The Politics of Religion: Father Michael
and the Argument with Catholicism

'How now,' Father Shawn crisply addressed the ghost
Wavering there, gauze-edged, smelling of woodsmoke,
'What manner of business are you on?
From your blue pallor, I'd say you inhabited the frozen waste
Of hell, and not the fiery part. Yet to judge by that dazzled look,
That noble mien, perhaps you've late quitted heaven?

In a voice furred with frost,
Ghost said the priest:
'Neither of these countries do I frequent:
Earth is my haunt.'
"Dialogue between Ghost and Priest" (CP: 38)

CONTINUITY AND INNOVATION
IN PLATH'S WRITING 1956–1963

THERE IS EVIDENCE THAT THOSE THINGS WHICH SO INTERESTED
Plath during her years with Hughes—astrology, spiritualism, mythology
and the Muse—continued to engage her during the period of conflict and
separation. Global politics may have encouraged her to view the intensity of her beliefs with more detachment and scepticism, but far from de-
molishing those kinds of interests the period of Cold War anxiety and
marital separation seems to have intensified her search for spiritual support from within the Christian church.

This is quite consistent with the politics of the period. One strand of
the nuclear disarmament campaign saw itself as being a moral campaign
that was outside politics. CND avoiding having a membership system until 1966 precisely for this reason: it did not want to find itself absorbed
into the British Labour Party, and forced to spend money on organisa-
tional matters. One of its most well-known leaders, John Collins, was a
Canon in the church, while the form of protest adopted by Betrand Russell's *Committee of 100* owed much to the non-violent, spiritual protest

212

of Gandhi. Ironically, as Richard Taylor explains in *Against the Bomb* [1] the Cuban Missile Crisis marks the high water mark of the Campaign for Nuclear Disarmament. In the aftermath it became apparent that at the moment of greatest crisis civilian demonstrations and protests had been completely ineffectual. It was the world leaders, Khrushcev and Kennedy, who had drawn back from the brink, despite all CND predictions to the contrary.

In the writing of late 1962 and early 1963 there is evidence that Plath even investigated, and found attractive, the spiritual certainties of rich ritual and intellectual superstructure offered by Catholicism. It was a religion to which she had been attracted before. On 3 August 1958 she had written in her journal: "Felt a sudden ridiculous desire this morning to investigate the Catholic Church" (JP: 253). But, this immediately qualified by: "—so much in it I would not be able to accept. I would need a Jesuit to argue me—" (J: 253–4). In her later imaginative work, she continued to write in a voice that is wary of this religion which eventually becomes the object of humorous observation. When Esther is carrying her contraceptive diaphragm she refers to her suspicion that Catholics have X-ray vision. And the Ghost's answer to the Priest in "Dialogue between Ghost and Priest," written some six years earlier confirms what is evident from the later dialogue with religion: the voice in the writing is always that of someone who has her feet firmly on the ground.

Tom Paulin[2] has spoken of the integration of religious traditions in Ted Hughes's writing, where the Yorkshire Dissenting Tradition in him that admired the rebelliousness and the fervour of Cromwell, Puritanism, and Calvin could sit comfortably alongside an admiration for Gerald Manley Hopkins and an appreciation of "Shakespeare the Catholic." Hughes felt that the richness of the English language was in its vitality and scope for linguistic improvization.

Plath, too, moves between these two Christian traditions, sometimes in a serious, sometimes in an apparently dismissive way. In "Three Women," for example, the Second Voice offers a variation in the belief in Original Sin, where only the unborn, or those who die before they are born, can be perfect and holy. The First Voice identifies with the Virgin:

> Dusk hoods me in blue now, like a Mary.
> O color of distance and forgetfulness!—
>
> (CP: 179)

The first line is almost a repetition of a line that appeared in "Heavy Women" (also about pregnancy), written one year earlier:

> Dusk hoods them in Mary-blue'
>
> (CP: 158)

In many of the poems exploring the specific experience of womanhood, the Virgin Mary appears as a presence or reference point. In "Widow" there is this poweful image of the effect of loss and bereavement:

> That is the fear she has—the fear
> His soul may beat and be beating at her dull sense
> Like blue Mary's angel, dovelike against a pane
> Blinded to all but the gray, spiritless room
> It looks in on, and must go on looking in on.

> (CP: 165)

Elsewhere, in the later poems of 1962, there is often a hint of irony in the religious allusions But the evidence that she had a sense of the ridiculous and a sharp satirical eye does not diminish the underpinning of seriousness. Wit is a significant weapon in the moralist's arsenal, and Plath was always going to be as resistant to elements of established religion when it took itself too seriously. It does not mean that she did not take the idea of "religion" seriously, or that Cold War politics had erased her strong sense of the spiritual.

THE LUDICROUSNESS OF INSTITUTIONS

The humor and irony which pervades those poems which are consciously self-dramatizing and performative is missed by those who regard Plath's more operatic poems as evidence of overblown melodrama. It is J. D. O'Hara's contention that the performative element in Plath's verse sometimes breaks through as a comic persona, so that the writer rages and argues with the world in the guise of someone who is as bizarre and eccentric as one of Beckett's solitary and desperate heroes. This is deliberate act of performativity. As a former Smith "girl" who went to extreme lengths to fit in, Plath is quite aware of what the world considers to be wild, irrational, eccentric, and dysfunctional. As Sandra Richards has said, Plath had a healthy sense of the ridiculous.[3] The recogniton of this sense of the ludicrous may have been behind Hughes's August 1962 gift to Plath of Joseph Heller's 1961 novel *Catch-22*, with its absurdist rendition of war. It is certainly evident in a letter Plath wrote to George MacBeth in the same month, congratulating him on coming up with the idea of a Penguin Book of Sick Verse, and including two of her own poems which are darker and "sicker" than her other dark, sick poems.[4]

MacBeth's poems, at times macabre, at times violent, at times comic and and at times all three show some superficial parallels with Plath's in their interrogation of the White Goddess myth ("Prayer to the White

Lady"), in their Catholic imagery ("Confession," "Mother Superior") and in their Cold War allusiveness ("Early Warning," "Missile Commander," and "The Crab-Apple Crisis"). George MacBeth also combined poetry with novel writing, and his successful career showed that the "nasty tone" that the *Time* Magazine reviewer had criticised in the 9 March 1962 article did not stand in the way of publication and recognition.

When one year earlier Plath had commented on the novel that was to become *The Bell Jar*, she had acknowledged the black comedy that it was, and had commented on the effect its tone had on her:

> I am over one-third through a novel about a college girl building up for and going through a nervous breakdown. . . . It's probably godawful, but it's so funny, and yet serious, it makes me laugh. (Letter to Ann and Leo Goodman, 27 April 1961, MRBR)

A similar reading of some of the poetry is supported by Plath's admiration for Stevie Smith, expressed in a letter written on the 19 November, the day on which "Mary's Song" was written, and a few days after "The Fearful." She had been listening to Smith's poems on some recordings made for the British Council, perhaps lent to her by Peter Orr, or recommended by him when she went to record her own poems at the end of the previous month. The special children's book review section of the *New Statesman* on the 9 November 1962 featured reviews by Smith (and Ted Hughes) alongside Plath's. Some of the comments included in an *Observer* review by Kathleen Nott of Smith's own *Selected Poems* might have appealed to Plath, for in a modified way they could be applied to the persona in some of her own poems:

> In a way she is extremely English—or rather British, of the Celtic and lunatic fringe; but one thinks quickly of Carroll and Lear—and as quickly rejects them. There is no Nonsense about her verse. It avoids whimsicality effortlessly and by miles, and, though often funny, it is never even "light." She has indeed some very serious and genuinely deep preoccupations. An old dyed-in-the-wool Rationalist has a continual, almost demonic, battle with the tortuosities of Christian theology, and seems to have got wounded in the struggle.[5]

Such a reading allows poems such as "The Tour," which otherwise seems to sit so oddly alongside the other other poems, to be regarded as less eccentric than they at first appear. For Susan Van Dyne, this Stevie Smith-like poem is a botched job, an unsuccessful attack on "bad mothering." Compared to the other poems written at this time it may appear to be unsuccessful, but it is precisely a willingness to adopt the ironical tone which here becomes the whole voice—that contributes to the success of the treatment of the more weighty subjects. A similar point is made by Raymond Smith, though here he is discussing Plath's respresentation of the male rather than the female:

> Plath's treatment of the male is not without its satiric humour, intended to deflate the masculine ego. The whole of "Gigolo" is in this mode. "By Candlelight" concludes with a satiric note as the mother sardonically comments to her child on the brass candlestick holder—a kneeling Atlas set off by a pile of cannonballs:
>
>> He is yours, the little brassy Atlas—
>> Poor heirloom, all you have,
>> At his heels a pile of five brass cannonballs,
>> No child, no wife.
>> Five balls! Five bright brass balls!
>> To juggle with, my love, when the sky falls.

The "little brassy Atlas," without wife or child, represents, of course, the absent husband. Such satiric diminution is reminiscent of Pope.[6]

W. H. Auden (a poet she had admired and imitated ever since his arrival as poet in residence at Smith while she was there as a student), provided another model of the way a poet could move successfully between the humorous and the serious. In his Introduction to the *Oxford Book of Light Verse*[7] Auden wrote that "light work can be serious" and that "poetry which is at the same time light and adult can only be written in a society which is both integrated and free." Yet the paradox of the poet's attitude to religion and belief, observed in the comments of Stevie Smith quoted above, is revealed in Auden's apparently contradictory footnote on the previous page:

> [I]t is perhaps no accident that the two best light-verse writers of our time, Belloc and Chesterton, are both Catholics.[8]

During the last three or so months of her life, Plath exchanged letters with a Catholic priest, a member of the Augustinian Assumption, who was attending Campion College in Oxford. He was an American, had attended a Boston school not far from Wellesley, and was intending to become a teacher. He was also a poet, which is why he had written to Plath. He was almost the Jesuit that in 1958 she had said would be needed to persuade her, and she comments on their correspondence in a letter to her mother:

> I feel Yeats's spirit blessing me. Imagine, a Roman Catholic priest at Oxford, also a poet, is writing me and and blessing me too! He is an American teacher

priest who likes my poems and sent me his for criticism. I thought this would please Dot. (14 December 1962, LH: 490)

Her mother had herself been Catholic in her childhood, and in her "Letters Home" Plath is eager to make links with her mother's former religion, noting on 3 March 1960, example, that she has met the British poet Elizabeth Jennings, "a Catholic." Many of Plath's relatives on her mother's side, including her Aunt Dotty, had remained Catholics. In *The Bell Jar,* Esther speaks about her family:

My mother had been a Catholic before she was a Methodist.
My grandmother and my grandfather and my Aunt Libby were all still Catholics. My Aunt Libby had broken away from the Catholic Church at the same time my mother did, but then she'd fallen in love with an Italian Catholic, so she'd gone back again.

Lately I had considered going into the Catholic Church myself. I knew that Catholics thought killing yourself was an awful sin. But perhaps, if this was so, they might have a good way to persuade me out of it.

Of course I didn't believe in life after death or the virgin birth or the Inquisition or the infallibility of that little monkey-faced Pope or anything, but I didn't have to let the priest see this, I could just concentrate on my sin, and he would help me repent.

The only trouble was, Church, even the Catholic Church, didn't take up the whole of your life. No matter how much you knelt and prayed, you still had to eat three meals a day and have a job and live in the world.

I thought I might see how long you had to be a Catholic before you became a nun, so I asked my mother, thinking she'd know the best way to go about it.

My mother had laughed at me. "Do you think they'll take someone like you, right off the bat? Why you've got to know all these catechisms and credos and believe in them, lock, stock and barrel. A girl with your sense!"

Still, I imagined myself going to some Boston priest—it would have to be Boston, because I didn't want any priest in my home town to know I'd thought of killing myself. Priests were terrible gossips. (BJ: 174–75)

Esther goes on to describe a nun sent by a nunnery to see Teresa, her Aunt Libby's sister in law and the Greenwood family doctor. Names are often significant in *The Bell Jar,* and it may be relevant, that a few years earlier, Plath had made copious notes on Saint Teresa, as part of an investigation into visionary women. Doctor Teresa is not a visionary, but Esther likes her, she combines her profession with a family (she has three children) and she is, presumably, Catholic like her brother.

In a letter written to Marcia Stern from Devon in December 1961, Plath says that a child can benefit from being couched in a rich religious tradition:

I know I always envied my mother's having been brought up in the Catholic church as a child because she had a rich & definite faith to break away from, & I think that it's better to have a child start this way, than be the only one who doesn't go to church at an age when religious and philosophical arguments mean nothing to them, & he only feels curious and outcast. (Letter to Marcia Stern, December 1961, MRBR)

Yet, *The Bell Jar* also contains a very different view of the Catholic Church, which in a passage (the italicized paragraph quoted below) that was subsequently cut by Plath is associated with that male hypocrisy that surrounds the control of female sexuality:

Ever since I'd learned about the corruption of Buddy Willard my virginity weighed like a millstone around my neck. It had been of such enormous importance to me for so long that my habit was to defend it all costs. I had been defending it for five years and I was sick of it.

In fact the whole dating game seemed a monumental, obscene farce, like bridal bouquets and satin and priestly words, when under all the folderol, like Peter's rock, lay the double bed.[9] (*Bell Jar* draft, p. 271 MRBR)

Such contradictory attitudes written into the 1961 text anticipate the complex argument with Catholicism that became more pronounced in the writing as Plath came to live the life of a single parent and writer in 1962. In a letter to Richard Murphy written on 7 October, announcing her plan (later abandoned) to move to Moyard in Ireland and employ a nanny she noted:

I shall try for a good Catholic, and maybe she can convert me, only I suppose I am damned already. Do they never forgive divorcees? I am getting a divorce.[10]

Yet, in her 1962 writing poems the speaker gives voice to a contempt for much of the spiritual and intellectual luggage that comes with Catholicism. In poems such as "Berck-Plage," "Medusa," "Fever 103°," and "Mary's Song" there is a searching interrogation of religion.

QUESTIONING THE CHURCH

This interrogation of institutionalized religion begins most strikingly in the exercise in verse of Autumn 1961, "The Moon and the Yew Tree." The speaker has fallen from grace, and she has exchanged the Virgin Mary for the Moon as symbol of motherhood. The speaker inhabits a world in which a belief in tenderness is no longer possible. It is a dark world, and the yew leads not to the serenity of the church as the speaker perhaps feels it should, but to its companion the cold, blank moon.

> The moon is my mother. She is not sweet like Mary.
> Her blue garments unloose small bats and owls.
> How I would like to believe in tenderness—
> The face of the effigy, gentled by candles,
> Bending, on me in particular, its mild eyes.
>
> I have fallen a long way. Clouds are flowering
> Blue and mystical over the face of the stars.
> Inside the church, the saints will be all blue,
> Floating on their delicate feet over the cold pews,
> Their hands and faces stiff with holiness.
> The moon sees nothing of this. She is bald and wild.
> And the message of the yew tree is blackness—blackness and silence.
>
> (CP: 173)

No matter that the church that is being described is Anglican rather than Catholic. The focus is on the gentleness of Mary, and the failure of that image to sustain the speaker who, like Plath in the autumn of 1961, is aware of a harsher, wilder world presided over by the indifferent, cold moon.

In the later, nightmare world of Berck—Plage, partly set in the French town that provides the title, Plath is recalling images conjured up from her visit in June 1961, as the speaker meditates on the death of a village neighbor in England. If the sweetness of Mary in the previous poem is false, the darkness of the priest here is sinister:

> This black boot has no mercy for anybody.
> Why should it, it is the hearse of a dead foot,
>
> The high dead toeless foot of this priest
> Who plumbs the well of his book,
>
> The bent print bulging before him like scenery,
>
> (CP: 196)

The priest, of course, is a convenient category of image for an individual man who "puts on dark glasses" and "affects a cassock" in the earlier part of the poem. In "A Birthday Present" there seems to be an allusion to the awful suggestion of a secret that must lie behind Hawthorne's "The Minister's Black Veil," and it is the inscrutability and silence of the man that is so terrible. He is as ghostly as Death, and the speaker imagines him asking questions about her: "Is this the one for the annunciation?" (CP: 206). Elsewhere in the poem, the speaker hints at the way that at times of crisis it is ritual and custom and routine that makes life bearable. Preparing food is an escape from uncertainty (Plath had been delighted to learn that Virginia Woolf found relief in just the same way):

> When I am quiet at my cooking I feel it looking, I feel it thinking
>
> 'Is this the one I am to appear for,
> Is this the elect one, the one with black eye-pits and a scar?
>
> Measuring the flour, cutting off the surplus,
> Adhering to rules, to rules.
>
> (CP: 206)

In other words, this is not an argument simply with the institution of the church, it is an argument with a set of dark judgmental practices and forms of behavior that overshadow and make insubstantial the tenderness of Mary. In order to come out from under that shadow the speaker must become strong, hard, pure, burning off "the beads of hot metal" in "Fever 103°." In that poem the speaker becomes a parody of Mary, celebrating an Assumption which is part baroque painting, part cookery program, and part rocket launch:

> I think I am going up,
> I think I may rise—
> The beads of hot metal fly, and I, love, I
>
> Am a pure acetylene
> Virgin
> Attended by roses,
>
> By kisses, by cherubim,
> By whatever these pink things mean.
> Not you, nor him
>
> Not him, nor him
> (My selves dissolving, old whore petticoats)—
> To Paradise.
>
> (CP: 232)

The cookery image is taken to even more daring levels in "Mary's Song," the manuscript version of which is dedicated to "Father Michael." The domestic ritual of the Sunday roast is the lamb of God crackling in the oven, but the image quickly shifts from the King of the Jews to the Jewish victims of anti-semitic burnings, from the "heretics" of the European past to the generation that was burnt in the camp ovens. It is a bold, highly risky leap, rescued from tastelessness by the quiet sadness of the tender concern of mother for child in the last three lines:

> It is a heart,
> This holocaust I walk in,
> O golden child the world will kill and eat.

(CP: 257)

In a version of "Nick and the Candlestick" written on the 24 October and retained in the final version, there is this set of lines:

> Those holy Joes.
> And the fish, the fish—
> Christ ! they are panes of ice,
>
> A vice of knives,
> A piranha
> Religion, drinking
>
> Its first communion out of my live toes.

(CP: 241)

In his discussion of Plath's "Piranha Religion," Tim Kendall (1999) emphasizes the link between religion and eating that characterises many of the 1962 and 1963 poems. Religion is predatory, its message a language that is taken in by word of mouth. Significant in this respect is the short story "Mothers" written in 1962 at about the same time as the sketches of North Tawton villagers that appear in the published journals and *Johnny Panic and the Bible of Dreams*.[11] The mouths of poppies, the mouthfuls of blood in "Ariel" all suggest an exploration of transubstantiation, which becomes a sinister cannibalism, the literal eating of flesh and blood.

Emerging during the middle of the Cuban Missile Crisis the assault on the world of "Nick and the Candlestick" is more than an assault on religion. The communion that is being celebrated at the speaker's expense is a rite that celebrates darkness, death and destruction not life (Nietzsche's complaint about Christianity). In "A Birthday Present," a poem which precedes the crisis by some three weeks, the disturbing presence that examines the speaker as she stands by the kitchen window is silver suited, like a spaceman, or a jet pilot or the super-people of "Brasilia." The black cassocked priest and the silver-suited are but two manifestations of the cold, clinical life-taking principle:

You are silver-suited for the occasion. O adding machine—

Is it impossible for you to let something go and have it go whole?
Must you stamp each piece in purple,

Must you kill what you can?

                                                    (CP: 207)

But, if this poem moves away from veiled priestly figure to silver-suited specter, then "Nick and the Candlestick" moves in the opposite direction. The image of the apocalyptic world of religious judgement (Plath had noted in a letter how the local vicar in Devon had equated nuclear war with just punishment for universal human wickedness) is then turned on its head as the speaker's baby, alone perhaps with the mother who lights the "cave" with the communion candle, becomes the Christ child, the "baby in the barn." The 6 November poem "Getting There" also ends with innocence and purity of infancy, but here it is the speaker who has achieved that state through suffering, following the journey through a war torn landscape in which nurses tend to the wounded with water flowing like a nun's veil. But, it is not just the old world that is destructive, the old war torn Europe subject to the ravages of a Napoleon and a Hitler. It is the new, modernist world of Brasilia, clinical and frightening with its steel-torsoed superbeings, winged at the elbows, a world that once again threatens the child in the poem. The speaker begs this super world to leave the child alone, to leave it to the motherly (Devon) world of sheep and red earth:

> O You who eat
>
> People like light rays, leave
> This one
> Mirror safe, unredeemed
>
> By the dove's annihilation,
> The glory
> The power, the glory.

                                                    (CP 259)

The failure of Christianity remained an issue for Plath and informs her final work. There are references to Christ in a number of the 1963 poems: "Totem" ("Let us eat it like Christ"), "Gigolo," ("My mouth sags / The mouth of Christ / When my enging reaches the end of it") and "Mystic." "Mystic" in particular seems to be an assault on the spiritual, possibly an assault on the unwordliness of Hughes, but also the abstract spirituality of Father Michael. The tone in which the speaker asks if religious practices and beliefs are the remedy for her suffering suggest that the answer is already known:

> What is the remedy?
>
> The pill of the Communion tablet,
> The walking beside still water? Memory?
> Or picking up the bright pieces
> Of Christ in the faces of rodents,
> The tame flower-nibblers, the ones
>
> Whose hopes are so low they are comfortable—
>
> . . . .
>
> Is there no great love, only tenderness?
>
> (CP: 269)

The speaker is not ready to humble herself. She still has life: "The heart has not stopped" (CP: 269).

As a student at Smith College, Plath had written an essay "Religion As I See It." The world is man-made and therefore imperfect: perfection is impossible on earth. It is this religious belief and the questioning of absolutes that characterises the final poems of 1963. Yet, the outer world, and the attempts of human beings to make it a better place still won her admiration. Sitting watching Camden Council meetings in the month before she died she was overwhelmed by the efforts of ordinary citizens to improve the living conditions of the poor.[12] The material presence of politics continued to exercise its influence on her thinking and writing, right until the last.

10

The Fusion of Discourses

[A]s I said in introducing a BBC reading of my poems, that, for the
practice of the style of truth to become a thing of the present, poetry
must become a thing of the past.
> —Laura Riding, Preface to *Selected Poems: In Five Sets*

I'm sure Sylvia's influences are hidden, as with most of us. . . . Believe
me, no one ever tells one's real influences—and certainly not on the
radio or the TV or in interviews. . . . I'd never tell anyone and she was
smarter than I am about such hidden things.
> —Anne Sexton, "The Bar Fly Ought to Sing"

You who have blown your tubes like a bad radio
Clear of voices and history, the staticky
Noise of the new
> Sylvia Plath, "Lesbos"

THE AMERICAN PHOTOGRAPHS OF SYLVIA PLATH OFTEN SHOW HER
with friends, but also alone, sometimes in a state of great happiness, but
sometimes downcast and morose. The published pictures taken in England depict her in one of two roles: marriage partner or mother. Later
images of Plath in a group, in professional or public places, are absent.
Unfortunately, Plath's poems and other writings are often regarded as literary photographs, in which the artist has turned the camera on herself.
If an analogy with photography is to work, however, we must discard the
idea of a modern camera with its snap shutter. Instead, we should imagine the pattern left on an early photographic plate, which was focused on
a scene but captured in cryptic and negative form many other subjects
which passed in front of the lens during the process of exposure. The central image may be that of an elm tree, but the movement of a rook has
sometimes left a blurred and puzzling trajectory across the glass.

In redirecting attention to, and arguing for, the significance of the
wider public world of politics and contemporary discourse in Plath's work
and in their mediation through the specific localities of England the aim
has been to read Plath in a new context which recognises the full scope
of her keen intelligence and the complex set of ideas that fed into her po-

etry, novels and other imaginative writing. This does not result in a new reading that should replace all other readings. There is substantial evidence in the Journals that the complicated feelings Plath had about her father and her mother, her intense feelings about herself as a woman, and the search for a language in which to express those feelings and thoughts in ways which took them beyond the merely personal all fed directly into the writing she did in England, and in particular into the final poems. The specific cause of the rage, and the immediate target of much of the anger is also beyond doubt. Yet, this does not do justice to the full range of influences that contributed to a poetry that is certainly concentrated and terrifying, but also has multiple resonances.

In the specific case of Plath's writing in England one of these important influences was the continual commentary on the Cold War and the destruction caused by atomic and hydrogen bombs. Plath came across these in magazines, in radio programmes, in newspapers and in the protest movement. They contributed to a discourse which was specific to its period, and which conjured up a terrifying picture of the destruction of all humanity.

Two contrasting examples will illustrate the many forms that this discourse took. In 1957, Norman Mailer wrote "The White Negro," published that year in *Advertisements for Myself* in the United States and four years later in England. In this essay Mailer described what it meant to be living as an adult in the post-Second World War world. Although the first sentence in the following paragraph takes us back to 1945, it is the continuing legacy of that experience and its expression in the daily fragility of the Cold War that is his principal point:

> Probably we will never be able to determine the psychic havoc of the concentration camps and the atom bomb upon the unconscious mind of almost everyone alive in these years. For the first time in civilized history, perhaps for the first time in all of history, we have been forced to live with the suppressed knowledge that the smallest facets of our personality or the most minor projection of our ideas, or indeed the absence of ideas and the absence of personality could mean equally well that we might still be doomed to die as a cipher in some vast statistical operation in which our teeth would be counted, and our hair would be saved, but our death itself would be unknown, unhonoured, and unremarked, a death which could not follow with dignity as a possible consequence to serious actions we had chosen, but rather a death by *deus ex machina* in a gas chamber or a radio active city; . . . (Mailer 1961: 282)

The gas chambers of the past now reappear in the form of the cities destroyed by atomic weapons. What was done to six million is now to be done to the entire population of the world. The human race dies unremarked, and without dignity.

The second example of what might be called a Cold War existential discourse is lighter, and the levity illustrates another response to terror. In 1963—and, perhaps earlier—Plath had taken an interest in the humorous London magazine *Punch*. She contributed an article for the series "Maids in School," a wry account of her schooldays in America which she called "America, America," a place and a culture which she now viewed very differently. The January issues of the magazine, whose book section she is likely to have scoured for reviews of *The Bell Jar* (in vain), has Cold War cartoons on the opening pages, which seem to have a more anxious edge than was usual in the magazine. One cartoon wistfully imagines the 1962 that did not happen: no Missile Crisis, no world tension, no fear. Another shows Prime Minister Macmillan riding on a Polaris missile as if riding a horse. A third has a young couple being addressed by a travel agent who is standing in front of a map of Australia and asking them if they want to go to the other side of the world just for the period of missile tension, or for ever.

It would be foolish to suggest that these constant reminders of a world on the edge were responsible for specific elements in Plath's thinking and writing, or that they made her a more serious or depressed individual. It may or may not be the case that specific poems such as "Waking in Winter" and "Elm" evoke nuclear winter, or the "now familiar photographic images of the visual aftermath of nuclear tests or bombs," as Tracy Brain argues.[1] My argument is that the texts frequently contain a wry, sardonic voice of a speaker who is adroit at concealing and disguising panic. Plath was, after all, capable of producing a poem considered suitable for an event at which Spike Milligan would be reading, suggesting either comic verse or something written in acknowledgement of his brave combination of mental breakdown, anti-nuclear bomb activism and manic humour. According to Anne Stevenson, on one occasion Plath read "Daddy" aloud in a comical voice to Clarissa Roche and both women burst out with laughter.[2] The picture is complex.

This reading of Plath is, as always, a tentative and provisional one. Devon is not central London: during the summer and Autumn of 1962 she was not mixing with political activists. But, in October of 1962, even young children at school were affected by the sense of tension that the nuclear powers confrontation brought about. Plath read the Sunday papers, she listened to the radio, she made visits to London. She was experiencing what she felt was her own personal apocalypse: the additional fear that world events induced contributed to the sense of betrayal, of the collapse of idealism and the loss of certainties. This merging and blending of discourses in the poetry and published novel indicates that she could tap into and respond to rhetoric suggesting that the world was about to destroy itself. In such a reading, specific references to deception, betrayal, nightmares, terror, atrocities, Hiroshima, ash, Ariel, tall clouds, mushrooms, and apocalyptic forces have a more contemporary resonance than is generally acknowledged. *The Bell Jar* and the *Ariel* poems are not "about" the Cold War. But, it needs reiterating, neither are they not about it.

Appendix 1
Experiments with Masquerade:
Gender, Identity, and the Body Politic

IN THE INTRODUCTION, I SAID THAT IT IS WITH THE MODEL OF PER-
formativity and masquerade in mind that I wished to examine the journal writings of the 1950s as this model offers an insight into the often un-
refined and untested political comments that Sylvia Plath makes during
this period. That is not to say that the later writing ceases to be a performance—it certainly does not. The difference is that the writing in
England becomes a more controlled performance, and one that is informed by greater self-awareness and purpose. Part of this is the consequence of a greater engagement with the world at large, through reading
(and discussion) as Plath defines herself less as an adjunct to another successful poet and more as a mature woman and mother who interacts with
the contemporary world beyond that of artists.

During these early Journal years the subject of the body, rather than
politics or society, is the site for the sharper moments of observation
and scrutiny. As a teenager—and as an adult too—Plath's journals show
that she was often troubled by human ugliness, and this carries through
into her 1962 writing. The corollary of this is that in her student entries
she comments frequently on the blond haired handsome young men, on
the beauty of women she saw as her rivals, and on the flaws in others which
made her feel inadequate. Because she is nearly 5' 10" inches and and her
male dates are often shorter, she feels forced to wear flat shoes, which
make her feel like an ox. Rather than compassion for those who are plain
or disabled, there is reluctant admiration for the body beautiful.

Yet, Plath's interest in the body goes beyond the chronicling of her excitement at meeting handsome boys who will impress her friends.
Women are scrutinized as often as men, and not simply as rivals. Sometimes these descriptions are more acute, more sensual, as she takes on
the role of artist and spectator:

> She is fluid. She smokes cutely. You are always aware of her insolent breasts
> which pout at you *very* cutely from their position as high and close to her
> shoulders as possible. (JPI: 38)[1]

Such writing can be read alongside theories of fetishism and gender-mas-
querade. As Angela Moorjani points out:

> If in accord with (the mother-father fantasy of breasted phallic sculptures) this
> fantasy—so closely repeated in the myth of the original hermaphrodite—we
> first conceive of our bodies as sexually complete, then the denial for this pow-
> erful fantasy results in mourning the missing parts in others and in oneself.[2]

Plath's 1959 short story "The Fifteen Dollar Eagle" (JP: 59) explores the
relationship between the body and art, and the body as art. Set in a tattoo shop it explores the way that fantasies of religion, nature, Hollywood,
politics and sexuality can be inscribed on the concealed parts of the body,
so that hidden from public gaze the movement of thighs, breasts, but-
tocks, and backs animate the snakes, mermaids, and naked movie queens
in erotic and wondrous ways. The narrator fantasizes about these bodily
marvels, imagining the tattooist's wife Laura:

> Up to this moment I had been projecting, fatuously, intimate visits with Laura
> at Carmey's place. I have been imagining a lithe, supple Laura, a butterfly
> poised for flight on each breast, roses blooming on her buttocks, a gold-guard-
> ing dragon on her back and Sinbad the Sailor in six colors on her belly, a
> woman with Experience written all over her, a woman to learn from in this
> life. I should have known better. (JP: 72)

Laura hates tatoos and her body remains unadorned. She is not the
woman of "Experience." The story ends with the narrator imagining her
"death—lily white and totally bare—the body of a woman immune as a
nun to the eagle's anger, the desire of the rose" (JP: 73). This expression
of disappointment—the image of nun-like woman and the paleness of
corpse-like flesh—reappears in Plath's later writing in ways usually suggesting failure, barrenness, lifelessness. Yet, this judgement is often undercut by the rhetorical sense of awe at the refusal of the woman to be
constructed in the way that the surrounding culture expects, and the final, sentence of this story, with its ambiguous "alone," conveys the con-
tradictions in Plath's reading of the resistant woman: "From Carmey's
wall the world's menagerie howls and ogles at her alone" (JP: 73).

If Plath's early social and economic politics are shallow, her gender politics are not. In the early Smith Journal she oscillates between protesting
at the constraints placed on women and on perfecting herself as the
model woman that her dates seem to desire:

> I dislike being a girl, because as such I must come to realize that I cannot be
> a man. In other words, I must pour my energies through the direction and
> force of my mate. My only free act is choosing or refusing that mate. And yet,
> it is as I feared: I am becoming adjusted to that idea. (J: 23)

> From the moment I was conceived I was doomed to sprout breasts and ovaries, rather than penis and scrotum, to have my whole circle of action, thought and feeling rigidly circumscribed by my inescapable femininity.[3] (J: 30)

It is Jacqueline Rose's contention[4] that in her writing—in her poetry in particular—Plath sought to challenge the limitations imposed by this "inescapable" femininity through language—through exploring what it was like to be the "other" by seeing and approaching and sexually exploring women as might a man. This argument, which Rose insists is limited to the sphere of a psychoanalytic reading of texts and has nothing to say about the person, the human being who was Plath, at all, is apparently supported by evidence in this early Journal entry:

> I am part man, and I notice women's breasts and thighs with the calculation of a man choosing a mistress. . . but that is the artist and the analytical attitude towards the female body . . . for I am more a woman; even as I long for full breasts and a beautiful body, so do I abhor the sensuousness which they bring. . . . I desire the things which will destroy me in the end. (J: 23)

Although Plath did not see herself as beautiful ("You are no golden-woman yourself—just a rather vivacious human one"),[5] she was comfortable with her own body and was not reluctant to celebrate it:

> God, for the sun, beating, bearing, melting my body to gleaming warm bronze; bronze-thighed, bronze-breasted, ripe and full, glowing. (Journal, p. 186, MRBR)

The writing combines these rushes of youthful self-esteem with an uncanny gift of prophecy, and one effect of reading her journals is an unnerving sense that she wrote her life before it happened to her. A simple example is the irony of this early entry, whose concern about abandonment is written into her very early poem *"Ballade Banale:"*

> I have alot [*sic*] to give someone, someday. But I must not be too Christian. I can only end up with one, and I must leave many lonely by the wayside so that is all for now. Perhaps someday someone will leave me by the wayside. And that will be poetic justice. (JPl: 23)

The sense of two voices—in this case the exuberantly youthful and the precociously prescient—is announced in the writing right from the beginning. But, in these early texts writing is an activity that is undertaken as part of the performance of being a writer. She is good enough to be published and to win prizes and competitions, but at this stage a great deal is being projected on to the fantasy of being a writer. Writing for Plath will always involve an element of masquerade, but at this stage the disguises are still tried on hurriedly and as a surrogate, a substitute for a voice: she does not have control of them. So that, when, for example, the narrator of "Tongues of Stone" describes the disenchantment with her body that the institutionalized girl experiences, the disgust is relentless, and the Body a mere spectacle:

> She felt the subtle slow inevitable corruption of her flesh that yellowed and softened hour by hour. She imagined the waste piling up in her, swelling her full of poisons that show in the blank darkness of her eyes when she stared into the mirror, hating the dead face that greeted her, the mindless face with the purple scar on the left cheek that marked her like a scarlet letter.
>
> A small scab began to form at each corner of her mouth. She was sure that this was a sure sign of her coming dessication and that the scabs would never heal but spread over he body, that the backwaters of her mind would break out on her body in a slow, consuming leprosy. (JP: 270)

The passing reference to Hawthorne's Hester Prynne anchors the writing in Massachusetts. The story had been written as an exercise for her writing class tutor Alfred Kazin during her final year at Smith.

Appendix 2
Becoming a Writer, Becoming a Smith Girl

AFTER THE NINE YEARS IN WINTHROP, SYLVIA PLATH LIVED IN THREE other places in Massachusetts: Wellesley, Northampton, and Boston. During each of these phases Plath's journals and letters suggest that her sense of identity was shaped less by the land (or sea) and more by her ambition and success in the practice of writing. Thus, in moving inland, in moving away from the landscape she associated with her father and grandparents, she withdrew from the outer world of sea and nature to the inner one shaped by constructions of human behaviour offered by school, college and city. Encouraged by a sense of ambition and congenial models of human activity (the life of the famous writer) presented by her English studies in school and college, particularly by the possibilities opened up for her by her English teacher at Bradford Senior High School in Wellesley, she quickly identified with the role of writer-artist. This category became increasingly important to the construction of the identity that was important to Plath—the identity being that of "a writer" or "a poet."

This evidence of a shift towards introspection is not to exclude other factors that had a bearing on Plath's adolescence and for which plenty of evidence can be found in the early journals and letters. It is simply to claim that the self-conscious identification with the role of writer provided a sense of stable identity which these other factors (relationships with family, membership of Girl Scout and Church groups, and later, boyfriends and depression) do not. It is a matter of what appears to provide the greatest source of strength for her reflections on herself (which are frequent) in the journals and letters from her student years, most notably from 1950 onwards, as she leaves school and childhood behind. It is not her appearance that is central to this developing identity (though it is important), it is not her intelligence (which she takes for granted) and it is not her religious beliefs (she later wrote to her mother that she was "not really a Christian in the true sense of the word, but more of an ethical culturalist" (LH: 201). What brought her to Smith College was her success as a high school student who won a scholarship available to those who suffered economic hardship, and to support her case she had pro-

vided evidence of her writing ability. Writing is an activity that is legitimate for the artist woman. Her patron, Olive Higgins Prouty, was a model
of the successful writing woman. But, there are two related problems
with this choice of identity.

The first became more apparent later in her life, when she sought to
combine the role of mother and writer in a firm (or performative) rejection of the model of the sterile, childless woman—Emily Brontë, Emily
Dickinson, Virginia Woolf—or the lesbian woman of the kind that carries
out the shock treatment on the secretary in "Johnny Panic and the Bible
of Dreams" and puzzles Esther in *The Bell Jar.* This later experience of
writing with the new identity of a mother of young children is considered
in the later chapters; it is central to her politicization.

The other problem is that with so much invested in writing there is a
danger that the writer feels that any critical comments on the text is a
judgment on the person. The Plath voice in the journal exposes its
fragility and conflation of identities when it confesses to an anxiety that
people will not be interested in her as a person unless she is successful in
her writing. In notes written after a conversation with her psychoanalyst,
Ruth Beuscher, she records:

> I felt if I did not write nobody would accept me as a human being. Writing,
> then, was a substitute for myself: if you don't love me, love my writing and love
> me for my writing. (Journal, 27 December 1958, J: 280)

Plath expressed dislike for the social and political detachment that wedding herself to this identity involves. A solipsistic life is rewarding in some
ways, but it leads to solipsistic writing:

> If I did not have this time to be myself, to write here, to be alone, I would
> somehow, inexplicably, lose a part of my integrity. As it is, what I have written
> here so far is rather poor, rather unsatisfactory. It is the product of an unimag-
> inative girl preoccupied with herself and continually splashing about in the
> shallow waters of her own narrow psyche.
> (Student Journal, p. 168, MRBR)

And, there is a risk. She is afraid of failure, as she says in her June/July
crisis journal entry in 1953 ("Letter to an Over-grown, Over-pro-
tected,Scared, Spoiled Baby" [J: 81]). Yet, this voice is also desperate to
succeed—a need arising from the hugely competitive culture which had
not only formed Plath but which she found she could manage quite easily. The string of successful "A" grades and prizes was testimony to this,
but as she realized, it was like riding a tiger, and there was no possibility
of jumping off. The voice in the journals felt that it had to go on winning
prizes, otherwise her peers would say she was in decline.

The longing for success in prose narrative—in particular the novel—above all other forms of imaginative writing, including poetry remained with Plath throughout her life.[1] She was determined to have her stories published in *The Ladies Home Journal* and and the other magazines she termed "the slicks," and she took her career as a writer of prose fiction extremely seriously. The Mortimer Rare Book Room at Smith houses her copies of the Writers Year Books for 1952, 1954, and 1955, and her hardback copy of *The Writers Handbook* for 1956 has heavily underlined passages in the sections devoted to "Stories" and "Writing a Novel," but has no sentence at all marked in the section supplying advice on the writing of poetry. The essay "Writing a Novel" by Anne Hamilton seems to have been taken particularly seriously, with annotations confirming the advice to allow a year for the novel's completion and to write between 2,000 and 2,500 words a day.

Plath's determination to succeed in narrative prose may be related, if not traced, to an experience she records in the second half of her journal, where she describes the way that a group of companions at her school used to "run away giggling together when I started to tell them a story." This experience was not so much painful as confusing: "I did not understand. Bewildered, breathless, I would run after them. And then I learned that they had arranged to run away so that they wouldn't have to listen to my lengthy, dull rambling." (Student Journal, p. 323, MRBR).

The voice in the journal seems determined that people will stop and listen: only publication would ensure that such an aim had been realized.

When things were going well, the voice was ecstatic. In Boston, several years later, after she had spent two years at Cambridge, England and one teaching at Smith College, she noted that she had hosts of ideas for prose: "I feel that this month I have conquered my Panic Bird. I am a calm, happy and serene writer" (Journal, 31 May 1959, J: 305).

The process of writing is likened to sexual activity, the aftermath of which is a pleasing tiredness:

> I feel in a rug-braiding mood today. Very sleepy, as after a good love-making after all that writing this week. My poems are far in the background now. It is a very healthy antidote, this prose, to the poem's intense limitations. (Journal, 31 May 1959, J: 307)

Plath's marriage to Hughes meant that there was an even greater concentration on writing. For the voice in the Northampton and Boston journals, a commitment to marriage—the idea, the institution, the permanence of marriage—is seen as a stabilizing act. The early student voice was able to imagine having relationships with several men at the same time—frequently the men in her life overlap. But, this playing the field obviously ends when she marries. In the dominant suburban American culture marriage is constructed as a final achievement for women. The voice of the journals dating from the Cambridge and Smith College teaching years invests an enormous amount in this marriage, which like the model New England marriage is mapped out to last for a lifetime. A summit has been reached. With so much hinging on the commitment she has made, a new set of anxieties appear.

Appendix 3
Disturbance, Panic, and the Fear
of World Politics

EVEN THOUGH THE PREDOMINANT THEMES OF THE PRE-MARRIAGE, 1950–53 student journal are writing, personal career plans and goals, anxieties about failure, and the satisfactory or unsatisfactory nature of the men currently in her life, the presence of the outer world and the undercurrent of fears about a military apocalypse is sometimes voiced, generally, however, world politics is presented as spectacle. Sometimes the two concerns overlap, so that the terror of failing as an individual is overshadowed by the possibility that war could extinguish us all:[1]

> They're really going to mash the world up this time, the damn fools. When I read that description of the victims of Nagasaki I was sick: "And we saw what first looked like lizards crawling up the hill, croaking. It got lighter and we could see that it was humans, their skin burned off, and their bodies broken where they had been thrown against something". Sounds like something out of a horror story. (Journal, Entry 51, pp. 84–86, MRBR) (JPI: 46)

This entry continues, railing against the futility of the spectacle of war.[2] Impatience and disgust with the leaders of nations is mingled with fear of extinction.

> Oh, America's young, strong. So is Russia. And how they can think of atom-bombing each other, I don't know. What will be left? War will come some day now, with all the hothead leaders and articles "What If *Women* are Drafted?" (Journal, Entry 51, p. 86, MRBR) (JPI: 46)

There is nothing unusual about sustained introspection and solipsism in the diaries of an intelligent student, though a strand of American culture has always believed that social activity is a healthy antidote to the unhealthy tendencies of too much intelligence and private thinking. In the student voice of Plath's journals there is an inevitable impatience with the possibility that others (men) can start a war which then invades and destroys her own life and plans. The voice acknowledges its own (unwitting) complicity through an uncritical subscription to the good life:

> When you come right down to it, I do believe in the freedom of the individual—but to kill off all the ones who could forge a strong nation? How foolish! Of what good-living and freedom without home, without family, without all that makes life? (JPI: 47)

And, in the periods of terror that are revealed towards the end of this student journal, as her first breakdown approaches in 1953, the voice's panic and sense of worthlessness finds desperate expression. It wishes to become the servant of some dark force, some tyranny, some masculine strength that seems to posses the power which is denied her and which could thus distribute it to her:

> Entry 154 November 3 God, if ever I have come close to wanting to commit suicide it is now. . . . I want to kill myself, to escape from responsibility, to crawl abjectly into the womb. I do not know who I am, where I am going—and I am the one who has to decide the answers to these hideous questions. . . . I want more than ever the stern, final, paternal directive. . . . I turn wearily to the totalitarian dictatorship where I am absolved of all personal responsibility and can sacrifice myself in a "splurge of altruism" on the altar of the cause with a capital "C". . . . I can begin to see the compulsion for admitting original sin, for adoring Hitler, for taking opium. . . . Why did Virginia Woolf commit suicide? Or Sara Teasdale—or the other brilliant women—neurotic? Was their writing sublimation (oh, horrible word) of deep, basic desires? (J: 58–59)

The depression that runs through the voice of the entries for November and January, when the former "golden boy" Dick, becomes a kissing mouth poisonous with TB germs, and when she breaks her leg skiing and is confined to her room, gives rise to written expressions of despair. The expressed wish of the "I" to throw itself at the mercy of a dictator (anticipating the irony of the 1962 line from "Daddy," "Every woman adores a Fascist") may be no more "literal" than the fantasies of rape which several times appear in this journal. They are imaginative projections of a deflated identity, and indicative of the feeling of worthlessness and depression. They are political metaphors for something still seeking to give itself shape, and at this stage in Plath's life she largely regards politics itself as instrumental, as a set of ideas which can be used to develop her own writing and which can provide exercises in thought and new metaphor. This is something she may have picked up from W. H. Auden. On 27 April 1953, in one of her later journal entries she describes listening to Auden, who was in residence at Smith. He spoke about the *The*

Tempest, and the way that the split between Ariel (the creative and imaginative force) and Caliban (the natural and bestial one) could be seen as life projections. The position of Miranda—pestered by Caliban, ruled by her father, alert to the power of the enslaved spirit Ariel but exiled on a Brave New World island—was a reminder of her own constrained position as a woman, whose ambition to work the magic of Prospero would cause others to represent her as other, as neurotic, as witch.

Appendix 4
The Bell Jar Manuscripts

SYLVIA PLATH'S USE AND RE-USE OF THESE MANUSCRIPT PAGES RAISES some provocative questions, the first of which is: which version of *The Bell Jar* appears on the reverse of these poems? It is not a carbon copy of the final manuscript because (a) the page numbers do not match and (b) experts in the Rare Book room say that some of the pages have the appearance of a top copy.

It does, however, deal with events that are missing from the end of Draft B. We may wonder, then, if the pink paper ran out at some point and that Plath had to use white typing paper. This is possible but the pagination does not match. Drafts A and B seem to be written in groups of pages roughly corresponding to chapters; at the beginning of a new chapter Plath would start a new cycle of numbers. When she has reached twenty or thirty, the numbers begin again at 1, and so it continues. She is not numbering all the pages sequentially, as she clearly was in the final manuscript and as she was in this white typing-paper version, where the text has reached numbers in the 200s. The last page of final manuscript is numbered 264 and the wording is identical to the page numbered 289 in this white-typing paper version. In between the two versions, material adding up to twenty-five typed pages has been cut.

We, therefore, seem to have evidence of a version of *The Bell Jar* that comes between Draft B and the final manuscript. It incorporates the name Victoria Lucas, unaltered. This could have been the top copy of the version sent off to the American publishers Knopf and Harper and Row, but it seems unlikely for this was rejected much later, in late December 1962 by Knopf, and by Harper and Row in January 1963. Even if Plath had sent off the carbon version to America, she would surely have held on to the original without recycling it. In any case, this typescript has handwritten corrections (by Plath) on it, and she never sent off manuscripts in this condition to publishers.

These separate manuscript states invited three major tasks. The first was to compare the text of these "new" pages of Typescript C—the unclassified ones that appear on the reverse of the Smith drafts "New Year on Dartmoor" and "Waking in Winter"—with the final manuscript to see if there were any differences in wording, as preliminary examination suggested there to be. Sequences have indeed been cut from these new pages, which detail incidents in the psychiatric hospital including the breaking of the thermometer and the arrival of Jane/Joan. The second task was to subject the pages that appear on the back of the drafts of "Fever" to a similar scrutiny.

The third task was to find out more about the fate of the manuscript(s) sent to Alfred Knopf and Harper and Row. There is something puzzling about the two rejections, and the short space of time between them.

DIFFERENCES BETWEEN THE "NEW" PAGES OF TYPESCRIPT C AND THE FINAL MANUSCRIPT

There are few enough pages on the reverse of these two poems to consider each one in turn, and in the following discussion I will use the abbreviations TC (for Typescript C) and FM (for Final Manuscript).

The page numbered 197 in TC corresponds to 196 in FM, except that the top half of TC includes an exchange between the doctor and Victoria in which Victoria says "I feel so cut off" and the doctor replies that it is not she but her father's leg that has been cut off. This is rather labored and does not work as a joke, and was rightly removed. The allusion to her father's amputation, however, is one of many found in Plath's work—though more usually in her poetry.

200 (TC) starts in the same way as 199 (FM) but a paragraph has been cut from the bottom of the page. 201 (TC) is the same text as 199/200 in FM, which incorporates changes made on TC in ink by Plath. For example, when the nurse discovers that Victoria has broken the thermometer and there are little bits of mercury all over the floor her reaction "What have you done" is altered to "Look what you've done."

203 (TC) is the same as 202 (FM) except that a sequence has been removed describing Victoria's response to a blue bound copy of the Bible that "a Christian Scientist lady I worked for one summer" had sent to her:

[A]ll I could read in the Bible was about Lazarus of Bethany.
I thought bringing Lazarus back must have been the worst thing Jesus did. Lazarus would be cold and white as a pressed root after those four days in the cave. What could the world be to him, risen. A senseless hell of smiles, a furnace of sun consuming petal and leaf. . . .

Lazarus would be sick with the death-stench of his own four-day dead limbs.

He would beg to return to the cave and be left in peace.

(MRBR)

Perhaps at this stage in her career—and, in this context—Plath was unhappy about making so explicit the parallels between Victoria's "death" in the basement and her "resurrection."

204 (TC) has text which is spread across 202 and 203 in the FM, while 205 (TC) picks up the text on 203, both pages then ending in the same place. Finally 207 (TC) is 205 (FM), plus half a page describing the meeting between what is presumably the Joan/Jane character and Victoria. A stocky, freckled girl appears at Victoria's door and asks "Would you like to go for a walk?" This scene has not survived in this form in the published version of *The Bell Jar.*

From this evidence, it is clear that in the process of rewriting Plath was more likely to cut than add passages, as the original length of the entire manuscript had already shown. There are several passages in these "new" pages of Typescript C which do not appear in the final manuscript—and because we do not have the equivalent passages in the earlier drafts, they are the only extant evidence of these deleted sections.

The differences between the "Fever" *Bell Jar* pages and the FM are revealing. The page numbered 186, for example, includes a comment on Catholicism's attitude to suicide, not included in the FM. Altogether eleven lines have been cut, lines in which the narrator says that in surviving a suicide attempt in these circumstances she has entered the hell that Catholics would have predicted for her.

196 has half a page describing a new doctor, a character who has been cut from the FM. Presumably, later pages, either missing or destroyed, describe the encounter with this doctor. 268, 269, 270, and 271 deal with events surrounding the narrator's disastrous sexual encounter with Irwin. Cuts include some brief comments about the meeting for coffee in a Boston cafe, including references to Radcliffe girls and the revelation that following the electric shock treatment the narrator finds she can now read again. On 270 Irwin is described as having a "studious, monkish face" while in the final version the word "studious" has been removed. A paragraph on 271 describing the farce of the dating game has also been cut. Some indication of the degree of cutting that has taken place can be gauged by the fact that 268 in TC corresponds to 244 in the FM.

279 contains a paragraph describing the search for Jane/Joan around the Boston area. 280 consists of only five lines, all of which survive in the later version and the page ends with a three quarter page break follow-

ing Doctor Quinn's announcement that Jane's body has been found and that she had hanged herself. In the end the two manuscripts are reunited, 289 corresponds to the last page of the FM, 264

TYPESCRIPT SENT TO THE UNITED STATES

This is not in the possession of either of the main two collections of Plath Papers—Smith and the Lilly Library—and may either be in the possession of the Plath Estate or destroyed. It is unlikely that Knopf/Harpers and Row still keep a copy. It is possible that it was an identical second carbon copy of the manuscript sent out to Heinemann, or even the second carbon copy itself. It seems unlikely that Plath would have sent out the only two finished copies of the manuscript, however, especially in carbon form.

What is interesting about the two rejection letters is that the one sent from Knopf is addressed to Sylvia Plath, which is what we would expect, while the one from Harper and Row is addressed to "Mrs. Ted Hughes." This either suggests that it had been sent to Harper and Row much earlier than is usually supposed (in other words when Plath was still happy to use the name Hughes in late 1961 or early 1962—or that it was simply a device to retain some sense of anonymity, or difference in identity from the Plath who Knopf knew about from Heinemann. If there were two separate manuscripts sent to the United States, it would explain the otherwise suspiciously quick (but not impossible) turn-around of a single manuscript posted no earlier than the 28 December and read and rejected in America, some 18 days later.

Appendix 5
The Drafts of "Wuthering Heights"

At the seventh page of the Lilly Library copies of the drafts of "Wuthering Heights" (discussed in Chapter 6) there is still some way to go before the poem is complete. The eighth page is also typed, but much corrected. A stanza describing the discovery of a broken winged moor bird is cut, as are lines describing the village in the valley. A ninth page, identified by Sylvia Plath as 8a, reworks the final stanza, and shows Plath eager to say something about the nature of the moor-grass, the bowing, acquiescent character of this grass. This is temporarily put aside—the image of the humble character of grass is reappears in the October (1961) poem "The Moon and the Yew Tree"—on the next page which revises and revises the final stanza, with the opening that will survive all further alteratons: "The sky leans on me . . ." (LL).

The process continues on the pages numbered 10, 11, 12, 13, and 14 with the same stanza being reworked and reworked. On 12, the image of the acquiescent grass returns, and Plath experiments with and then rejects line after line about the grass and its bowing, millions of filaments. The page numbered 14 is actually an unfinished version of "The Surgeon at 2 a.m.," and has six lines of the poem about the moors she is working on, all about the grass, and all to be rejected. The matter is only resolved by having two whole pages (14a and 14b) devoted to lines about the grass. 14a has the title: "The bald truth about: Grass at Wuthering Heights" and has 46 lines of free verse, including lines which explore the grass's amnesia, an idea that informs a number of poems of this period. 14b is simply called "The Grass" and has 43 lines, many of them repeated words and ideas from 14a, including the references to amnesia. The page numbered 15 is typed and has one final reworking of the last stanza, the poem is now ready to be typed out in its finished form, and sent away for publication.

What is clear from all this is that a poem rooted in a visit made five years earlier has taken on a life of its own, but that life is given character by the proximity of the moors, memory and the loss of memory, and the contemporary world brought into collision with the past of literary history. The two visits made by Plath to Top Withens are triggers for a much more abstract, unfamiliar discourse on place and memory.

Hughes's own poem "Wuthering Heights" does not mention the second visit at all. They start from Haworth, and during the course of the poem Hughes weaves in a comparison between Sylvia and Emily, emphasing difference: the Plath who climbs a tree to have her picture taken is not like the serious Emily, the Emily Brontë (who may also be partly constructed from a memory of Plath?) who appeared in Hughes's poem "Emily Brontë" published in 1979 (Hughes 1979: 96). The intermingling of America and England informs Hughes's writing about this place—in another poem published in 1979, "Top Withens" the speaker talks of American news, of dreams and the hope of the past. Yet, the 1950s visits were not without their own disturbances. In a piece of writing that appeared in an American angling magazine not long before he died, Hughes recalled the journey to Top Withens he made with Plath and an incident that is not recorded in her journals:

> I was taking her over the moor, to visit the old farmhouse said to be the original of Wuthering Heights.
>
> Halfway across this moor, a grouse got up out of the heather. It was obviously wounded or sick and just fluttered away and collapsed again. I caught it. My instinct was that if it were sick or wounded, you just killed it. So I killed it. And she went berserk. "How could you do it?" It turned out that grouse were part of her mythology.
>
> When she was a little girl in Massachusetts, she'd been on some bus and the fellow sitting beside her had begun to tell a story of "the heather bird's eyebrows." She had treasured this vision of the heather bird's eyebrows. She'd no idea what a heather bird was. From the moment of first meeting her, I used to hear about this wonderful bird. Of course it turned out to be a damned red grouse. And she'd realised this by the time this event happened in Yorkshire.
>
> So I'd not only killed this helpless thing in front of her, I'd killed the legendary bird.[1]

The incident may not have been recorded in the journals, but it is possible that this is the "broken-winged moor bird" that appears in one of the drafts of Plath's poem "Wuthering Heights." If so, the thought was excised. Plath at this stage in her career acts as a censor of her own writing, removing that which is inadmissible in her own work.

Appendix 6
The Politics of Abjection and Desire

In trying to locate Sylvia Plath's later writing at the intersection of the political and the psychoanalytical, it can helpful to draw on Helga Geyer-Ryan's discussion of "Fables of Desire".[1] Geyer Ryan starts by considering the way that for Levinas the unbridgeable distance of the Other (to use Lacan's term to describe the existence of a world whose discovery constitutes for the infant both loss and the beginning of consciousness) is the origin of desire. Concepts of desire, transcendence and infinity emerge from what Geyer-Ryan, drawing on Levinas's reading of absence, calls the "existential abyss." The simultaneous appeal and impenetrability of the Other is expressed, for Levinas in the face, an observation that throws light on Plath's fascination with the bald madonnas, the Munich Mannequins, and those sisters with their featureless, stitched faces, the Disquieting Muses.

Geyer-Ryan argues that Plath's writing differs from more recent attempts by women to explore what is meant by a feminine aesthetic through a concern with a feminine sexuality, or more specifically a lesbian femine sexuality (she cites Verena Stefan's *Shedding* and Monique Wittig's *Les Guerilleres*): "The work of Sylvia Plath, by contrast, still bears witness to an agonizing struggle between the compulsive claims of reproductive sexuality and a profound desire to break free of them."[2]

One strand of Geyer-Ryan's argument about the ethics of art and fables of desire takes us into the familiar—though no less important for that reason—territory of the silencing of women by men. In "The Castration of Cassandra," Geyer-Ryan discusses the way that the double silencing of Cassandra and Philomela is written into Greek narrative. Cassandra, already a prisoner, is a prophet whose prophecies are ignored because they are not understood. She is later put to death, killed by Clytemenestra, precisely because Cassandra has been brought back as her husband's Agamemnon's concubine and a symbol of his male power.

Earlier in the story of the conquest of Troy Cassandra is raped by Ajax in the goddess Athene's shrine. Her body is, thus, appropriated, mutilated, subjected, ignored, and then destroyed. As if this were not enough, Geyer-Ryan points to the satirical vase depictions of the narrative, in

245

which it is Ajax, and not Cassandra, who is clinging to Athene's statue for protection. In this male fantasy, it is argued, Cassandra is the predator and Ajax the victim. This is a triple silencing, through parody.

Less complex, but equally terrible, are the silencing of Philomela (tongue cut out to silence her after she has been raped by Tereus, King of Thrace), Echo (silenced by the jealous goddess of patriarchal marriage, Hera—or in another version, torn to pieces by shepherds on Pan's instructions after Echo has resisted his advances) and Xanthippe, who is again silenced through ridicule, she being the "shrill" shrewish wife of the philospher, Socrates.

Geyer-Ryan characterizes these silencing as the castration of women. By denying women their voice, they are denied what is seen as their source of power. In ridiculing their voice—and more recent examples would be The Wife of Bath, Shakespeare's tamed "Shrew" and the infantalization of women in the Victorian period (in 1852 Florence Nightingale attacked this misogynistic practice in her *Cassandra*)—women have no voice.

The pathologizing and even the gendering of Plath's voice in her writing can be seen as part of the process of controlling the voice. The troubling voice of "Daddy," with its childish refrain, is perhaps an attempt to retrieve that voice through a parody of the parody.

A second strand of Geyer-Ryan's argument takes the reader towards a consideration of Abjection, particularly with reference to Walter Benjamin. Benjamin's interest in Goethe's Faust is cited as an example of Benjamin's desire to "salvage images." Faust descends to the Mothers to retrieve the unsullied image of Helen. As Geyer-Ryan describes it: "Faust must immerse himself in the pre-symbolic real of the imaginary in the space of the pre-Oedipal mother with its menacing destruction of the 'I.' The horror of this is its emptiness, which is beyond all experience and consequently all identification."[3]

This emptiness represents both an end and a beginning. There is no subject-object division, so it is the end of unity, but it is also the beginning of differentiation and language. The themes of Plath's own writing are seductively resonant of Geyer-Ryan's description of this process:

> The splitting towards difference is brought about through the child's identification with the father of his "personal prehistory," a Third Party towards which the interest of the mother is diverted, away from the child.
>
> By turning away from its mother, the child rejects her and she becomes abject, In this first detachment of mother and child, a position is created for the later formation of the subject-object relationship, but the traumatic and fundamental loss of the first object is also introduced. The ambivalent nature of the archaic relationship with the mother again becomes apparent as an ambiguity, in the response of revulsion. Revulsion is a mixture of fear of losing one's

identity and a fascination with this loss, where the pleasure of fusion, the pleasure derived from the abandonment of identity in the undifferentiated, becomes discoverable.[4]

The representation of the mother in *The Bell Jar,* and in "Medusa," seems to endorse this kind of reading Plath's discovery of feelings of abandonment are targetted at nations (apparent rejection of England and America), institutions and reckless war-gaming nuclear powers. The actual mother is only a part of this whole process.

Another of the features of Abjection that is relevant to a consideration of Plath's writing is the inability to create clear boundaries between that which is rejected and thrown away and that which a culture keeps to define its own status. These limits and boundaries are transgressed through writing and creativity, in which the "pure" mingles with the "impure." Benjamin sought to escape the "prison-house of language" by retrieving and restoring outcast images, thus violating taboos. The fact that Benjamin, too, committed suicide (a significant taboo) and the fact that the retrieval of the taboo images of female bodily processes (menstruation, childbirth, masturbation) are inscribed in the "confessional" poetry of Anne Sexton, seems to be leading towards biographical readings of Plath's writing again, and this is something I wish to resist. Yet, the return of the repressed is a powerful trope. What Geyer-Ryan calls the "banishment of corporeality from literary communication" means the effective castration of the body, and more precisely the mother's body:

> As a functional image, woman is always killed off anyway, since the patriarchal gaze turns the woman's body into an object, rendering it silent. Memory is linked to representations of the body and of objects, and consequently to images. The resurrection of the maternal body from pre-Oedipal space would in any case always be the presentation of a corpse lying concealed beneath the appearance.[5]

Psychoanalytic theory meets with politics through the specificity of geopolitics and place: individual experience is culturally and historically determined. Electro Convulsive Therapy was not used in America in 1900, nor is it used routinely in 2000. It was a standard form of treatment in 1950, however. It, and the huge psychiatric hospitals in which it took place, were cultural expressions of the medical ideology of their time. Equally, the small Wellesley house in which Plath lived as a teenager and young woman and the "Houses" at Smith were models of what was thought to be the ideal "home." Plath sought to reconstruct her own version of that ideal and discovered it to be based on a myth. Geyer-Ryan is always eager to locate her discussion among the fables of desire in art, and this frequently leads her back to the narratives of Classical myth, the significance of place and *nostalgia*. In her discussion of *The Iliad* and *The Odyssey* she argues convincingly that the former has received more critical attention because women are either absent, or if they are present they are powerless, and subject to conventional mutilation or deification for their beauty. Men are killing machines, warriors: even the love story element, as Simone Weil has pointed out, is a "love story between men" and its "true hero . . . is force."[6] *The Odyssey*, on the other hand, has women in control, women exercising power, while Odysseus is constantly thwarted in his attempts to return home. The ending of *The Odyssey* may superficially seem to suggest a happy conclusion as Odysseus climbs into bed with Penelope, but the prospect of a fight with the families of the slain suitors, and the shadow of Teiresias's prophecy that he will have to leave Ithaca again, undercuts the sense of a happy return:

> Homecoming—justs like repetition is impossible. for time and the passing of time continue to be written back into the very point of departure, with the result that there is no longer any origin to come back to.[7]

Or, as Plath says in her anthem of forgetting "Amnesiac:"

> O sister, mother, wife,
> Sweet Lethe is my life.
> I am never, never,never coming home!

                                                    (CP: 233)

Appendix 7
Final Reading

There is no reason why I should not last quite a long time yet. I seem to have an uncommon reserve of energy. To keep my mind firm, that is the essential thing, to fix it firmly in my reasonable hopes, and lull it there. Encourage it. Mesmerise it slightly with a sort of continuous prayer. Because when my mind is firm, my energy is firm. And that is the main thing here—energy.
> —from "Snow," written and read by Ted Hughes
> on the BBC Third Programme, 8 January 1963

As I HOPE I HAVE MADE CLEAR, ALL MY READINGS OF SYLVIA PLATH'S 1962 poems took place alongside a close reading of contemporary newspaper, principally copies of the London *Observer*, which Plath read and to which she contributed. Having arrived in London on the 12 December, she made a note in her week-to-week diary to order both *The Observer* and *The Radio Times* on the 16 December, and Trevor Thomas, the man who lived in the flat below Plath at, 23 Fitzroy Road, has described the way that on a Sunday not long before Plath's death (it would have been 27 January) she showed him a copy of a page of the *The Observer* with a review of *The Bell Jar*, followed by a page on which a poem by Ted Hughes appeared. Ironically, this poem is "Full Moon and Little Frieda."

At the end of a long day trawling through the September and October copies of *The Observer*, I thought that it was worth glancing at the next reel of microfilm, which covered the Spring of 1963. There were the three poems by Ted Hughes, dominating an Arts page on 4 January. There, indeed, was Plath's poem "Winter Trees," which was to be praised by Al Alvarez (the editor of the poetry column who was a friend and supportive reader of her poetry) in the tribute he wrote immediately following her death. Plath's poem appears in the "Weekend Review" section on 13 January, one of five. The poem immediately to the left of it is "Separation" by David Wevill. That cannot have failed to have an impact on Plath's reading of her own poem: Assia Wevill had left her husband to begin a relationship with Hughes.

As we have seen, there was more painful reading on 27 January, when the very positive review by Anthony Burgess of *The Bell Jar* by "Victoria Lucas" was almost certainly eclipsed by the bitter irony of an adjacent affectionate poem about a daughter by a father who had seemingly abandoned her.

Yet, what was puzzling to me, as a reader who had seen the letters that Plath was receiving during January and early February, was the evidence that Plath's writing career was clearly on the up. A letter from Tony Dyson, one of the editors of *Critical Quartlerly*, and dated 8 January, asks Plath for another poem and invites her to dinner at the magazine's expense. A letter dated 12 January from Morocco (which we presume was read) announces that her friend, Ruth Fainlight, is coming to London, and is eager for a copy of Plath's second novel. A letter from Bangor invites Plath to contribute to an Arts Festival, while best of all (again, assuming it was read), a letter dated four days later, 8 February, from Leonie Cohen at the BBC, accepts the script for the prose reminiscence "Ocean 1212W" and asks when Plath can come in to record it. There was one big professional blow, in the form of a letter dated 16 January from Harper and Row in the United States, rejecting *The Bell Jar* for publication there. If one works on the theory that Plath was finding the material and emotional conditions of life in England intolerable, but would only return to the United States if her reputation as a writer was firmly established, then this would have come as a great disappointment. But, this remains at the level of speculation. It is quite possible that a letter written in America on 16 January still had not been delivered to Plath one month later.

A smaller professional blow was John Richardson's letter of 7 February. Richardson was Chair of the Library and Arts Committee at Camden Library and the contact for the 1963 St. Pancras Arts Festival. Plath had clearly sent him a poem—which one he is unable to recall—and he had written to say that he would pass it to the Spike Milligan group, or to the Highgate Poetry group. This refers to two festival events—a jazz and poetry evening with readings from Spike Milligan, Dannie Abse, Laurie Lee and others on Saturday 3 March, and an event called "Poetry in St. Pancras, Yesterday and Today" on the 21 March at Hamilton House. This latter event, organised by the Highgate Poetry Circle, was introduced by Huw Weldon, and included David Wevill as one of the advertised readers. Ironically, neither Milligan nor Wevill actually appeared at these events, according to the Library Report. The point about Richardson's response, a polite rejection, is that it suggested that Plath remained a relatively unrecognized poet in February 1962, despite her publication history. Friends of Plath have argued that she found it difficult to enter these circles now that she was no longer part of the clique.

I then looked at *The Observer* for the final two Sundays of Plath's life. There is no writing by either Plath, or Hughes in either edition. However, there is an article by Dr. Spock on 10 February that has a particular poignancy and relevance for anyone who is familiar with Plath's poems, letters and earlier journals. We know that much of Plath's writing explores the meaning and consequence of having a missing father. Her poems, such as "Colossus," "Full Fathom Five," "Electra on the Azalea Path," her journals and parts of *The Bell Jar* reveal her attempts to come to terms with this, and how her suicide attempt was an attempt to get back to him. She felt keenly not only that the desertion by Hughes meant that was without a husband, but that her children were without a father, would grow up as she had grown up with the danger that she would turn into her mother. On 26 September she had written the poem "For a Fatherless Son," a poem which in many ways launches the "Ariel" sequence.

The Spock article is called "The fatherless family" and is the third in a series. The first dealt with the problem of couples arguing, and the second considered the problem of divorce. In "The fatherless family" Spock's intention is to be reassuring, but statements such as "We know that a child wants both a father and a mother," "[A] human being is a creature who *must* have a father and a mother," and "It's obvious that when a mother has no husband it won't be as easy to keep her relationship without her son as ordinary as it would otherwise be" seem likely to have the opposite effect. In saying categorically that "[t]here is every evidence that a girl needs a father as much as a boy does" Spock seems unwittingly determined to unsettle someone in Plath's position. We know that Plath went out and bought Spock when she gave birth to her first child, and thought his advice worth considering when she had her second. A note in her calendar for 6 May 1962 says "Read Spock" and in the review of *Dr. Spock Talks with Mothers* published in the *New Statesman* on 18 May she writes:

> Dr. Spock, of course, is by now apocalyptic; he makes splendid sense. In case of crisis, minor and major, his fine, wise voice (made immediately accessible by a convenient index) is both sedative and salubrious. This is a complementary volume to his *Baby and Child Care* and covers general health, a child's position in the family, discipline, behaviour problems, attachments and anxieties—and more. And admirable aid to weathering the horrors and astonishments of parenthood. (From "Oblongs" Plath 1962)

How numbing it may have been to read, therefore, his recommendation that the mother "keeps alive the memory of the boy's father, and respects him as the boy's father." For in her exorcism of the absent father she had demonized this figure, not only in letters but in poems that had been recorded for the BBC and submitted for publication. This article could be taken by Plath to mean that the very works that she knew were going to make her reputation were going to do damage to her children.

A number of qualifications act as a brake on this kind of conjecture, however. Although it is likely that Plath read the article, we cannot be certain that she did. She had been staying with friends over the weekend and returned on the Sunday. The newspaper may not have been there in her flat when she returned, or if it was she may have ignored it. Even if the article was read, we cannot know its effect. It may have contributed to the decision to take her own life, but her own immediat experience of marital breakdown, the bitterly cold weather, the power cuts and water failures which made the physical business of living and looking after two small children extremely hard—all of these must have been contributory factors.[1] We just do not know. But, this article, whether it was read or not, provides in Richard Larschan's words, a further "cultural" index to the complexity of the discourses that surround Plath writing in England.

Appendix 8
Supporting Evidence

From the Plath MSS in the Lilly Library
Manuscript Department, University of Indiana
at Bloomington, From the Ted Hughes Papers in the
Special Collections, Robert W. Woodruff Library
at Emory University, Atlanta, Georgia,
and from other published material.

1. In a letter to Aurelia Plath dated 20 October 1960, in a section not included in *Letters Home*, Plath urges her mother to vote for Kennedy as he does not exhibit what Plath sees as the complacent stupidity of the uncritical attitude towards America of Eisenhower and Nixon. In an unpublished section of a letter written to her mother on 7 December 1961, Plath argues that the American Legion, the Boy Scouts of America and other "ghastly" anti-communist organizations should be forced to sit down and watch films every Sunday showing the victims of Hiroshima, and that the generals should be forced to live with a victim of an atomic bomb explosion (Plath MSS II, Correspondence 1961–1976, Lilly Library).

2. In chapter 5 I discuss the importance of radio programs, particularly those broadcast by the BBC in England. In a letter to Aurelia Plath dated 31 January 1962 Plath tells her mother that she and Hughes have just bought a new VHF radio for the three British broadcasting frequencies, and that it will replace their old, inadequate wireless (Ibid.).

3. In a section from a letter to her mother dated 25 October 1962, omitted from *Letters Home*, Plath accuses her mother of shying away from the hardest things, and cites Hiroshima, the Inquisition and Belsen (though not the Missile Crisis) as examples (Ibid.). In an important recent article Susan Gubar has defended Plath from the charge of exploitation, larceny, and sensationalism in her use of Holocaust imagery in the poetry. See Susan Gubar: "Prosopopoeia and Holocaust Poetry in

English: Sylvia Plath and her Contemporaries" in *The Yale Journal of Criticism* 14.1 2001 191–215.

4. In Chapter 9 I refer to the correspondence between Plath and Father Michael, the priest at Oxford with whom she exchanged letters on the subject of poetry and religion in late 1962 and early 1963. These letters were published as an Appendix in Toni Salvidar's *Sylvia Plath: Contesting the Fictive Self* New York Peter Lang 1992 pp 201–06. In one of these letters, dated 21 November, 1962, Plath writes: "I am myself, ironically, an atheist. And like a certain sort of atheist, my poems are God obsessed, priest obsessed. Full of Marys, Christs and and nuns. Theology and philosophy fascinate me, and my next book will have a long bit about a priest in a cassock." (See Salvidar, p. 203). I think it is reasonable to read such comments as evidence of a shift towards a sceptical reading of religion, which is why I am not persuaded that Plath should be regarded as a mystical writer and other-wordly, a view encouraged by Hughes's later comparison of Plath with Emily Dickinson.

5. In chapter 8 I refer to Plath's poem "Poppies in October" suggesting that it is unusual, though not impossible, for poppies to flower that late in the year. A letter to Aurelia Plath, written on 25 October has a section not included in *Letters Home* in which Plath describes the late poppies and cornflowers that she currently has on her desk. Her awareness of the wearing of poppies on Remembrance Day is shown by the article she wrote at Cambridge on this subject.

6. In chapter 2 I discuss the apparently unfinished novel started at Cambridge. The changing name of the hero (Gerald/Ian in "Venus in the Seventh," Leonard in the notes for "Falcon Yard" suggest the frequent revisions Plath made to this material. The additional pages at Emory relating to "Falcon Yard" are as follows:

a) Three pages of notes, listing names of characters, 'real people', a character notebook (which, next to the name of the Pan-like hero Leonard, wonders how Pan can be drawn into a world of nappies and toast) and under the heading 'Peregrine" a set of notes 'On God'. On this last page the writer poses the problem of how the fallible man can be accepted as divine. The speaker sees herself as Godmaker, and likens herself also to the Lamia, the Medusa and the Corn Mother, both the maker and destroyer of life. (Hughes MSS 644 Series 3 Sylvia Plath Subseries 3-2)

b) Six pages with the chapter heading "Venus in the Seventh." These are later than the page at Smith College, which is numbered 25 and describes Winthrop and Jess's journey to Munich. The pages at Emory are numbered 35, 43, 64, 65, 73, and 76 and detail Jess and Winthrop's experiences in Venice, the train journey to Rome the final parting with Winthrop as Jess flies back to London, dreaming of Gerald, and her arrival at Ian's Rugby Street flat. (Hughes MSS 644 Subseries 3.2)

c)   One page with the title "Hill of Leopards" (Hughes MS 644 Series 3 subseries 3.2). This was the original title of "Falcon Yard" but may subsequently have been relegated to a chapter heading, and part of the sequence which includes "Venus in the Seventh." Like "Venus in the Seventh," its main character is called Jess, and the hero is called Ian. This page has a Cambridge setting, and its reference to a character called Luke who lives near a fish and chip shop links it to the Smith-held pages describing unnamed characters visiting a fish and chip shop. The two characters in the Emory-held page are Jess and Ian. Jess has a brown scar on her cheek.

7. There are may other unpublished prose fragments at Emory and Lilly that could have been fed into "Falcon Yard," such as a description of a character on a runaway horse, the long description of "The Matisse Chapel" (drawn to my attention by Kathleen Connor) based on the visit to Venice made by Plath and Sassoon, and the extraordinary page with the title "The Mummy." But these pages do not have characters with "Falcon Yard" names, and in their existing form are more likely to be fragments of unpublished short stories either preceding or post-dating the Cambridge novel.

8. There are several additional discarded pages from the typed version of *The Bell* Jar, apart from those held at Smith College and discussed in chapter 4. At Lilly the Plath mss contain the following numbered pages: 136, 236, 269, 269, 270, 271, 279. The Ted Hughes papers at Emory contain the following pages: 152, 166, 171, 207, 236, 237, 238, 239, 240, 241, 245, 242, 243, 244, 247, 249, 250. In some cases there is more than one page with the same number, as the same page was revised.

Notes

1. SYLVIA PLATH: WRITING, HISTORY, AND POLITICS

1. Allen Tate, "Narcissus as Narcissus" (1938); reprinted in *The Heath Anthology of American Literature Volume Two*, ed. Paul Lauter (New York Houghton Mifflin Company, 1998), 1882–90.

2. Peter Orr, ed., "Sylvia Plath," in *The Poet Speaks* (London: Routledge and Kegan Paul, 1967), 169.

3. Jacqueline Rose, *The Haunting of Sylvia Plath* (London: Virago Press, 1991). See chapter 4 of Rose's book.

4. Janice Markey, *A Journey into the Red Eye, The Poetry of Sylvia Plath—A Critique* (London: The Women's Press, 1993) 18–30.

5. Letter from Sylvia Plath to Anne Sexton, 21 August 1962 (Harry Ransom Centre, University of Texas at Austin).

6. Judith Kroll, *Chapters in a Mythology: The Poetry of Sylvia Plath* (Harper and Row: New York, 1976).

7. Mary Kurtz, "Plath's 'Ariel' and Tarot," *Centennial Review* 32 (Summer 1988): 286–95.

8. Timothy Materer, *Modernist Alchemy: Poetry and the Occult Ithaca* (Cornell University Press, 1995).

9. David Holbrook, *Sylvia Plath: Poetry and Existence* (London: The Athlone Press, 1976).

10. Rose, *The Haunting of Sylvia Plath*.

11. See, for example, essays by these writers and others in *New French Feminisms: An Anthology*, ed. with introductions by Elaine Marks and Isabelle de Courtivron (Brighton: The Harvester Press, 1981).

12. Sandra Gilbert and Susan Gubar *No Man's Land: the Place of the Woman Writer in the Twentieth Century, vol. 3, Letters from the Front* (London: Yale University Press, 1994).

13. Judith Butler, *Gender Trouble: Feminism and the Subversion of Identity* (London: Routledge, 1990).

14. Susan R. Van Dyne, *Revising Life: Sylvia Plath's Ariel poems* (University of North Carolina Press, 1993).

15. Christina Britzolakis *Sylvia Plath and the Theatre of Mourning* (Oxford: Clarendon Press 2000).

16. Hugh Kenner, "Sincerity Kills" in Gary Lane, ed., *Sylvia Plath: New Views on the Poetry* (London: The John Hopkins University Press, 1979), 33—44.

17. David Shapiro, "Sylvia Plath: drama and melodrama," in Gary Lane, ed., *Sylvia Plath: New Views on the Poetry* (London: The John Hopkins University Press, 1979), 45–53.

18. Gary Lane, ed., *Sylvia Plath: New Views on the Poetry* (London: The John Hopkins University Press, 1979).

19. J. D. O'Hara, "Plath's Comedy" in Gary Lane, ed., *Sylvia Plath: New Views on the Poetry* (London: The John Hopkins University Press, 1979), 74–96.

20. Beyond the Fringe was a satirical show performed by Peter Cook, Alan Bennett, Jonathan Miller and Dudley Moore in the early 1960s.

21. Gilbert and Gubar, *Letters from the Front,* 289–92.

22. Daniel Weissbort, "Sylvia Plath and Translation," in Anthony Rudolf, *Theme and Version/Plath and Ronsard* (London: The Menard Press, 1994) 1–16.

23. Gilbert and Gubar, *Letters from the Front,* 297.

24. Sylvia Lehrer, *The Dialectic of Art and Life: a portrait of Sylvia Plath as Woman and Poet* (Salzburg: Institut für Anglistik und Amerikanistik Universitatät Salzburg, 1985).

25. Renée R Curry, *White Women Writing White* (London: Greenwood Press, 2000), p. 124.

26. Lawrence Langer, *The Holocaust and the Literary Imagination* (New Haven and London: Yale University Press, 1975).

27. Jerome Mazzaro, "Sylvia Plath and the cycles of history" in *Sylvia Plath: New Views on her Poetry* edited by Gary Lane. (London: The John Hopkins University Press, 1979).

28. Margaret Dickie Uroff, *Sylvia Plath and Ted Hughes* Urbana, Ill.: University of Illinois, 1980).

29. Alan Sinfield, "Women Writing: Sylvia Plath" in *Literature, Politics and Culture in Postwar Britain* (Berkeley and Los Angeles: University of California Press, 1989).

30. Rose, *The Haunting of Sylvia Plath,* pp. 209–27.

31. Al Strangeways, *Sylvia Plath: The Shaping of Shadows* (Madison, N.J.: Fairleigh Dickinson University Press, 1998), p.

32. Tracy Brain, "Or shall I bring you the sounds of poisons?": *Silent Spring and Sylvia Plath* in *Writing the Environment: Ecocriticism and Literature* (London and New York: Zed Books, 1998), p 146–64.

33. Fredric Jameson, *The Political Unconscious: Narrative as a Socially Symbolic Act* (London: Routledge 1981 p17)
In this book Jameson argues strongly against readings which privliege a separateness of the individual:

> To imagine that, sheltered from the implacable influence of the social, there already exists a realm of freedom—whether it be that of microscopic experience of words in a text or the ecstasies and intensities of the various private religions—is only to strengthen the grip of Necessity over all such blind zones in which the individual subject seeks refuge, in pursuit of a purely individual, a merely psychological, project of salvation. The only effective liberation from such constraint begins with the recognition that there is nothing that is not social and historical . . . indeed, that everything is 'in the last analysis' political. (20)

34. Wendy S Hesford, "Reading Rape Stories: Material Rhetoric and the Trauma of Representation" in *College English* 62, no. 2 (November 1999) p. 192–229. Cited quotation is from p. 205.

35. Orr, *The Poet Speaks,* p. 171.

36. The advertisement proposes that wives, children, and relatives of Russian military officials live in towns next to missile-launching bases in the U.S. and in NATO countries, and that Americans and NATO officials would live in equivalent localities in the USSR.

37. "Operation Safety Catch: A Memorandum to the Governments of Nuclear Nations," *The Observer* 27 January 1963, p. 8. Eric Fromm (Fromm and Maccoby 1962) had

predicted just this kind of response in his citing of William Longer's assessment of the impact of the Black Death on towns which lost a third of their population in just a few months:

> It is perfectly clear that disaster and death threatening an entire community will bring on a mass emotional disturbance, based on a feeling of helpless exposure, disorientation and common guilt. (See Driver 1964: p 190)

38. "Follow the Leader" (Science and the Citizen column) in *Scientific American* September 1962, *Arms Control: Readings from Scientific American* ed. Frank Herbert (San Francisco: W. H. Freeman and Company 1973).

39. Barrie Axford, Gark K. Brown, Richard Huggins, Ben Rosamond and John Turner *Politics: An Introduction* (London and New York: 1997), p. 4.

40. Fredric Jameson, *The Political Unconscious* (London: Routledge, 1989) p. 9.

41. Catherine Belsey, "Literature, History, Politics," in *Literature and History* 9 (Spring 1983): 17–27.

42. Ibid, 19.

43. Stan Smith, *Inviolable Voice: History and Twentieth Century Poetry* (Dublin: Gill and Macmillan, 1982), p. 202.

44. Ibid., 3.

45. Gilbert and Gubar, *Letters from the Front.*

46. In his review of Jeffrey Cox's *Poetry and Politics in the Cockney School* (Cox 1999) John Bayley says that Cox shows how this can be done. In his book "he avoids the hunt-the slipper determination which has caused some zealous critics to see a covert political message lurking in every Romantic line." Yet the poetry cannot be uncoupled from political discourse. The very term "Cockney School" was coined by Blackwoods to discredit the republican beliefs of Leigh Hunt and his followers. Sylvia Plath's writing has not been disparaged in quite this way, but criticism has tended to uncouple it from debates about global politics. Poetry is a very special discourse, and it is a fine line between treating it as holy writ and treating it as just another language.

John Bayley ("Hottentot in Jackboots," in *The (London: Review of Books* [10 June 1999]: 10), like Ted Hughes, has always been keen to speak up on behalf of "the poetically unique imagination," as he does in this review when he says that:

> A poem that comes off, and takes off, does so in terms of its own language, irrespective of ideological impulses and overtones.

My view is that the first part of this sentence is right, but the second seems to create too simplistic a binary opposition. Preferable is Robert Alter's description of the potentially reductive effect of *bad* historicism:

> [T] he literary imagination at the height of its vigour is generally two moves ahead of us—let us say a knight's move, and a reinvention of the game. . . . ("A Readiness to be Surprised: The Recovery of Open-mindedness and the Revival of the Literary Imagination," Robert Alter's Presidential Address to the Association of Literary Scholars and Critics, reprinted in the *Times Literary Supplement*, 23 January 1998, 15).

Plath reinvents, but draws on her reading of world events in carrying out her "knight's move."

47. Linda Wagner-Martin, *Sylvia Plath: A Biography* (New York: Simon and Schuster, 1987), 212.

48. John Hersey, *Hiroshima* (London: Penguin Books, 1946). Hersey' account was originally published in *The New Yorker,* August 1946.

49. See, for example, biographies by Anne Stevenson (*Bitter Fame: A Life of Sylvia Plath* [London: Penguin Books, 1989]), Linda Wagner-Martin (*Sylvia Plath: A Biography* [New York: Simon and Schuster, 1987]), Paul Alexander (*Rough Magic* [New York: Viking Penguin, 1991]), and Ronald Hayman (*The Death and Life of Sylvia Plath* [London: Heinemann 1991]).

50. Kristin Thompson and David Bordwell, *Film History: an Introduction* [London: McGraw-Hill, Inc., 1994), 394.

51. Adam Bresnick, "They've been cheated," in the *Times Literary Supplement* (11 December 1998): 11.

52. Alan Trachtenberg, "The Social and Cultural Context," in *American Literature*, ed. Boris Ford (London: Penguin, 1991), 299.

53. "On Poetic Influence" *Three Contemporary Poets: Thom Gunn, Ted Hughes and RS Thomas* A Selection of Critical Essays, ed. by A. E. Dyson (London: Macmillan, 1990), 104.

54. John Lucas, *Modern Poetry from Hardy to Hughes* (London: BT Batsford Limited, 1986), 191.

55. Adrienne Rich, *The Fact of a Doorframe: Poems Selected and New 1950–1984* (London: WW Norton and Company, 1984), xv.

56. Stan Smith, *Inviolable Voice: History and Twentieth Century Poetry* (Dublin: Gill and Macmillan, 1982), 219.

57. A. Alvarez, "Sylvia Plath," in A. Alvarez, *Beyond all this Fiddle: Essays 1955–67* (London: Allen Lane The Penguin Press, 1968), 63. The essay originally appeared in 1963.

58. This New York Random House edition of *Thus Spake Zarathustra*, with the inscription "Christmas 1949 / To my Sylvia / Mother" is kept in the Mortimer Rare Book Room at Smith College.

59. Joan Riviere, "Womanliness as Masquerade" (1929) in Victor Burgin, James Dondald, and Cora Kaplan, Ed., *Formations of Fantasy* (London: Methuen, 1986), 38.

60. Judith Butler, *Gender Trouble: Feminism and the Subversion of Identity* (London: Routledge, 1990).

61. George Steiner, "Dying is an art," in *Language and Silence* (London: Faber and Faber, 1967, rpt. 1985), 324.

62. Michael Hulse, "Formal Bleeding" *Spectator* 14 (November 1981): 20.

63. Sylvia Plath wrote in her week-by-week calendar a reminder to herself to order *The Observer* and the *Radio Times* in London on Sunday 16 December 16. It is likely that both were read selectively: *The Observer* primarily for its arts supplement, the Radio Times for its radio listings, notes on which were sometimes transferred to the week-by-week calendar.

The Radio Times for this period shows what a complex cultural soup England was becoming at the end of her life, that is, in December 1962 and the beginning of 1963. Although Plath seems to have avoided television, *The Radio Times* featured illustrated articles on new television shows such as *That Was The Week That Was*, the much-featured police series *Z Cars* and a play with a guest appearance by a very young Bob Dylan.

In the context of the argument that Plath disguised, and did not ignore, contemporary global politics in her writing and that the Cold War crisis of 1962 is relevant to a reading of her work, it is interesting to note Antony Scaduto's description of Bob Dylan's song/poem "A Hard Rain's Gonna Fall":

> At almost precisely the same time the nation was enmeshed in the Cuban Missile Crisis and marched along the edge of nuclear war [Bob Dylan] went to a friend's apartment and wrote "A Hard Rain's Gonna Fall". . . . Never mentioning nuclear war or fallout, the evils of segregation or man's inhumanity to his own kind, but

forcing the listener to conjure such terrors out of his own emotions. (Scaduto 1972: 126–27)

Plath's life also overlapped with the beginning of the recording career of The Beatles, something also drawn attention to in *The Radio Times*. The Beatles had "Please Please Me" at Number 2 in January 1963 (it was released on 11 January), and recorded the ten songs for the album "Please Please Me" at the Abbey Road studios—not very far from Fitzroy Road—on 11 February. This was a free day in the middle of their touring schedule: it was the same day that Sylvia Plath died.

Yet England remained a predominantly conservative country and the social changes that were to occur later in the decade were not obvious in the early 1960s. Brian Epstein had met The Beatles as early as 3 December 1961, but although the Light Programme had The Beatles on Saturday Club it had little space for recorded popular music of the kind that Plath played on the piano (Ted Hughes recalls her playing the hit songs of the forties and fifties: see the poem "Fingers" in *Birthdays Letters*, the note on "Morning Song" in Newman [1970: 193] and the quotation cited by Margaret Shook in Linda Wagner [1988: 18–20]). The radio listings reflect a resistance to popular culture, with much classical music on both the Home Service and the Third Programme and talks and plays, arts reviews, and poetry readings. "Light entertainment," like television itself, was regarded as lowbrow culture by the arts circle which Plath knew. For the same reason that they were dismissive of the Ginsberg and the Beat Movement in the 1950s, they would not have impressed to learn that that on 12 July, the day after Plath had written "Word Heard, by Accident, Over the phone" the Rolling Stones had made their first appearance at the Marquee·Club in London.

64. Letter to George MacBeth dated 4 April 1962, BBC Written Archives Centre, Caversham, Reading, England. George Macbeth was in the BBC Talks Department at the time and was Plath's contact for any readings she was commissioned to do. The letter draws attention to a reference to Macbeth's poetry in a recent edition of *Time* (research shows that it was 9 March 1962) and is a covering letter for poems that Janice Markey suggests have disappeared (Markey 1993: 199). Plath's reference to "Ash," "Afterlife" and "Mother Superior" sound likely Plath poems, but are in fact poems written by MacBeth himself (See MacBeth 1989). MacBeth's poetry and its relationship to Plath's is touched on in chapter 9).

65. *The Observer* Weekend Review, 3 February 1963. On 4 February Plath wrote the poem "Contusions" which seems to be a series of lines inspired by a bad bruise. Quite possibly that is a satisfactory explanation, and the bruising is an image intended to connote the emotional bruising of the individual. There is nothing in the poem to suggest it bears any relationship to the Polaris discussion. But Plath had written a poem called "Cut" on 24 October 1962, and as I argue in chapter 8, this can be read differently if it is noted that this was written in the middle of the Cuban Missile Crisis.

66. Transcript of Official Secrets Trial, 12 February–12 July 1962. In Christopher Driver, *The Disarmers: A Study in Protest* (London: Hodder and Stoughton, 1964), 165.

67. Interview with the author, May 1999

68. Eugen Kogon, *The Theory and Practice of Hell: The German Concentration Camps and the System Behind Them* (London: Secker and Warburg, 1950).

69. Hannah Arendt *Between Past and Future: six exercises in Political Thought* (London: Faber and Faber, 1954); Hannah Arendt, *The Human Condition* (Chicago: The University of Chicago Press, 1958); Hannah Arendt, *The Origins of Totalitarianism* (London: George Allen and Unwin, Ltd. 1961).

70. Hannah Arendt, *Eichmann in Jerusalem: a report on the banality of evil* (London: Faber and Faber, 1963).

71. A. Alvarez, "The Literature of the Holocaust," in *Commentary* 38, no. 5 (November 1964): 65.

72. Al Strangeways, *Sylvia Plath: The Shaping of Shadows* (Madison, NJ: Fairleigh Dickinson: Associated University Press, 1998), 106.

73. "Got seats at 'Beyond the Fringe' by way of Ruth's employer who is in ITV . . . raved over Jonathan Miller." In *The Journals of Sylvia Plath 1950–1962*, ed. Karen V. Kukil (London: Faber and Faber, 2000), 633.

2. Writing novels in Cambridge, London, and Devon: Exchanging White Goddess for WASP

1. Sylvia Plath, "Platinum Summer" Unpublished manuscript Indiana University: Lilly Library, (1955). Sylvia Plath refers this story in a letter to her mother dated 19 July 1955 in which she says that she intends to start the story (formerly to be called "Peroxide Summer") the following day and hopes to have completed it by the time she sees her mother the following week (LH: 177).

2. Letter to Olive Higgins Prouty, 22 November 1962, MRBR.

3. Allen Ginsberg "America" (written 17 January 1956), in *Howl and Other Poems* (1956), reprinted in Allen Ginsberg, *Selected Poems* (London: Penguin Books, 1997).

4. Sylvia Plath's 1955 story "Tongues of Stone" is sometimes seen as an apprenticeship piece for *The Bell Jar*. Published in JP: 267.

5. Ted Hughes, *Winter Pollen: Occasional Prose,* ed. William Scammell (London: Faber and Faber, 1994) 185.

6. Ibid.

7. Edward Butscher, *Sylvia Plath: Method and Madness* (New York: Seabury Press, 1976), 21.

8. Pat Macpherson, *Reflecting on The Bell Jar* (London: Routledge, 1991).

9. On 7 November 1955 Plath had written to her mother "[I] saw a rather good production of my favorite *I am a Camera* . . . which made me want to turn immediately to writing again" (LH: 194). The phrase comes from Christopher Isherwood's *Sally Bowles* (1937) which was dramatized in 1951 by John Van Druten as *I am a Camera* and then turned into the stage musical *Cabaret* in 1968. Plath was clearly fond of the play, which she saw at Cambridge.

10. Sylvia Plath, "Suffering Angel" (book review) in *New Statesman* (7 December 1962): 828–129.

11. Denis Donoghue, Review of *The Collected Poems of Sylvia Plath* in *The New York Review of Books* (22 November 1981): 1, 30. Donogue says that the analogy between the death of the Rosenbergs and the electric shock treatment is "blatant rather than just," and the charge of petulance is also levelled at later poems such as "Tulips" and "Lady Lazarus." As for the charge of self-centredness, it is slighly qualified: "Self-absorbed, she shows what self-absorption makes possible in art."

12. Margaret Dickie Uroff, *Sylvia Plath and Ted Hughes* (Urbana: University of Illinois Press, 1980).

13. Strangeways, *The Shaping of Shadows,* 78.

14. See "Leaves from a Cambridge Notebook" part 2, by Sylvia Plath, in *The Christian Science Monitor,* Boston Massachusetts (Tuesday 6 March 1956): 15b. (Part 1 appeared on Monday 5 March).

15. Sylvia Plath, "B. and K. at the Claridge," in *Smith Alumnae Quarterly* (November 1956) 16–17 (Smith Archives: Sophia Smith Collection).

16. "What made you stay" was a radio programme broadcast on Friday, 7 September 1962 on the BBC Home Service between 3.30 and 4.00 in the afternoon. In the *Radio Times* it appears in the regular slot entitled *A World of Sound* and as the first in a series of programmes in which Marvin Kane asks "What made you stay?" of seven Americans who have chosen to live and work in England. Plath is described as "Sylvia Plath, poet" (*Radio Times* 30 August 1962): 46.

17. "Hughes Depicts Cambridge Scene" by Bonnie Joseph. *The Sophian* (7 November 1957): 3–4. Used with permission of Smith College Archives.

18. Richard Larschan, letter to the author, 12 January 1999.

19. Nancy Chodorow *The Reproduction of Mothering: psychoanalysis and the sociology of gender* (Berkeley: University of California Press, 1978).

20. Alan Sinfield, "Women Writing: Sylvia Plath" in *Literature, Politics and Culture in Postwar Britain* (Berkeley and Los Angeles: University of California Press, 1989).

21. See Christopher Driver, *The Disarmers: A Study in Protest* (London: Hodder and Stoughton, 1964).

22. Anne Stevenson, *Bitter Fame: a Life of Sylvia Plath* (Boston: Houghton Mifflin Co., 1989).

23. Ibid., 192.

24. The collage, or photomontage as it was known in the 1920s and 1930s, was used from the very earliest days of photography and film, and became a serious art form in the hands of the Dadaists, Contructivists, and Surrealists. For an account of its history and dvelopment, see Dawn Ades's *Photomontage* (1996). Plath's anti-military collage is reproduced on the jacket.

25. Rose, *The Haunting of Sylvia Plath.*

26. Brain, *The Other Sylvia Plath,* 91–93.

27. Driver, *The Disarmers,* 98.

28. W. B. Yeats, *The Autobiography of WB Yeats* (New York: Doubleday Anchor, 1958), 248.

29. Letter to Lynne Lawner, 3 September 1960 (Lilly Library, Indiana and copy at MRBR, Smith College).

30. Anne Sexton, "The Barfly Ought to Sing" *Triquarterly* 7 (Fall 1966): 92.

31. *The New Yorker* May 28 1960, 72.

32. Sylvia Plath 'A War to End Wars' School assignment, Class II SS February 1946 (MRBR).

33. Sylvia Plath 'The World and the United States' 1946 (MRBR). This project is mainly about the the United Nations and the problems surrounding its foundation.

34. "Context," in JP: 92.

35. Letter to Marcia Stern, 21 March 1956 (MRBR).

36. Letter to Marcia Stern, 15 December 1956 (MRBR).

37. See J: 332.

38. "Franny" appeared in *The New Yorker* in 1955 and "Zooey" in 1957. They appeared as books in the United States in 1961, and in England in 1962, and in this form were too late to have influenced *The Bell Jar.*

39. This alteration is made in Typescript B of the manuscript on the page that appears on the back of "The Tour," Draft 5, page 2. There the name "Frieda Lucas" is changed to "Victoria Lucas" and the title "Diary of a Suicide" crossed out in favour of "The Bell Jar" (MRBR).

40. See Ian Hamilton, "In Search of J. D. Salinger" (London: Bloomsbury, 1998), p. 82. Hamilton says that in Devon Salinger "was made to feel like an American soldier at whom the locals were inclined to stare" but the key difference between his expeerience and Plath's was the wartime proesence of a huge number of Americans in the area so that

for possibly the first time in his life, he felt a sense of 'tribal solidarity.' (Ibid). Plath was not part of any such American community, committed to any such worthy cause.

41. BJ: 215.

42. Helga Geyer-Ryan, *Fables of Desire: Studies in the Ethics of Art and Gender* (Oxford: Polity Press, 1994), 162.

43. Robert Lowell, "Memories of West Street and Lepke" (1959), in Robert Lowell, *Life Studies* (London: Faber and Faber, 1985), 9.

44. Jerome Mazzaro, "Sylvia Plath and the cycles of history," in Gary Lane, ed., *Sylvia Plath: New Views on the Poetry* (London: The John Hopkins University Press, 1979), 218–40.

45. Marion Harris, Review of *The Bell Jar* in *West Coat Review* (October 1973): 54–56. Reprinted in *Sylvia Plath: The Critical Heritage,* ed. Linda Wagner-Martin (London: Routledge, 1988), 109.

46. *The Nation* (New York) 193, no. 14 (28 October 1961): 277.

47. JP: 92. Originally in *London Magazine* (February 1962): 45.

48. *London Magazine* (February 1962): 44.

49. Letter to Aurelia Plath, 17 December 1961 (Lilly Library, Bloomington, Indiana).

50. Linda Wagner-Martin, *Sylvia Plath: A Biography* (New York: Simon and Schuster, 1987), 203.

51. Ernest May and Philip Zelikow *The Kennedy Tapes: Inside the White House during the Cuban Missile Crisis* (Cambridge, Mass.: the Belknap Press, of Harvard University Press, 1997), 297.

52. Ibid., 288

53. Journals January 12 1958 MRBR.

54. LH: 135, dates this letter as March 1954 but Anne Stevenson (*Bitter Fame* p56) says that it is dated 1955

55. The image of the broken statue links this scene with another, very American piece of writing, called "Mrs McFague and the Corn Vase Girl," which drew on Plath's experiences the previous summer on holiday with Hughes on Cape Cod. The Corn Vase Girl is a statue which Plath had sketched in her notebooks, and it too is to be an idol around which Mrs. McFague moves. A page from the Cape Cod notebook, written up some time after the pen drawing (page 41 to the drawing's page 27 [MRBR]) has the heading "Mama McFague and the The Corn Vase Girl/A House for Mama McFague" and has notes on the Spauldings, Myrtle and Lester. She is hard working, cleans the cabins, works herself to exhaustion, is dependent and "blithely impractical." They live in a trailer in the summer, and have no house. Then a "kid breaks one of McFague's statues. Now she can bear to sell the other." Similarly, in the journal, the statue is guarded "through an invasion by barbarian hordes in Tookies cabin, and Mrs McFague has sluggard, unhelpful husband." This is Plath the American writer, conscious of the *New Yorker* market, strict with herself to ensure she satisfies the demands of American magazine editors.

56. Letter to Lynne Lawner, 11 March 1959 (Lilly Library, Bloomington, Indiana, copy in MRBR).

57. It is possible that a typed page included among the Hughes manuscripts kept at the British Library is from the novel (Hughes has used the versos of a number of Plath's draft pages for his own work: these include typed versions of "Mushrooms" and "Sleep in Mojave Desert"). The page is an extract from a narrative set on a Cambridge farm, in which a character called Sheila receives an airmail letter that revealed that "Sassoon" was on his way. Richard Sassoon and Plath were lovers immediately before she met Hughes, but she rarely used "real" names in her writing, and the piece may be by Hughes himself (British Library Manuscript Add 53784). [Additional pages of "Falcon Yard" have appeared among the Hughes papers acquired by Emory University, Georgia.]

58. Stevenson *Bitter Fame,* 251.

59. CP: 223.

60. Ted Hughes, *Birthday Letters* (London: Faber and Faber, 1998), 14.

61. In the rough draft of a letter to Jane Prouty Smith (the daughter of Olive Higgins Prouty, who had part funded Plath's scholarship to Smith, and continued to supply financial and practical help in the years that followed) Aurelia Plath wrote: "This was to be the companion book to *The Bell Jar* (although written in rough draft first) and was the story of an American girl's experience in Cambridge, England. It was 'the view of life seen through the eyes of health' with Ted its hero, that Sylvia destroyed before my eyes in the summer of 1962" (Draft dated 26 November 1963, MRBR).

62. See Linda Heller, "Aurelia Plath: a lasting commitment," in *Bostonia* (Boston University Alumnae Magazine, Spring 1976): 36.

63. Letter shown to author and in possession of owner. In the manuscript of *Letters Home*, a copy of which is kept at the Mortimer Rare Book Room (the original is in the Lilly Library, Indiana), Aurelia Plath refers to this "third novel" in a paragraph of her own commentary (drawn from a letter she wrote to Warren and Margaret) which describes the burning of the Cambridge novel. The paragraph is not included in the published version of *Letters Home*.

64. Letter from Sylvia Plath to Douglas Claverdon, dated 19 November 1962. BBC Written Archives Centre, Caversham Park, Berkshire

65. Stevenson, *Bitter Fame*, 289.

3. WINTHROP TO WINKLEIGH:
PERFORMANCE, POLITICS, AND PLACE

1. Patricia Macpherson, "The Puzzle of Sylvia Plath" *Women's Studies Occasional Papers* no. 4 (University of Kent at Canterbury, 1983), 3.

2. Ibid.

3. Edward Butscher, *Sylvia Plath: Method and Madness* (New York: Seabury Press, 1976), 35.

4. In her account of her own life Friedan has always given the impression that she was just such a trapped suburban housewife and mother herself. Ironically she appears to have concealed her own achievements as a political activist, first at Smith College (over ten years before Plath) and then as a Popular Front Labor journalist for the left-wing news service Federated Press. As Daniel Horowitz argues in his study of the relationship between Friedan, the American Left, the Cold War, and modern feminism (Horowitz 1998) this was largely due to Friedan's fear of her feminist agenda being undermined by an association with Communism, which during the Cold War period during which *The Feminine Mystique* was being written would have been very damaging.

5. Richard J. Ellis, "The Forgotten Betty," *Times Literary Supplement* no. 5007 (19 March 1999), 5.

6. Joan Riviere, "Womanliness as Masquerade," (1929) in Victor Burgin, James Dondald, and Cora Kaplan, eds., *Formations of Fantasy* (London: Methuen, 1986), 38.

7. Linda Wagner-Martin, *Sylvia Plath*.

8. Anne Stevenson, *Bitter Fame*.

9. Ronald Hayman, *The Death and Life of Sylvia Plath*.

10. Paul Alexander, *Rough Magic*.

11. Nancy Hunter Steiner, *A Closer Look at Ariel: A Memory of Sylvia Plath* (New York: Harpers Magazine Press, 1973 and London: Faber and Faber, 1974). The longer quotation reads:

The generation to which we both belonged spent its formative years listening to radio newscasts from the battlefronts of the Second World War—the one that would end all wars. Those years were a time of new opportunities, new fortunes, and new dimensions for the American Dream. We watched as our mothers went off to work in unprecedented numbers, as the nation achieved unparalleled prosperity, and as the people of this country united in unquestioning devotion to a single national cause. We thrived on a diet of tuna fish and macaroni and discovered, when we were old enough to wear silk stockings, that they had all been turned into parachutes. We grew accustomed to sacrifice. When the war ended, we listened in numbing disbelief to tales of Hitler's nearly successful attempt to exterminate the Jews and learned to live with the realities of the Cold War and atomic capability. Most of us remained sanguine; if we could not look outward without shuddering, we would turn our gaze inward, instead. Korea was a dark shadow hanging over the boys we knew, but we girls raced off to colleges and universities without them. Dwight Eisenhower was in the White House, and if Joe McCarthy was in the Senate, building a career on accusation and innuendo, what had that to do with us? We had been encouraged since childhood to believe that all would soon be well in the best of possible places and we had no reason, now, to abandon our optimism. We packed our cashmere sweaters and our unshakable convictions in a set of brand-new luggage and we were on our way. (10–11).

12. Lameyer writes that Sylvia sent him a Valentine card telling him of her evening listening to the English novelist Esther Forbes in the Hampshire Bookshop (Gordon Lameyer, "Sylvia at Smith," in Edward Butscher, *Sylvia Plath: The Woman and her Work* [London: Owen, 1979], 35). The relationship with Lameyer is interesting because he spent three years in the navy and during Plath's final year as a student at Smith was stationed at the American base in Cuba.

13. The full entry reveals the meditative character of these early Smith entries:

This is my first snow at Smith. It is like any other snow, but from a different window, and there lies the singular charm of it. . . . The house across the street is melting and crumbling into whiteness. . . . Now there is a stippling of white caught on the edge of things, and I wonder what would happen to us all if the planes came, and the bombs. . . . It's one thing to look at snow from a light, steam-heated room; it's one thing to walk out into it with lifted face and woolen clothes a few inches thick. But to live out in that white world, to scratch for a living from the withdrawn lavendar trees, the pale frozen ground. No, no. But the squirrels would still be there, and the birds. Long after, unless the smoke and the radioactivity (oh, Marie Curie, if you could know!) got them. I can only hazard. In the back of my mind there are bombs falling, women and children screaming, but I can't describe it now. I don't know how it will be. But I do know that nothing will matter much— I mean whether or not I went to House Dance or to a party at New Year's. It is amusing to wonder whether dreams would matter at all, or "freedom" or "democracy." I think not; I think there would only be the wondering what to eat and where to sleep and how to build out of the wreckage of life and mankind. Yet, while America dies like the great Roman Empire died, while the legions fail and the barbarians overrun our tender, steak-juicy, butter-creamy, million-dollar stupendous land, somewhere there will be the people that never mattered much in our scheme of things anyway. In India, perhaps, or Africa, they will rise. It will be long before everyone is wiped out. . . . And so I will belong to a dark age, and historians will say "We have a few documents to show how the common people lived at this time. Records lead us to believe that a majority were killed. But there were glorious men." And school children will sigh and learn the names of Truman and Senator McCarthy. Oh, it is hard for me to reconcile myself to this. But maybe this is why I am a girl—so I can live more safely than the boys I have known and envied, so I can bear children, and instill in them the eating desire to learn and love life which I will never quite fulfill, because there isn't time, because there isn't time at all, but instead the quick desperate fear, the ticking clock and the snow which comes too suddenly upon the summer. . . . Now I am living on the edge. We are on the brink, and it takes a lot of nerve, a lot of energy, to teeter on the edge, looking over, looking down into the windy blackness. . . . (Journal 1950–53, Entry 37, pp. 53–57, MRBR; JPL: 31–32)

14. This entry into new patterns and resources of language is one way in which writing evolves. It can also parallel the way identity is formed, and in *Critical Desire* Linda Williams (London: Edward Arnold, 1995) shows how psycho-analytic theory can be useful in a discussion of the literary subject. In classical Freudian theory identity is rooted in sexuality, and the suppressed desire for the parent. Seduction theory thus provides one explanation for fantasy, and the displacement of desire acted out through art. For D. W. Winnicott and Melanie Klein (Melanie Klein, "Infantile Anxiety Situations Reflected in a Work of Art and in the Creative Impulse" [1929], in Melanie Klein, *Love, Guilt and Reparation and Other Works, 1921–1945* [London: Hogarth, 1975] "objects" such as the breast are important in helping individuals construction a relationship with the world, and object relations theory argues that desire for objects can translate into the fetishisation of objects, so that they do not simply stand for the absent object of desire, they assume its power. Strangeways discusses the role played by Winnicott and other object-relations theorists in the psycho-analytic approaches to Plath's poetry in her chapter "The Psychoanalyzing of Sylvia" (*Sylvia Plath: The Shaping of Shadows*, 132–74) which also discusses the influence of Lacanian theory and theories of Abjection.

It is Lacan's emphasis on the defining and segregating role of language (See, for example, Jacqes Lacan, *Ecrits* [Paris: Seuil 1966] and Jacques Lacan, *Ecrits: A Selection,* trans. Alan Sheridian [New York Norton, 1977] that is particularly useful for a reading of Plath's writing, and the way that it rejoices in separation (the American construction of the individual) but then expresses a longing for union, sublimation and rebirth. As Raman Selden says:

> Lacan's theory of the individual's entry into the social world involves our adopting a "subject" position. We achieve this situatedness on entering the symbolic system of language, which gives us a place in the chain of discourse—an "I" and a gender orientation within the family (he/she, daughter/son). (Raman Selden, ed., *The Theory of Criticism from Plato to the Present* [London: Longman, 1988])

Although Lacan's initial concern is with the very early pre-linguistic stages of a child's development, this is only the beginning of a long, cyclic process. In his study of Hamlet, Lacan concentrates on Hamlet's insubstantial image of his father. In Plath's case, the access to political discourse allows her to construct models of an imaginary and imagined father that carry the weight of her feelings and anxieties about global politics:

> In the German tongue, in the Polish town
> Scraped flat by the roller
> Of wars, wars, wars.
> But the name of the town is common.
> My Polack friend

> Says there are a dozen or two.
> So I never could tell where you
> Put your foot, your root,
> I never could talk to you.
> The tongue stuck in my jaw
>
> ("Daddy," CP: 222)

A simple biographical reading would point to the genetic father Otto, born in the Polish corridor and German speaking. His home town may well have had a common name: everything may be related to some autobiographical fact. But the repetition of "wars," the flatness of landscape and the indistinguishable nature of the towns, together with the inability to speak suggest a fear and a dread that spreads from "Daddy" to country, and from country to martial juggernauts, crushing humanity under its rollers.

The *Ariel* poems seek to rid the world of the patriarchal drive towards destruction and to achieve a rebirth. The rebirth of the body is the subject of the writing, and represents an attempt to start afresh. The vulnerable, digesting, animal body is the problem—the muck funnel and flaking skin images of the *Ariel* poems convey a Puritanical disgust with the body, and in her early writing this is concealed by a tendency to avoid the particularities of politics, whilst still commenting on the contemporary issues and fears.

15. Tony Tanner, *City of Words: American Fiction 1950–1970* (London: Jonathan Cape, 1971), chapter 15, "On the Parapet (Norman Mailer)."

16. Larschan, letter to the author.

17. Note to the author, 1999.

18. Angela Moorjani, "Fetishism, Gender Masquerade, and the Mother-Father Fantasy," in J. Smith and Afaf Mahfouz, eds., *Psychoanalysis, Feminism and the Future of Gender*, Psychiatry and the Humanities vol. 14 (London: The Johns Hopkins University Press, 1994), 27.

19. This image can be found in many poems, including "The Disquieting Muses" (1957), "On Deck," (1960), "Three Women," (1962) and "The Munich Mannequins" (1963). Another image, that of the veil hiding the female face, occurs in Plath's later work, including her final piece of commissioned prose, "Ocean 1212W." Here she describes the "motherly pulse of the sea" which taught her early lessons about deception and the counterfeit:

> Like a deep woman, it hid a good deal; it had many faces, many delicate terrible veils. It spoke of miracles and of distances; if it could court, it could also kill. (JP: 117)

20. Rose, *The Haunting of Sylvia Plath*, chapter 2, 29–64.

21. Letter from Leonie Cohn, acknowledging the script that Plath had sent on 28 January. The letter is dated 8 February 1962 and may not have been delivered before Plath died. Copy in BBC Written Archives Centre, Caversham Park, Berkshire.

22. Letter to Richard Murphy, Friday, 17 August 1962. Published in Stevenson, *Bitter Fame*, 355.

23. Robyn Marsack, *Sylvia Plath* (Buckingham, England Open University Press, 1992), 56.

24. Terry Eagleton *Exiles and Emigres* (London: Chatto and Windus, 1970).

25. See chapter 2, n. 16, above.

26. See "Cambridge Letter" by Sylvia Plath, *Isis* (Oxford University) 6 May 1956. Republished in *The Sunday Times* (15 April 1990): H8.

27. Ted Hughes, *Winter Pollen: Occasional Prose,* ed. William Scammell (London: Faber and Faber, 1994), 185.

28. In *Birthday Letters* (London: Faber and Faber, 1998) Hughes acknowledged that the move was a mistake:

> I brought you to Devon. I brought you into my dreamland.
> I sleepwalked you
> Into my land of totems. Never-never land:
> The orchard in the West
>   I wrestled
> With the blankets, the caul and the cord,
> And you stayed with me
> Gallant and desperate and hopeful,
> Listening for different gods, stripping off
> Your American royalty, garment by garment—
> Till you stepped out soul-naked and stricken
> Into this cobbled, pictureless corridor
> Aimed at a graveyard.
>   What had happened
> To the Italian sun?
> Had it escaped our snatch
> Like a butterfly off a nettle? The flashing trajectory,
> The trans-continental dream express
> Of your adolescence—had it
> Slammed to a dead-end, crushing halt, fatal
> In this red-soil tunnel?
>
>   ("Error," Hughes 1998: 122)

Hughes's poems are in part a record of the disillusionment with place that coincides with their marriage. Here he is describing the troubling omen of a bloodstain on a pillow, a reminder of a former occupant of their first home in Cambridge:

>   It confirmed
> Your idea of England: part
> Nursing home, part morgue
> For something partly dying, partly dead.
>
>   ("55 Eltisley," Hughes 1998: 49)

But it is the later move out of London: to the country that heightens Plath's sense of exile. They are inland in a county famous for its coastline. Plath longs for a sight of the sea:

> England was so filthy! Only the sea
> Could scour it. You ocean salts would scour you.
> You wanted to be washed, scoured, sunned.
> That 'jewel in the head'—your flashing, thunderclap miles
> Of Nauset surf. The slew of horse-shoe crabs
> And sand-dollars. You craved like oxygen
> American earlier summers, yourself burnt dark—
> Some prophecy mislaid, somehow. England
> Was so poor! Was black paint cheaper? Why
> Were English cars all black—to hide the filth?
> Or to stay respectable, like bowlers
> And umbrellas ? Every vehicle a hearse.

The traffic procession a hushing leftover
Of Victoria's perpetual funeral Sunday—
The funeral of colour and light and life !
London a morgue of dinge—English dinge.
Our sole indigenous art-form—depressionist !
And why were everybody's
Garments so begrimed?
Grubby-looking, like a camouflage? 'Alas
We have never recovered,' I said, 'from our fox-holes,
Our trenches, our fatigues and bomb shelters.'

("The Beach," Hughes 1998: 154)

Hughes's final comment is no consolation. In his (re) writing of the life together, he recalls another visit to the coast, the occasion that inspired the writing of 'The Rabbit Catcher':

We tried to find the coast. You
Raged against our English private greed
Of fencing off all coastal approaches,
Hiding the sea from roads, from all inland
You despised England's grubby edges when you got there.

("The Rabbit Catcher," Hughes 1998: 144)

The very plainness of the language of *Birthday Letters* is part of their rhetorical effect: the reader is being encouraged to read the poems as notices, as reports, as a setting down of the details with the sad feeling of hindsight. They provide another set of pictures, intended to be read in relation to Plath's published journals, correspondence and poems, showing her anxieties about her new homeland.

29. Elizabeth Sigmund (Elizabeth Compton), "Sylvia in Devon 1962," in Edward Butscher *Sylvia Plath: The Woman and the Work* (New York: Dodd Mead and Co., 1977), 100–107. Elizabeth Sigmund not only recalls Plath's delight at Elizabeth's interest in Liberal Party politics but also that they discussed national government's armaments policies with Plath expressing anger at the involvement of American big business in the weapons industry (102).

30. "Sylvia Plath" entry written by Judith Kroll for *Notable American Women: The Modern Period: A Biographical Dictionary*, ed. Barbara Sicherman and Carol Hurd Green (Cambridge, Mass. and London: Belknap Press of Harvard University Press, 1980), 548–51.

31. Richard Larschan, letter to the author.

4. Revising and Revising: *The Bell Jar* Manuscripts, Two January 1962 Poems, "Elm," and *Ariel*

1. See Jacqueline Rose, *The Haunting of Sylvia Plath* (London: Virago Press, 1991) and Susan R. Van Dyne, *Revising Life: Sylvia Plath's Ariel poems* (University of North Carolina Press, 1993).

2. The quotation from Draft B of *The Bell Jar* manuscript is taken from the manuscripts held at Smith College in the Mortimer Rare Book Room. All references to manuscripts held at Smith College refer to this collection.

3. Copy 1 of "Waking in Winter," Mortimer Rare Book Room.

4. Copy 2 of "Waking in Winter," Mortimer Rare Book Room.

5. Copy 1 of "Fever," Mortimer Rare Book Room.

6. Copy 2 "Fever," Mortimer Rare Book Room.

7. Copies 3–8 of "Fever," Mortimer Rare Book Room.

8. Ted Hughes, *Birthday Letters* (London: Faber and Faber, 1998), 141.

9. Photograph captioned "Baluba mothers and their babies wounded . . . in Elisabethville," *The Observer* (Sunday, 17 December 1961): 2. It is extremely likely that Plath read *The Observer:* her poem "The Rival" appeared on Sunday, 21 January 1962 and when she moved to (London: one of the early reminders on her week-by-week calendar was to order "Observer and Radio Times" (Mortimer Rare Book Room).

10. *The Times,* (13 January 1962): 2.

11. Sylvia Plath, "Context" (1962), republished in Sylvia Plath, *Johnny Panic and the Bible of Dreams* (New York: Harper and Row, 1980), 92.

12. *The Observer* (4 February 1962): 1.

13. Letter dated 30 October 1961, in Aurelia Schober Plath, ed., *Letters Home (by Sylvia Plath)* (New York: Harper and Row, 1975), 434.

14. *The Observer* (Sunday, 29 October 1961): 2.

15. *New Statesman* (10 November 1961), 697.

16. "Fever," Copy 2, Mortimer Rare Book Room.

17. Sylvia Plath, "Context," in *Johnny Panic,* 92.

18. Anne Stevenson, *Bitter Fame: A Life of Sylvia Plath* (Boston: Houghton Mifflin, 1989), 239.

19. Stevenson, *Bitter Fame,* 238.

20. Draft 4c of "Elm," Mortimer Rare Book Room.

21. "Fever in Winter": "Fever" Copy 1, Mortimer Rare Book Room.

22. "Fever" Copy 3, Mortimer Rare Book Room.

23. "Elm" Draft 3b, Mortimer Rare Book Room.

24. "Fever" Copy 4, Mortimer Rare Book Room.

25. "Waking in Winter" Copy 4, Mortimer Rare Book Room.

26. "Fever in Winter" ("Fever" Copy 1), Mortimer Rare Book Room.

27. "Waking in Winter" in CP 151.

28. "Little Fugue" Draft 1, p. 3, Mortimer Rare Book Room.

29. Tim Kendall, "Plath's 'Piranha Religion'" in *Essays in Criticism* 49, no. 1 (January 1999): 44–61.

30. Ted Hughes, Introduction to CP: 13.

5. Women and Politics on the Wireless: Sylvia Plath, Laura Riding, and the BBC

1. Letter from George Macbeth to Sylvia Plath, 5 July 1962 (BBC Written Archives Centre, Caversham Park, Buckinghamshire).

2. Letter from George Macbeth to Sylvia Plath, 22 June 1962 (BBC Written Archives Centre, Caversham Park, Buckinghamshire).

3. See Stevenson, *Bitter Fame,* 224.

4. Richard Perceval Graves, *Robert Graves and the White Goddess* (London: Weidenfeld and Nicolson, 1995).

5. Robert Graves, *The White Goddess* (London: Faber and Faber, 1948).

6. Robert Graves had seen sufficient direct action during his experiences in the

trenches in the First World War, and had subsequently dedicated his life to poetry: the important business of poetry was a contract between the poet and his/her Muse. Earlier in the Second World War, in writing his novel *Wife to Mr Milton* (*The Story of Mary Powell: Wife to Mr Milton* [London: Methuen, 1943]; in New York as *Wife to Mr Milton: the Story of Mary Powell* [Creative Age Press, 1944]) Graves had scorned Milton's commitment to the Parliamentary project of Puritanism, and was sceptical about Milton's own commitment to the control of passions and to the improvement of the world. Such a secular, prosaic, political compromise of his art, in Graves's view, disqualified him from being regarded as a true poet. For Robert Graves, poetry and world politics occupied different spheres, and the poet was wise to keep well out of politics.

7. Laura Riding and sixty-five others, *The World and Ourselves* (London: Chatto and Windus, 1938), 16.

8. Richard Perceval Graves, *Robert Graves: the years with Laura* (London: Weidenfeld and Nicolson, 1990), 269.

9. Robyn Marsack, *Sylvia Plath*.

10. Laura Riding, "Introduction to 'Laura Riding,'" broadcast on the BBC Third Programme, 1 April 1962, p. 1. Script copyright of the BBC Written Archive Centre. Includes amendments made by Laura Riding to the published version "Introduction For a Broadcast," *Chelsea* 12 (1962): 3–5.

11. Laura Riding, "Introduction," 1.

12. Ibid.

13. Ibid., 2.

14. Jacqueline Rose, *The Haunting of Sylvia Plath*, 220.

15. Laura (Riding) Jackson *The Poems of Laura Riding* (Manchester: Carcanet Press, 1980), 76.

16. Jacqueline Rose, *The Haunting of Sylvia Plath*, 219.

17. Laura (Riding) Jackson, *The Poems*, 36.

18. Laura (Riding) Jackson, *The Poems*, 111.

19. Louis Simpson *Studies of Dylan Thomas, Allen Ginsberg, Sylvia Plath and Robert Lowell*, 1978, p 119.

20. See chapter 2, n. 16, above. In the interview Plath discusses what it means to see England—and America—through the eyes of an American who has decided to settle in England. She talks about the surprise of going into an English butcher's shop and seeing the cuts of meat on display, and she bemoans the way that American children are given too much license nowadays. The tone of mildly offended dignity is not unlike that of the fictional Peter Walsh, in her favourite Virginia Woolf novel, *Mrs Dalloway:* "Those five years—1918–23—had been, he suspected, somehow very important. People looked different. Newspapers seemed different. Now, for instance, there was a man writing quite openly in one of the respectable weeklies about water closets. That you couldn't have done ten years ago—written quite openly about water closets in a respectable weekly" (Virginia Woolf, *Mrs Dalloway* [London: The Hogarth Press, 1954]; Sylvia Plath's library copy held in Mortimer Rare Book Room, Smith College).

21. Letter from John Powell to Sylvia Plath, 17 September 1962 (BBC Written Archive Centre, Caversham Park, Buckinghamshire).

22. The coda proposes two episodes. The first is the return to college and involves the Doestoevski and the bleaching of her hair. The second has the heading "Summer School," and was presumably going to deal with the sexual odyssey that took place at Harvard, including the hemorrhaging that was transposed to an earlier time and included in the novel. (MRBR).

23. See, for example, Linda Wagner-Martin's *Sylvia Plath: A Literary Life* (London: Macmillan Press, 1999) and Tracy Brain's *The Other Sylvia Plath* (London: Pearson, 2001).

6. Institutions and the Formation
of Political Judgement: Arenas, Ruins,
Hospitals, and Other Troubling Places

1. See R. Peel, A. Patterson, and J. Gerlach, *Questions of English* (London: Routledge, 2000).

2. Frank R. Stockton, *The Lady or the Tiger?* (New York: Charles Scribner and Sons, 1914). The story was originally published in *The Century* magazine in November 1882 and in 1888 was the subject of an operetta.

3. Louise J. Kaplan, *Female Perversions: The Temptations of Emma Bovary* (New York: Doubleday-Anchor, 1991), 362–407; Sigmund Freud, *The Standard Edition of the Complete Psychological Works of Sigmund Freud,* ed. and trans. James Strachey, 24 vols (London: Hogarth, 1953–74), vol. 20 *Inhibitions, Symptoms and Anxiety,* 143; Melanie Klein, "Infantile Anxiety Situations Reflected in a Work of Art and in the Creative Impulse" in M. Klein, *Love, Guilt and Reparation and Other Works, 1921–1945* (London: Hogarth, 1975) 213.

4. See appendix 7, n. 2 below.

5. "Monday Night: February 17 [1958] A moment caught . . . My own tigress perfume . . . " (Journals MRBR, Smith College). Elizabeth Compton (1977: 106) refers to Plath's two cats, Tiger and Skunky, in her memoir of Plath (Compton: *Sylvia in Devon 1962,* in Edward Butscher, *Sylvia Plath,* 106).

6. Al Strangeways, *The Shaping of Shadows,* 36.

7. This was not strictly Woolf's first published piece, as Clive Bell points out in his biography of Virginia Woolf. On 14 December *The Guardian* published her review of a book by W. D. Howells, but as this had been written—and presumably submitted—after the Haworth piece, Bell feels it appropriate to identify this as the first published work. The essay appears in *The Essays of Virginia Woolf, Volume 1 1904–1912,* ed. Andrew McNeillie (New York: Harcourt Brace Jovanovich, 1986).

8. Sandra Gilbert and Susan Gubar, *No Man's Land Volume 1 The War of the Words* (London: Yale University Press, 1988), 200.

9. This notebook (a carbon book dated 26 June [1956]—December 1958 and later) is kept at the Mortimer Rare Book Room, Smith College. The short story notes appear on the first page 31 (There are two sheets for each page number). See JPL: Appendix 10 p 579.

10. Strangeways, *The Shaping of Shadows,* 36.

11. See n. 9 above.

12. Notebook: see n. 9 above. The short story "All the Dead Dears" appears in JP: 177. The 1957 poem of the same name (CP: 70) is singled out by Steiner in "Dying is an Art" (Steiner 1965) as an example of Plath's fascination with Webster and seventeenth-century Gothic which he thinks is sometimes over-indulged.

13. "A Walk to the Withens," *Christian Science Monitor* (6 June 1959): 12.

14. Ibid.

15. See appendix 5 for some further comments on the developments in this poem. Ted Hughes's article for *Wild Steelhead and Salmon Magazine,* Seattle Washington, was reprinted in *The Guardian* London (9 January 1999): Saturday Review, 1.

16. Alice Miller, *For Your Own Good: Hidden Cruelty in Childrearing and the Roots of Violence* (New York: Farrar, Straus and Giroux, 1983).

17. Terry Eagleton, "Myths of Power: a Marxist Study on Wuthering Heights" in Emily Brontë, *Wuthering Heights,* ed. Linda H. Peterson (Boston: Bedford Books St. Martins Press); Terry Eagleton, *Heathcliff and the Great Hunger* (London: Verso, 1995).

18. Michael J. Moore, *The Life and Death of Northampton State Hospital* (Northampton: Historic Northampton Press, 1994), 5.

19. See "Zoo Keeper's Wife" (CP: 154) and the discussion of "Thalidomide" in chapter 7.

20. Interview recorded on 30 October 1962. Published in Peter Orr, gen. ed., *The Poet Speaks: Interviews with Contemporary Poets* (London: Routledge and Kegan Paul, 1967), 169.

21. See Michel Foucault, *The Archaeaology of Knowledge,* trans. A. M. Sheridan Smith (London: Tavistock, 1972); *The Birth of the Clinic: an Archaelogy of Medical Perception,* trans. A. M. Sheridan Smith (London: Tavistock, 1973); *Discipline and Punish: The Birth of the Prison* (New York: Random House, 1972); *The History of Sexuality Volume 1: An Introduction,* trans. Robert Hurley (New York: Random House, 1978); Volume 2: *The Use of Pleasure, The History of Sexuality* trans. Robert Hurley (New York: Random House, 1985); Volume 3: *The Care of the Self, History of Sexuality* trans. Robert Hurley (New York: Random House, 1986).

22. Strangeways, *The Shaping of Shadows,* chapter 3. "The Psychoanalyzing of Sylvia," 132.

23. Nancy Chodorow, *Feminism and Pscho-analytic Theory* (Oxford: Polity Press/Blackwell, 1989).

24. Davod Holbrook, *Sylvia Plath, Poetry and Existence* (London: Athlone Press, 1976).

25. Stephen Gould Axelrod, *Sylvia Plath: the Wound and the Cure of Words* (Baltimore and London: Johns Hopkins University Press, 1990).

26. Lynda K. Bundtzen, *Plath's Incarnations: Woman and theCreative Process* (Ann Arbor: University of Michigan Press, 1988).

27. *Voices and Visions,* part 13 Sylvia Plath (South Carolina Educational Television and New York Center for Visual History Production, 1988).

7. "The Issues of Our Time": *The Observer*, Poetry and "Thalidomide"

1. Susan R. Van Dyne, *Revising Life: Sylvia Plath's Ariel poems* (University of North Carolina Press, 1993).

2. Ibid., 152.

3. Ibid.

4. "The Effects of Weapons Tests," Scientific American (July 1962). Reproduced in Frank Herbert York, *Arms Control: Readings from Scientific American* (San Francisco: W. H. Freeman and Company, 1973), 85.

5. "The Thalidomide Babies: An *Observer* Inquiry," in *The Observer* Weekend Review section (London: 4 November 1962): 1.

6. The specific inspiration for the poem does not discredit Renée Curry's argument concerning the significance of blackness in this poem (Renée R. Curry, *White Women Writing White,* 153–54) but it does qualify it. It is odd that Curry reports that the poem was written in 1960, however.

7. In "Zoo-keeper's wife," a poem written in February 1961 when she was living near (London: Zoo, Plath speaks of the disturbing effect of seeing such a large spider:

> *And the bear-furred, bird-eating spider*
> Clambering around its glass box like an eight fingered hand
> I can't get it out of my mind

Such a spider appears in *The Incredible Shrinking Man* (1957), a film which reflects anxieties about the effects of radiation on the human body. The tiny shrunken man, is attacked by a "monstrous" spider in the basement of his house.

Linda Wagner-Martin (*Sylvia Plath*, 184) sees "Zoo-keeper's wife" as an early example of Plath's argument that what men can do to animals they can do to women, an argument also to be found in "The Rabbit Catcher." The first dog sent into space in Sputnik 2 in September 1957, Licha, was female, and the perceived cruelty of this experiment was the subject of contemporary comment in America.

8. Virgina Woolf, *Mrs Dalloway* (1925; London: The Hogarth Press, 1954), 98.

9. Pamela J. Annas, *A Disturbance in Mirrors New York* (Greenwood Press, 1981).

10. Judith Butler, *Gender Trouble: Feminism and the Subversion of Identity* (London: Routledge, 1990).

11. "Context" essay: *London* Magazine (February 1962) (JP: 92). The essay opens by citing the article by Fred Cook "Juggernaut, the Warfare State" referred to earlier. Although there is no concrete evidence that she had read it, Plath is likely to have been aware of another popular analysis of corporate power, C. Wright Mill's *The Power Elite* (1956).

8. THE LANGUAGE OF APOCALYPSE:
THE *ARIEL* Poems and the Discourse of Warfare

1. Susan R. Van Dyne, *Revising Life: Sylvia Plath's Ariel poems* (University of North Carolina Press, 1993).

2. Linda Wagner-Martin, *Sylvia Plath: A Biography* (New York: Simon and Schuster, 1987). Published in England by Chatto and Windus, 1989 and by Macdonald and Co., 1990. Quotation taken from 1990 edition, 219.

3. Al Alvarez, ed., "Introduction" to *The New Poetry* (Harmondsworth, England: Penguin Books, 1962) 26–27.

4. *The Observer* (2 September 1962): 9.

5. *New Statesman* (27 April 1962): 602.

6. Peter Orr, *The Poet Speaks*, 169.

7. Sylvia Plath, "Oregonian Original" (book review), *The New Statesman* (9 November 1962): 660.

8. Ibid.

9. Ibid.

10. Sylvia Plath, "Suffering Angel" (book review), in *New Statesman* (7 December 1962): 828–29.

11. Ibid.

12. Ibid.

13. Barnett Guttenberg, "Plath's cosmology and the house of Yeats" in Gary Lane, ed., *Sylvia Plath: New Views on her Poetry* (London: The John Hopkins Press, 1979), 150.

14. Judith Kroll, *Chapters in a Mythology*, 180–81.

15. See Christopher Driver, *The Disarmers: A Study in Protest* (London: Hodder and Stoughton, 1964), 146.

16. Anne Sexton, "My Friend, My Friend," *Antioch Review* 19, no. 2 (Summer 1959): 150.

17. From George Steiner, "Dying is an Art," in Charles Newman, *The Art of Sylvia Plath: a Symposium* (London: Faber and Faber, 1970), 218.

18. Hannah Arendt, *Eichmann in Jerusalem: a report on the banality of evil* (London:

Faber and Faber, 1963), 43. This was published after Plath's death, as was the serialization in *The New Yorker.*

19. Ibid., 44.

20. Ibid., 43.

21. Hannah Arendt, *The Origins of Totalitarianism* (London: George Allen and Unwin Ltd., 1961).

22. Ibid., 441.

23. Ibid.

24. Gayle Wurst, "'We See—Comparatively'": Reading Rich/Reading Plath/Reading Dickinson" in Antoine Caze, ed., *Profils Americains 8* (Emily Dickinson) (Montpellier, France: Presses de l'Université Paul Valery, 1996).

25. Gayle Wurst, "'The Clearest Thing I Own': Metaphor, Myth and Identity in Plath's *Ocean 1212W,*'" in Wurst and Raguet-Bouvert, eds., *Sounding the Depths: Writing as Metaphor in North American Literature* (Liège: Liège University Lan, 1998).

26. Helga Geyer-Ryan, *Fables of Desire: Studies in the Ethics of Art and Gender* (Oxford Polity Press, 1994), 78.

27. John Hersey, *Hiroshima* (London: Penguin Books, 1946). First published in *The New Yorker,* August 1946.

28. Peter Orr, *The Poet Speaks,* 169.

29. Peter Orr, *The Poet Speaks,* 169–70.

30. Kristin Thompson and David Bordwell, *Film History: an Introduction* (London: McGraw-Hill, Inc., 1994), 450.

31. "Follow the Leader," in *Scientific American* (September 1962). See chapter 1, n. 35.

32. In Hughes's explanatory note in *The Collected Poems,* 295, he quotes the very specific (and, presumably, tongue-in-cheek) explanation given by Plath in a reading prepared for BBC Radio:

> "In this poem, the speaker's horse is proceeding at a slow, cold walk down a hill of macadam to the stable at the bottom. It is December. It is foggy. In the fog there are sheep."

33. Ted Hughes, "Sylvia Plath: the evolution of 'Sheep in Fog,'" in Ted Hughes, *Winter Pollen: Occasional Prose,* ed. William Scammell (London: Faber and Faber, 1994), 198.

34. Ibid., 193.

35. Ibid.

36. Ibid., 194.

37. Ibid.

38. Ibid., 206.

39. Ibid., 195.

40. "Water," in "Three Poems by Ted Hughes," *The Observer* (6 January 1993): 19.

41. Unattributed verse 'Operation Safety Catch' *The Observer* 27 Jan 1963, 8.

9. THE POLITICS OF RELIGION: FATHER MICHAEL AND THE ARGUMENT WITH CATHOLICISM

1. Richard Taylor, *Against the Bomb: The British Peace Movement 1958–68.* (Oxford: The Clarendon Press, 1988).

§2. Tom Paulin, Opening address at *Ways with Words,* Dartington, Devon, England, 9 July 1999 (not published).

3. Sandra Richards, "Is there Humour in Sylvia Plath?" *English Review* 4 (4 April 1994): 28–31.

4. Letter from Sylvia Plath to George MacBeth, 15 August 1962 (BBC Written Archives Centre, Caversham Park, Buckinghamshire).

5. *The Observer* (23 September 1962): 19,

6. Raymond Smith, "Late Harvest," *Modern Poetry Studies* 1972, pp. 91– 93; in L. Wagner, *Sylvia Plath: The Critical Heritage* (London: Routledge, 1988), 181.

7. W. H. Auden, H ed., *The Oxford Book of Light Verse* (Oxford: Oxford University Press, 1938), xx.

8. Ibid., xix.

9. *The Bell Jar* draft, 271. On reverse of "Fever" Copy 4, p. 2, MRBR, Smith College.

10. Letter to Richard Murphy, 7 October 1962, in Anne Stevenson, *Bitter Fame*, 358.

11. JP: 226–44.

12. Colin Hughes Stanton, telephone conversation with author. Hughes Stanton was a reporter in 1962–63 and recalls that Sylvia Plath was extremely moved when she witnessed in a council meeting the efforts of the local council to improve the housing conditions of the poorer members of the community.

10. THE FUSION OF DISCOURSES

1. Tracy Brain, *The Other Sylvia Plath* (2001). Tracy Brain also reminds us of th elink made by Al Alvarez between images in the poem "Fever 103°" and the film *Hiroshima Mon Amour.* She also draws an interesting parallel between the West's representation of communism as disease and the representation of sickness in *The Bell Jar.* For discussion of these points see pages 89, 109, 118, and 151.

2. Anne Stevenson, *Bitter Fame*, 277.

APPENDIX 1. EXPERIMENTS WITH MASQUERADE

1. The passage continues at some length, becoming quite a discursive essay on the subject of the fellow student's breasts, perhaps because they approximate to the 1950s screen and advertisers' model of the desirable female body.

2. Angela Moorjani, "Fetishism, Gender Masquerade, and the Mother-Father Fantasty," in J. Smith and Afaf Mahfouz, eds., *Psychoanalysis, Feminism and the Future of Gender,* Psychiatry and the Humanities Volume 14 (London: The John Hopkins Press, 1994), 23.

3. The surrounding text registers annoyance that it is a man's world, that there are double standards in sexual relations, that woman is relegated to the role of servant to man. The greatest annoyance is reserved for the obstacle all this this puts in the way of her writing: because she is a woman she cannot enter the company of ordinary men as observer/writer interested in their lives without this interest being misconstrued.

4. Jacqueline Rose, *The Haunting of Sylvia Plath* (London: Virago Press, 1991). See especially the chapters "The Body in Question" (p. 29) and "No Fantasy without Protest" (p. 114).

5. Journals 1950–53, p. 363, Mortimer Rare Book Room, Smith College.

Appendix 2. Becoming a Writer

1. The continuation of the entry quoted from p. 168 of the student journal describes how Plath sees the journal writings as notes and experiments for future stories. At the same time she acknowledges the jump from fragmentary descriptions to the creation of character and the knitting of plot (see Journal 1950–53, p. 168, MRBR). Published as *The Journals of Sylvia Plath 1950–1962*, ed. Karen V. Kukil (London: Faber and Faber), 83.

Appendix 3. Disturbance, Panic

1. The continuation of this entry makes reference to the war, bombing and bloodshed in Korea, Germany and Russia but this is described as a personal problem for the writer who feels powerless to do anything about it (see J: 24)

2. The entry continues with references to radiation and electrocution that reveal guilt and compassion, but no signs yet of a developed political consciousness:

> God save us from doing that again. For the United States did that. Our guilt. My country. No, never again. And then one reads in the papers "Second bomb blast in Nevada bigger than the first!" What obsession do men have for destruction and murder? Why do we electrocute men for murdering an individual and then pin a purple heart on them for mass slaugher of someone arbitrarily labeled "enemy"? Weren't the Russians communists when helped us slap down the Germans? And now: what would we do with the Russian nation if we bombed it to bits? How could we "rule" such a mass of foreign people—we, who don't even speak the Russian language? How could we control them under our "democratic" system, we who are even now losing that precious commodity, freedom of speech? (Mr. Crockett, that dear man, was questioned by the town board, a supposed "enlightened" community. All because he is a pacifist. That, it seems, is a crime.) Why do we send the pick of our young men overseas to be massacred for three dirty miles of nothing on earth? Korea was never divided into "North" and "South" (Journal, Entry 51, pp. 84–86, MRBR; *The Journals of Sylvia Plath*, ed. Kukil, p. 46)

Appendix 5. The Drafts of "Wuthering Heights"

1. *Wild Steelhead and Salmon Magazine*, Seattle, Washington. Reprinted in *The Guardian* (London): 9 January 1999, Saturday Review, p. 1

Appendix 6. The Politics of Abjection and Desire

1. Helga Geyer-Ryan, *Fables of Desire: Studies in the Ethics of Art and Gender* (Oxford: Polity Press, 1994).
2. Ibid., 191.
3. Ibid., 106
4. Ibid., 108

5. Ibid., 198

6. Simone Weil, "The Iliad: A poem of force" in Peter Mayer, ed., *The Pacifist Conscience* (New York/London: Rupert Hart-Davis, 1966) 292.

7. Helga Geyer-Ryan, *Fables of Desire*, 241.

APPENDIX 7. FINAL READING

1. For those puzzled by the circumstance of that death—Alvarez has long been of the opinion that she did not wish it to end the way it did—there is one more detail, unmentioned by others, to complicate the picture. Plath may have had no telephone, but it is likely that she had a radio—the radio that is pictured in *Letters Home.* Biographers have noted that on Saturday, 9 February the Third Programme broadcast a repeat of a Ted Hughes play, "Difficulties of a Bridegroom," first broadcast on 21 January, less than two weeks after his short story "Snow." The Radio Times described "Difficulties of a Bridegroom" as a "divertissement" by Ted Hughes in which he examines the illusion and reality of love." It was one of the "Highlights of the Week" and having described the basic situation in which the central character Sullivan is driving to London to meet a girl when he runs over and kills a hare, the *Radio Times* quotes Hughes:

> The drama or myth which to be worked to a resolution is whether he shall be permitted to meet and fall for a certain woman: certain inner things are against it, others are for it, and resulting myth is typical of all such situations. (*Radio Times,* 17 January p. 3)

Ronald Hayman (1991) believes that if Plath heard the play at all, she would have heard it at the time of its first broadcast, and that the reference to the powerful perfume of the woman Sullivan is going to meet would have suggested that woman was based on Assia. This ignores Hughes's assertion that his principal inspiration was *The Chemical Wedding* of Christian Rosencreutz, a Rosicrucian text, which had influenced his work throughout 1962, raising the possibility that Plath knew of the play before it was broadcast. In the "Introduction" to the collection of short stories *Difficulties of a Bridegroom,* which does not include the play,° Hughes (1995) writes:

> Some time around 1962 I hit on the phrase "Difficulties of a Bridegroom" and this became the working title for almost everything I wrote for the next few years

The manuscript of the play, which does not seem to have been published, shows Sullivan confronted with the image of the bride, whose associations with whiteness and the moon suggest the continuing influence of Graves's *The White Goddess.* The play is highly abstract and opaque, and more concerned with mood and symbolism than narrative realism. Sullivan even calls the beautiful maiden, "a metaphysical parallel," and the woman instructs him to dress in pantherskin trousers and to wear an adderskin tie. As the play climaxes there are tiger roars, but it ends on a note of realism as Sullivan presents the woman with two roses, which he has bought with the five shillings he received for the dead hare. It is tempting to see a connection between this and the "two roses" at the end of the February 1st poem "Kindness," though there is a similar event in "The Chemical Wedding."

One of the reasons for listening to records at the Becker house that Saturday evening may have been to avoid the possibility of hearing the repeat broadcast, but on the following evening there was a repeat broadcast that Plath may have been much more willing to hear. Between seven and seven thirty the Third Programme was broadcasting a reading of selected poems from Yeats's *The Tower*, first transmitted on 23 October in the middle of the Cuban Missile Crisis. Some accounts of that final evening say that Gerry Becker, the husband of the couple she had been staying with in Islington that weekend, dropped her at her flat and had returned home by seven, others say that it was much later. If she had turned on the radio after putting the children to bed, she would have had the uncanny experience of hearing (in Yeats's house) a reading of Yeats's poems whose title was taken from the tower she had visited less than sixth months earlier. "I feel Yeat's spirit blessing me" she had written to her mother on 14 December 1962 (*Letters Home*), and whether ironically or faithfully, she continued to believe in the significance of the Yeats connection. A reading of "Sailing to Byzantium," a poem whose third and fourth stanzas, with their longing for eternity and escape she had heavily underlined in her own copy of Yeats's poems (Smith Collection) would have had a pariticular significance, as would a reading of "The Wheel":

> *Through winter-time we call on spring*
> And when abounding hedges ring
> Declare that winter's best of all;
> And after that there's nothing good
> Because the spring-time has not come
> Nor know what disturbs our blood
> Is but its longing for the tomb

But, as with the Dr. Spock article, the signficance of this remains at the level of conjecture and speculation. There is no evidence that Plath heard this reading, and it is not even certain that these particular poems were read.

*This collection does include the story "Snow," however, a first person monolog in which a man whose aircraft has crashed into a snow covered wilderness sits in his chair contemplating what to do next.

Bibliography

By Sylvia Plath

The Journals of Sylvia Plath. Edited by Frances McCullough and Ted Hughes. New York Dial/Ballantine, 1982.

The Journals of Sylvia Plath. Edited by Karen V. Kukil. (London: Faber and Faber, 2000.

"Sylvia Plath" in *The Poet Speaks: Interviews with Contemporary Poets.* Edited by Peter Orr. London: Routledge and Kegan Paul, 1967, pp. 167–72.

"Suffering Angel" (review of *Lord Byron's Wife*). *New Statesman,* 7 December 1962, pp. 828–29

Letters Home: Correspondence 1950–1963. Edited by Aurelia Schober Plath. (London: Faber and Faber, 1978.

"Platinum Summer" (1956). Unpublished manuscript. Indiana University: Lilly Library.

"General Jodpur's Conversion" (review). *The New Statesman,* 10 November 1961, pp. 696–98.

"A Walk to Withens." *Christian Science Monitor* 6 June 1959, p. 12.

"Context" (1962). Republished in Sylvia Plath, *Johnny Panic and the Bible of Dreams.* New York: Harper and Row, 1980 pp. 92–93.

"Oregonian Original" (review). *The New Statesman,* 9 November 1962, p. 660.

"Pair of Queens" (review). *The New Statesman,* 27 April 1962, p. 602–3.

"Oblongs" (review of four books, including *Dr Spock Talks with Mothers*). *New Statesman* 63, 18 May 1962, p. 724.

Collected Poems. Edited by Ted Hughes. London: Faber and Faber, 1981.

The Bell Jar (1963). London: Faber and Faber, 1988.

Johnny Panic and the Bible of Dreams and Other Prose Writings. London: Faber and Faber, 1977.

Books and Articles on Sylvia Plath

Alvarez, A. "Sylvia Plath" in Alvarez, A., *Beyond all this Fiddle: Essays 1955–67.* London: Allen Lane The Penguin Press, 1968. Reprinted in *The Art of Sylvia Plath: A Symposium.* Edited by Charles Newman. London: Faber and Faber, 1970, pp. 56–68.

Annas, Pamela J *A Disturbance in Mirrors,* New York Greenwood Press, 1981.

Armstrong, Isobel and Sinfield, Alan "'This Drastic Split in the Functions of a Whole Woman' An Uncollected Article by Sylvia Plath, "Cambridge Letter", *ISIS* May 1956" in *Literature and History* Volume 1: 1 Spring 1990 pp. 75–79

Brain, Tracy. "'Or shall I bring you the sounds of poisons?': *Silent Spring* and Sylvia Plath" in *Writing the Environment: Ecocriticism and Literature.* London: and New York Zed Books, 1998, pp. 146–64.

————. "'Your Puddle-jumping daughter': Sylvia Plath's Midatlanticism." *English* 47, no. 187 (1998): 17–39.

————. *The Other Sylvia Plath*. London: Pearson, 2001.

Britzolakis, Christina. *Sylvia Plath and the Theatre of Mourning*. Oxford: Clarendon Press, 2000.

Bronfen, Elisabeth. *Sylvia Plath*. Writers and their Work Series. London: British Council, 1998.

Butscher, Edward. *Sylvia Plath: Method and Madness*. New York: Seabury Press, 1976.

Curry, Renée R. *White Women Writing White*. London: Greenwood Press, 2000.

Easthope, Anthony. "Reading the Poetry of Sylvia Plath." *English* 43, no. 177 (1994): 223–35.

Guttenberg, Barnett. "Plath's cosmology and the house of Yeats." In Gary Lane, ed., *Sylvia Plath: New Views on her Poetry*. London: The John Hopkins Press, 1979, pp. 138–42.

Hall, Caroline King Barnard. *Sylvia Plath, Revised*. London: Prentice Hall International, 1998.

Hayman, Ronald. *The Death and Life of Sylvia Plath*. London: Heinemann, 1991.

Holbrook, David. *Sylvia Plath: Poetry and Existence*. London: The Athlone Press, 1976.

Hughes, Ted and Godwin, Fay. *Remains of Elmet*. London: Faber and Faber, 1979.

Hughes, Ted. *Winter Pollen: Occasional Prose*. Edited by William Scammell. London: Faber and Faber, 1994.

————. *Birthday Letters*. London: Faber and Faber, 1999.

Hughes, Ted ed., Introduction to *The Collected Poems of Sylvia Plath* London: Faber and Faber, 1981.

Kendall, Tim. "Plath's 'Piranha Religion.'" In *Essays in Criticism,* January 1999, No 1.

Kendall, Tim. *Sylvia Plath: A Critical Study*. London, Faber and Faber, 2001.

Kenner, Hugh. "Sincerity Kills." In Gary Lane, ed., *Sylvia Plath: New Views on the Poetry*. London: The John Hopkins Press, 1979, pp. 33–44.

Kroll, Judith. *Chapters in a Mythology: The Poetry of Sylvia Plath*. Harper and Row: New York, 1976.

Kurtzman, Mary. "Plath's 'Ariel' and Tarot." *Centennial Review* 32 (Summer 1988): pp. 286–95.

Lameyer, Gordon. "Sylvia at Smith" In Edward Butscher, *The Woman and her Work*. New York Dodd Mead and Co., London: Peter Owen, 1977, pp. 32–41.

Lane, Gary, ed., *Sylvia Plath: New Views on the Poetry*. London: The John Hopkins Press, 1979.

Lehrer, Sylvia. *The Dialectic of Art and Life: a portrait of Sylvia Plath as Woman and Poet*. Salzburg: Institut für Anglistik und Amerikanistik Universitatät last A) Salzburg, 1985.

Macpherson, Pat. *Reflecting on The Bell Jar*. London: Routledge, 1991.

Macpherson, Patricia. "The Puzzle of Sylvia Plath." *Women's Studies Occasional Papers,* Pamphlet no. 4, 1983. University of Kent at Canterbury.

Markey, Janice. *A Journey into the Red Eye, The Poetry of Sylvia Plath—A Critique*. London: The Women's Press, 1993.

Marsack, Robyn. *Sylvia Plath*. Buckingham, England: Open University Press, 1992.

Mazzaro, Jerome. "Sylvia Plath and the cycles of history." In Gary Lane, eds., *Sylvia Plath: New Views on her Poetry*. London: The John Hopkins Press, 1979, pp. 218–40.

Newman, Charles. *The Art of Sylvia Plath: a Symposium*. London: Faber and Faber, 1970.

O'Hara, J. D. "Plath's Comedy." In Gary Lane, ed., *Sylvia Plath: New Views on her Poetry*. London: The John Hopkins Press, 1979, pp. 75–96.

Ostriker, Alicia. "The Americanisation of Sylvia." In Linda W. Wagner, ed., *Critical Essays on Sylvia Plath*. Boston: G. K. Hall, 1984, pp. 97–109.

Quinn, Sister Bernetta. "Medusan imagery in Sylvia Plath." In Gary Lane, ed., *Sylvia Plath: New Views on the Poetry*. London: The John Hopkins Press, 1979, pp. 97–115.

Richards, Sandra. "Is there Humour in Sylvia Plath?" *English Review* 4 (4 April 1994) pp. 28–31.

Rose, Jacqueline. *The Haunting of Sylvia Plath*. London: Virago Press, 1991.

Shapiro, David. "Sylvia Plath: drama and melodrama." In Gary Lane, ed., *Sylvia Plath: New Views on her Poetry*. London: The John Hopkins Press, 1979.

Sigmund, Elizabeth (Elizabeth Compton). "Sylvia in Devon: 1962" In Edward Butscher, ed., *Sylvia Plath: The Woman and her Work*. London: Peter Own, 1979, pp. 100–107.

Sinfield, Alan. "Women Writing: Sylvia Plath." In *Literature, Politics and Culture in Postwar Britain*. Berkeley and Los Angeles: University of California Press, 1989.

Smith, Stan. *Inviolable Voice: History and Twentieth Century Poetry*. Dublin: Gill and Macmillan, 1982.

Steiner, G. "Dying is an art." In *Language and Silence*. London: Faber and Faber, 1967. Reprinted in *The Art of Sylvia Plath*. Edited by Charles Newman. London: Faber and Faber, 1970, pp. 211–18.

Steiner, Nancy Hunter. *A Closer Look at Ariel: A Memory of Sylvia Plath*. New York: Harpers Magazine Press, 1973.

Stevenson, Anne. *Bitter Fame: a Life of Sylvia Plath*. Boston: Houghton Mifflin Co., 1989.

Strangeways, Al. "'The Boot in the Face'": The Problem of Holocaust in the Poetry of Sylvia Plath." *Contemporary Literature* 37, no. 3 (Fall 1996): 370–390.

———. *Sylvia Plath: The Shaping of Shadows*. New Jersey: Associated University Presses, 1998.

Uroff, Margaret Dickie. *Sylvia Plath and Ted Hughes*. University of Illinois Press, 1980.

Van Dyne, Susan R. *Revising Life: Sylvia Plath's Ariel poems*. University of North Carolina Press, 1993.

Wagner, L. *Sylvia Plath: The Critical Heritage*. London: Routledge, 1988.

Wagner-Martin, Linda. *Sylvia Plath: A Biography*. New York: Simon and Schuster, 1987.

Wagner-Martin, Linda. *The Bell Jar: A Novel of the Fifties*. New York: Twayne Publishers, 1992.

———. *Sylvia Plath: A Literary Life*. London: Macmillan Press, 1999.

Weissbort, Daniel. "Sylvia Plath and Translation." In Anthony Rudolf, ed., *Theme and Version/Plath and Ronsard*. London: The Menard Press, 1994, pp. 1–15.

Wurst, Gayle. "'We See—Comparatively'": Reading Rich/Reading Plath/Reading Dickinson." In Antoine Caze, ed., *Profils Americains* 8 (Emily Dickinson). Montpellier, France: Presses de l'Universite Paul Valery, 1996.

Wurst, Gayle. "'The Clearest Thing I Own': Metaphor, Myth and Identity in Plath's Ocean 1212W." In Gayle Wurst, and Raguet-Bouvert, eds., *Sounding the Depths: Writing as Metaphor in North American Literature*. Liege Liege University Lan, 1998.

Other Works

Ades, Dawn. *Photomontage*. London: Thames and Hudson, 1996. Original large format edition 1976.

Alvarez, A. "Beyond the Gentility Principle" [Introduction to *The New Poetry*, ed. A. Alvarez,] in A. Alvarez, *Beyond all this Fiddle: Essays 1955–67*. London: Allen Lane The Penguin Press, 1968.

———. "The Literature of the Holocaust" (1964). In A. Alvarez, *Beyond all this Fiddle: Essays 1955–67*. London: Allen Lane The Penguin Press, 1968.

———. "The Literature of the Holocaust." *Commentary* 38, no. 5 (November 1964) 65.

———. *Beyond all this Fiddle: Essays 1955–67*. London: Allen Lane The Penguin Press, 1968.

———. *The Savage God: A Study in Suicide*. Harmondsworth, England: Penguin Books, 1974.

———. "Sylvia Plath." In Charles Newman, ed., *The Art of Sylvia Plath: A Symposium*. London: Faber and Faber, 1979.

———. ed., "Introduction" to *The New Poetry*. Harmondsworth, England: Penguin Books, 1962.

Arendt, Hannah. *Between Past and Future: six exercises in Political Thought*. London: Faber and Faber, 1954.

———. *The Human Condition*. Chicago The University of Chicago Press, 1958.

———. *The Origins of Totalitarianism*. London: George Allen and Unwin Ltd., 1961.

———. *Eichmann in Jerusalem: a report on the banality of evil*. London: Faber and Faber, 1963.

Aristotle *Poetics*. Translated by Gerald F. Else. Ann Arbor: Univerity of Michigan Press, 1970.

Auden, W. H. ed., *The Oxford Book of Light Verse*. Oxford: Oxford University Press, 1938.

Axford, Barrie, Gark K. Brown, Richard Huggins, Ben Rosamond, and John Turner. *Politics: An Introduction*. London: and New York, 1997.

Belsey, Catherine. "Literarature, History, Politics." *Literature and History* 9 (Spring 1983): 17–27.

Burgin, Victor, James Dondald, and Cora Kaplan, eds. *Formations of Fantasy*. London: Methuen, 1986.

Butler, Judith. *Gender Trouble: Feminism and the Subversion of Identity*. London: Routledge, 1990.

Chodorow, Nancy. *The Reproduction of Mothering: psychoanalysis and the sociology of gender*. Berkeley: University of California Press, 1978.

———. *Feminism and Pscho-analytic Theory*. Oxford: Polity Press/Blackwell, 1989.

Cox, Jeffrey. *Poetry and Politics in the Cockney School*. London: Cambridge University Press, 1999.

Driver, Christopher. *The Disarmers: A Study in Protest*. London: Hodder and Stoughton, 1964.

Duff, Peggy. *Left, Left, Left: A Personal Account of Six Protest Campaigns 1945–65*. London: Alison and Busby, 1971.

Eagleton, Terry. "Myths of Power: a Marxist Study on Wuthering Heights." In Emily Brontë, *Wuthering Heights*, (edited by Linda H. Peterson.) Boston: Bedford Books St. Martins Press, 1992.

———. *Exiles and Emigres*. London: Chatto and Windus, 1970.

———. *Heathcliff and the Great Hunger*. London: Verso, 1995.

Ellis, A. E. *The Rack*. London: William Heinemann, 1958.

Ellis, Richard J. "The Forgotten Betty." *Times Literary Supplement* no. 5007 (19 March 1999): p. 5.

Freud, Sigmund. *Inhibitions, Symptoms and Anxiety* (1926). Volume 20 of *The Standard Edition of the Complete Psychological Works of Sigmund Freud*. Edited and translated by James Strachey. 24 vols. London: Hogarth, 1953–74.

Fried, Richard M. *The Russians are Coming! The Russians are Coming! Pageantry and Patriotism in cold-war America*. Oxford: Oxford University Press, 1999.

Fromm, Erich and Michael Maccoby. "The Question of Civil Defence." In L. Mumford, et al., *Breakthrough to Peace*. New York New Directions 1962.

Geyer-Ryan, Helga. *Fables of Desire: Studies in the Ethics of Art and Gender.* Oxford: Polity Press, 1994.

Gilbert, Sandra and Susan Gubar. *No Man's Land: The Place of the Woman Writer in the Twentieth Century. Volume 1: The War of the Words*. London: Yale University Press, 1988.

———. *No Man's Land: the Place of the Woman Writer in the Twentieth Century. Volume 3: Letters from the Front*. London: Yale University Press, 1994.

Ginsburg, Alan. "America" In *Howl and Other Poems* (1956), reprinted in Alan Ginsburg, *Selected Poems*. London: Penguin Books 1997.

Graves, Richard Perceval. *Robert Graves: the years with Laura*. London: Weidenfeld and Nicolson, 1990.

———. *Robert Graves and the White Goddess*. London: Weidenfeld and Nicolson, 1995.

Graves, Robert. *The Story of Mary Powell: Wife to Mr Milton*. London: Methuen, 1943; in New York as *Wife to Mr Milton: the Story of Mary Powell*. Creative Age Press, 1944.

———. *The White Goddess: A Historical Grammar of Poetic Myth*. London: A. P. Watt and Son, 1966.

———. *The White Goddess*. London: Faber and Faber, 1948.

Gray, Richard. *American Poetry of the Twentieth Century*. London: Longman, 1990.

Greer, Germaine. *Slip-shod Sibyls* London: Viking 1995

Griffiths, John *The Cuban Missile Crisis*. Hove, England: Wayland, 1986.

Hersey, John. *Hiroshima*. London: Penguin Books, 1956. First published in *The New Yorker*, August 1946.

Homberger, Eric. *The Art of the Real*. London: Dent, 1977.

Horowitz, Daniel. *Betty Friedan and the Making of the Feminine Mystique: The American Left, the Cold War and Modern Feminism*. Amherst Mass.: University of Massachusetts Press, 1998.

Hughes, Ted. *Difficulies of a Bridegroom: Collected Short Stories*. London: Faber and Faber, 1995.

———. *Birthday Letters*. London: Faber and Faber, 1998.

———. "A Woman Unconscious." In *Lupercal*. London: Faber and Faber, 1960.

Hulse, Michael. "Formal Bleeding" *Spectator* 14 (November 1981): p. 20.

Jackson, Laura (Riding). *The Poems of Laura Riding*. Manchester Carcanet Press, 1980.

Jameson, Fredric. *The Political Unconscious: Narrative as a Socially Symbolic Act* London: Routledge, 1989.

Kaplan, Louise J. *Female Perversions: The Temptations of Emma Bovary*. New York: Doubleday-Anchor, 1991

Klein, Melanie. "Infantile Anxiety Situations Reflected in a Work of Art and in the Creative Impulse." In M. Klein, *Love, Guilt and Reparation and Other Works, 1921–1945*. London: Hogarth, 1975, p. 213.

Kogon, Eugen. *The Theory and Practice of Hell: The German Concentration Camps and the System Behind Them*. London: Secker and Warburg, 1950.

Kristeva, Julia. *Powers of Horror: An Essay on Abjection*. Translated by Leon S. Roudiez. New York: Columbia University Press, 1982.

Lacan, Jacques. "Desire and the Interpretation of Desire in *Hamlet*" (1959). Translated by James Hulbert. *Yale French Studies* no. 55/56 (1977): 11–52.

Langer, Lawrence. *The Holocaust and the Literary Imagination*. New Haven and London: Yale University Press, 1975.

Levy, Ann Deborah. "Ishtar" In Pierre Brunel, *Companion to Literary Myths, Heroes and Archetypes.* Translated by Wendy Allatson, Judith Hayward, and Trista Selous. London: Routledge, 1992. 603–10.

Lowell, Robert. *Life Studies.* London: Faber and Faber, 1959.

MacBeth, George. *Collected Poems 1958–1982.* London: Hutchinson, 1989.

Mailer, Norman. *Advertisements for Myself.* London: Andre Deutsch, 1961.

Marks, Elain and Isabelle De Courtivron, eds. *New French Feminisms: An Anthology.* Brighton: The Harvester Press, 1981.

Materer, Timothy. *Modernist Alchemy: Poetry and the Occult Ithaca.* Cornell University Press, 1995.

Miller, Alice. *For Your Own Good: Hidden Cruelty in Childrearing and the Roots of Violence.* New York: Farrar, Straus and Giroux, 1983.

Mills, C. Wright. *The Power Elite.* Oxford: Oxford University Press, 1956.

Moore, Michael J. *The Life and Death of Northampton State Hospital.* Northampton Historic Northampton Press, 1994.

Moorjani, Angela. "Fetishism, Gender Masquerade, and the Mother-Father Fantasy." In Joseph H. Smith, and Afaf M. Mahfouz, eds., *Psychoanalysis, Feminism and the Future of Gender.* London: The Johns Hopkins University Press, 1994, p. 27.

Nightingale, Florence. "Cassandra." In Ray Strachey, ed., *The Cause.* London: Virago Press, 1978, pp. 395–418. Originally appeared as Nightingale, Florence. "Suggestions for Thought." In *Searchers after Religious Truth, pt II; 'Practical Suggestions,'* privately printed 1859.

Peel, R., A. Patterson, and J. Gerlach. *Questions of English.* London: Routledge, 2000.

Riding, Laura. Preface to "Selected Poems: In Five Sets" (1970) in Jackson, Laura (Riding). *The Poems of Laura Riding.* Manchester: Carcanet Press, 1980, p. 416.

———. "Introduction" to "Laura Riding," broadcast on the BBC Third Programme 1 April 1962. Script copyright of the BBC Written Archive Centre. Includes amendments made by Laura Riding to the published version "Introduction For a Broadcast," Chelsea 12, 1962, pp. 3–5.

———, and sixty-five others. *The World and Ourselves.* London: Chatto and Windus, 1938.

Riviere, Joan. "Womanliness as Masquerade." (1929) In Victor Burgin, James Dondald, and Cora Kaplan, eds., *Formations of Fantasy.* London: Methuen, 1986.

Rose, Lisle A. *The Cold War Comes to Main Street: America in 1950.* Lawrence: Kansas University Press, 1999.

Salewicz, Chris. *McCartney.* London: McDonald 1986.

Scudato, Anthony. *Bob Dylan.* London: W. H. Allen, 1972.

Sexton, Anne. "The Barfly Ought to Sing." *Triquarterly* 7 (Fall 1966): 92.

Simpson, Louis. *Studies of Dylan Thomas, Allen Ginsberg, Sylvia Plath and Robert Lowell.* London: Macmillan, 1978.

Stockton, Frank R. *The Lady, or The Tiger?* New York: Charles Scribner and Sons, 1914.

Tanner, Tony. *City of Words.* London: Jonathan Cape, 1971.

Taylor, Richard. *Against the Bomb: The British Peace Movement 1958–68.* Oxford: The Clarendon Press, 1988.

Taylor, Richard and Colin Pritchard. *The Protest Makers: The British Nuclear Disarmament Movement of 1958–65 Twenty Years On.* Oxford Pergamon Press, 1980.

Thompson, Kristin and David Bordwell. *Film History: an Introduction.* London: McGraw-Hill, Inc., 1994.

Weil, Simone. "The Iliad: A poem of force." In Peter Mayer, ed., *The Pacifist Conscience.* New York/London: Rupert Hart-Davis, 1966, p. 292.

Williams, Linda Ruth. *Critical Desire: Psychoanalysis and the Literary Subject*. London: Edward Arnold, 1995.

Woolf, Virginia. *Mrs Dalloway* (1924). London: The Hogarth Press, (Sylvia Plath's copy: 1954).

Yeats, W. B. *The Autobiography of WB Yeats*. New York Doubleday Anchor, 1958.

Index